THE STATE AND ECONOMIC LIFE

EDITORS: Mel Watkins, University of Toronto;
Leo Panitch, Carleton University

This series, begun in 1978, includes original studies in the general area of Canadian political economy and economic history, with particular emphasis on the part played by the government in shaping the economy. Collections of shorter studies, as well as theoretical or internationally comparative works, may also be included.

3 PAUL CRAVEN
'An Impartial Umpire': Industrial Relations and the Canadian State 1900–1911

This book is an insightful and detailed analysis of Canadian labour relations policy at the beginning of the 20th century, and of the formulation of distinctive features which still characterize it today. The development and reception of this policy are explained as a product of ideological and economic forces. These include the impact of international unionism on the Canadian working class, the emergence of scientific management in business ideology, and the special role of the state in economic development and the mediation of class relationships.

The ideas and career of Mackenzie King, including his 'new liberalism,' and his activities in regard to the Department of Labour are examined, revealing how he moulded Canada's official position in the relations between capital and labour. With a focus on King's intellectual qualities in an international context, the author brings out another dimension, portraying him as Canada's first practising social scientist.

The book examines implementation of policy through an analysis of the work of the Department of Labour and through detailed case studies of government interventions in industrial disputes. The initial acceptance of the labour relations policy by the labour movement is explained and its repudiation in 1911 is examined against a background of setbacks which reflected its practical limits as much as its philosophical orientation.

The result is a study which moves beyond a particular concern with labour policy to illuminate the contours of Canadian life in a crucial period of national development.

PAUL CRAVEN is a member of the Division of Social Science at York University.

PAUL CRAVEN

'An Impartial Umpire'
Industrial Relations and the
Canadian State 1900–1911

S. McBride
Dec. 1980

UNIVERSITY OF TORONTO PRESS
TORONTO BUFFALO LONDON

© University of Toronto Press 1980
Toronto Buffalo London
Printed in Canada

ISBN 0-8020-5505-2 bd.
ISBN 0-8020-6401-9 pa.

Canadian Cataloguing in Publication Data

Craven, Paul, 1950-
　'An impartial umpire'

　(The state and economic life ; 3)
　Bibliography: p.
　Includes index.
　ISBN 0-8020-5505-2 bd. ISBN 0-8020-6401-9 pa.
　1. Industry and state – Canada – History – 20th
　century. 2. Industrial relations – Canada – History –
　20th century. 3. Mediation and conciliation, Industrial
　– Canada – History – 20th century. I. Title. II. Series
　HD3616.C32C72　　322'.3'0971　　C80-094522-0

The cartoon on the cover is by George S. Shields,
Toronto *Telegram*, 20 July, 1910.

Rightly conceived, law and order in Industry is the equivalent of fair-play in sport, and of the means and methods taken to ensure it ... There is usually an impartially selected umpire or referee to whom, in cases of dispute, appeal can be made, and whose decision is accepted as final. [William Lyon Mackenzie King, *Industry and Humanity*, 1918]

We will hardly submit to the decision of an umpire, much less to the interference of a meddler with only a smattering of the knowledge of the real facts of the case, even though that meddler be called the High Court of Parliament. [A cotton manufacturer, in Elizabeth Gaskell, *North and South*, 1854–5]

So much has been written about Labour and Capital and the legislation relating to them that it is scarcely possible to say anything new upon this subject. Not only is there an immense literature of controversial pamphlets bearing upon the matter, but there is also a superabundance of facts and information. What seems now to be needed is a careful attempt to understand the principles of legislation which emerge when we analyse the actions of the Legislature, and the state of public opinion with reference to the conflict of labour and capital and the regulation of industry. The all-important point is to explain if possible why, in general, we uphold the rule of *laisser faire*, and yet in large classes of cases invoke the interference of local or central authorities. This question involves the most delicate and complicated considerations ... Specific experience is our best guide, or even express experiment where possible; but the real difficulty often consists in the interpretation of experience. [W. Stanley Jevons, *The State in Relation to Labour*, 1894]

Contents

Acknowledgments

This book could not have been written without the aid, example, and (sometimes unwitting) suggestions of a very great number of people. It would hardly be possible to name them all here, but I should like to thank especially some of those most closely associated with its progress from rough sketch to final proof.

The book began as a doctoral dissertation at the University of Toronto, where Bernd Baldus chaired my thesis committee. The Social Science Division at York University permitted me to arrange my teaching schedule to expedite its completion, provided computer time, and arranged for the final drafts of both the thesis and the book to be typed. At York, the staffs of the Secretarial Services and computer facilities were most helpful.

The burden of research would have been far more onerous had it not been for the unfailing patience, assistance, and advice of the staffs of a number of institutions: the Public Archives of Canada, the National Library, the Libraries of Labour Canada and the National Research Council, the Public Archives of Ontario, the Archives and Robarts Library at the University of Toronto, and the Government Documents section at the York University Library. I can single out for special gratitude only three: Nancy Stunden and John Smart, the extremely knowledgeable and helpful archivists at PAC, and York's very resourceful government documents librarian, Vivienne Monty. A number of other researchers, notably Wayne Roberts, were free with the results of their own investigations. The hospitality of several Ottawa friends made my research trips far more pleasurable than they might otherwise have been.

Three friends in particular must be singled out for special notice and thanks. Mel Watkins, who was associated with this project almost from the beginning, has inspired a whole generation of 'new political economists,' and

I know I am not alone in my indebtedness to his enthusiasm and intellectual generosity. Tom Traves has been a wellspring of ideas and support during five years' association at York: I have learned a great deal from him about a surprising number of things. R.I.K. Davidson has been a patient and sympathetic editor, and it has been a pleasure to work with him.

This book has been published with the help of a grant from the Social Science Federation of Canada, using funds provided by the Social Sciences and Humanities Research Council of Canada, and a grant to the University of Toronto Press from the Andrew W. Mellon Foundation.

It is a commonplace of the scholarly idiom to assign credit broadly for what is worthwhile in one's work while assuming sole responsibility for its failings. The claim may be hackneyed but, in the case of this book at least, it is very close to the truth.

P.C.
Toronto
May 1980

'AN IMPARTIAL UMPIRE'

Abbreviations

Some frequently cited sources are abbreviated as follows throughout the notes:

CHR	*Canadian Historical Review*
IC	*Industrial Canada*
LG	*Labour Gazette*
TLC	Trades and Labor Congress of Canada, *Minutes and Proceedings* of annual conventions
Dawson	R.M. Dawson, *William Lyon Mackenzie King: A Political Biography*, 1874–1923 (Toronto: University of Toronto Press, 1958)
Debates	Canada, House of Commons, *Debates*
Ferns and Ostry	H.S. Ferns and Bernard Ostry, *The Age of Mackenzie King: The Rise of the Leader* (London: Heinemann, 1955)
Jamieson	Stuart M. Jamieson, *Times of Trouble: Labour Unrest and Industrial Conflict in Canada* (Ottawa: Privy Council Office, 1968)
Pentland	H. Clare Pentland, 'A Study of the Changing Social, Economic, and Political Background of the Canadian System of Industrial Relations,' unpublished draft study for Task Force on Labour Relations, Ottawa, 1968

Introduction

In both Canada and the United States the commission of inquiry has long been favoured for supplying at least the semblance of official action regarding what have been perceived as pressing social problems. In April 1914 this tradition was triply confirmed when the United States Commission on Industrial Relations heard testimony about the efficacy of investigative bodies in the settlement of industrial disputes from a man with a lengthy record of service on Canadian Royal Commissions. The Dominion's former Minister of Labour, William Lyon Mackenzie King, had been invited to answer the Walsh Commission's questions about his experience with Canada's Industrial Disputes Investigation Act (IDIA) and his views on the applicability of a similar measure to the American situation.[1]

King explained to the commissioners that he had drawn on extensive personal experience as a mediator in drafting the Canadian legislation. The idea for the Act had come to him while he was attempting to reach a settlement in an Alberta coal miners' strike in 1906. The protracted dispute was threatening a severe fuel shortage as winter approached, yet the coal company and the striking miners remained oblivious to the larger public consequences of their quarrel. 'My experience there and in connection with other disputes,' King informed the Commission, 'had led me to believe that if we could put together an act which would compel the parties to a dispute to act together and provide some legislation that would get at the facts when they got together, that a large percentage of the industrial disputes would be saved.'

1 For an account of the Walsh Commission, see James Weinstein, *The Corporate Ideal in the Liberal State* (Boston: Beacon Press, 1968), 172–213. For King's testimony, see *Industrial Relations*, Final Report and Testimony Submitted to Congress by the Commission on Industrial Relations, US Senate Document no. 415, 64th Congress, 1st Session (Washington: Government Printing Office, 1916), vol. 1, 713–18, 732–8.

With Prime Minister Laurier's blessing, King drew up a measure which prohibited strikes and lock-outs in certain industries, defined as public utilities, pending the report of a tripartite investigating board. Once the report had been made, a strike or lock-out could take place without penalty: the principle of the Act was compulsory investigation without compulsory arbitration. According to King, it worked well. Of those disputes for which an investigating board had been constituted, only a small fraction had resulted in strikes or lock-outs. Moreover, he explained, the mere presence of the Act on the statute books was sufficient to dissuade workers and employers from pressing other disputes to the point at which recourse to a board would become necessary. Fear of an investigation and subsequent publicity would temper hot-headedness and facilitate sensible negotiation and adjustment of grievances. For the most serious cause of industrial unrest was the unwillingness of the parties to sit down and talk things over in a reasonable and responsible way: 'I might say that such limited experience as I had in dealing with these disputes showed clearly that one of the great difficulties in every strike was to get the parties together. That same thing came up on one occasion after the other. Employers would not meet so-and-so because they were belonging to a union, because they had become obnoxious, through personalities or other causes.'

The commissioners pressed King for a justification of the Act's interim prohibition of strikes and lock-outs and its prescription of penalties in the form of fines for violators. King insisted that the penalty clause had rarely been invoked, and never at the instance of the government. He justified the prohibition of work stoppages by explaining that there was a trade-off involved:

We knew that as soon as the measure was brought down that at once the employers would say and the public would say, 'You are setting up a tribunal at the expense of the State, giving rights that have never been given to labor before, namely, the right to choose a chairman, the right to call witnesses and to have those witnesses paid for by the State, the right to appear for themselves, or by their own representatives. You do all this at the expense of the State. What is the State getting in return for it?' The government of the day did not think the measure could be put through unless there was some answer to that question. The answer was this: 'What you get in return is the continuous operation of the utility that is concerned,' and the only way that could be put in words before the public was to impose a penalty which would be collectible in the event a violation of that took place. That is the nature of the understanding, so to speak, between the State and one of the parties to an industrial dispute.[2]

2 *Industrial Relations*, 714, 716

Two other witnesses attended the Walsh Commission hearings that day to discuss King's testimony. They could hardly have been a more unlikely pair. But Samuel Gompers, president of the American Federation of Labor, and James A. Emery, counsel for the National Association of Manufacturers, agreed on at least one thing: the inadvisability of modelling American legislation on the IDI Act.

As Gompers saw it, the line between compulsory investigation and compulsory arbitration was exceedingly narrow. The penalty clause, in so far as it prevented workers from leaving their employment before the board made its report, was an inadmissible interference with the freedom of labour, tantamount to slavery:

A system of compulsory arbitration, or a system of compulsory investigation, as it obtains in Canada, wherein and whereby workers are given the choice of continuing to labor, enforced compulsory service for any given period, when the worker regards it as his interests and his rights to leave that employment, call it by whatever name you please, compulsory arbitration or compulsory investigation, compulsory work, pending the final determination of that investigation, the system of slavery has been established and I doubt that the workingmen of the United States will ever be ready to accept legislation of that character without a protest.[3]

Emery managed to differ with both Gompers and King simultaneously. He agreed with King that the increasing interdependency of all sections of the economy made it necessary that transportation and communication services be maintained in continuous operation. 'You can starve New York to death in three days.' But in his view, special labour legislation was not needed. The existing criminal law, if adequately prosecuted, would ensure sufficient protection against strikes and other 'forms of assault.' He gave two arguments against the passage of an American IDIA. First, he considered it would give rise to enormous difficulties of administration. Second, the American case could not be compared to the Canadian, for there was 'a difference in our fundamental organic law which raises objections which seem to me insuperable.' He summed up by paraphrasing Burke: 'You could not indict the Nation then. You can not imprison a union of employers or employees.'[4]

King replied to Gompers by re-emphasizing the significance of the trade-off implicit in the Canadian Act. Workers gained far more than they lost under the IDIA because, in exchange for postponing their work stoppage,

3 *Ibid.*, 721
4 *Ibid.*, 732

they received an alternative method for obtaining justice that was better than the strike. 'It seems to me you have substituted a wider liberty rather than helped to enslave people.' To Emery, he quoted Burke in return: 'Burke said somewhere that justice was the common concern of mankind. That being so, an act of this kind is framed with the view of enabling the public, which is mankind, to know in regard to the justice of the situation, and bring public opinion to bear on the side of the party that is in the right. That is the underlying motive of it.' To the Commission as a whole, King outlined the underpinnings of his conception of society, the philosophy behind the Act:

I was going to mention that in the discussion here before, as we have listened to it, the entire discussion seems to have been confined to the two parties to the industrial dispute. Nothing has been said about the rights or obligations of the third party, which is the community as a whole; and the Canadian act proceeds on this basis, that neither would capital be able to gain dividends nor would labor be able to gain wages unless it were for what the community, organized as a community, does for both. In other words, Government maintains law and order; it makes possible the development and organization both in labor and in capital. It enables modern industrial society to be carried on under the methods in which it is carried on, and therefore makes possible to each whatever gains are made. Now, if that is true, certainly something is owing to society in return, whereby the community shall not be adversely affected where it is not in fault one way or another, and the Canadian act proceeds on that line, that the public are to be given an opportunity to know, in regard to something which affects the public, the right and wrong of the situation.[5]

The Industrial Disputes Investigation Act was the culmination of seven years of unprecedented legislative activity in Canadian industrial relations policy. It formed the basis for what has been most characteristically the Canadian method of state intervention in labour disputes ever since. State-sponsored conciliation during an enforced suspension of active hostilities (the 'cooling-off period') and a special statutory concern with 'public utilities,' 'essential industries,' or, most recently, 'essential workers' have remained at the centre of modern labour relations policy. Despite the significance of compulsory collective bargaining, introduced during the Second World War, these turn-of-the-century principles continue to dominate the Canadian scene, especially in those industries and services whose disruption by strike or lock-out receives the most widespread public attention. Since 1950, when *ad hoc* back-to-work legislation was enacted for the first time in a

5 *Ibid.*, 734

national railway strike, the role of the state in 'public interest' disputes has taken on a new guise. Nevertheless, the underlying principles of the IDIA have exhibited remarkable staying power. The machinery of compulsory conciliation has been tacked on to the collective bargaining apparatus in most jurisdictions, and the trend towards ever-increasing exercise of the *ad hoc* statutory prerogative merely serves to underline the lasting significance of the IDIA's concern with 'public utilities.' The extension of collective bargaining and the right to strike to workers in the public service has brought with it an extension of the scope of this term. Like Australia and New Zealand, Canada was a leading experimenter in industrial relations at the beginning of the century, and, like theirs, Canada's experiments took root and spread, so that, behind all the modifications and modernizations, the old structure is still plainly visible.

Arguing that the measures introduced before 1910 'were more clearly of Canadian origin and more deliberately designed for Canadian conditions than those introduced at other times,' H.C. Pentland has posed the obvious questions: 'why a vigorous labour policy should appear at that time, what it was intended to accomplish or might have accomplished and, perhaps the most important question, why this energetic initiative was succeeded by forty years of inactivity.'[6] This study speaks directly to the first and second of these, while it has some bearing on the third as well. Its main object is to render intelligible the policy and practice of state intervention in industrial relations during what appears to be the critical period, the first decade of the century.

At least three broad approaches to this project of making the Canadian policy intelligible can be isolated.

In the first place, the policy might be viewed as an intellectual production, involving ideas about the proper relations of labour and capital, the legitimacy of class organizations and their programmes or strategies, the extent to which government should become involved in economic relations, and so forth. Such an approach would seek to discover an intellectual prime mover, and would find him in Mackenzie King. It would attempt to identify the sources of King's ideas, show how he came to adopt them, and examine the extent to which they were altered in transmission and application. Finally, this approach would have to explain why these particular ideas gained fluency in the period under study and how it was they were able to supplant earlier formulations.

---

6 Pentland, 148. I am indebted to the late Professor Pentland for permission to quote from this study.

A second approach would view the policy as the outcome of some more or less rational bargaining process carried out between the parties directly involved in industrial relations, labour and capital, taking the state to fulfil a brokerage function, whether honestly or corruptly. In this view, the principal determinant of change in industrial relations policy would be change in the relations of labour and capital. Such change might in turn be explained either in terms of changes in the balance of market forces that follow from internal reorganizations of labour and/or capital, or in terms of external changes in the industrial relations environment, or both.

A third approach would find its point of departure in the theory of the state. Rejecting the simple brokerage model of the state in favour of a more sophisticated view of that institution as a complex of imperfectly co-ordinated components with a dynamic of its own, it would seek to explain the emergence of the policy as the consequence of specific contradictions implicit in the structure and role of the state as they are brought into prominence by particular historical contingencies.

While there is a great deal to be said for each of these approaches taken separately, a wholehearted commitment to any one of them runs the risk of obscuring almost as much as it reveals. Canada's industrial relations policy – and it is to be understood throughout that this term subsumes both the formal policy and its practice – was not solely a tissue of ideas, the outcome of a market transaction, or the product of institutional tensions. Indeed, it is even insufficient to say it was all of these, for the three elements suggested here cannot be simply added up to produce an explanation: rather, they must be seen as interacting in complex ways, each setting limits to the others and bounding the direction in which the policy developed. For example, the ideational content of King's policy can only be fully grasped when the analysis of his intellectual formation is linked to an understanding of how the trade union movement's stance on compulsory arbitration was transformed, while labour's reception of the policy was conditioned not only by its immediate experience of costs and benefits, but also by its changing image of the state.

Perhaps enough has been suggested here to account for the methodology of this study, which seeks to integrate the critical elements of the three approaches outlined above. The approach adopted here might be described as an attempt to fashion a political economy of Canadian industrial relations policy at the turn of the century. It seeks to provide a historically grounded explanation in terms of a complex of structural, institutional, and ideological factors. Implicit in this approach is an attempt to weigh the extent to which the social forces whose interaction produced the Canadian policy were typical of liberal societies in general, and the extent to which they must be explained in terms of the peculiarities of the Canadian political economy.

The methodological complexity of this study has imposed upon it some empirical simplifications. In preparing a net to be cast so broadly, it has been necessary to sacrifice fineness of mesh. Inevitably, this introduces some distortions into the picture, but it has been felt that the fine shading must wait upon the broad outline, and it is the latter that is presented here. Perhaps the grossest oversimplification amounting, in fact, to reification, lies in taking the views and activities of two national organizations, the Trades and Labor Congress of Canada and the Canadian Manufacturers' Association, to represent the organized workers and the organized capitalists respectively. In the last few years, historians of the Canadian working class in particular have introduced dimensions into the study of class formation that cannot be touched on here. Suffice it so say, first, that to the extent that the claims of these organizations to speak for their constituencies were accepted by each other and by the state, their views and activities retain a special relevance to our problem, and second, that any consistent attempt to build in special considerations of ethnicity, religion, culture, community, or occupational characteristics here would have meant the uncontrolled expansion of what is already a lengthy book.

This study falls into two parts. The first, comprising chapters 1 to 6, examines the structural, institutional, and ideological preconditions for the emergence and reception of the new industrial relations policy, while the second part, chapters 7 to 10, discusses that policy in its practice.

Chapter 1 outlines the broader context for understanding the Canadian policy that is implied by the general approach. Beginning with some questions about the peculiar role of Mackenzie King, it argues that the problem of interpreting his role can be recast in terms of the relation between ideas and society, while the substance of his policy can be understood in terms of the problem of social order. King is then viewed as an intellectual engaged in a search for the roots of social order at a point in the history of ideas when new challenges to theory, and new solutions, are in the air. Chapter 2 places King in his intellectual context and discusses what use he made of the new ideas about social order in his early writings; this is followed by a discussion of *Industry and Humanity*, which he published in 1918, showing the continuing significance of these concerns in his later thought. Chapters 4 and 5 turn to the discussion of class relations, class organization, and class ideologies as they took shape in Canada during the wheat boom, stressing their bearing on the practice of industrial relations. Chapter 6 raises some theoretical questions about the nature and role of the Canadian state, and explores the relations of workers and industrialists to each other and to the state through an examination of the tariff debate and its implications for industrial relations.

The second part of the study begins in chapter 7 with a survey of the Department of Labour in its early years, emphasizing King's use of the Conciliation Act. Chapter 8 undertakes a case study of conciliation proceedings in the western Canadian mining industry. The origins, interpretation, and reception of the Industrial Disputes Investigation Act are treated in chapter 9, and a case study of intervention in an industry covered by that statute follows in chapter 10, where King's role in the 1910 Grand Trunk strike is examined. The concluding chapter attempts to draw together the theoretical implications of the study for understanding Canadian industrial relations policy.

One last comment is necessary by way of introduction. As will become clear in the pages that follow, the methodology pursued here inevitably raises questions about the ideological character of social analysis in general. This study is itself not immune from such questions. To say this is not to embrace cynicism, but to acknowledge that our understanding of society, like society itself, has a history, and one that unfolds with a subtle dialectic. If this study contributes, however tentatively, to that unfolding, it will have served its purpose.

1
The labour problem and the problem of order

He might as well say that there is no better rule needful for men than that each should tug and rive for what will please him, without caring how that tugging will act on the fine widespread network of society in which he is fast meshed. If any man taught that as a doctrine, we should know him for a fool. [George Eliot, 'Address to Working Men, by Felix Holt,' 1868]

To write about the development of Canadian labour policy without discussing William Lyon Mackenzie King would be like mounting a production of *Hamlet* without the prince. It could be done – no doubt the latter has been done – but the exercise would have very little point. King dominated the formative period of federal labour policy in the Dominion as much as Hamlet does the working out of the play. There the simile ends, for while the melancholy events at Elsinore follow on its prince's passivity, King was activity personified. He was the principal architect of the new labour policy, its chief theorist and propagandist, and its most prominent executive. He was also a compulsive packrat, leaving an enormous body of personal and official papers from which to reconstruct his role.[1]

Ironically, this poses a special difficulty. King's contribution was so great, and its record so extensive, that it is easy to lose sight of more shadowy figures in the background. There is the risk of accepting a 'Great Man' account of the subject, of adopting a King's eye view that would do violence

1 Besides the Diary, there are many volumes of personal and official correspondence, speeches, memoranda and notes, and other materials in Manuscript Group 26-J at the Public Archives of Canada. Official Department of Labour files are located in Record Group 27 at the same depository. In addition, there are the files of the *Labour Gazette* and the printed testimony and reports of the several Royal Commissions on which King served. Despite occasional lacunae, the record is enormous.

to a broader, and ultimately more valuable, perspective. But while the object of this study is not biography, without a little biography it would be incomplete.

William Lyon Mackenzie King was born at Berlin, Ontario, in 1874. His father was a lawyer, his mother the daughter of the radical intellectual and political leader, William Lyon Mackenzie. After graduating from high school, King attended the University of Toronto, where he was active in student affairs including the *Varsity*. Following the completion of his BA degree, King was offered a fellowship in economics at the University of Chicago, but he turned it down and worked for a year, first in his father's law office, and later as a reporter for the Toronto *News* and the *Globe*. Although he had rejected the idea of a law career, King used this year to complete the course of reading for an LL B degree, apparently to please his father. In the subsequent year, 1896, he accepted a renewed offer from Chicago where, in addition to his academic work, he became briefly involved with the Hull House social settlement. Dissatisfied with Chicago, he arranged to transfer to Harvard in 1897. During the vacation, he prepared a series of articles on social problems for the Toronto press, which resulted in the passage of the 'Fair Wages' Resolution by the federal government. In 1899, his residency at Harvard over, King went to London, England, to pursue his studies. While there, he received the offer of a teaching post at Harvard, but declined it in order to become editor of the Canadian government's new *Labour Gazette*. He went on to become the country's first Deputy Minister of Labour and, following his election to Parliament in 1908, the first full-time Minister of Labour. He lost his seat in the Liberal collapse in 1911, and shortly thereafter became industrial relations consultant to the Rockefeller Foundation. In 1919 he was chosen leader of the federal Liberal party, and from then until his retirement in 1948 spent some of his time as opposition leader and the greater part as Prime Minister. King died in 1950.

I

The most recent popular version of King is that made familiar by newspaper condensations of Stacey's *A Very Double Life*[2]: a plump little man on a furtive and euphemistic stroll, ever conscious of the position of the hands of his watch, and plunged into periodic misery over the position his own hands have adopted. The source for much of this, of course, is King's diary, and the revelations of his personal life which might have been expected to illuminate his public activities have, instead, overshadowed them.

2 Subtitled *The Private World of Mackenzie King* (Toronto: Macmillan, 1976)

But alongside Stacey's King, there are other versions that focus their attention on the man's political career. There is the three-volume official biography, a number of laudatory and journalistic lives that appeared at the time of his death, the systematic attack by Ferns and Ostry, and the stalwart defence by F.A. McGregor, together with a long list of more specialized works.[3] The present study is not intended to add to this literature nor to try to reconcile the various Kings that it presents: there will be little to say about King as a practising politician except when it is necessary for broader purposes. The King to be examined here is an intellectual King, sometimes even King the social theorist. This King is a man with an intellectual vocation, a vocation that comes into frequent conflict with other tendencies; a man who attempts the resolution of this conflict by translating his theorizing about the world into practical action; above all, a man whose social role is that of the intellectual.

This is not a broadly accepted view of King, although it may be gaining in respectability. The most eminent dissenter is King's second official biographer, Blair Neatby: 'To put it bluntly, Mackenzie King was incapable of any coherent presentation of his political philosophy.' The statement is blunt indeed, and what follows only underscores it:

To say, however, that King had no ideas, no political philosophy, because he never articulated any philosophy worthy of the name, would indeed, in King's words, be making of logic an end in itself. It is possible to have ideas without expressing them. King was not a political philosopher. He was an active practitioner of the art of government, a politician. He was necessarily concerned with immediate problems and choices of action. To govern is to choose – to decide what is necessary, what is desirable, what is possible. But all of these decisions imply a scale of values, imply that a man is equipped with ideas or preconceptions. These ideas may be unconscious or undefined, they may be little more than attitudes or sentiments, modified by experience, or even by logic. King's political ideas were not articulated but he was human – he had ideas.[4]

King's reputation in some quarters is such that that penultimate bit of reassurance may be necessary. So far as King the intellectual is concerned,

---

3 The official biography for the period covered by this study is Dawson: the two subsequent volumes are by H. Blair Neatby, *The Lonely Heights* (1963) and *The Prism of Unity* (1976). The most popular of the journalistic accounts was Bruce Hutchison, *The Incredible Canadian* (Toronto: Longmans, 1952). F.A. McGregor, *The Fall and Rise of Mackenize King: 1911–1919* (Toronto: Macmillan, 1962)

4 In M. Hamelin, ed., *The Political Ideas of the Prime Ministers of Canada* (Ottawa: University of Ottawa Press, 1969), 121

though, it amounts to damning with the faintest praise imaginable. And if the pronouncement of an official biographer is not enough, King himself takes a hand in a diary entry: 'The truth is I am not suited to theoretical work, but to practical and need the active touch with men and affairs to give vitality to what I write.'[5] But it is not the vitality of his style that is at issue here – King may safely be deferred to on that point, while the rest of the claim stands.

What grounds can be produced to support our view of King as an intellectual, in the face of such opposition? Much of what follows, of course, speaks to the question: for the time being, two sorts of answers – descriptive and analytic – may be outlined.

A descriptive definition of King as an intellectual would point to his possession of any attributes or activities that would generally be considered characteristic of intellectuals. First, education might be taken into account: King took a BA, LLB, and MA at the University of Toronto, and went on, *via* Chicago, to acquire a PhD from Harvard. Intellectuals are given to abstract thought: King developed a general theory of society which he discussed in a book, *Industry and Humanity*. The publication of a book of this sort might itself be considered an intellectual activity; to it may be added a number of articles and speeches on topics which would generally be considered the intellectual's preserve. Against the judgement of Neatby might be placed that of the president of Harvard, Charles W. Eliot, who considered King sufficiently an intellectual to offer him a teaching position on at least two occasions. And it might be noted that on the first occasion that King turned down this invitation, it was to become editor of a journal that he did so: another typically intellectual pursuit. Other descriptive criteria might be invoked, but these will probably do for the present.

Analytically, the intellectual may be viewed not so much as a collection of personal characteristics, but as an identifiable social role, as a position in the social order. Then it may be asked whether King might reasonably be considered to have occupied such a role. The obvious advantage of this approach is that it permits King to be situated within a larger social setting, and rescues the analysis from some of the interpretative difficulties alluded to earlier. The distinction between what are here called descriptive and analytic approaches to the definition of the intellectual has been clearly stated by Gramsci:

The most widespread error of method seems to me that of having looked for this criterion of distinction [to characterize intellectuals as a group] in the intrinsic nature of intellectual activities, rather than in the ensemble of the system of relations in

5 Quoted in Dawson, 250

which these activities (and therefore the intellectual groups who personify them) have their place within the general complex of social relations. Indeed the worker or proletarian, for example, is not specifically characterized by his manual or instrumental work, but by performing this work in specific conditions and in specific social relations ... All men are intellectuals, one could therefore say, but not all men have in society the function of intellectuals.

Gramsci's analytic view of the place of the intellectuals in the system of social relations is a dynamic one: he views the intellectual role as an emergent counterpart to the development of new forms of material production in society, forms that are characterized by the emergence of new social classes:

Every social group, coming into existence on the original terrain of an essential function in the world of economic production, creates within itself, organically, one or more strata of intellectuals which give it homogeneity and an awareness of its own political function not only in the economic but also in the social and political fields. The capitalist entrepreneur creates alongside himself the industrial technician, the specialist in political economy, the organisers of a new culture, of a new legal system, etc.[6]

These, in Gramsci's terminology, are the 'organic' intellectuals, in contrast to the residual intellectual strata of previous forms of social organization, the 'traditional' intellectuals. The latter exhibit a remarkable degree of staying-power within the new order, presenting themselves as autonomous, or 'free-floating.' Part of the social role of the new organic intellectuals is to win over the traditional strata to support of the new order. The most significant stratum of traditional intellectuals is often the ecclesiastic one; Gramsci notes however that in new societies (he discusses the United States in particular) traditional strata may be, if not wholly lacking, at least relatively insignificant. In this situation, the task of the organic intellectual is not so much to win over older intellectual groups to the new order, as to 'fuse together in a single national crucible with a unitary culture the different forms of culture imported by immigrants of differing national origins.'[7]

---

6 Antonio Gramsci, *Selections from the Prison Notebooks*, ed. and trans. Q. Hoare and G.N. Smith (New York: International, 1971), 8f., 5. For another applicaton of Gramsci's concepts to King, see R.F. Mahood, 'Ideology in the Work of Mackenzie King,' unpublished MA dissertation, Regina, 1972.
7 *Ibid.*, 20. Gramsci argues that the persistence of a two-party system in American politics may be explained, at least in part, by the absence of traditional strata. The analysis seems to have elements in common with Gad Horowitz's version of Hartz's 'fragment theory.' *Cf.* his *Canadian Labour in Politics* (Toronto: University of Toronto Press, 1968), chap. 1.

Organic intellectuals emerge with a new social class founded in changed relations of production. Their relationship with the world of production is '"mediated" by the whole fabric of society and by the complex of super-structures, of which the intellectuals are, precisely, the "functionaries".' Gramsci distinguishes between two 'superstructural levels' which form the immediate context for the intellectual role, 'civil society' and 'the State': 'These two levels correspond on the one hand to the function of "hege-mony" which the dominant group exercises throughout society and on the other hand to that of "direct domination" or command exercised through the State ... The functions in question are precisely organizational and con-nective. The intellectuals are the dominant group's "deputies" exercising the subaltern functions of social hegemony and political government.'[8]

There will be occasion later on to explore the implications of this analysis. For the time being, there is the immediate problem of determining whether there exist analytic grounds for defining King as an intellectual, and, it may now be added, as an intellectual with a high degree of 'organicity.' These grounds, unfortunately, cannot be briefly spelled out: the answer must emerge from a detailed analysis, which may, however, be guided by a tenta-tive hypothesis suggested by Gramsci's frame of reference. King's task, such an hypothesis might run, was the advocacy, development, and implementa-tion of a system of state intervention in industrial relations that formed a 'superstructural' complement to changes in the structure of material produc-tion in the Canada of his day, and that facilitated the smooth working of these changed structures. This task[9] had both 'hegemonic' and 'command' aspects, and it had implications that extended beyond the relatively narrow field of industrial relations policy to embrace very broad aspects of his society.

To bring an hypothesis of this sort to the data is an inherently exacting enterprise. It implies the sort of case study approach that requires particular attention to the detail of concrete 'mediations.' To paint in the broad outlines of King's policy in such a way as to fit it to an equally broad hypothesis would

8 *Prison Notebooks*, 12
9 The term 'task' must, of course, be considered metaphorically: it is as though, at the end of the study, it were possible to say, 'Looking back, it seems that King behaved in this context *just as if* he had been given, or had consciously adopted, this specific task at the outset,' or, perhaps better, '... just as he would have behaved had he been given ...' But all this is a very complicated way of stating a very simple metaphorical idea, and the attempt to unpack it merely confuses the issue. In other words, 'task,' like Gramsci's 'function,' is a *post hoc* analytical descriptor and does not carry any implication that such a task 'existed' in any concrete sense.

be self-serving and scientifically futile. Perhaps it is never possible to 'prove' such an hypothesis beyond the point of demonstrating its plausibility in detail, and, if possible, to the exclusion of variant interpretations. If this can be accomplished, the 'intellectual' approach to King will have been justified. Moreover, it follows that this treatment of King, indispensable as it is here claimed to be to the understanding of early Canadian industrial relations policy, is also useful as a point of access to a more general social analysis.

King's testimony before the Walsh Commission, summarized at the beginning of the introduction, will serve to make this clear. We might begin by pointing out that King had at his command what was at least a rather sophisticated ideological justification for the measures he advocated. The notion that there exists a 'community' which serves as both the precondition and the ultimate end of economic activity and which derives from this rights that supersede those of particular parties is, whatever its merits, not a simple one. Against Gompers' assertion that any intervention amounts to slavery, or Emery's, that strikes should be put down because they are bad for business, it appears almost donnish. But the point of this observation is not that King was more erudite than Emery or Gompers: it is that having thought through the nature and broad implications of his policy, he had available to him a language of justification which spoke to higher-level concepts than the scrappy phenomena of strikes and lock-outs with which that policy had immediately to do.

Of course, the fact that he could use this language does not necessarily imply that he meant what he said. Reading the Commission debate, it is impossible to decide whether the ideas used by any of the participants amounted to highly internalized and powerful sources of motivation, or mere debating points to be used as *post hoc* rationalizations of positions taken for rather different, and perhaps more thoroughly self-serving, reasons. History knows both zealots and opportunists, and there is undoubtedly a largely populated middle realm. But in Mackenzie King's case, it is possible at least to say that the ideas he used were not formed after the fact. What King thought about society in the abstract had been put in place, to all intents and purposes, before he realized the opportunity to act on a particular society. He had an educated knowledge of social theory, and had embraced a particular school of social thought which not only organized his observer's perceptions of the social world, but provided him with an explicit task as an actor within it.

Once this has been established, the distinction between opportunist and zealot becomes slightly reduced in importance. After all, even the most rank of opportunists must frame his acts according to some organized perception of what is likely to be opportune: if Machiavelli himself were to be transplanted to the Canada of today and pointed towards the 'national unity' crisis, it is conceivable that he might stumble a little. But the view that King can be 'explained' purely and simply in terms of his opportunism is rejected here.[10] We begin instead with the superficially naive assumption that King meant what he said in elaborating his justification of his industrial relations policy. After all, for the zealot no less than the opportunist, the end may justify the means. It may just have been that Mackenzie King was exceptionally fortunate in that his personal ambitions coincided nicely with his broad vision of the just society.

Be that as it may, it does point towards one salient consideration. It is one thing to say that King possessed a sophisticated ideology which informed his policy; it is quite another thing to point out that he was permitted to translate his thought into action, that this particular social thinker was able to become a highly successful practitioner as well, at least in so far as longevity is a measure of success. This would seem to suggest some goodness of fit between King's ideology and the policy it informed, on the one hand, and some characteristic of his society, on the other. It is to suggest that how King made sense of his society somehow made sense for that society as well. To the extent that this follows, what had been a purely idiosyncratic problem in biography reveals itself as a general and rather profound sociological problem. This is the problem that is variously described as that of theory and practice, consciousness and action, or ideology and social structure; and, in this last form at least, it has a bearing on what may be an even more vexed opposition, that of base and superstructure. To what extent are people's ideas about the world conditioned by particular aspects of the society in which they live? What does 'conditioned' mean in concrete terms? To what extent is the society in which they live conditioned by what people think about it? What does 'conditioned' mean here? If 'society' both 'conditions' ideas and is 'conditioned' by them, what is the nature of this 'conditioning' process? Can any process of causation or determination be said to obtain?

Thus in seeking to understand Canadian labour policy from the springboard of King's ideas, we are at the same time carrying out a sort of case study that might be expected to inform some of these more general theoretical problems, problems which have become identified with the 'sociology of knowledge.' Beyond this, when we come to examine the substance of King's thought, we find that it is of a rather apocalyptic sort. King was concerned, at

10 On this point see my 'King and Context: A Reply to Whitaker,' *Labour/Le Travailleur*, 1979.

bottom, with the most fundamental of all sociological inquiries, the search for the roots of social order, the questioning of the very possibility of society. In King's view, the social world was on the verge of breaking up. Conflict was endemic and might at any time take on the proportions of a Hobbesian war. Of course, for King 'society' meant liberal capitalist society, and what threatened its possibility was class conflict. His enterprise, both as theoretician and as policy-maker, was to place that society on new foundations, to discover a fount of social harmony that would wash away the soil in which class ideas have thrived.

While King's experiments in labour policy were unique, his general enterprise obviously was not. The 'labour problem,' as it was known to two or three generations of Anglo-European social thinkers, was significant for two interconnected reasons. In the first place, the rise of trade unionism and working-class political movements in the mid-nineteenth century seemed to threaten directly the capitalist social order. In the second place, they threatened quite successfully to destroy the foundations of liberal social theory. If these two threats are related, as they obviously are, then the nature of the relationship must be sought in the sociology-of-knowledge problem touched on above. Both King's ideas and his practical activity may be placed in this more general context. His ideas were formed during his vicarious participation, as a student, in the great theoretical debate that transformed political economy at the end of the nineteenth century. His labour policy was designed to solve the labour problem as he saw it developing in Canada at the turn of the century – and this perception was shaped by that theoretical debate and his position within it. It is in this context that the sociology-of-knowledge problem bears on the problem of order. We are suggesting that, on the one hand, King made sense of his society by using a framework developed to cope with the intellectual problems raised by the emergence of a working-class movement in nineteenth-century Europe. On the other hand, this 'sense' that King made could be translated into political action in early twentieth-century Canada with such goodness of fit that, first, King could erect an enormously successful political career on it, and second, the basic policy elements have been retained to the present day. Clearly we are saying something about social theory, and something else about Canada in, say, 1900, and these two things are related through the historically specific mediation of Mackenzie King.[11] To begin, then, what is there to be said

---

11 This is not to claim, of course, that King constitutes the only link. It should be added that to pose the problem in terms of thought and action, ideology and society, or various cognates, is to presuppose at the outset a dichotomy that may obscure as much as it illuminates.

about social theory? Here we must make a fairly considerable detour into the shaping of liberal social thought, to identify in its evolution the moment that determined King's point of departure.

II

The increasing (albeit, one suspects, non-linear) sophistication of the social sciences and the general retreat from positivism among intellectuals everywhere have contributed to a noticeable revival of interest in the claims of social theory to scientific status and in the *soi-disant* 'ideological' character of the enterprise. Sociology, to take one example, has been warned of its 'coming crisis,' and the received norm of value-freedom has been challenged on both political and epistemological grounds. The 'end of ideology' has itself been shown to have been thoroughly ideological, and historians of the discipline have been far more reluctant than formerly to advocate a thoroughgoing Whig interpretation of inexorable scientific progress.

It is to economists, however, and not to sociologists, that we are indebted for one of the more interesting debates about ideology and science. Economics, far more than sociology, has been a paradigmatic discipline, in the Kuhnian sense, and it has been far more successful than other fields of social investigation in clothing its models in scientific, which is to say mathematical, dress. Furthermore, it has been viewed as more immediately a practical science than the others, and this has meant far more opportunity to find its prescriptions wanting when brought against the measure of affairs than sociology, say, or political science have yet received. So it is not surprising that the more critically minded among economists have paused in the business of fitting elegant epicycles to yet more elegant, if practically inadequate, theoretical models to question their discipline's claim to analytic validity and political neutrality. Because economics has been paradigmatic, the ensuing debate has turned on the interpretation of the history of the discipline.

It was not long before the debaters realized – and they had here Marx's comment about 'apologetics' to guide them[12] – that the history of economic

---

12 'With the year 1830 came the decisive crisis ... Thenceforth, the class-struggle, practically as well as theoretically, took on more and more outspoken and threatening forms. It sounded the knell of scientific bourgeois economy. It was thenceforth no longer a question, whether this theorem or that was true, but whether it was useful to capital or harmful, expedient or inexpedient, politically dangerous or not. In place of disinterested enquirers, there were hired prizefighters; in place of genuine scientific research, the bad conscience and the evil intent of apologetic.' Author's preface to *Capital*, 2nd ed. 1873 (Moore-Aveling-Engels ed., New York: Modern Library, n.d. [1906]), 19

thought must be viewed against the history of the social formation that gave it birth. To what extent have models in economics been responses to emerging factors in the political economy of the theorists' times? What part has been played by non-scientific – 'ideological' or 'metaphysical' – considerations in the theory that is made? Of course, the questions are in some degree separable: the new data that are pushed into prominence by social change must be incorporated within the theory, but it does not automatically follow that the theory itself is 'ideology,' as opposed to 'science.' Schumpeter thought that a distinction might be drawn between what economists argued for, and how they argued, and that the latter could serve as the basis for a history of economics as a science divorced from ideology, a history of economic *analysis*. Thus what is scientific is the tool kit, refined over time, and the history of economics need not be a history of ideologies: while ideology 'enters on the very ground floor, into the preanalytic cognitive act,' 'the rules of procedure that we apply in our analytic work are almost as much exempt from ideological influence as vision is subject to it.'[13]

Joan Robinson argues (along lines similar to Myrdal's[14]) that while 'metaphysical propositions' abound, and indeed are necessary as a source of hypotheses, 'economics is not only a branch of theology.'[15] Economics ought to try to make the progress towards science, as much by seeking to illuminate its own ideology, and to combat it, as by anything else. Maurice Dobb held that the Schumpeterian distinction between economics-as-ideology and economics-as-science (and this seems to underlie Robinson's position as well) was untenable unless 'analysis' was taken to mean merely the formal logical or mathematical framework of economic reasoning, devoid of specifically economic content, and devoid equally of any relevance to the task of the economist, and he put the case for a moderate version of historicism: 'new concepts and theorems have to be envisaged simultaneously as being fashioned in response to (and hence patterned upon) older ones – as critical assessment of their adequacy to fulfil the role for which they have been cast – and as a reflection of changing human experience and of the problems and conflicts involved in human social activity that is itself motivated by the use of abstract notions applied to human beings in general, to their artifacts and to "things".'[16] The first half of this statement seems to permit of

13 Joseph Schumpeter, *History of Economic Analysis* (New York: Oxford University Press, 1954), 42, 43
14 See his introduction to the English edition of *The Political Element in the Development of Economic Theory* (London: Routledge and Kegan Paul, 1953).
15 *Economic Philosophy* (Harmondsworth: Penguin, 1964), 25
16 *Theories of Value and Distribution since Adam Smith: Ideology and Economic Theory* (London: Cambridge University Press, 1973), 37

scientific progress; whether the second vitiates this in part or wholly remains undecided.[17] Dobb here introduces, although he does not pursue, the other, heretofore missing, half of the economists' debate. They have principally been concerned with the extent to which economic theory is determined by social and political factors which ought to be exogenous to the scientific enterprise. The reverse of this question, as we have seen, asks about the effect that a theory might have on the society in which it is held.

We shall have to return to this debate. Just now, we must turn our attention to the matter over which so much fuss is being made, the interpretation of the rise and fall of economic paradigms. The account which follows draws heavily on ammunition mustered by the writers mentioned above for the debate about ideology and science. As it translates economic paradigms into sociological ideal types, accentuating radical contrasts, it inevitably does violence to the subtleties of analysis and the continuities in thought. Perhaps it leans too far in one direction: to insist on a slant in the other, however, is to obscure a genuine revolution in thought.

The late nineteenth century saw the transformation of political economy. The classical concern with production and accumulation was supplanted by the neoclassical emphasis on equilibrium and exchange. Where Ricardo had seen classes with competing interests, Jevons, Walras, and the rest now posited a collectivity of individual utility-maximizers meeting as equals in the market-place. The old tradition, culminating in J.S. Mill, had conceived of the science as a unified field with anchors in both social philosophy and practical policy. With the rise of the neoclassical school, political economy became economics, a special discipline within the general field of the social sciences, to be distinguished from sociology, psychology, history, and the rest. The classical writers had developed the theory appropriate to the heroic origins of industrial capitalism: the new school, so Bukharin claimed, supplanted it with a model devised for the comfort of the absentee owner, the finance capitalist, the rentier.[18] The continuities served mostly to accentuate the change. Neoclassical economics could trace its ancestry, through the classical school, to the natural law doctrines of the Enlightenment, and to the

17 For a critical review of some of the positions taken in this debate, see the title essay in R.L. Meek, *Economics and Ideology and Other Essays* (London: Chapman and Hall, 1967).
18 Nikolai Bukharin, *Economic Theory of the Leisure Class* [1919] (New York: Monthly Review Press, 1972). E.g., the 'three initial fallacies of the Austrian school' are 'connected' with 'the three basic mental traits of the bourgeois rentier.' But, 'both their psychic and logical systems are complicated quantities in which various elements are variously united and fused, their efforts becoming now stronger, now weaker, depending on the other concomitant factors.' Pp. 57, 58

Benthamite utilitarianism that had so excited the principal figures of the old school. Indeed, as Myrdal put it, 'utilitarian influence reached its peak with the introduction of the theory of marginal utility,' in the new economics.[19] Neoclassicism rescued the doctrine of *laissez-faire* from the failing hands of its classical parent and placed it on a new foundation. But in truly fundamental ways, the new school broke with the old. T.W. Hutchison has identified four 'pillars' of the old political economy, three of which were abandoned in the new synthesis. Malthusian population theory, the wages fund doctrine, and the labour theory of value were all renounced: only the Ricardian theory of rent 'was to survive ... like some Anglo-Saxon masonry left in a Norman cathedral.'[20]

What accounts for a change so radical that it is best described by a metaphor of conquest? There were limitations to the explanatory power of classical theory, particularly with respect to distribution and price-formation, but these in themselves are insufficient to account for the overthrow of the paradigm. Robinson and Eatwell lay out, in simplified form, an explanation that is largely shared by many of the writers we have met:

[I]t was not so much a weakness in pure theory as a change in the political climate, that brought the reign of the classics to an end. Classical doctrines, even in their most liberal form, emphasize the economic role of social classes and the conflicts of interest between them. In the late nineteenth century, the focus of social conflict had shifted from the antagonism of capitalist and landlord to the opposition of the workers to capitalists. Fear and horror aroused by the work of Marx were exacerbated by the impact throughout Europe of the Paris Commune of 1871. Doctrines which suggested conflict were no longer desirable. Theories which diverted attention from the antagonism of social classes met a ready welcome.[21]

When economists discuss this episode in the history of their discipline, they are likely to talk about changes in theories of value and distribution. Our purpose may most simply be served, however, by talking specifically of *class*. Social classes, defined in terms of property relations and functions in the process of production, may figure prominently or not at all in various theories of value and of distribution. In classical theory, they occupied a significant, if somewhat ambivalent, position; in the neoclassical model, if

19 *Political Element*, 17
20 *A Review of Economic Doctrines, 1870–1929* (Oxford: Oxford University Press, 1966), 14
21 Joan Robinson and John Eatwell, *An Introduction to Modern Economics* (London: McGraw-Hill, 1973), 35

they were not utterly banished, they were at least placed under house arrest. What is germane in the analysis of class models, as Robinson and Eatwell remind us, is that they are conflict-of-interest models. Moreover, the conflict is far more basic than that of, say, buyer and seller in the market-place, each concerned with maximizing his own return. The higgling of the market is an expression of the similarity of the higglers' respective ends. It is the essence of the social bond in liberal theory. The conflict of classes, on the other hand, is a threat to that social order. For the equilibrium theorist, class conflict appears as the consequence of false consciousness or vice. For the class theorist, it is a structured inevitability of the way society is organized, so that only a change in social organization can put it to rest.

David Ricardo, whose *Principles* stands at the apex of the classical achievement, was, however reluctantly, a class theorist in this sense. The basic position was stated in the first sentence of the preface: 'The produce of the earth – all that is derived from its surface by the united application of labour, machinery, and capital, is divided among three classes of the community, namely the proprietor of the land, the owner of the stock or capital necessary for its cultivation, and the labourers by whose industry it is cultivated.'[22] The principal area of conflict with which Ricardo dealt (here and in the correspondence with Malthus) was that between capitalists and landlords. Since the share of the produce which is to go to labour is fixed by the wages fund doctrine and limited to subsistence by the tendency for population growth to outstrip increases in the food supply, the great battle is between the rentiers who desire income for conspicuous consumption, and capitalists whose goal is accumulation. Rent is a deduction from the value of production which is not balanced by any corresponding contribution to value: it is a millstone holding back the pace of economic growth. So far as relations between workers and capitalists are concerned, their relative shares, as classes, are fixed within the total value of production minus the deductions of the landlords. The absolute income of the worker approximates to subsistence, although this could change were the rate of population increase to be kept down, below the rate of increase in the social product. This last is determined technically. It would seem to follow that the worker has a common interest with the capitalist in lessening the share going to rent, and a positive class interest in birth control. In this model, then, there seems to be no endemic conflict between capitalist and worker; indeed, they would seem to share a second area of common interest in technical progress, increasing the size of the pie.

22 *The Principles of Political Economy and Taxation* [3rd ed., 1821] (London: Everyman, 1973), 3

But here Ricardo, in the edition of 1821, introduced a new note: 'In the present chapter I shall enter into some inquiry respecting the influence of machinery on the interests of the different classes of society ... It is more incumbent on me to declare my opinion on this question because they have on further reflection, undergone a considerable change ...'[23] In his earlier view, Ricardo had considered that 'an application of machinery to any branch of production as should have the effect of saving labour was a general good,' benefitting all classes by a reduction in the prices of some of the commodities on which they would be spending their rents, profits, or wages. The wage rate would remain as before, although some labour might be diverted from the trade into which machinery had been introduced to other fields of employment. Since the demand for labour would remain the same across the whole field of production, notwithstanding its reduction in a particular trade, wages would be maintained and the worker, too, would gain in purchasing power from the introduction of machinery. 'These were my opinions, and they continue unaltered, as far as regards the landlord and the capitalist; but I am convinced that the substitution of machinery for human labour is often very injurious to the interests of the class of labourers.'[24]

The point of this somewhat detailed exposition is to demonstrate that Ricardo's thought encompassed, not just the ungerminated seeds of class conflict which would blossom in the Ricardian socialists' use of the labour theory of value, but also an explicit admission of structural contradictions in the community-of-interest theory of the ever-expanding pie. If one key to the pie's aggrandizement is technological innovation, and if such innovation may be 'often very injurious to the interests of the class of labourers,' the traditional basis for arguing a ground for social solidarity in an ever-increasing national income is radically put into question.

But it would be a serious misrepresentation of Ricardo's position to end our account of it here. For alongside the class model, with its inexorable logic of conflict, stood the utilitarian model of the market, the old political theory of 'possessive individualism'[25] and its calculus of satisfactions in exchange, passed on to Ricardo by his friend and (in these matters) tutor, James Mill. It is pointless to attempt a reconciliation of these two inherently contradictory models, for to do so would be to deny to one or the other of them the analytic bearing that Ricardo apparently intended for both. This

23 *Ibid.*, 263
24 *Ibid.*, 264
25 C.B. Macpherson, *The Political Theory of Possessive Individualism* (Oxford: Oxford University Press, 1962). There is a useful summary of the theory by Macpherson in his *Democratic Theory: Essays in Retrieval* (Oxford: Oxford University Press, 1973), 199.

immanent contradiction in his thought pointed the way to the two great schools which arose in competition, each claiming to transcend Ricardo's defects while incorporating its own version of what was most pregnant in his theory. One, following to its logical end the labour theory of value and placing class conflict at the centre of the stage of world history, culminated in the work of Karl Marx. The other, responding as much to the challenge of the socialist critics as to the irreconcilables in Ricardo's work, sought a new basis for harmony in attempts to conceive of a liberal capitalist economy without classes. The history of this conflict is brilliantly presented in Meek's essay, 'The Decline of Ricardian Economics in England,'[26] and need not be pursued in any detail here. It is sufficient to point out that the tortuous history of revisions to J.S. Mill's *Principles* indicates that the debate was very much alive, and very far from resolution, between 1848 and 1871,[27] and to quote Bladen to the following effect: 'For ten or twenty years after the publication of Mill's *Principles* English political economy was stagnant. True it was at the zenith of its popularity, but the science was resting on its laurels, showing no signs of growth, believed by its chief expositor, and even more firmly by the public, to have reached finality.'[28] Then came the Jevonian revolution, which found the end of history in analysing the equilibrium state, and banished class concerns from the economist's curriculum as much by a narrowed definition of the discipline's field as by its achievements within those bounds.

III

It is necessary now to step back a little, and take up a thread that has woven its way through the preceding discussion of economic theory. This is the liberal political theory that provided the underpinning for free market economics and that, emerging out of Adam Smith's contextual analysis, co-existed uneasily with class notions in Ricardo's work before it effected a lasting marriage with economics in the neoclassical school. It is worth mentioning in passing that liberal market theory had to wait upon the era of imperfect competition before it achieved its fullest flowering.

The most penetrating discussion of this political theory is to be found in Macpherson's *Possessive Individualism*, where it is couched in the language of

26 In his *Economics and Ideology*
27 See the critical edition compiled by J.W. Robson and published as volumes II and III of Mill's *Collected Works* (Toronto: University of Toronto Press, 1965).
28 V.W. Bladen, *From Adam Smith to Maynard Keynes* (Toronto: University of Toronto Press, 1974), 319

the search for a valid theory of political obligation in liberal democracy. But the preconditions for a theory of political obligation are equally preconditions for social order in a capitalist society founded on voluntarism. Social solidarity in a collectivity of individual utility-maximizers, where market relations are taken to be the very type of social relations, must be founded on the possibility of ultimate common interests expressed through allegiance to a state, notwithstanding that those same common interests may dictate elaborate constraints on the state's role. Thus the liberal theory of possessive individualism, no less in economics than in politics, is the theory of the possibility of liberal society, which is to say the liberal theory of social order.

Macpherson sets out two preconditions. First, we must be able to postulate the ability of members of the society to see themselves as equal in some respect more fundamental than those respects in which they are unequal. This first condition, he argues, was supplied until about the middle of the nineteenth century by the apparent inevitability of everyone's subjection to the laws of the market. The second condition is that 'there must be a cohesion of self-interests, among all those who have a voice in choosing the government, sufficient to offset the centrifugal forces of the possessive market society.' This condition was also at one time met, by the restriction of the franchise to owners of property. Both these preconditions were more or less adequately fulfilled until about the middle of the nineteenth century:

Thereafter, both conditions ceased to be met. Although possessive market relations continued to prevail in fact, their inevitability became increasingly challenged as an industrial working class developed some class consciousness and became politically articulate. Men no longer saw themselves as fundamentally equal in an inevitable subjection to the determination of the market. The development of the market system, producing a class which could envisage alternatives to the system, thus destroyed the social fact ... which had fulfilled the first prerequisite ...

The second prerequisite condition was similarly affected. Although the society continued to be class divided, and the possessing class continued to be cohesive, its cohesion ceased to fulfil the prerequisite when the possessing class had to yield its monopoly of power by admitting the rest of the society to the franchise. With the democratic franchise, there was no longer that assurance of cohesion, among all those with a political voice, which had been provided by class interest during the time when only one class had had the franchise.[29]

29 *Possessive Individualism*, 272–3, 273–4

As we have seen, the assault on the possibility of the liberal market society came on two fronts: from the utopian socialists and Marxists who spun out the Ricardian web to the embarrassment of orthodoxy, and from the economic and political movements created by the working class itself. These movements, from Chartism through the 'new unionism' and beyond, led to the demolition of the combination laws and other props of the *laissez-faire* state and the eventual achievement of manhood suffrage, and signalled the emergence of new forces that could not be accounted for by existing theories. The message borne by the assailants on both fronts was at bottom the same, no matter what twistings and turnings the path to its realization took: liberal society is a class society; against the doctrine of economic freedom we assert that the employing class and the working class have nothing in common.

The response of the liberal intellectuals, political and economic theorists alike, was twofold. On the one hand, they attempted to amend their models so as to make it possible for society to continue to exist. On the other hand, they launched an attack on the opposing model. This dual enterprise took on some curious contortions, and led, as we have seen, to the eventual abandonment of the pillars of classical doctrine. One example, roughly sketched in, ought to suffice: the wages fund doctrine.

As originally enunciated by Ricardo, the wages fund may have been of no further consequence than an analytic device to keep the labouring class out of the picture while the conflict of landlord and capitalist was under discussion. In essence, the doctrine asserted that the proportion of the social product going to labour was fixed at any level of technique. The 'hired prize-fighters' among political economists seized on this analytic device to demonstrate that trade unions and strikes were incapable of achieving anything for the workers. At most, they could increase the incomes of one group of workers, but only at the expense of all the others. Trade unionism, and by implication the class model, was thus an irrational outburst against a law of nature. The market, and with it liberal society, remained intact so long as reason held the field.

But the doctrine of the wages fund was taken over by the enemy. Lassalle announced the Iron Law of Wages, denounced the economic system that was ruled by it, and called for the workers to rise in revolt. If, under capitalism, workers could never hope for anything more than subsistence, and this dearly bought at the price of sexual abstinence, then capitalism must go. The more clear-thinking of the liberal social theorists dropped the wages fund doctrine like the red hot brand that, in fact, it had turned out to be. The most dramatic of these about-faces was John Stuart Mill's.[30] But at the same time, the wages fund changed hands again when Brentano took it up as one weapon in the Böhm-Bawerk school's fight against Marxism.[31] With the rise of the neoclassical school after the 1870s, and its abandonment of the Ricardian paraphenalia, the debate petered out. Thus when F. W. Taussig resurrected it in the course of his attempt to reconcile classical and neoclassical economics, he acknowledged that it had no practical bearing on trade unionism, but was, in effect, an interesting if irrelevant technical puzzle for the professional economists.[32] Exhausted ideologies never die: they retire to the senior common rooms.

The old liberalism's approach to strikes saw in them evidence of the extent to which the working classes were insufficiently enlightened. The trade unions struck not only against an employer but against the natural laws of political economy as well.[33] Practical measures, severe or humane, might have to be taken in order to cope with these rash and inevitably self-defeating acts,[34] but they posed no challenge to theory except, perhaps, the psychological one of how men could be so obtuse as to behave contrary to their own and the general interest. But the new liberal critique of classical political economy cast doubts on the doctrine of simple identity of economic interests – as, indeed, did the obstinate refusal of the new trade unions to behave as though such identity was the case. The new thinkers, therefore, were faced with a choice. Either they must accept the principle of fundamentally conflicting interests, the class struggle, or they must reinvent common interests on a new plane.

Ultimately, in the neoclassical synthesis, the problem was again relegated to the back shelf. But in the interval between Mill's first doubts and the final victory of the marginal utilitarians, a number of attempts were made to place the 'labour problem' on a theoretical foundation. Recognizing that this was

30 Dobb, *Theories of Value and Distribution*, 131–4, discusses Mill's use of the doctrine and his recantation.
31 Lujo Brentano, *The Relation of Labor to the Law of To-Day*, trans. Porter Sherman (New York: Putnam's, 1891)
32 See page 57 below.
33 Among the many examples that might be given of this view, one is especially interesting in that it is both early and Canadian. See the 'case for the contractors' set out in H.C. Pentland, 'The Lachine Strike of 1843,' *CHR*, vol. xxix, 3 (1948), esp 269–77.
34 The notion that a strike must be self-defeating, inasmuch as the wages fund doctrine means that a raise in wages of some workers will mean a decline for others, is a curious one. In denying the possibility of class action benefitting the whole class, it is impelled to assume the very model – class conflict – that it is designed to explode.

but a brief interlude in the history of their discipline, and concluding perhaps that it marked an unfortunate deviation from the Whig progression leading from eighteenth-century political philosophy to modern economic science, most writers on the history of the subject have relegated it to little more than a footnote. Thus Bladen, who may be taken as typical.[35] This new liberalism, short-lived as its influence on theoretical economics may have been, is of some significance to our inquiry, as from its school came Mackenzie King. This is discussed at length in the following chapter; for the time being, we should merely note that the new liberalism, in its search for commonality of interest, was forced to jettison the principles of *laissez-faire*. State intervention in the relations of labour and capital found theoretical acceptance, first in exceptional cases, later as a general principle. It is in the context of this theoretical debate, and this set of solutions to it – the search for a new commonality with which to rebuild the edifice of social order and escape the otherwise inescapable conclusion that liberal society is by its nature a house divided – that the ideology of Canadian labour policy must be placed.

35 'I do not propose to discuss the work of the Historical School ...' *Smith to Keynes*, 319. Bladen does go on to provide two quotations from leading figures in this movement but these are intended merely to demonstrate the dissatisfaction with classical economics that 'is necessary as an introduction to the work of Jevons and Marshall.'

2
The intellectual formation of
Mackenzie King

'I was reading a work the other day,' said Egremont, 'that statistically proved that the general condition of the people was much better at this moment than it had been at any known period of history.

'Ah! yes, I know that style of speculation,' said Gerard; 'your gentleman who reminds you that a working man now has a pair of cotton stockings, and that Harry the Eighth himself was not so well off. At any rate, the condition of the classes must be judged by the age, and by their relation with each other. One need not dwell on that.' [Benjamin Disraeli, *Sybil* 1845]

White it would be fatuous to deny the influence of a host of social, familial, and religious factors, young Mackenzie King's ideas about the nature of modern society and his place in it were most immediately conditioned by his exposure to academic social thought. His education as a political economist was largely in the hands of men who were in the vanguard of a new movement within the discipline. The new political economy, whether it be called the historical school, the inductive movement, or sociology, represented a break with traditional positivism and deductivism and shaded into a variety of forms of ameliorative social activism. While some of its adherents may have seen themselves as involved first and foremost in a methodological debate, the significance of the new movement was in the final analysis a political one. Dissociating themselves from the *laissez-faire* orthodoxy of an earlier generation, the new political economists were willing to countenance, and even to prescribe, a positive role for the state. They endorsed trade unionism, in some at least of its forms, and they supported social reform movements. At the same time, most of them did battle with Marxism and 'collectivism,' although many approved of, and worked for, other forms of 'socialism.' Out of this struggle between Ricardian orthodoxy, on the one hand, and revolutionary socialism on the other, emerged a new form of liberalism better suited than the old to the changed circumstances of late nineteenth-century capitalism.

The debate within political economy did not occur in isolation, of course. It was a response to changing social conditions, and to the perceived failure of the discipline either to explain these or to change them. As Arnold Toynbee put it, 'Political Economy was transformed by the working class.'[1] With the rise of the trade union movement, the Chartist agitation, and the emergence of reformist and socialist politics, the 'immutable laws' of Smith, Malthus, Ricardo, and Say were seen to be discredited by events. Abstract political economy was increasingly divorced from practical application. With changes in the social relations of production, there emerged a new intellectual orientation with a self-proclaimed mission of explication and reform.

Many of the new political economists shared with Toynbee a 'genuine but not uncritical sympathy with the aspirations of the working class,'[2] a sentiment which King was to make his own. The spirit of the new movement, along with several of its undigested presuppositions, imbued his thought and practice. It was largely responsible for his 'intellectual formation' in both senses of the phrase: it conditioned the content of his social thought, and it established the horizons of his role as a new kind of intellectual, the activist social scientific expert. An exhaustive account of the emergence of the new political economy would fall outside the scope of this study: this chapter examines some of its aspects as they bore, more or less directly, on King's academic experience and social thought.

I

Although the German historical school and *Katheder Sozialisten* played at least as great a part in the development of the new political economy,[3] it is convenient to begin with Arnold Toynbee. King was himself deeply affected by reading Toynbee, and several of his teachers had been among Toynbee's pupils or associates, or had otherwise been influenced by him. As Dawson has shown, King saw in Toynbee's social and religious ideals a model for his

1 *Lectures on the Industrial Revolution of the 18th Century in England, Popular Addresses, Notes and Other Fragments* (New York: Humboldt, 1884), 10
2 Alfred Milner (Viscount Milner), 'Arnold Toynbee,' *Dictionary of National Biography*, XIX, 1064
3 W.J. Ashley, 'Historical School of Economists,' in H. Higgs, ed., *Palgrave's Dictionary of Political Economy*, 2nd ed. [1925–6] (New York: Kelley, 1963), vol. 2, 310ff

own life,[4] but none of his biographers seems to have realized the extent to which Toynbee's analysis of modern society influenced King.

Arnold Toynbee was born in London in 1852 and died, aged thirty, in 1883. His father, an aural surgeon and Fellow of the Royal Society, had been interested in social betterment projects, including model housing for the poor. Arnold Toynbee originally intended to pursue a military career, but when he discovered an interest in political economy he devoted a year in solitary reading on the subject and then entered Oxford. As an undergraduate, Toynbee's personal qualities and intellectual abilities attracted the notice and friendship of a circle of professors and fellow students, including Benjamin Jowett, Master of Balliol, and the idealist philosopher, Thomas Hill Green. He took his pass degree in 1878, and was immediately appointed tutor at Balliol, a post which he occupied for the four and a half years remaining until his death. In addition to his research and teaching in economic history and political economy, Toynbee became deeply involved in charitable work and church reform, and spent one vacation term living among the poor in Whitechapel. He delivered a number of addresses on political and social subjects to audiences of employers and workmen in various industrial centres; following his death, these were collected and published, together with his Balliol lectures, under the title, *Lectures on the Industrial Revolution of the 18th Century in England*. The book went through four editions between 1884 and 1894; notwithstanding its lasting impact, Toynbee's contemporaries agreed that the influence of personal contact with him had been even greater.[5]

Toynbee's influence had two aspects. There was his formal political economy, with a range of methodological and substantive concerns, and there was, too, the Christian reformism and insistence on moral obligation that anticipated the Social Gospel movement.[6] W.J. Ashley summed up the first of these in 1889:

4 Dawson, 45–7 and *passim*
5 See Milner, 'Arnold Toynbee'; F.C. Montague, 'Arnold Toynbee,' *Johns Hopkins University Studies in Historical and Political Science*, 7th series, no. 1 (Baltimore: N. Murray, 1889); W.J. Ashley, 'Arnold Toynbee,' in his *Surveys Historic and Economic* [1900] (New York: Kelley, 1966), 428–31 (first published as a review of Montague's study in 1889); and Benjamin Jowett, 'Memoir,' in Toynbee, *Lectures*, v–xxvii.
6 For Salem Bland's acknowledgment of a debt to Toynbee, see Richard Allen, *The Social Passion* (Toronto: University of Toronto Press, 1973), 9. Bland's contribution to the reconstruction debate, moreover, shares some remarkable similarities with King's, even to the use of common metaphors. Salem Bland, *The New Christianity* [1920] (Toronto: University of Toronto Press, 1973)

First, at a time when the study of political economy had sunk to its lowest point in England, he did perhaps more than any other man to create a new interest in it, a new belief in its seriousness as a scientific discipline, a new hope that in it might be found some help towards the solution of pressing economic problems.

Secondly, he turned this new interest in the direction of the historical investigation of social development, and of the direct examination of existing phenomena ...

Thirdly, Toynbee was the first professed economist in England to distinctly recognise the element of good in modern socialism, and to see in a cautious extension of the functions of the State one of the most effectual preventives of revolution.[7]

The second aspect is suggested by Mrs Humphry Ward:

Let me pause to think how much that phrase ['a useful life'] meant in the mouths of the best men whom Balliol produced, in the days when I knew Oxford. The Master, Green, Toynbee – their minds were full, half a century ago, of the 'condition of the people' question, of temperance, housing, wages, electoral reform; and within the University, and by the help of the weapons of thought and teaching, they regarded themselves as the natural allies of the Liberal party which was striving for these things through politics and Parliament. 'Usefulness,' 'social reform,' the bettering of daily life for the many – these ideas are stamped on all their work ...[8]

Toynbee thought that the old political economy, which he identified particularly with the work of Ricardo, had become overly abstract and divorced from social reality. Inasmuch as the logical deductions of the political economists had been appropriated by journalists, politicians, and businessmen, and elevated into immutable precepts for action, its influence had become pernicious and reactionary. Changing social conditions had swept away the premises on which these deductions had been based: the practical utility of laissez-faire had ended with the achievement of free trade, and the wages fund doctrine, never completely valid, represented a perversion of economic science when it was used to justify the prevailing rate of wages and to ridicule the aspirations of the trade unions. He attacked the naive positivist view that these doctrines amounted to iron laws as immutable as the Law of Gravity: 'Economists have failed to distinguish between laws of

7 'Toynbee,' 429f

8 *A Writer's Recollections* (Collins: London, 1918), 133. Mrs Ward might have been somewhat partisan in her association of Toynbee with the Liberal party; Jowett ('Memoir,' xiv) claimed that 'he was not a party politician at all.' But Toynbee did once stand as Liberal candidate for Oxford Town Council, and on another occasion he addressed a party meeting (Montague, 'Toynbee,' 51).

physical and laws of social science. They have refused to see that whilst the former are inevitable and eternal, the latter ... express, for the most part, facts of human nature, which is capable of modification by self-conscious human endeavour.'[9]

Toynbee did not disparage the deductive method in favour of a naive empiricism, but he did insist on the complementarity of induction and deduction. Historical research would furnish deductive premises, and the results of deduction must be brought to empirical test. He criticized those, like Cliffe Leslie, who thought that the historical method would completely supplant deductive theory, arguing that 'there is no real opposition between the two.' At the same time, however, he insisted that the new political economy was radically different from the old: 'The historical method has revolutionised Political Economy, not by showing its laws to be false, but by proving that they are relative for the most part to a particular stage of civilisation. This destroys their character as eternal laws, and strips them of much of their force and all their sanctity. In this way the historical method has rescued us from intellectual superstitions.'[10]

Toynbee insisted on the interdependence of the science of political economy and the developmental process that was its subject matter. He advised his students to study economics through the history of theory, 'and see if you can make out the way in which various doctrines have arisen and been modified,'[11] as society has changed. He realized that the historical method could have profoundly conservative implications, by picturing a constant progression towards perfection and thus indicating that the present is, for the present, the best of all possible worlds; but he insisted that the same method 'may exercise a precisely opposite influence by showing the gross injustice which was blindly perpetrated during this growth': 'The historical method is supposed to prove that economic changes have been the inevitable outcome of natural laws. It just as often proves them to have been brought about by the self-seeking action of dominant classes.' He urged his students to 'pursue facts for their own sake, but penetrated with a vivid sense of the problems of your own time.'[12]

Toynbee put his methodological principles to work in his lectures on the history of the industrial revolution. He was among the first to insist that the period between 1760 and the 1840s witnessed a complete and rapid transfor-

---

9 *Lectures*, 22
10 *Ibid.*, 29, 25
11 Ashley, 'Toynbee,' 430
12 *Lectures*, 58, 28

mation of English society.[13] His book remained the standard work on the subject for at least twenty years, and his central thesis of immiseration remains a contentious issue among economic and social historians.[14] Toynbee held that the 'most vital' consequence of the industrial revolution lay in the impact of changes 'in the external forms of industry upon its inner life.'[15] 'These effects were terrible.' On the one hand, the old personal relation between employer and labourer was destroyed, to be replaced by the cash nexus, while, on the other, the standard of life of the newly freed working class was drastically reduced. It was 'a period as disastrous and terrible as any through which a nation ever passed ... because, side by side with a great increase of wealth was seen an enormous increase of pauperism; and production on a vast scale, the result of free competition, led to a rapid alienation of classes and to the degradation of a large body of producers.'

An 'irreconcilable antagonism of interest' between workers and employers emerged with the destruction of the old bonds of society. The old political economy, with its concentration on problems of production, failed to deal adequately with the distribution of wealth, and thus contributed to the looming class conflict. As its precepts hardened into dogma, political economy became a class ideology attacked both by radical Tories like Carlyle and by the working class as it organized the trade unions. The working class saved political economy from itself: with the Chartist agitation and the extension of the franchise, 'Democracy saved industry' from the terrible effects of class war.[16]

Toynbee believed that, devastating as it had been for the masses of the working population, the industrial revolution was a transitory phenomenon. The destruction of the personal relation in industry, and the immiseration of the workers, laid the foundations for a new and higher stage of social existence. 'The detested cash-nexus was a sign, not of dissolution but of growth; not of the workman's isolation, but of his independence.' The new stage rested on the extension of the rights of citizenship to the workers, and on their ability, through the trade unions, to place relations with employers on a basis of 'indifference.' By this, Toynbee meant that employers and workers could meet to make a bargain on equal terms, when workers united to bargain collectively. He quoted with approbation a saying of Mundella's, the

13 W.J. Ashley, *The Economic Organization of England* (London: Longmans, Green, 1921), 140

14 Cf E.P. Thompson, *The Making of the English Working Class* (Harmondsworth: Penguin, 1968), 222ff

15 *Lectures*, 205

16 *Ibid.*, 84, 191, 195

pioneer of conciliation boards and collective bargaining: 'We consider in buying labour we should treat the seller of labour just as courteously as the seller of coal or cotton.' The gulf between the classes could be bridged with 'the full, ungrudging recognition by the employer of the workman's equality and independence,' as the conciliation boards had shown. 'Democracy transforms disputes about wages from social feuds into business bargains.'[17]

The trade unions and the extended franchise, both of them working-class institutions that were condemned by orthodox political economy, saved England from revolution. Revolutionary socialists in Europe might call for the abolition of private property as the only way to secure improvement in the conditions of working-class life: 'We in England laugh at such conceptions, but if we are able to laugh at them, it is because we have here institutions like Trades-Unions, which have enabled working men to hold their own against employers, and to effect a considerable improvement in their condition.' But trade unions and other voluntary associations alone were not sufficient to ensure the most equitable distribution of wealth possible under existing social conditions. Toynbee 'reluctantly admitted' the necessity for state intervention, on condition that, 'first, the matter must be one of primary social importance; next, it must be proved to be practicable; thirdly, the State interference must not diminish self-reliance.'[18]

Beyond this, the new order of society required a new morality. The rise of democracy meant an end to the irreconcilable antagonism of the classes, 'for workman and employer parted as protector and dependant to unite as equal citizens of a free state.' But this did not mean an end to conflict: it would be a mistake to conclude that 'questions of wages can be treated as business bargains and nothing more.' Moreover, there was now the unpleasant possibility that workers and employers in any industry might join together to hold the rest of the community to ransom: 'There is already one great antagonism of interest – that between employer and labourer – and here you would be creating a second antagonism of interests between one group of producers and the producers of the whole community, and the result would be an industrial war within the community.' So although the conflict of classes could now be translated into the far less threatening conflict of interests, future stability would have to depend on the development of a new moral order: 'In spite of a fundamental identity of interest between employers and workmen revealed by the subsidence of social strife, there always will be, there always must be, antagonisms of interest; and these can only be met by

17 *Ibid.*, 192, 199, 171, 173, 198
18 *Ibid.*, 175, 220, 219

moral ideas appropriate not to the feudal, but to the citizen, stage. Men's rights will clash and the reconciliation must come through a higher gospel than the gospel of rights – the gospel of duty.'

Thus, in the final analysis, Toynbee's new political economy ended where it began: with his claim that the 'facts of human nature [are] capable of modification by self-conscious human endeavour.' While much of mid-nineteenth century economic liberalism was discarded in his work, the great postulate of eighteenth-century liberalism – the ultimate perfectibility and rationality of man – survived.

II

Granting the seminal character of Toynbee's work, it is hardly surprising that Mackenzie King should have come into contact with it at some point in the course of a student career which spanned three universities in two countries, and eight years of reading and lecture-going. What could not have been as readily foretold was that so many of King's professors should have identified their own work with Toynbee's, on the strength either of personal acquaintance or of some more remote connection. It must be remembered that Toynbee's special brand of political economy was still on the youthful leading edge of the discipline; while it had gained important disciples since his death, it was still by no means the received version of the subject in most university departments. All the same, and more, in all likelihood, by chance than by design, King's student contacts with academic political economists were in great part contacts with men who saw themselves in one way or another cast in the Toynbee mould.

The first evidence that King read Toynbee is found in a diary entry for 23 April 1894, when with his friend Charlie Cross he was studying for final examinations: 'Charlie and I have done a splendid day's work today. This morning we worked at our economics at the Ricardian period. We read some 5 or 6 chaps. in Toynbee's industrial revolution, and have found them very useful.'[20] For examination purposes, it is likely that King and Cross concentrated on the first sections of the book, Toynbee's formal Oxford lectures on economic history. That summer, however, King opened the book again, this time to its aphoristic final section: 'Tonight I read ... some notes & jottings by

19 *Ibid.*, 200, 166
20 Mackenzie King's personal diary (which has been published in microfiche by the University of Toronto Press) is located at PAC, in MG 26 J13. The earlier volumes were written in longhand, but a typewritten transcription exists and it is this that is used here. It is referred to henceforth as Diary.

Arnold Toynbee. I was simply enraptured by his writings and believe I have at last found a model for my future work in life.'[21] The following summer he took his copy of the *Industrial Revolution* with him on a holiday in Muskoka.[22] Shortly before he left, he had attended a public lecture by Jane Addams, the organizer of Chicago's Hull House settlement, which was modelled on Toynbee Hall in London.[23] After the lecture, King met Miss Addams: 'The history of the movement, taking it back to the influence & practical work of Arnold Toynbee was more than delightful to me. I love Toynbee & I love Miss Adams [*sic*]. I love the work in which the one was and the other is & which I hope soon to be, engaged in.'[24]

While the first diary reference to Toynbee occurs in the spring of 1894, it is not unlikely that King's first reading of parts of his book occurred two years earlier. He began his diary in September 1893: in September of 1891 he had enrolled as an undergraduate in the Faculty of Arts at the University of Toronto. In his first year there, he attended a course in economics taught by the University's Professor of Political Economy and Constitutional History, William James Ashley. Ashley, who was later to be described as Toynbee's most eminent disciple,[25] had been responsible for the editing and publication of the *Industrial Revolution* and had been tutored in economics by its author: while no reading list for his 1891–2 course survives, it seems unlikely that Toynbee's book should not have had a place on it. King studied for only one year with Ashley at Toronto, as the latter took a position at Harvard in the fall of 1892, but when King went to Harvard as a graduate student in 1897–9 he became Ashley's student again.[26]

The creation of a department of political science at the university (rather than the college) level was one of the conditions attached to the federation of

21 Diary, 11 July 1894. The final section of Toynbee's book was entitled 'Notes and Jottings.'
22 See the inventory at page 278f. of the Summer Diary for 1895.
23 For an account of the founding and work of Toynbee Hall, see Philip L. Gell, 'The Work of Toynbee Hall,' appendix to Montague, 'Toynbee,' 57–64
24 Diary, 21 July 1895
25 The description is Lujo Brentano's, in a testimonial written for Ashley: 'Testimonials in Favour of W.J. Ashley ... A Candidate for the Drummond Professorship of Political Economy in the University of Oxford,' pamphlet, 1890, 12f. Copy in University of Toronto Archives
26 C.M. Toynbee, 'Prefatory Note,' Toynbee, *Lectures*, xxx–xxxi; Anne Ashley, *William James Ashley: A Life* (London: King, 1932), 19, 22. Ashley assigned Toynbee in his 'History of Economic Development' course at Toronto in 1889–90; Vincent Bladen, *Bladen on Bladen* (Toronto: Scarborough College, 1978), 22. See also n 72 below.

denominational schools that became the University of Toronto in 1887–9.[27] The selection of a professor for the new department became a problem in Ontario politics, inasmuch as control over appointments rested with the provincial Minister of Education (and later Premier), George W. Ross. Political Science – the name of the chair was subsequently changed, apparently at Ashley's request, to Political Economy and Constitutional History – was viewed by Ontario's Liberal government as a particularly controversial appointment. While the documentary evidence is not conclusive, it appears that two inextricably interrelated issues were involved. First, there was a policy difference in the ranks of the Ontario Liberal party concerning Macdonald's National Policy of tariff protection. Toronto industrialists favoured the maintenance of the tariff, and the federal wing of the party was being pushed by Edward Blake towards the reluctant admission that any 'incidental' protection consequent on the imposition of a revenue tariff might not be altogether a bad thing. In rural Ontario, however, Liberal farmers were committed free traders. Ross, together with Blake, Mulock, and Mowat among the party leadership, had the problem of appointing a political economist whose views would not alienate either faction within the party. The second, related, problem was that of patronage. University patronage was taken more or less as a matter of course: that G.M. Wrong occupied the chair of history was due not only to his abilities in the field but also to the fact that he was Blake's son-in-law. But the really vexatious difficulty lay in the fact that there were two candidates for the political science job, each equally deserving of patronage, and each supported by one of the contending factions within the party. Ross considered the problem for some time, and finally rejected the two Canadian applicants as well as the suggestion offered by one of his correspondents, that both be hired. It was the better part of wisdom to go outside the country and hire someone whose liberalism was sufficiently well established to satisfy the party as a whole, whose remoteness from Ontario politics was sufficient to by-pass the internecine squabbling, and whose distinction was sufficient to quash the agitation for the appointment to go to a Canadian. Ashley was finally offered the post, but not before he had been interviewed by Ross, Ontario Premier Mowat, and federal Liberal leader Blake.[28] It was a happy choice: not only did Toronto acquire an outstanding political econo-

---

27 For details, see W. Stewart Wallace, *A History of the University of Toronto, 1827–1927* (Toronto: University of Toronto Press, 1927), chaps. v and vi; Alan F. Bowker, 'Truly Useful Men: Maurice Hutton, George Wrong, James Mavor and the University of Toronto, 1880–1927' (unpublished PH D dissertation, University of Toronto, 1975), chap. I.

28 On this point, Anne Ashley, *Ashley*, 48

mist, but a rift in the party was successfully avoided. In testimonials written on Ashley's behalf in 1890, Blake commented that 'you have dealt judiciously with the special difficulties surrounding you growing out of the present tariff policy of Canada,' while Sir Daniel Wilson, president of the University, noted that, 'he has successfully encountered the special difficulties of a subject closely related to the questions of party politics.'[29] Blake's satisfaction was no doubt enhanced by the fact that Ashley came down, judiciously, on the side of protection.

Ashley was born in 1860, the son of a journeyman hatter whose fortunes declined with the rise of machine industry in his trade. A brilliant student, he attended Oxford on scholarships, and took a First Class in History in 1881. Supporting himself by tutoring, he continued his studies until 1885 when he was elected to a Fellowship at Lincoln College. It was during this period that he came into contact with Toynbee and made the first of his short vacation trips to Germany, establishing relations with some of the members of the 'Younger Historical School' there. Ashley was trained as an historian in the institutionalist school of Regius Professor William Stubbs, and this orientation influenced his approach to problems of political economy. His major work in economic history, the *Introduction to English Economic History and Theory*, concentrated on the Middle Ages: its title reflected Toynbee's teaching about the interrelation of history and theory, and the first volume was dedicated to the memory of his former tutor. Ashley's choice of period may well have arisen from his interest in Toynbee's work on the industrial revolution and his historian's instinct for pushing the frontier of analysis further back in time: at any rate, it is recorded that one of his instructors, impressed by this proclivity, told him, 'You needn't go back to protoplasm, Ashley.'[30] But like Toynbee, Ashley was impressed with the need for political economy to relate to practical pro-

29 The Blake and Wilson quotes are from the 'Testimonials ...' pamphlet. This reconstruction of the politics of the Ashley appointment is based on a number of manuscript sources. They include: correspondence to George Ross in the Department of Education files (PAO: RG2 D7, box 10; file labelled 'Political Economy'); the Blake papers (three boxes of correspondence relating to the University, at the University of Toronto Archives); correspondence with Blake in the papers of University of Toronto President Loudon (Box 13, University of Toronto Archives); and the journal of Sir Daniel Wilson (University of Toronto Archives) which contains some spirited comments on the (deficient) character and ability of one of the Canadian candidates. For Blake's views on protection in 1888, and the division within the Liberal party, see R. Craig Brown, *Canada's National Policy 1883–1900: A Study in Canadian American Relations* (Princeton: Princeton University Press, 1964), esp. chap. 6.
30 Anne Ashley, *Ashley*, 18. The comment was J.F. Bright's.

blems of contemporary society, and he went further than Toynbee in dismissing the significance of abstract theory in the deductive tradition. While in Toronto and completing the second volume of his *Introduction*, he devoted much effort to studying the political economy of Canada and published a book on Canadian constitutional history. His 'practical' work lapsed somewhat during his Harvard years, apparently because he felt that as a non-citizen he should remain aloof from political debate (although he did some charity work), but on returning to England to organize the new school of commerce at Birmingham in 1901 he resumed this activity. He was an informal economic adviser to a number of British politicians, including Joseph Chamberlain, contributed articles to newspapers and journals, and published a book on the tariff question.[31]

Ashley set out his political credo in a letter to his fiancée in 1886, and according to his daughter and biographer it remained for the most part unchanged for the rest of his life. He began by laying out his objections to 'what are usually known as Socialists in England,' principally criticizing Marx's doctrine of surplus value, the tendency of socialists to ignore agriculture and non-factory industry, and their faith in the possibility of a rapid and fundamental change in social organization: against the latter, he opted for evolution rather than violent revolution. But he went on to say that the socialist analysis of factory industry is essentially correct (and in the tradition of Ricardo and Cairns); that 'in private industrial undertakings, certain arrangements are coming into existence, which point to ultimate socialization' ('e.g. the transition from individual entrepreneurs to great companies, the increased importance of the managing director, the clearer distinction between that part of profit that is due to skill, and that which is due to the mere possession of capital and goes to the shareholder') and that 'new views are arising of the functions of the State.' He continued, developing a theme which was to be repeated in his inaugural lectures at Toronto and Harvard:

Therefore, it seems to me that the work of the *Economist* should be, (i) the investigation of economic history – no facts are too remote to be without significance for the present, and both Lassalle and Marx have given a great impulse to investigation in this direction, and (ii) the examination of modern industrial life *in the piece*.

And for the immediate present and the *politician*, (i) to urge a new organization of existing Government works on the basis of fair wage and not competition wage ...;

31 Biographical details are from *ibid*.

(ii) the extension of State ownership to railways, waterworks and gasworks; (iii) the increase of *municipal* property in land and houses.'[32]

Ashley's views on trade unionism closely parallelled Toynbee's: 'Though Trade Unionism in itself may not be the ideally best means of remedying social inequalities,' he had written in 1881, 'yet it is really the only means towards that end.' While in Toronto, he advocated this position both within the university and to a wider audience through public addresses and journalism. That he should do so followed naturally from his conception of the role of the new political economist. In his inaugural lecture at Toronto he sketched in the field: 'All the studies of this course are concerned ultimately with society in its organized form as the State: and in all of them, accordingly, the final test in any matter must be the welfare of the State ... [S]ince the very exercise of individual rights rests on the existence of society, of which the State is the organized expression, the State can justly claim, in the interest of the common good, to modify individual rights.'[33] And he made it clear in this lecture that this new political economy was not to be merely an academic exercise: like the German economists with whom he identified his approach,[34] he saw himself as engaged in the training of practical men of affairs: 'I think it may be said that the introduction of Political Science is due

32 This letter is reproduced in *ibid.*, 34f
33 The Toronto inaugural address is published in *ibid.*, 49–52. See also his introductory lecture at Harvard, 'On the Study of Economic History,' and his 1899 address to the American Historical Association, 'On the Study of Economic History: After Seven Years,' both in his *Surveys*, 1–21, 22–30.
34 That Ashley identified himself with the German school is suggested in the two *Surveys* articles referred to above. *Surveys* was itself dedicated to one of the intellectual leaders of the German school, Gustav Schmoller. Ashley seems to have been accepted as a colleague by the Germans, as well: the 'Testimonials ...' pamphlet contains letters from Knies, Schmoller, Brentano, and Cohn. But for some strictures on Ashley's relationship to the German school, see Schumpeter, *History*, 822n. I have not included a discussion of the German school here because King's exposure to it was indirect, coming from men like Ashley, Veblen, and others. This may be a good point, as well, to indicate that by 'the new political economy,' as I use the term in this chapter, I do not mean to imply that there existed a formal school among English-speaking political economists as there existed in Germany, but merely that a new and describable orientation was emerging, many of whose adherents were acquainted with one another and shared, to a greater or lesser degree, some significant professional, intellectual, methodological, and political opinions. Whether these were sufficient to justify grouping them under the rubric, 'new organic intellectuals,' in the sense described above, is, it seems to me, quite independent of the question whether they may be described as forming a 'school' in the strict sense which Schumpeter apparently intended (*History* 808, 822; the unfinished chapter on 'sociology of economics' was to provide a narrow definition of the term – see p. 46f).

to a widening conception of personal duty. The work of governing a great modern State is not an easy one: it is not one which average common sense, and party management can be left alone to control. I will not here lay stress on the advantages of such a course to the man who intends to "enter politics," to the man who looks forward to journalism, to the future civil servants of the country ...'

Mackenzie King, the future journalist, civil servant and politician, was not in Ashley's audience that day, but there can be little doubt that had he read these words a few years later he would have agreed wholeheartedly. 'I believe a sound theoretical basis is what I need,' he wrote early in 1897; 'I am strongly inclined practically [,] I need a solid basis, I believe in conservative as opposed to radical measures for reform.'[35]

III

When Ashley left for Harvard in 1893, he was replaced at Toronto by James Mavor. This is not the place to attempt charting the course taken by this eccentric figure from his early adventures with the Socialist League to the *laissez-faire* hysteria of his last work.[36] In his long career at the university, Mavor gained a reputation as Toronto's own bohemian intellectual. He maintained a correspondence with Tolstoy and Kropotkin, was acquainted with Shaw and Havelock Ellis, and in general kept up an international network of intellectual, business, and artistic contacts from the library of his home on the university campus. In several important respects, Mavor's thought underwent a profound change in the course of the years, although a continuous thread of libertarian individualism may be seen to run through his work. Here, it is only necessary to discuss his ideas and teaching as they had developed to 1896, when Mackenzie King ceased to be his student.

By the time of his arrival in Toronto at the age of forty, Mavor had already run through the gamut of *avant-garde* political, social, and artistic move-

---

35 Diary, 12 Jan. 1897
36 There have been two worthwhile attempts recently to write Mavor's intellectual biography, although the definitive work has yet to be done. They are Bowker, 'Truly Useful Men,' chap. IV, and S.E.D. Shortt, *The Search for an Ideal: Six Canadian Intellectuals and their Convictions in an Age of Transition, 1890–1930* (Toronto: University of Toronto Press, 1976), chap. 7. I have used these extensively in this and the following two paragraphs, although the speculation about 'libertarian individualism' is my own. Mavor's autobiography, *My Windows on the Street of the World* (London: Dent, 1923; 2 vols.) is not as useful as it may seem, inasmuch as hindsight seems to have modified a great many opinions.

ments in his native Scotland. He had been intimate with William Morris and with Patrick Geddes, who had been involved in a Scottish version of Toynbee Hall; he had been successively a member of the (Marxist) Social Democratic Federation, Morris's Socialist League, the Glasgow Fabian Society, and the Liberal party; and he had participated in urban reform, sanitary, suffragist, co-operative, trade unionist and adult education movements, among others. He had more or less trained himself in political economy, befriended the leading British and European economists, become active in the British Association for the Advancement of Science, and lectured in political economy at Edinburgh and Glasgow universities (concurrently) and at the Glasgow Athanaeum. In his capacity as a political economist, Mavor 'established himself as the foremost British expert on labour colonies, studied co-operative societies, trade unions, and other systems of production and social organization, and in 1891 endorsed a bimetallist programme as a means of stimulating world trade and stabilizing currency.'[37] At the same time, he was making his living in journalism, had become editor of the *Scottish Arts Review*, and stood for the Liberal nomination in an 1892 parliamentary election. In a letter recommending Mavor as his successor, Ashley informed Ross that 'his desire to move across the Atlantic is due not to any want of success at home, but to a desire to give up the literary labours of which he has hitherto in large measure secured an income.'[38] Once in Toronto, however, Mavor set out to spread himself every bit as thin as he had in Glasgow.

Unlike Ashley and Toynbee, whose background had been in history, Mavor came to political economy from applied science. His formal education had been curtailed when he was apprenticed to a drysalter, but even before this he had been a youthful assistant to Sir William Thompson (later Lord Kelvin), and later on, as assistant editor of *Industries*, his contacts were with technicians and engineers. This background in the 'hard' sciences undoubtedly influenced his approach to political economy: while Mavor could be as suspicious as Ashley or Toynbee of the claims of abstract deductive theory, his grounds for empiricism were quite different. While the historians abjured positivism, Mavor championed the possibility of a social science, similar to the physical sciences to the extent that its laws would be formed by painstaking generalization from carefully acquired empirical evidence. While he

37 Bowker, 'Truly Useful Men,' 119
38 This letter is in the Department of Education files, PAO, RG2 D7 Box 16, Mavor dossier. I am indebted to M. Starkman of the University of Toronto Archives for bringing the letter to my attention and permitting me to use his copy of it.

would have differed with the historians in this respect, he heartily agreed with their conviction that political economy should be a *practical* science. In his early years, he would have committed it to the goal of rational state intervention: later, he seemed to see its greatest practical utility in showing the futility of public interference in business affairs.

By the time he was appointed to Toronto, Mavor had clearly allied himself in politics with Gladstone's Liberals, and was so much aligned with the 'centre' of that party that in 1892 he stood for nomination against a candidate of a Labour faction: 'Mavor believed that his "neutral position as regards capital and labour" and his "known sympathy alike with the advancement of labour, and with liberal policy generally" could reunite the party behind him.'[39] Mavor's views on the 'labour problem' had been spelled out in two studies written a short time before: 'On Wage Statistics and Wage Theories,' read to the British Association in 1888, and *The Scottish Railway Strike*, a little book published in 1891.

In the former, Mavor aligned himself with the position already taken by Toynbee and Ashley, that 'how the product is distributed among the contributories to production is at once the most practically important and the most difficult question in the whole field of economic science.' The paper called for the collection of better statistics on wage rates and living costs, and agreed with the Ricardian view that 'the normal tendency when competition is free, is for actual wages to approximate to actual maintenance.' He claimed, however, that his position differed from that of Jevons – 'that "ultimately" actual wages tend to be identical with the amount of the produce' – in that in his view, 'the tendency to approximation only operates when free competition is replaced by control either on the part of the labourers as in trade unions, or on the part of the employers as in the case of [profit-sharing co-operatives].' In other words, he accepted the view that trade unionism could affect the distribution of the product, and banished the wages fund doctrine to the abstract realm of perfect competition.

In his study of the 1891 railway strike, Mavor devoted himself to the question of the impact of large organizations of capital and of labour on the common good. He noted that 'the modern joint-stock company and the modern trade union were born together, and have grown together,' and claimed that 'the dominant motive in both cases is self-interest': 'The danger which may arise to society lies in the circumstance, that one or other of these masses of combined labour or combined capital which may happen to exercise some socially necessary function may fold its hands and say, "we do no

39 Bowker, 'Truly Useful Men,' 121. The internal quotations are Mavor's.

work until such and such terms be granted."'' In addition, he raised the point earlier made by Toynbee, that workers and employers might combine to hold the community to ransom: 'a danger so great,' he quoted Marshall, 'that if these compacts cannot be bent by public opinion they may have to be broken up by public force.'[40]

Developing his theme, Mavor expounded an organic conception of society, stressing 'the close interdependence of the parts of our highly organised society, and the dependence of the groups which constitute the commercial world upon each other and upon the public.'[41] The public is the 'real sufferer' in major industrial conflicts, and for this reason it is entitled to interfere: 'The interest of the public as the holder of the great insurance fund from which all the losses due to all such catastrophes must be paid, is really paramount. The objection that it has no business with industrial conflicts, and that these are best left to be settled by the brute forces of the combatants, will not hold water for a moment.' Should the public, then, prohibit 'combinations' of workers in industries which 'exercise some socially necessary function'? Mavor argued that this would place the public service and the railways at a competitive disadvantage, so that they would in any case have to pay higher wages in order to attract workers away from industries where unionism was permitted. Furthermore, if an industry combined opposition to unionism with 'excessive severity of work' – as the railways had – 'rebellion' would inevitably follow. The best solution to the problem, he argued, was 'wisely conducted and strongly supported unions, with appeals to arbitration where disputes cannot be prevented otherwise.' But this solution, he continued, is not much more than a 'palliative': '[T]he trade union and the joint-stock company ... do not supply a permanent solution of the labour problem, though they may contain the germs of a mediate solution. The difficulty, so far as both of these forms of combination are concerned, is, that men in a position of considerable power are apt to use it badly, ... Meanwhile, the existing checks to these tendencies – publicity and criticism – may

40 The quotation is from Marshall's Presidential Address to Section F of the British Association, 1890. This may be the place to point out that a similar fear of a form of 'class war' breaking out between producers and consumers was expressed by Jevons in a book assigned in a number of the courses King took: '... the supposed conflict of labour with capital is a delusion. The real conflict is between producers and consumers.' W.S. Jevons, *The State in Relation to Labour* (London: Macmillan, 1894), 101. But Jevons also thought that a 'vertical' organization of producers would be preferable to the present 'horizontal' one, despite this problem; see 149, 167. For King's view on this question, see below.
41 *The Scottish Railway Strike, 1891: A History and Criticism* (Edinburgh: William Brown, 1891), 60

well be applied constantly, and much may be hoped from the growing discredit which is overtaking short-sighted self-regarding and socially injurious action on the part of individuals or of corporations.'[42]

In his 1892 nomination address, Mavor reflected on the experience of the strike and the necessity for state intervention, arguing that '*laissez-faire* is dead': 'I am bound to say that while before the railway strike I was of opinion that trade unions might probably actually secure shorter hours before the public were brought to the pitch of demanding legislative interference, the strike convinced me that in securing shorter hours the way to cause least disturbance to industry, and the way to save unnecessary friction between employers and employed was by legislation.'[43]

From the 1890s on – at any rate, until the no-holds-barred vituperation of *Niagara in Politics* (published posthumously in 1925) – Mavor adopted the stance of the objective social scientific observer, engaged in 'criticism' and the formation of public opinion. He described this stance in his inaugural lecture at Toronto: 'If we are to build up a science of economics we must do so with our eye on, but with our minds and voices away from, the market place or the hustings. We must have as little emotional interest in this or that theory, or this or that policy, as we should have in the examination of the evolutions of an oyster feeding under the microscope ... Any student of history knows more of battles than the soldiers who were there ... The onlookers see most of the game.' The role of economics in the study of practical problems, then, 'is to give a man that sane and all-round view which our dual system of party government tends to prevent him from having; it is to show a man that the result of his action is at best uncertain, but that in proportion as step by step he reasons rightly and comprehensively, he is the more likely to bring his action to good issues.'

Mavor insisted in this lecture that social problems like poverty could only be effectively met on the basis of extensive empirical investigation and analysis: 'The methods that are now being employed in the study of poverty are simply the methods by which other sciences than economics have succeeded in enlarging the domain of knowledge, viz., observation, induction and deduction. The same order of skill with which beasts, birds, fishes and insects have been classified and arranged is at last being brought to bear upon mankind. It is beginning to be possible to understand ourselves.' He gave as examples of the sort of empirical investigation he had in mind the work of

42 *Ibid.*, 60, 61, 64
43 'The Political Situation and Labour Problems: An Address Delivered to the Electors of Tradeston, 30th March, 1892,' pamphlet (n.p., n.d.), 9

Frederic Le Play on the social organization of families, and Charles Booth's surveys of working- and lower-class London. Mavor had corresponded for some years with the Le Play societies and had personally accompanied Booth on some of his investigations. He argued that unscientific charity breeds pauperism: it is only with painstaking empirical investigations like those of Le Play and Booth that effective solutions to this and other social problems may be designed. The ultimate justification for public, or state, charity is the desire of the society to preserve itself so long as every man does not have 'a perfectly alert regard to his own interest, and the most ample opportunity to secure his interest.'[44] Ultimately, problems like poverty must be dealt with on a technical basis, on a foundation of objective social scientific knowledge.

Mavor had an acute sensitivity to the failings of mankind, and to the tendency of power to corrupt. There appears to be justification in his writings for classing him with the traditional conservative, with an organic conception of society and a belief that man is inherently evil. On one occasion, he defined the major political positions: 'The most favorable view of the Conservative position is that in conservatism society is conceived as an organism, and that certain institutions form a vital part of it. Men rather than institutions are to be blamed when necessary. The least favorable view of the Liberal position is that the Liberal regards society as a mechanism, and holds that when things go out of gear the machinery is at fault, and must be altered.'[45]

Mavor still defined his politics as Liberal in 1895, when this was written, but he was coming to believe that there was increasingly little real difference between the British parties. On the basis of this quotation, it is hard to place Mavor: the enterprise is probably pointless, in any event, for there were obvious inconsistencies in his thought. But it is interesting to note that he adopted a Tory approach to the critique of trade unionism: the 'futility of the working-class movement in the U.S.' was put down to 'the centralization of control of these organizations in the hands of a few exceedingly expert but doubtfully honest labor politicians,'[46] while in Britain the 'working class does not trust its leaders, and the leaders do not trust each other ... They have been easily won over by social and political influence ... The working class is

44 'The Relation of Economic Study to Public and Private Charity,' *Annals Am. Acad. Pol. Soc. Science*, vol. IV (1893). This is an 'Inaugural Lecture delivered before the University of Toronto, February 6th, 1893.' Quotations are from pp. 34, 37, 38, 40, 53.
45 'Labor and Politics in England,' *Pol. Sci. Quarterly*, vol. X, 3 (1895), 489n. King wrote in his Diary on 28 November 1894: '... went to a public lecture by Prof. Mavor on "the Labour movement in Eng. politics" the best lecture I ever heard Mavor deliver.'
46 'Prof. Mavor on Labor in the U.S.,' *Toronto Evening News*, 5 Nov. 1898

divided into innumerable sections ... It is too selfish or too astute to pay the expenses of labor candidates. If these think they can win a collectivist state for it, they are welcome to make the attempt.'[47] By 1895 it appears as though his stance of objectivity and science had become a barely veiled cynicism. But it would be a mistake to identify this as the only trend in Mavor's thought: he persisted with various schemes of social amelioration and economic betterment, and the eager reformer was to coexist uneasily with the disappointed sceptic for many years.

Mavor's influence on King is extremely difficult to pin down. There is no doubt that many of the ideas and approaches discussed here became part of King's intellectual apparatus, but it is just as certain that the relationship between the two, once extremely friendly, became equally hostile. Two events, the student strike of 1895 and King's failure to win a graduate scholarship at Toronto, have been suggested as leading to the falling-out. Ferns and Ostry, who are extremely hostile to Mavor, organize their account of the 1895 affair around his behaviour.[48] Briefly, the Political Science Club, of which King was a member, submitted its lecture program to Mavor for approval, as required by the University regulations, and it was accepted. But then the club invited two Toronto labour leaders, Alf Jury[49] and Phillips Thompson, to speak without obtaining authorization. Mavor, 'who was already hostile to the trade union and socialist movement,' was enraged and cancelled the entire programme. In the ensuing conflict, a host of festering issues related to the authoritarianism of university officials and the alleged incompetence of certain faculty members, including Mavor, received an airing, and the students, led by a triumvirate one of whose members was King, decided to boycott classes. Eventually an Ontario Royal Commission was appointed to inquire into the affair.

Ferns and Ostry did not have access to the King diary: if they had, they would have found that King remained on good terms with Mavor in the wake of the strike, defended him before his fellow students during the

47 'Labor and Politics in England,' 516
48 Ferns and Ostry, 20–8. For their hostility to Mavor, see 18–19.
49 This was not the first time that Jury, a tailor and socialist, had been banned from campus. In April of 1886, Daniel Wilson refused to let the Political Economy Club invite Jury, as part of his on-going war of attrition against a faculty member who later became one of the Canadian contenders for the job that eventually went to Ashley. See Wilson, 'Journal,' 21 April and 17 June 1886. In October 1895, King visited Jury to get information for an article on 'the condition of male labour in Toronto.' Diary, 7 Oct. 1895

affair,[50] and believed his own testimony before the Royal Commission supported not only the students but Mavor as well.[51]

Mavor did not recommend King for a graduate fellowship, apparently because – on King's own showing – more senior candidates had applied. King, who had stood second in his year, was upset: 'I think Mavor has acted very shabbily.'[52] John King, Mackenzie's father, was furious and pursued the matter, and Mavor, with a vengeance, asking questions in the University Senate, of which he was a member, and writing angrily to Ross.[53] But John King was a disappointed man, and ever alive to the possibility of a conspiracy against himself and his family. His son seems to have gotten over his own disappointment: a week later he was visiting Mavor to discuss possible essay topics, and a little later still King reported on another visit, 'I quite enjoyed my afternoon with him.'[54] Perhaps both the strike and the fellowship chapters were merely occasions for King's legendary duplicity; in any event, it is difficult to reach a final verdict. There can be no doubt, however, of King's later hostility to Mavor: in 1905 he told the Governor General, Lord Grey, that he 'would not believe [Mavor] on oath.'[55] But despite this antagonism, Mavor seems to have had a significant influence on the development of King's thought and career aspirations: in the final analysis, perhaps they were too much alike in some important respects to remain on good terms.[56]

IV

King's biographers have minimized the significance of his undergraduate years at the University of Toronto, arguing that his intellectual awakening came as a graduate student at Chicago and Harvard. Noting that his undergraduate record was an excellent one, Dawson comments that 'it is nevertheless impossible to indicate any specific benefit or inspiration which he derived from these studies.'[57] Ferns and Ostry claim that 'King's life as a

50 Diary, 11 Jan. 1895
51 On 13 April, King went through his diary and took out his comments on Mavor, presumably in preparation for the commission hearings. On the 15th, he called on Mavor, 'to get my notes' – could these be the diary extracts? King gave his testimony on the 17th. See Diary for these dates.
52 Diary, 25 and 30 Sept. 1895
53 These letters are in Department of Education, Mavor dossier.
54 Diary, 9 and 23 Oct. 1895
55 Quoted in Bowker, 'Truly Useful Men,' 134
56 For a psychoanalytic interpretation of King's relationship with Mavor, see Joy E. Esberey, *Knight of the Holy Spirit: A Study of William Lyon Mackenzie King* (forthcoming).
57 Dawson, 41

student at the University of Toronto would hardly be worth recording were it not for a dramatic event which filled a part of his last year of undergraduate study' – the student strike. Conversely, they argue that 'in the making of his career as a politician the years 1896–1900 [the Harvard and Chicago years] were, for Mackenzie King, the most important of his life.'[58] Their interpretation is the antithesis of the position taken here.

King's ideas and vocation were essentially formed during his University of Toronto years. Chicago and Harvard were important, and they left their mark. But that mark was made on an already formed mind: to pursue a rather unwieldy analogy, the ornamental excrescences and architectural detail supplied by the graduate schools ought not to be granted more importance than the less subtle, but perhaps more solid, structure which predated them and to which they were affixed. King's diaries contain much more intellectual detail about the Harvard and Chicago years than they do about Toronto; his lecture notes are more extensive and insightful;[59] but in the last analysis these sources reveal far less about what he really learned than his own intellectual productions, which are examined later in this chapter. Partly for this reason, and partly because the Chicago and Harvard environments have been extensively described elsewhere, it is not necessary here to go into as much detail about King's contacts at the two American universities as it was for Toronto.

At Chicago, King studied sociology with Charles R. Henderson, the university chaplain, and political economy with J. Laurence Laughlin and Thorstein Veblen. At Harvard, he took courses in the history of economic theory with Frank W. Taussig and with Ashley, studied sociology with Edward Cummings, and took a course offered by the visiting economic historian, William Cunningham. He was also a member of the senior 'seminary' in economics, supervised by Ashley, Cummings, Taussig, and the department chairman, C.F. Dunbar. He had originally intended to take the two-year PHD course at Chicago, but left after a year, submitting his thesis to Toronto in 1897 for an MA degree. He attended lectures at Harvard in 1897–99 and passed the qualifying examination for the doctorate, although he did not receive the degree until 1909, and then under somewhat unusual circumstances.[60]

---

58 Ferns and Ostry, 20, 30
59 Some of King's lecture notes are preserved at PAC (MG26 J4): vols. 45 through 50 contain Toronto notes; 43 and 44 Chicago notes; 7 through 12 Harvard notes. Henceforth referred to as Student Notes
60 King sent Harvard a collection of the official reports he had compiled as a civil servant, in lieu of a thesis: the University agreed to accept one of them, and he was awarded the degree only a few days before his election to the Cabinet. See Dawson, 198f.

Neither Chicago nor Harvard had succumbed as completely as Toronto to the claims of the new political economy. The chairman at Chicago, Laughlin, was a Harvard man and a traditionalist, although his preference for the older economics did not preclude him from hiring Veblen, albeit in a very junior capacity. Dunbar at Harvard was equally of the old school, and one of the most influential younger men, Taussig, was busily reconciling the older economics of Ricardo with the marginal utility theory of Jevons and the Austrians in what amounted to an end run around the followers of the historical school.[61] But there was a general reconciliation taking place between the old guard and the young progressives in American economics. When the American Economic Association was formed in 1885, it included in its statement of principles this commitment: 'We regard the State as an agency whose positive assistance is one of the indispensable conditions of human progress.'[62] Not surprisingly, the traditionalists did not join. But by 1892 peace had been made, the offending clause had been dropped, and Dunbar was made president of the Association. There is some evidence that he felt it politic to reciprocate, and that this is how Ashley came to be appointed to the new chair of economic history at Harvard.[63] Among the reasons for this reconciliation was the fact that many of the 'social questions' which had troubled American economists and led to the division in their ranks could now be passed on to the sociologists, who occupied separate departments at several universities, including Chicago. With the delegation of the more politically awkward topics to the realm of sociology, some of the political economists and economists pure and simple could satisfy themselves with more technical and 'scientific' claims for their own subject. At Harvard, however, sociology remained within the political economy department for many years, as, incidentally, it did at Toronto, where Mavor's long-lasting influence may well have been responsible for the broader view that was taken of the discipline's scope.

---

61 The Austrian school of Böhm-Bawerk *et al.* had some influence on Mavor, as his work on wage theories indicates. In an essay on the development of political economy in Canada, one of Mavor's colleagues wrote that he 'adheres to the Austrian school.' S.M. Wickett, 'The Study of Political Economy at Canadian Universities,' Appendix to the *Report of the Ontario Bureau of Industries, 1897* (Toronto: Ontario Department of Agriculture, 1899), 103

62 Quoted in Joseph Dorfman, *The Economic Mind in American Civilization*, vol. 3 [1949] (New York: Kelley, 1969), 207

63 Robert L. Church, 'The Economists Study Society: Sociology at Harvard 1891–1902),' in P. Buck, ed., *Social Sciences at Harvard 1860–1920* (Cambridge, Mass.: Harvard University Press, 1965), 67f

King met the chairman of Chicago's sociology department, Albion Small, almost on his arrival at the university, but he was displeased by Small's aggressive entrepreneurship, which involved pressing a copy of his recently published book into King's hands and offering him a large fellowship in the following year if he would agree to major in sociology, all on an hour's acquaintance; it appears that King did not attend his classes. Henderson taught sociology 'as an instrument of Christian social reform.' He wrote a textbook for Chautauqua, was involved in organizing the University Settlement, another descendant of Toynbee Hall,[64] and was later active in prison reform. He was a founding associate editor of the *American Journal of Sociology*. His teaching practices apparently involved sending his students to observe conditions in the Chicago slums, and in an appendix to his 1898 textbook, *Social Elements*, he gave extensive 'directions for local studies,' emphasizing social cartography and the inquiry methods of Le Play and Booth.[65] He insisted that the social scientist become involved in practical affairs, and claimed that, because of his disinterested stance, the scholar had a special role to play: 'It is the duty of the scholar to place and keep before the public the supreme criterion of social conduct, the common welfare ... The scholar's duty is to aid in forming a judicial public opinion, as distinguished from the public opinion of a class and its special pleaders.'[66]

In all this, his views closely resembled Mavor's. He agreed with Ely that 'the labor movement is a force pushing toward the attainment of the purpose of humanity ... the full and harmonious development in each individual of all human faculties,' but he insisted that there existed a larger 'social movement' which crossed class lines, and included 'managers of trusts' among its leaders. His reformism rested on idealist premisses: '[T]he oppression of one class is an injury to all others, and most of all to the oppressor. It is better to suffer wrong than to do wrong; and there is no element in the community to which universal justice is so vital as the small class of the rich. It is not only necessary that they should be just, but that other men should believe that they are just. The smallest class is the most helpless.'[67]

Thorstein Veblen, of course, had a rather different analysis. By 1896 he was working on the first draft of *The Theory of the Leisure Class*, and had

---

64 Richard J. Storr, *Harper's University: The Beginnings* (Chicago: University of Chicago Press, 1966), 77, 186f. The Chautauqua book was *The Social Spirit in America* (Meadville, Pen.: Flood and Vincent/The Chautauqua-Century Press, 1897).
65 *Social Elements: Institutions, Character, Progress* (New York: Scribner's, 1898), 395ff.
66 'Business Men and Social Theorists,' *AJS*, vol. I, 4 (Jan. 1896), 389, 390
67 *Social Elements*, 169, 170

sorted out his distinction between 'industrial' and 'pecuniary' employments.[68] King took his courses on economic theory and on socialism. In the former, the readings covered not only Malthus, Senior, Ricardo, and Cairnes, but, characteristically, looked at Hegelianism, Santanyana's *Sense of Beauty*, and Hoffman's *Race Traits and Tendencies of the American Negroes and Indians* as well. Readings for the socialism course ranged from St Simon, Proudhon, and Owen through the anarchists to the Chartists, Christian Socialists, and Fabians. Students were expected to read *Capital* and Böhm-Bawerk's criticism of it, as well as the Fabians, Bellamy, William Morris, and Hobhouse. 'Veblen is the best lecturer I have as yet listened to,' King reported. Again, 'This course I must admit has influenced me greatly. I believe that Socialistic tendencies are coming to be the prevailing ones.'[69]

The inability of his students to discover 'the slightest inkling' of Veblen's own stand on socialism was legendary: Laughlin was less opaque. He denounced 'any appeal to the state by labour, because such socialistic appeals are confessions of individual weakness.'[70] But Laughlin was not unaware of the effect his views had on his students, as one incident recorded by King shows: '[W]ent to Prof. Loughlin's [*sic*] house to have a talk with him on my paper. We had a most interesting conversation for nearly two hours on the condition of the working classes & the poor in this century. The early part of my paper was strongly socialistic & I was glad to hear the opposite side so strongly & ably represented. I felt sorry to think that Prof. Loughlin thought I or others believed him to be unsympathetic etc.'[71] Laughlin was the last of the old school to remain outside the American Economic Association, not joining until 1904.

At Harvard, King studied under Ashley again,[72] and found his lectures 'well delivered & full of first class material.' When Ashley went on sabbatical in 1898, his friend and mentor William Cunningham, of Cambridge, took his place. Cunningham was author of *Growth of English Industry and Commerce* [1882], which Ashley had read while in residence at Oxford, and his methodological and social views were very similar to Ashley's. Cunningham had also been an intimate of Toynbee's, and conveyed more of the latter's

68 Joseph Dorfman, *Thorstein Veblen and his America* [1934] (New York: Kelley, 1961), 132 and *passim*
69 Student Notes, vol. 44, files 237 and 238; Diary 12 May and 18 June 1897
70 Dorfman, *Veblen*, 120, 138
71 Diary, 2 Feb. 1897
72 Dawson, 70, claims that 'King had not actually met Ashley in Toronto before the latter's departure from the University.' However, there are notes on Ashley's course in economics in the Student Notes, vol. 45, file 246.

Christian idealism in his teaching than did Ashley. King attended his lectures and read his books, and was enthralled by him: 'He speaks of the need of high ideals & self-discipline as the great factors in individual progress. He is right. This man is having an influence on me. He is the sort of personality I have sought most, & I meet him now at the close of my course. A Christian Economist. The Harvard men present the Utilitarian point of view most strongly. Taussig is a strong utilitarian. It is well that Cunningham asserts so strongly the Christian point of view [;] it goes to show the completeness in life which wd be wanting but for religion.'[73]

Edward Cummings, whose sociology courses King took, was another Toynbee devotee. It is unlikely that he had ever met the master, but he had spent a year in residence at the original Toynbee Hall and shared the enthusiasm for 'practical' work that he found there. In other respects, though, he was very far from men like Ashley and Cunningham: 'Cummings was one of those fascinating, confused, contradictory conservatives so prominent at the turn of the century. A Social Darwinist, he used rigidly objective standards of social investigation to show that individual initiative and the free operation of natural selection were essential to social progress. Yet he was a social gospeler and headed many, many charity organizations in the Boston area.' Cummings' resolution of this conflict between philanthropy and natural selection is reminiscent of Henderson's idealism and Mavor's strictures on charity: 'Thus is the real paradox solved, the sacrifice of the strong to the weak reconciled with progress, because *intelligent* self-sacrifice of the strong to the weak makes the strong stronger and the weak more strong. To him that hath the capacity to receive shall be given the priceless boon of opportunity, and from him that hath not shall be taken away the power of degrading himself and society.'[74]

King took Cummings' course on 'Principles of Sociology,' which was devoted in large part to the evolution of the family, and found it a waste of time. He gave Cummings his notes on Veblen's course, 'thinking he would be glad to look them over & feeling that Veblen's lectures could not but bring him closer to the truth,' but the experiment was evidently unsuccessful, and King concluded that 'there is something about Sociology which is loose & flabby.'[75] He was a little more positive about Cummings' course on 'The Labor Question in Europe and the United States,' commenting on one lecture that 'there is lots of good material, how I would like to be giving it to

73 Diary, 6 Oct. 1897, 17 March 1899
74 Church, 'Economists Study Society,' 37, 43f
75 Diary, 11 Feb. 1898, 6 Oct. 1898

an audience of 500 working men.'[76] Cummings defined the 'labor problem' as the problem of obtaining 'for the great multitude of people who work for hire the possibility of gaining such a standard of life as will enable them to develop and realize those capacities of threefold nature which every individual in a greater or less degree is born heir to.' 'Threefold nature' referred to the material, intellectual, and spiritual existences of man: it would be interesting to know what King's '500 working men' would have made of Cummings' definition of the last of these as 'an existence which, ceasing to regard the individual as a means, looks to him, however deformed, and however defaced, as an end in himself ...'[77]

Some account of Frank W. Taussig's position has already been given. King took two of his courses, one on taxation and the other on modern economic theory, both of which he enjoyed, and he became quite friendly with Taussig. Like Laughlin at Chicago, Taussig 'insisted on the substantial validity of the classical school,' but unlike Laughlin he was open to considering new ideas even if, in the end, he rejected them. Dorfman gives several examples of his conservatism: his belief that 'the proponents of labor legislation were guided by an excessive humanitarian spirit; his doubts about the effectiveness of disability insurance, 'because of the enormous clerical staff needed'; his conviction that minimum female wage legislation was 'injurious to the interest of women workers.'[78] But in his attempts to rescue classical theory, he introduced a pragmatic touch. Thus while he wrote a book on the wages fund doctrine, attempting to demonstrate its lasting usefulness, he noted that 'the conclusions of the economist as to the theoretical relations of wages and capital have little or no bearing on the disputes between laborers and capitalists as they usually appear in the specific case.' The wages fund doctrine set the upper limit beyond which wages could not increase: however, 'proximately, the success or failure to get higher wages will depend much on the accidents of the particular situation.'[79] King rather sagely noted, on reading the book, 'it seems to me these writers have different things in mind when speaking of the Wages Fund,' and later: 'I believe Taussig is right though I think his conception of the Wages Fund is somewhat different to that held by the old orthodox economists.'[80] It should be clear that Taussig's approach was just that which the historical school dismissed: King's contrast

76 *Ibid.*, 11 Oct. 1898
77 Student Notes, vol. 11, file 65
78 Dorfman, *Economic Mind*, 264, 267
79 *Wages and Capital: An Examination of the Wages Fund Doctrine* (New York: D. Appleton, 1896), 100f., 104
80 Diary, 7 and 10 Jan. 1898

of Taussig and Cunningham has already been cited. Despite his encounters with Taussig's conservatism, and despite his friendship with Taussig, King retained his belief in the efficacy of state action. Thus, on one occasion King read a report to the 'seminary' on Canada's new 'fair wages' legislation: 'I had quite a discussion with Meyer re Gov't interference in matters of this kind with wh. my subject dealt. He said he is a strong individualist & differs strongly from my point of view. Is inclined to look on Gov't as a ring of politicians & not as representing the people. We shall talk the matter over again.'[81]

V

We have now glanced at several of the key intellectual figures with whom King came into contact in the course of his student career. While the economics they taught ranged from the unfettered classical model to the marginal utilitarianism that was replacing it, it is significant that an influential group based its position on the English historical school's critique of classical theory, a critique that diverged significantly from the new justification of *laissez-faire* in neoclassical economics.

Implicit in the historical school's analysis of the emergence of capitalist social relations was a sentimental regard for the mutual interdependence of worker and employer which was taken to be characteristic of pre-industrial relations. At the same time, Carlyle's longing for a return to the old ways was rejected in favour of an attempt to reconcile modern property relations with a humanitarian concern for the well-being of the working class. The old paternalism of master towards men had been destroyed by changes in the organization of industry, and a return to the old way was not only impossible but undesirable because it would mean losing all the advantages and promise of the new industrialism. "Indifference' could become the basis for a new liberal order if it was accompanied by the 'gospel of duty.' In practice, 'duty' translated into the recognition of an identity of interests among workers and employers, encouraged by the new paternalism of the state. Factory legislation, social insurance, and conciliation of disputes might be implemented by the state to ensure that the dictates of the gospel of wealth did not overrun those of the gospel of duty.

In industrial-relations terms, the classical model merely denied the ability of trade unionism, in any guise but that of the benevolent society, to increase the share of the working class in the social product. Out of the critique of classical theory, several alternatives were to emerge. The English historical school leaned heavily towards the view that trade unions could improve the position of the workers, and advocated the positive role of a paternalistic state against the claims of *laissez-faire* individualism. In a similar revolt against *laissez-faire*, the programme of the German *Katheder-Sozialisten* culminated in Bismarck's social insurance schemes. American institutionalism, rid of the Veblenian burden of a general critique of capitalist society, was translated into advocacy for compulsory collective bargaining in the work of John Commons and his associates, although it had to compete for many years with the rigorous *laissez-faire* prescriptions of the mainstream of professional economists. In Britain, the renewed commitment to the negative state that followed from the neoclassical orthodoxy of Alfred Marshall lay behind the continuing reluctance to intervene in relations between employers and employees.

While King's mature position constituted an eclectic amalgam of parts of all these positions, the most prominent strain was that of the English historical school. Out of its analysis of the nature and implications of property and social relations in modern society, he pieced together a view of the strains and tensions in Canadian industrial relations and a programme for their amelioration.

During his university years, King became imbued with a sense of mission, and much of his involvement with various of the social movements of the day must be put down to his attempts to discover precisely what that mission entailed. The term, mission, may be used advisedly, for it was some time before King's sense of his life's work became largely secularized. His biographers have described the numerous projects of social amelioration into which he threw himself during these years. He visited hospitals and prisons, occasionally preaching a lay sermon within their walls; he started clubs for newsboys and devised a highly idiosyncratic strategy for the reformation of prostitutes; he attended charity organization conferences and took office in the YMCA; he had a short-lived experience in the Toynbee pattern at Chicago's University and Hull House settlements. Throughout all this, as his diaries reveal, he was attempting to map out a conception of his future role that would link his reformist aspirations with his developing estimate of his own strengths and shortcomings.

'What am I to be? That question presents itself to me continually and I am not unambitious in the reply I make.'[82] That question, along with various replies, is a frequent refrain in King's early diaries. Three vocations pre-

82 *Ibid.*, 31 Aug. 1895

sented themselves to him as worthy ones: he could be a minister, an academic political economist, or a politician. As time went on, he found he could subsume the essential contents of the first of these in the others: eventually, he was to link the remaining two in a career as an expert civil servant and, finally, cabinet minister.

In November 1893, shortly after beginning his third year at the University of Toronto, King experienced a call to the ministry. It appears to have been his first contact with the supernatural: for seven nights in a row he opened his bible to 'Chapters in which I found some verse which spoke of my going into the ministry.' The call was not at first wholly convincing, it seems, for he continued: 'I am trying to turn my thoughts to this end & hope soon to be determined.' On New Year's Eve, summing up the events of the year, he wrote: 'I have decided, I may say, to become a Minister of the Gospel of Christ.' But this vocation was competing with another. Only two weeks later, the question arose again: 'What course am I to take in Life [?] I have decided [I] might say on the Ministry and yet I have a very great desire to go into politics which Goldwyn Smith says "is the noblest of all callings tho; the worst of all trades". I would add [,] except the Ministry which I believe to be the highest and best of all callings [.] I will leave all to my Maker. He has guided me in the past and will open up the way for me in the future.'[83] Then, that April, the third option was entered in the diary for the first time. '[I] find that I am [?taking] in this Pol. Ec. in great style. I am very fond of this subject and take great pleasure in working at it.'[84]

His political ambition was linked to his liking for political economy; evidently politics would mean putting the lessons of the science into practice, as the new political economists taught. The two interests appear together for the first time in 1894, when King and Charles Cross were studying together for examinations: 'Tonight Charles and I have been working up the Austrian theories & had one or two heavy disputes. I walked up with him & remarked that it would be strange if we should ever be on the floor of H. of Prlt. together. I have a grt. longing for Politics but do not think I may go in it.'[85]

Similarly, there was a link between his religious vocation and his political one. By 1895, when the thought of actually becoming a minister had receded from his horizon, King had managed to subordinate the former to the latter. He heard Sir Wilfred Laurier address a meeting at Massey Hall: 'I felt more

---

83 *Ibid.*, 7–14 Nov. and 31 Dec. 1893; 15 Jan. 1894. Here, as later, the supernatural was not decisive.
84 *Ibid.*, 3 April 1894
85 *Ibid.*, 27 April 1894

than inspired with the speaking and feel that my ambition may carry me into political life. I want to have first a solid Christian basis.'[86]

King's academic vocation was later in developing. There is a hint of it on 27 July 1895 – 'I would like to give all my time to Political Science[.] I will work very hard at it & endeavour to accomplish something as my whole heart is in the work' – and later that summer it is fully enunciated for the first time. This passage is especially interesting, for it indicates how politics and scientific work were becoming integrated in King's aspirations, and how a religious career was subsumed by them:

I might as well record here thoughts that are constantly flooding my mind. I feel that I have a great work to do in this life, I believe that in some sphere I shall rise to be influenced and helpful. As yet I do not know where it is to be, I believe it may be a professor of Political Economy, an earnest student of social questions. Or it may be in public life, parliament perhaps, – what if [it] might be both. – Here is my ambition, if it is right, if it is going to make my life good and useful [,] if it make me helpful to others and a good faithful servant of my great Master, may it be granted. If it is to take me a step farther from Heaven than I am today may it be blighted as cursed, e'er the desire unfolds itself.[87]

That same summer, King professed a 'great faith ... in the "historical method" & theories as being the theoretical counterpart of the practical activities of the time.' By that fall, as be prepared for a year of newspaper work, the 'practical' had become a necessary adjunct of his academic vocation: 'I think the practical work in Journalism will be good for me, it will call into service my college reading & fit me better to understand practical movements. I will keep before me always an academic future.'[88]

It was this notion of the 'practical,' of course, which knit together King's vocations. The common element was that desire for a 'useful' life which Mrs Ward had discerned in Toynbee and his circle, and for King, as for them, this meant a life dedicated to improving the condition of the people. As a minister, he would have followed in the steps of Toynbee's Reverend Bartlett, living among the poor and preaching a social gospel. As an academic, he would have modelled himself on Toynbee or Ashley, seeking solutions to practical problems of the day, unafraid to challenge the prejudices of received political economy. As a politician, his mentor would have been Grandfather

86   *Ibid.*, 5 Feb. 1895
87   *Ibid.*, 27 Aug. 1895
88   *Ibid.*, 6 Sept. and 1 Oct. 1895

Mackenzie, the fearless reformer who died in penury as a consequence of his struggles on behalf of a down-trodden people. These were the figures who peopled King's daydreams, and sometimes it seemed to him that they had existed only to smooth the way for his arrival on the scene: 'I was at the office all day and spent most of my time reading Mackenzie's life. As I read of his many marvellous escapes from death the thought occurred to me [:] why should this man escape the many many attempts made to end his life, suffer imprisonment, experience poverty in its worst form, be exciled [*sic*] from his native country, that to him a young child should be born, the 13th & last of a large family, who should bare[*sic*] of [a] son to inherit the name of his grandfather W.L. Mackenzie[? S]urely I have some great work to accomplish before I die.'[89]

As he had noted, King was 'not unambitious' in his aspirations. But these ambitions, he felt, were selfless ones. In September 1894 he recorded attending 'an excellent sermon on helping the degraded poor, just the line of thought I have often contemplated,' and a few weeks later he decided 'to devote my whole life to mission work.' By November, this aspiration had been linked to his academic vocation: 'I am going to make a careful study of the poorer classes and the worst social evil with a view to remedying to some degree the latter, and bettering the condition of the former,' a resolution that he repeated the following spring: 'I feel more anxious than ever to work at Economics most thoroughly and seek to learn all I can of the masses, the labouring classes and the poor, to understand their needs and desires and how to alleviate them, and better their condition.'[90] By the time King left for Chicago in the summer of 1896, the vocation of usefulness had attained an intensity which can only be described as morbid. He wrote to his friend Albert Harper:

The world, the toiling weary world is crying loudly for you and me [,] why do we pass by on the other side [?] Poor suffering humanity and the erring many [,] how they need our help, our comfort, our strength! I can hear their voices tonight, some crying from beds of loneliness & pain for a heart to appeal to. Some weeping in factories & sweat-shops for the arm of a deliverer to shorten their hours & secure them their bread, some thrown deep into the mire of despair praying only for a gleam of light. In this ever heaving and surging ocean of human despair, in this wild hurricane of thoughtless indifference & maddening haste to ruin, in this night destitute of hope & peace you can hear from every side the moanings, the shrieks & the echos of

89 *Ibid.*, 18 July 1895
90 *Ibid.*, 16 Sept., 11 Oct., 29 Nov. 1894, and 27 April 1895

unanswered calls rising ever & saying always 'Oh who will help'. Long have I heard the awful din, often have I recoiled back into my selfish rest but other voices tell me now to go, no longer to wait, & surely I will heed them. I have gazed & pitied – who has not, – I have even thrown a life rope but have been afloat myself and had not the power to hold it fast, but now I must go myself, live for them, die for them, & through Eternity rejoice with them ...[91]

As this letter makes painfully clear, King had a rather Galahad-like conception of the role of the reformer. At times, he exhibited an unequivocally condescending attitude to those who were to be reformed: 'I helped a drunken man home this afternoon along King St.,' he wrote on one occasion; 'I felt very sorry for him, he looked so respectable.' 'I like to see the poorer classes enjoying themselves,' he commented on Orange Day, 1895.[92] But this was only one side of King's reformism, a side that seemed to be drawn out particularly in his association with that Galahad *aere perennius*, Albert Harper, as their letters and King's *Secret of Heroism* make so plain.[93] It would be a mistake to consider King a sort of magic-lantern reformer, pure and simple. The sentimentality and condescension were there, to be sure, but for the most part, and increasingly with the passage of time, they were relegated to the background and to the diaries. So while as late as April 1899 he could write in his diary, 'I love the working classes, I long [to] be more consecrated to my work and their cause,' he was equally capable of a tough-minded assessment of social conditions: 'My views are changing on the matter of the small store. I see in it a possible detriment to the welfare of the community, espec. to the welfare of those employed in it, & while I regret to see men of independence being crushed to the wall, yet their preservat'n with conditions as they are means little for themselves or society at large.'[94]

As his studies progressed, King came to refer less and less to the 'poorer classes' and to such social evils as prostitution and godlessness, and focused instead on the 'working classes' and labour problems. As early as June 1895, he had established some contacts in the Toronto trade union and socialist movements, and during that summer he seems to have spent a good deal of time with members of the Socialist Labour Party, although he disliked its 'scepticism.' The following autumn, he followed up these contacts, intending to write on 'the condition of male labour in Toronto,' and gathering

91 7 June 1896; appended to 1896 diary
92 Diary, 3 Jan. and 12 July 1895
93 (Toronto: Ontario Publishing Co., 1906)
94 Diary 5 April 1899 and 2 Nov. 1898

information on unemployment. In October he gave a brief speech to the SLP, 'pointing out that it was not so much Socialism [,] single tax &c that we were to argue about but [should] rather consider the question of more immediate reforms.'[95] During this period, King was working as a reporter for the Toronto press, and it is likely that many of his researches were intended for newspaper publication. But it is clear that he enjoyed his contacts with working-class leaders for their own sakes, and when he arrived at Chicago in October 1896 he immediately set about meeting local labour figures. He was not uniformly taken with them all: while he was favourably impressed with one Chicago socialist another he 'sized up as a shark at the outset.' He came back to Toronto for the Christmas vacation, and gave a talk to the SLP on 'Industrial Conditions in Chicago,' 'making this a means of reaching that body on the higher principles of life': 'In my closing address, when I spoke best, with ease & I believe a little power, I broached only on the need for improvement in morality & honesty among workingmen & all classes as being the most effective remedy for the evils of today or of any day. They applauded me loudly & responded heartily to a vote of thanks moved by Roland – a brick mason & seconded by Hepburn a tailor, both old friends.'[96]

In June 1897, he visited Pullman, the company town that had been torn apart by a violent strike three years before: 'I must say I was very much impressed with the place & the condition of the working men & their sur-roundings as they outwardly appeared. It was evident that they were "con-trolled" & well under the hands of the authorities, but they certainly seemed to be better off than workmen in crowded centres. We had a very happy day.' A year later he heard Eugene Debs, who had just organized the American Socialist Party, speak. In King's comments on this event are summarized both his sense of mission and his view of his own place, as an expert political economist, in the movement for social reform: '[Debs] said nothing in explanat'n of principles of his party, indulged in generalities about rights of man, etc [.,] spoke much of rich & poor, God's free air, the sun etc. I think his heart right, his desire good, but this sort of thing is terrible. Now the world needs *men* in the movement, trained minds. Oh God fit me for this work, to see & know the problem & how to direct people ...'[97]

By the time he left Harvard, King had come to see himself as a member of the intellectual vanguard of reform. He was sympathetic to some aspects of

---

95 *Ibid.*, 13 July, 7 Oct. (King met with Alf Jury, of student strike fame, to discuss this subject), 11 and 20 Oct. 1895
96 *Ibid.*, 21, 22, 23 Oct., 27 Dec. 1896
97 *Ibid.*, 5 June 1897, 27 Oct. 1898

socialism, suspicious of great accumulations of wealth, and committed to the alleviation of social injustice. He identified himself with the aspirations of the working class, although he doubted the integrity or ability of many of its leaders. He considered himself a trained social scientist who could bring his special knowledge to bear on working-class problems, and at the same time he could envision a role as the political champion of the oppressed. He seems to have had no misgivings in principle concerning this role: that the working class might have to develop its own leaders from within its ranks seems not to have occurred to him. He was fitted, by virtue of his training, his faith, and his ancestry for the task and, *deo volente*, he would fill it. 'I am coming more and more round to the view that other classes as well as those who actually work at manual labour are producers,' he had written in January 1898: 'After [all] in society as it is each man can only play a part, & it seems to me he does best to choose the part [in] wh. he has a comparative advantage & plays it well.'[98] Mackenzie King, conscious of his comparative advantage, was prepared to play his part.

VI

While King's mature self-concept was beginning to take shape, so too was his intellectual work developing along the lines that would lead him to the Department of Labour. In particular, his studies of the structure of the American trade union movement and his investigations of the 'sweating system' in the clothing trades, drawing on his growing familiarity with the new political economy, brought him within the sphere of 'practical' work that was to shape his career for the next decade.

On the day of his arrival at Chicago (3 October 1896), King met with Laughlin to discuss a thesis topic. Laughlin suggested that King study the rate of interest in the US but, although he 'outlined the subject in a very interesting manner,' it appears to have been too far beyond the range of King's enthusiasms for him to take it up. He wanted to write on a labour topic, and eventually settled on the International Typographical Union. The paper was submitted as an MA thesis to Toronto in 1897, and King published two articles based on his research in the University of Chicago's *Journal of Political Economy*.[99] This work, concentrating on an analysis of the structure

98 *Ibid.*, 26 Jan. 1898
99 'The International Typographical Union,' unpublished MA thesis, University of Toronto, 1897 (Copy in University of Toronto Archives. Mavor was the reader for the thesis: he considered it a 'very competent paper. The only drawback is that there are no references to authorities.' Henceforth Thesis); 'The International Typographical Union,' *JPE*, vol. v

of the American trade union movement, represents a fairly mature stage in King's thinking about working-class organizations. There is little evidence that his views changed materially in the next twenty years.

King does not question whether trade unions are in general a good thing, beyond stating that 'labor has sought many forms of organization by which to protect its rights and advance its interests; of these none has proved more continuous in existence or effective in operation than the trade union.' It is plain that he considers trade unionism more commendable than other forms of working-class organization, 'which in the end prove ephemeral.' The successful trade union is one whose members 'recognize that as a class they are destined to continue subject always to the conditions of hire,' and govern themselves accordingly. Legitimate trade unionism, then, acknowledges and accepts capitalist property relations: its development is ancillary to that of the factory system which both 'stimulated, and to a degree rendered necessary' the organization of unions. Indeed, union development in the United States has been more 'commendable' than in England, because 'the struggle for existence and subsequent recognition, which was so earnestly fought out by the trade unions of England at the beginning of the present century, is a feature which, happily enough, has been almost entirely wanting in the development of trades unionism in America.'[100]

The best and most successful form of trade unionism, King urged, is that which eschews politics: 'Next to internal dissension no other single factor has been so ruinous to successful association among workingmen as political intrigue, and for this reason the wisest leaders have always deprecated the introduction of politics into their unions or trades assemblies.' The most thorough-going form of apolitical unionism is the American Federation of Labor, and notwithstanding the fact that the more reform-minded Knights of Labor is still 'the most prominent federation in the country today,' King's typology makes the AFL 'the last and still higher form of organization.' AFL unionism is the best hope of the working-man, and when its organization is 'complete,' 'disturbances within the ranks' will cease to exist. It is the best antidote to radicalism: 'In this age, when there is a tendency, especially among large sections of workingmen, to seek for better conditions along new and somewhat radical lines, and a parallel tendency to "cry down" old and existing institutions, laborers will do well to consider what these older organi-

(1897), 458–84; 'Trade-Union Organization in the United States,' *ibid.*, 201–15. At Harvard, King wished to write a PHD thesis on the American Federation of Labor, but Ashley dissuaded him because another student had already begun work on the topic. Diary 6 Oct. 1897

100 'Trade-Union Organization,' 201, 202; 'International Typographical Union,' 458

zations have accomplished in the past, what their more perfect development promises for the future, and what are the reasons which should lead them at this particular time to accept or reject a plan of social and industrial betterment which never before has had more reasonable opportunities or better facilities for ultimate success.'

In describing the increasing level of organization from the independent local union through to the federation of many national unions, King notes the tendency for American unions to become 'international' by extending their jurisdiction to Canada. 'The trade interests of Canada and the United States are so nearly identical that this method is all the more imperative.'[101] International unionism is not problematic for King. In his study of the typographical union, he paid special attention to the problems inherent in organizing female and black workers, but seems not to have considered nationality worthy of a parallel discussion.

Increasing scale of organization is indicative of greater perfection in a trade union movement. Large-scale organization has its dangers of 'clique rule' and 'possible tyranny,' but on the whole a large union is a moderate one. In his thesis, King gives an extensive account of the International Typographical Union's defence fund: 'Paradoxical as it may appear, the perfection of the fund has been accompanied by greater conservatism on the part of the national body in its attitude towards strikes. There is not now the same likelihood [sic] of an unfair strike occurring as there was before the fund came into existence; for, with the increased funds at the disposal of the governing body, has come increased authority on the part of the executive officers in deciding upon the justifiableness of a strike, and increased responsibility on the part of the union that advises it.' The union's constitution contains elaborate safeguards against local strike action, and centralizes authority over the fund. The 'wisest leaders' have forsworn strikes in favour of arbitration, and the existence of the defence fund is principally useful in so far as it can back up an arbitration demand, by confronting the wealthy employer with an equally wealthy union. This proto-Galbraithean analysis concludes that 'the merit of the defence fund lies as much in the number of strikes which it prevents, as in the aid which it affords to those which are undertaken.' In Toynbee's terms, the large defence fund fosters indifference.

It is the task of the union to 'guarantee that the members have attained that degree of efficiency as handicraftsmen which the union may claim for those who belong to it.' This, of course, is an extension of the principle that

101 'Trade-Union Organization,' 207, 215, 206

the good union is one that is ancillary to capitalist property relations. This principle may conflict with the policy of including all the workers in the union's trade; in any event, so long as women and blacks maintain the standards of skilled white males, they should be accepted into the union without pay or other discrimination. Employers were excluded from the ITU in 1886, not 'in consequence of any hostility on the part of the workingmen towards those in whose employ they are,' but 'due exclusively to the desire for greater freedom of debate than might otherwise be enjoyed.'

Among 'the features most commendable in trades unions' are the various welfare and benefit plans they offer to their members. Such institutions as the home for indigent printers and various local charities 'are evidence that trades-unions develope [sic], to some extent, the nobler side of humanity.' Another evidence of the maturity of the typographical union is that there have been few efforts to 'influence the party colour of the union.' 'The insinuation of party politics into a union is almost certain to work disruption.'[102]

King's view of the good trade union may be summarized briefly. It eschews strikes, politics, and recognition disputes. It makes every effort to place relations with employers on a business basis, and avoids discrimination on racial or sexual grounds. It is large and bureaucratically organized, because centralization leads to moderation. It is reconciled to existing property relations, seeking only to advance the legitimate interests of its members along constitutional lines. Finally, it engages in benefit and insurance activities for its members, and is responsible for the discipline and qualifications of workers in its trade. The American Federation of Labor, then, is the very model of the modern trade union, and every effort should be made to help its organization become 'complete.' What part King was to play in this effort remains to be seen.

King's intellectual infatuation with the work of Arnold Toynbee is widely recognized and has already been discussed. In December 1896, he experienced a similar enthusiasm, although perhaps more short-lived, for another book, Charles Kingsley's *Alton Locke, Tailor and Poet*. This has not been noticed by King's biographers, although it was to have an important consequence for the direction of his career. King began reading *Alton Locke* while he was attending a charity conference, and the two seem to have worked together to fire him with enthusiasm. He memorized Kingsley's defence of the church in its relation to social problems, 'in case I need to use it at Conference,' but the need apparently never arose, and 'the church with-

102 Thesis, 7, 28, 30, 15, 25, 1, 42, 36

stood the attack as it ever will.' Nevertheless, 'it is a wonderful book. I find my own feelings so admirably expressed in many of its pages I could not get but great inspiration from reading it. I felt I must get to work & *do* something.'[103]

Alton Locke is a rather dreadful novel of Christian Socialism and class relations, organized around a tailor who, by dint of his poetic talents, becomes a favourite of the middle class and in the process becomes alienated both from his own roots and from his new patrons. Kingsley introduces him to the Chartist agitation, principally in order to demonstrate the folly of working-class politics. This accomplished, the author seems not to know quite what to do with his hero, so he sends him on an emigration voyage and kills him *en route*. It was one among a number of Victorian novels that attempted to find a solution to class problems: for Kingsley, a Liberal, individual effort and talent was the legitimate entry to upward mobility, while in Disraeli's *Sybil*, the working-class hero who rises to heights of personal nobility and can stand above the mundane world of manufacturer and worker turns out in the final chapter to be descended from an old aristocratic family. This is the only significant difference between the two: for both Tory and Liberal the average member of the working class is nasty, brutish, and, oddly enough, short.

There are two themes in *Alton Locke* that seem to have appealed to King. The first, already mentioned, is the defence of the church as an instrument of social reform. The other is the description of the 'sweating system' of tailoring in the 'dishonourable trades,' whereby the old craft traditions were destroyed and wages and working conditions extraordinarily depressed through the practices of subcontracting and outwork. Kingsley's descriptions of the sweatshops are particularly vivid and, for the most part, ring true to life:

I stumbled after Mr. Jones up a dark, narrow, iron staircase till we emerged through a trap-door into a garret at the top of the house. I recoiled with disgust at the scene before me; and here I was to work – perhaps through life! A low lean-to room, stifling me with the combined odours of human breath and perspiration, stale beer, the sweet sickly smell of gin, and the sour and hardly less disgusting one of new cloth. On the floor, thick with dust and dirt, scraps of stuff and ends of thread, sat some dozen haggard, untidy, shoeless men, with a mingled look of care and recklessness that made me shudder. The windows were tight closed to keep out the cold winter air:

103 Diary, 6–11 Dec. 1896.

and the condensed breath ran in streams down the panes, chequering the dreary outlook of chimney-tops and smoke.[104]

King had already encountered some aspects of the sweating system as a reporter in 1895, when 'a rather clever Jew' gave him a full account of its practice in Toronto.[105] Reading Kingsley seems to have given him a new impetus, however, for he spent the summer vacation of 1897 in Toronto, as a journalist for the *Mail and Empire*, carrying out detailed investigations of sweating and related social problems.[106] In the course of these researches, King stumbled upon the fact that clothing being made under government contract was 'sweated.' It appears that, rather than have this appear in a Conservative newspaper, King decided to inform the government. He visited Sir William Mulock, a family friend, colleague of King's father on the university senate, and Postmaster-General in the Laurier administration, who immediately had a new 'anti-sweating' contract form drawn up, and commissioned King to carry out a special study of methods used in the manufacture of government clothing.[107] This report was submitted in 1898.[108] Discussion of the government's action must be put off to another chapter: here, it is King's analysis of the sweating system that is to be considered.

King was not the first to report on the sweating system in Canada. The Royal Commission on the Relations of Labour and Capital had stated, in 1889, that the system existed 'only in exceptional cases in Canada,' but enumerated several 'abuses which lead inevitably to the sweating process,'

104 *Alton Locke, Tailor and Poet* [1850] (Everyman edition, 1970), 38. There are some particularly grisly descriptions of conditions in the homes of sweated tailors later in the book: see, e.g., chap. XXXV, 'The Lowest Deep,' and also Kingsley's prefaces.
105 Diary, 23 Oct. 1895. This seems to have been Benjamin Gurofsky, who supplied much of the information for Wright's investigation: see n. 110.
106 Four unsigned articles in the *Mail and Empire* are attributed to King by Dawson (65 n25). They are: 'Crowded Housing, Its Evil Effects' (18 Sept. 1897), 'Foreigners Who Live in Toronto' (25 Sept. and 2 Oct. 1897), 'Toronto & the Sweating System' (9 Oct. 1897).
107 For the terms of this contract see the *Globe*, 30 Sept. 1897, 'Adds A Labor Clause.' See also chap. 5 below. ╱
108 'Report to the Honourable the Postmaster General on the Methods Adopted in Canada in the Carrying Out of Government Clothing Contracts,' 1898. This report was published as a pamphlet, and assigned Sessional Paper number 87 for the year, but it was not printed in the annual volume of Sessional Papers. There is a copy in PAO, filed as pamphlet #22 for 1898. Henceforth referred to as 'Sweating Report.'

and called for legislation to suppress them.[109] In 1895, Alexander W. Wright was appointed a Commissioner by the Mackenzie Bowell government, 'to inquire whether, and if so, to what extent the sweating system is practised in the various industrial centres of the Dominion.' He reported that sweating was becoming fairly prevalent in the clothing industry, and recommended legislation, but the Conservatives, who had apparently established the inquiry for electioneering purposes, declined to act.[110] King's newspaper articles and official report differed from these, however, in two important respects. First, in pointing to sweating on government contract work, he created a potentially dangerous political issue. Second, he provided not only a description of the sweating system, but a political economist's explanation of it as well.

King defined the sweating system as 'a condition of being in which the remuneration is quite disproportionate to the amount of work done': 'It is also usually understood that the hours of labor are long, and that the place in which the work is done, and the environments to which the workers are subjected, are unhealthy, and such as to prove injurious to their physical and moral well-being. Excessive work, low wages, long hours and unhealthy surroundings are the distinguishing characteristics of the so-called sweating system.' These conditions arose because of the tendency of wholesale clothiers to avoid the provisions of the Factory Acts by contracting out work to be performed in small shops and private homes. There were several advantages for the wholesalers: they could avoid payment of the (Quebec) business tax; the contractors' profits, when working for government at a fixed sum, were 'calculable almost to a certainty,' and the wholesalers were able to keep contract prices below those 'sufficient to meet the gross expenses of a large factory with adequate labor-saving machinery and a division of labor minutely apportioned.' That wages could be kept sufficiently low to justify the system was due to vicious and unrestricted competition: 'The industries of one country are competing with those of others; within the one country those of one city or town with those of others; within the one city one wholesale merchant with the other wholesale merchants; among those employed by each, one contractor is set off against the others; his employees are set off against each

---

109 Greg Kealey, ed., *Canada Investigates Industrialism* (Toronto: University of Toronto Press, 1973). This is an abridgement of the reports and testimony of the 1889 Royal Commission. See 25–9 and *passim*.

110 Alexander Whyte Wright, 'Report upon the Sweating System in Canada,' Sessional Paper #61 (1895), 1. Cf. Sir Charles Tupper, in *Debates* (1896), 5052f. There were charges, as well, that Wright campaigned for the Conservatives during or immediately after the investigation. *Ibid.*, 1620–1

other; the small home-shops are arrayed against the workshops, and against each other; while the home workers are opposed to the home-shops and engaged in an endless conflict among themselves. In such a struggle the weakest are continually going to the wall and the last surviving on each plane help to bring down the others to their level.'

King argued that in its historical development, the clothing industry passes through three stages: from home, to shop, to factory. But the transition to the highest stage had not been completed, and 'methods common to all three stages have been retained, and are in operation at the present time.'[111] Sweating, then, was not properly the most recent stage in the history of the exploitation of labour by capital; rather, it was a throw-back to an earlier, less perfect form of organization of industry.[112] The problems arose because the clothing industry had not kept up with industrial evolution. King implied that the factory system, properly regulated, was the most advanced and humane method for organizing production. This view resembles his position on the 'small store,' mentioned above. Thus the sweating system was not one of the consequences of maturing industrialism: it was an 'abuse' traceable to the incompleteness of that process of maturation in a particular industry. Government intervention was necessary to overcome this backwardness.

The implications of King's views on the large-scale organization of industry, and indeed the implications of that trend in the Canadian political economy itself, are discussed later in this study. For the time being, it is sufficient to point out that both King's sense of mission and his developing analysis of industrialism and the labour movement flowed from the new political economy that he encountered at Toronto. While there are obvious difficulties with the proposition that particular authors and university lecturers have a determining influence on the thought of their readers and students, it is argued here that King's 'intellectual formation' took place in an environment, partly of his own selection, rich in the ideals and interpretations that he was to make his own. In a broader sense, moreover, this environment was an international one with specific national consequences. In Britain, it was to crystallize into the 'New Liberalism'; in the United States it was to feed the sources of 'Progressivism.'[113] The intellectual contents of

---

111 'The Sweating System in Canada,' *Globe*, 19 Nov. 1898; 'Sweating Report,' 21
112 For Marx's opposing view, see Charles Lipton, *The Trade Union Movement of Canada 1827–1959* (Toronto: NC Press, 1973), 64.
113 See, *inter alia*, L.T. Hobhouse, *Liberalism* [1911] (New York: Oxford University Press, 1974), and Michael Freeden, *The New Liberalism: An Ideology of Social Reform* (Oxford: Oxford University Press, 1978). There have been a number of recent attempts to iden-

these movements had resemblances, traceable in part to the body of thought considered here, but they were not identical. Mackenzie King's brand of industrial peace policy was an important part of the Canadian response to this environment: but as in the case of its British and American counterparts, this response was to be unique. King was neither a New Liberal nor a Progressive, but with the leaders of those movements he shared a common ancestor.

tify King with the American progressives, none of them particularly convincing. See, for example, Keith Cassidy, 'Mackenzie King and American Progressivism,' in John English and J.O. Stubbs, eds., *Mackenzie King: Widening the Debate* (Toronto: Macmillan, 1977).

3
Excursus: *Industry and Humanity*

Thought and life move through conflict to unity. [Salem Bland, *The New Christianity*, 1920]

Mackenzie King's articles on trade unionism and the sweating system were written just as he was about to embark on his career as labour expert: his work on sweating led, as we shall see, both to the creation of the labour department and to his employment in its service. No excuses need be made for the proposition that the ideas and principles set out in these early articles informed his approach to labour problems in the course of that career. Here, however, we leap some twenty years to 1918 and the publication of *Industry and Humanity*, a date that marks the close of that career and the opening of another. The writing of *Industry and Humanity* was both King's final contractual obligation to the Rockefeller Foundation, for which he had been working as an industrial relations consultant during the war,[1] and, some commentators would have it,[2] his entrée into the leadership of the Liberal Party of Canada. That *Industry and Humanity* represents King's reflections on two decades of experience in industrial relations is clear: what is somewhat more difficult to maintain is that the ideas set out in that book, like those in his earlier writings, informed his approach to labour problems from 1900 to 1911. This claim is made here: what is an excursus chronologically need not be a digression analytically.

This claim should not be taken too broadly. It is not intended to imply that King's thought underwent no change in the intervening period. The content

1 For an interesting new account of King's work with the Rockefellers, drawing on Gramsci's analysis of the intellectual, see Stephen Scheinberg, 'Rockefeller and King: The Capitalist and the Reformer,' in English and Stubbs, eds., *Mackenzie King*.
2 Cf. Ferns and Ostry, chap. IX.

of *Industry and Humanity* was undoubtedly influenced by King's experiences with the Rockefellers and by the climate of the wartime years. The book's rhetoric was shaped by the ideology of postwar reconstruction, as well as by the swelling currents of the Social Gospel. Much of this, however, is veneer. *Industry and Humanity* owes its greatest debt to King's pre-war experiences, and its great themes are ones with which we have already familiarized ourselves. Toynbee and Ashley, Mavor and Veblen – each has an identifiable presence in this book whose very title seems to be modelled on Toynbee's 'Industry and Democracy.' Where the book's approach is only dimly heralded in King's university years, precedents may frequently be discovered in speeches he gave during his tenure in the labour department,[3] as well as in articles published in the *Labour Gazette* and elsewhere. Moreover, several of the main arguments of *Industry and Humanity* are clearly anticipated in a five-page outline King drafted sometime between 1907 and 1911.[4] If we had as our principal concern the need to show that there is little new matter in *Industry and Humanity*, the task would not be overwhelming.

But that, of course, is not our principal concern. We are interested, rather, in understanding King's practice in the labour department, and this chronological excursus is necessary because some important aspects of that practice are intelligible only in light of the book's argument. That King should have dreamt up so complicated a rationale after the fact is unlikely, and the speculation is in any event unnecessary. While King's thinking about labour problems undoubtedly developed over the twenty years in question, it exhibited no radical discontinuity. In the final analysis, while it cannot be demonstrated that King acted in such and such a way before 1911 *because* he held to an idea that is only fully set out in the 1918 book, many of those actions are best understood in the context of those ideas. To examine *Industry and Humanity* here is a necessary compromise. Whether it is a debilitating one, the reader must decide.

I

King's youthful articles dealt with structural aspects of the organization of labour and production: the focus of *Industry and Humanity*[5] is on the dyna-

---

3 See for example the report of his speech on technical education in the *Toronto Daily Star*, 1 April 1910.
4 This is at PAC in MG 26 J4, vol. 15, 10512–6. The most likely date is 1910.
5 *Industry and Humanity* [1918] has been reprinted with an introduction by David J. Bercuson (Toronto: University of Toronto Press, 1973). Page references from this edition are incorporated into the text of this chapter.

mics of industrial relations, particularly industrial conflict. In the reconstruction rhetoric of *Industry and Humanity*, class conflict is set against the recent
war to illustrate its imminent danger:

Countries cannot continue to watch antagonistic groups in Industry assume the proportions and attitudes of vast opposing armies, without some day witnessing conflict
commensurable with the strength of these rival aggregations. If, to-day, nation can
rise against nation, under the incitement of ambition, or fear, or cherished ideals; if,
overnight, men of all classes can be led to forget differences and remember only the
flag which typifies unity; with human nature what it is, is there not also the possibility
that men may be equally willing to sacrifice their lives, through impulses of fear, of
love, and of hate, not one whit less real, and which have been cherished just as
ardently, just as secretly, and just as long? In many particulars, the horrors of international war pale before the possibilities of civil conflicts begotten of class hatreds.
This, the world is witnessing, even now! [p. 24]

King's explanation for the emergence of industrial disorder is almost a
paraphrase of Toynbee's. The essential difference is that while Toynbee
argued that the 'gospel of duty' was already becoming apparent in an environment of industrial democracy, spelling an end to class antagonism, for
King the danger of class war is still imminent. But like Toynbee, King sees
the origins of conflict in changes in the organization of production, which
have led in turn to altered social relations of employers and employees:

[T]he substitution of large-scale organization in industry for the domestic system ...
has wrought more change in the social order than the combined forces of many
preceding centuries. The transition has been accompanied by inconceivable hardship
and injustice. The large-scale organization of industry has been mainly, if not all but
exclusively, responsible for the shifting of industrial areas, the subdivision of industrial processes, the divorce between agriculture and manufacturing, the congestion of
cities, the rivalry between men and machines, the increased competition of foreign
with domestic labour, and the competition of women and children with men. It has
helped to break up communities and households, and to scatter their families over all
quarters of the globe. Worst of all, it has occasioned the instability characteristic of
modern industrial life, and has rendered inevitable the commercial depressions, the
financial panics, and the violent industrial crises which have become recurring
phenomena of our times. [p. 74]

King follows Toynbee in asserting that the social disorganization consequent
upon these changes has been the source of much suffering for labour, and

that industrial conflict has been its result. Toynbee would also have agreed with the next step in the argument:

What so many fail to see is that large organization of Industry and vast wealth are *in themselves* neither good nor evil. The *control* of either may contribute to vast injustice; it equally affords opportunity for the largest measure of service to mankind ... It is not against the *form*, but against the possible *abuses*, of industrial organization, whatever the system, that protests should be uttered. [p. 76]

Large-scale organization of industry offers, in principle, labour's greatest hope. Its development has meant the substitution of democracy for serfdom and of contract for status. It makes possible the production, and hence the distribution, of wealth beyond the dreams of the past, and it forms the essential precondition for the regulation of industry by the democratic state.

All this Toynbee had argued, in 'Industry and Democracy' and elsewhere. Now, however, King breaks with Toynbee, turning him, for the time being at least, on his head. Why has the control of vast wealth meant, not 'the largest measure of service to mankind,' but 'vast injustice'? To put it another way, is class conflict an inevitable concomitant of capitalist development, or is it merely the consequence of 'abuses' that can be reformed away, of a disease that can be healed without killing the patient? While Toynbee had argued that 'indifference' opened the way to a new harmony, for King indifference explains the persistence of social disorganization. The growth of large-scale industry has led to disorder because organizational complexity has led to the disappearance of the personal relation between employers and employed. This indifference, together with the cash nexus – which for Toynbee had been a key to the new social order – leads to the development of 'impersonal attitudes,' in which Capital is reified by labourers and Labour by capitalists. In consequence, opposed and conflicting interests have supplanted common ones. For King, then, 'indifference' is the villain of the piece. It is an attitudinal category that is introduced to help deny an ultimate structural basis for class conflict.

Impersonal attitudes have meant that each of the parties to industry, Labour and Capital, have pursued their own special interests without regard to the interests of the other party or the interests the two hold in common. Industry has become an end in itself rather than what it ought to be, a means to common social ends. Industry ought to be viewed as the highest form of social service, in which personal gain is merely a by-product. In this way, King reduces the apparent contradiction between the potential outcome of industrial growth and its observable consequences to a failure in communication. The implications of the materialist foundation of Toynbee's analysis are shrugged off by an appeal to radical idealism:

Ideas are the determining factors ... Herein lies the way of escape from what, in the maze of ever-changing conditions, seems to render the Labor Problem impossible of solution. It rests with man to determine his own fate. The social order is not unchangeable. Like all the rest, the social order is itself subject to change in accordance with ideas that may be made to prevail. [p. 71]

Of course, Toynbee had also eventually found refuge in eighteenth-century liberal premises and in the idealism of his 'gospel of duty.' But there is a significant difference between his version and King's. While Toynbee had located the ultimate cause of class conflict in material conditions, and had then gone on to propose that these might be transcended by a new idealism, for King the cause of class conflict itself lies in the realm of ideas. Toynbee had pointed to political and social changes caused by changes in the organization of production – 'Political Economy was transformed by the working class,' and 'Democracy saved industry' – as laying the groundwork on which this new idealism could be erected. For King, the idealist potential is located in the developing structure of industry itself: the choice simply lies in the ends to which Industry is to be turned.

With this, King has wrestled himself into a corner. Either the large-scale organization of industry gave rise to social dislocation and class formations which *in turn* brought about (or promise to bring about) new possibilities for social harmony – the Toynbee position – *or* the destruction of personal relations in industry, as a consequence of large-scale organization, has alienated workers from employers, causing the emergence of antagonistic class ideas which continue to breed conflict. King wants to have it both ways: he wants to have the bad ideas with their material antecedents, and the good ideas without them. Whereas Toynbee's idealism was ultimately grounded in a political analysis, King's is free-floating. This drives him to embrace a metaphysic of good and evil which constitutes one of the recurring themes in the book.

This metaphysic is based on the idea that certain social institutions, like Industry, Science, and, as we shall see, Management, are amoral – they can be turned to good ends or bad. Good and evil exist independently of these institutional forms: they reside in abstract 'laws' of Peace, Work and Health and of Blood and Death. In his opening chapter, King brings Louis Pasteur onto the stage to introduce these laws: ostensibly, Pasteur represents Science, the amoral force of discovery and invention, but there is surely an additional significance in Pasteur's other *persona*, the doctor, the healer. The implication is that social disorder and industrial unrest are diseases: they are not the natural condition of the organism, but malfunctionings, malignancies. Industry and Science may be turned to good ends (order, harmony) or bad (disorder, strife), but Pasteur is clearly the Good Scientist (Dr Frankenstein has already been introduced as the Bad one) and what in medicine may be termed diseases are, in King's language of social reform, 'abuses.' For in King's dualistic metaphysic, Good and Evil are not evenly matched. The good is the orderly is the *natural*: evil is abnormal, an abuse. This is made plain in King's attempt to define the natural condition of society by means of an analogy with the Newtonian universe:

If such an order exists in Nature; ... if all material things of the heavens and of the earth are thus related in a perfect harmony ... is it conceivable, is it rational to believe that underlying the social relations of men and of nations, an order is not discoverable somewhere, obedience to which will bring as perfect a harmony? [p. 107]

This is supported by a lengthy comparison of the Law of Peace, Work and Health with the Law of Conservation of Energy and the Law of Gravity. Pasteur is again trundled on to give the impress of science to the argument. The significance of this train of thought is revealed in this comment [p. 110]: 'A universal cosmic order which is wholly rational and law-abiding is the fundamental assumption of all Science.' This, of course, is the assumption King wishes to make about social relations. The problem with King's metaphysic here, is that there is no apparent analogue in science to the Law of Blood and Death, the evil principle. Once again, King wants to have his cake and eat it. Science is at one and the same time an amoral institution and the ultimate proof of the triumph of good over evil. Having accepted order as the natural condition of things, King is left to demonstrate whence disorder arises, and to show that disorder is in fact a disease-state, and not the normal condition. There is an ambivalence in *Industry and Humanity* about what can be put down to social conditions, and what must be considered the Devil's work.

At the same time, it should be noted that a dualistic theory, be it Heaven *vs.* Hell, Eros *vs.* Thanatos, or Peace, Work, and Health *vs.* Blood and Death, is inevitably a conflict theory. In escaping from conflict, King will have to demonstrate that order is natural and disorder merely epiphenomenal. His analysis of the social consequences of the large-scale organization of industry is the first attempt at this, but his appeal to radical idealism is a two-edged sword. Perhaps ideas about social harmony may one day be made to prevail: at present, class ideas are rapidly gaining ground. The metaphysic of order is insufficient for King's purposes. The next step in his argument, the most interesting section of the book, is his attempt to demonstrate the inadequacy of class models themselves. This is the analysis of the 'Four Parties to Industry.'

II

Very early in *Industry and Humanity*, King claims that 'the Labor Problem' does not adequately name the phenomenon he is seeking to elucidate: 'Nor is the problem of Labor and Capital any longer one which concerns only, or even mainly, these two essential parties to production. As never before, it is a Community problem, and a Community gradually expanding to the limits of human society.' [p. 32] This notion of 'community' is one familiar from Mavor's analysis of the Scottish railway strike: King carries it to much greater lengths, however. Following his analysis of the large-scale organization of industry, he points out that this discussion of industrial relations has been carried on as though two parties only were involved: Labour, the source of productive effort, and Capital, the results of past efforts. The breakdown of industrial harmony has been explained in terms of the 'impersonal attitudes' that each of these parties has come to bear towards the other as large-scale organization has proceeded. But Labour and Capital are not the only parties to Industry: two others have emerged to significance under the influence of the same agent – the increasing size, complexity, and interdependency of modern industry – that has been responsible for the antagonism of the first two. The new parties are Management and the Community.

The growth of large-scale industry has led to a separation between ownership, Capital, and direction, Management. Management is first and foremost a form of labour, but it is a special form inasmuch as it is concentrated mental labour and organizing genius. Notwithstanding this kinship, Labour has looked upon Management as identical to Capital, and has subjected it to the same sort of 'impersonal attitude.' The origins of King's notion of Management are not hard to find. Toynbee and Ashley had both pointed to the separation of ownership and direction, and Veblen had made it the basis of his distinction between 'industrial' and 'pecuniary' employments. (King's 1898 view, 'that other classes as well as those who actually work at manual labour are producers,' has already been quoted: it may have been inspired by Taussig's teachings on the theory of value.) The advantage of having a third party to mediate between Capital and Labour, sharing some of the attributes of each, is obvious. It opens up a far more promising path to social peace than the involuted metaphysic of good and evil, and it may to some extent be grounded in the historical analysis of social development which King uses to explain other phenomena. For King, Management comes to represent, like Industry and Science, an amoral institution, capable of being turned to good ends or bad. He does not travel precisely the same route as did, for example, Veblen, in proposing a sort of technocracy of managers and engineers whose only interest would be in the most efficient possible operation of the economy, but, as will be seen, his road ran a good part of the distance in parallel.[6]

The fourth party to Industry, as much so as Capital, Labour and Management, is the Community. King's account of the Community's claim to partnership is reminiscent of Mavor's analysis of the Scottish railway strike: it is this party, King argues:

which provides the natural resources and powers that underlie all production ... It is the Community which creates the demand for commodities and services, through which Labor is provided with remunerative employment, and Capital with a return on its investment. Apart from the Community, inventive genius, organizing capacity, managerial or other ability would be of little value. Turn where one may, it is the Community that makes possible all the activities of Industry and helps to determine their value and scope. [p. 97]

As a party to Industry, Community has its own reward. Labour receives wages; Capital receives rent; Management receives a salary:

What Labor, Capital, and Management receive as reward is in reality so much purchasing power wherewith to obtain commodities and services. The Community receives its reward in increase of quantity or improvement of quality of services and commodities available in exchange for purchasing power. This gain, it will be seen, is the equivalent of additional purchasing power. The Community is also entitled to reward in the shape of an orderly organization in the development and conduct of Industry. This is but return in kind for the service the Community renders the other parties to Industry in preserving law and order and promoting orderly organization and peaceful behavior throughout the State. [p. 97]

At first sight, King's 'community' is nothing more or less than the sum of the other three parties to Industry. This would imply just another version of

---

6 This is, however, an oversimplification of Veblen's position. See his *The Engineers and the Price System* [1921]

the very old liberal argument, the argument Mavor likely had in mind, that labour and capital have a common interest in their mutual interpendence to keep on producing wages and profits. But King makes it clear that whatever he means by Community, it is not a simple sum in arithmetic, but a kind of *Gestalt*. 'While the Community comprises the three parties to Industry known as Labor, Capital and Management,' he writes in a footnote [p. 96]:

it is not the sum of the three. It is not only something more; it is something different. It is, in reality, a separate and distinct entity. There is good reason, on account of the services the Community renders Industry, for regarding it as a distinct party and deserving of special consideration.

But this is quite unsatisfactory, for while it recognizes the problem, it hardly meets it. King seems to be having some difficulty with the concept, for the footnote continues:

The use of the word 'Community' seems preferable to the use of the word 'Public', though the two are often interchangeable. There is a greater definiteness about the word 'Community'. At the same time, it is sufficiently flexible to lend itself to con-traction and expansion in meaning where it is necessary to emphasize *the area within which a people share a common interest with respect to the subject under consideration*. [emphasis supplied]

Once again, King wants to have his cake and eat it. The Community does not represent the simple lumping together of the other three parties. Nor does it mean capitalists, labourers, and managers in their common role as consumers, as opposed to their special roles in production. King dismisses the old fear of a combination of capital and labour to force up prices at the expense of the community, for 'Capital, Labor and Management are in themselves representatives of individuals who are consumers as well as pro-ducers' [p. 167]. In fact, King is perpetrating a sort of conjuring trick here. He is purporting to pull out of his hat a white rabbit – the Community – which will provide the common interest his model so far lacks. On close inspection, however, the rabbit has multiplied before our eyes: it is not one beast, but two.

The first is the notion of the Community as 'the area within which a people share a common interest' – although 'a people' might be begging the question even here. King argues that this common interest is the order and stability supplied by the State as the basis for the successful prosecution of industry. This is identical to Mavor's conception of the community, and it is closely related to the rather shopworn notion that all the parties to industry have a common interest in increasing the size of the pie so that, even if the relative distribution remains unaltered, everyone will end up with a bigger bite:

However opposed the interests of the parties may seem to be as respects the distribution of income derivable from total production, as respects production itself they are concurrent, since it is to the advantage of each that the total available for distribution should be as large as possible. [p. 98]

The second creature to emerge from King's rhetorical hat is a logical dilemma, a problem of logical types or units of analysis. It is made possible by King's celebration of the flexibility in the meaning of the term Community, and its possible contraction and expansion. Although King refers to all four parties to industry in generic terms, capitalizing the initial letters of their names and speaking of them in the sense of Industry-in-general, the application of the concepts is very different. In the real world of particular industrial disputes – in the world, that is to say, of his practice in the labour department – capital-letter Labour, Management, and Capital have no play. It is the local representatives of each of these who go on strike, impose lock-outs, raise and lower wages, and so on. The second sense of Community, which King does not distinguish from the first, is the common interest of all those not directly involved in a particular strike or lock-out in the maintenance of industrial production. Under this head, Labour as such has nothing to gain from the actions of a particular group of labourers on strike for better wages or union recognition, because Labour is here subsumed under the category, Community. To distinguish this second sense of Community the term Public will be used here: in the later sections of the book, King uses this term without explanation.

It is essential to the logic of *Industry and Humanity* that the distinction between Community and Public be overlooked. It is equally essential to the understanding of King's practice that it not be neglected. Classes and class interests have no meaning in King's schema, beyond whatever meaning can be attached to 'wrong attitudes' and 'irrationality,' because what the members of a class have in common is precisely that which they have in common with all the other classes. Conflict and disorder is by definition local, and it is by definition contrary to the Public interest.

It may be helpful here to anticipate the argument a little and spell out some of the implications of this dual notion of Community. King's accomplishment is to replace class concepts with a notion of the Public that is far more powerful ideologically than the simple Community notion of shared interests. The Public grows out of the Community idea that capital and labour have a common interest in the growth of the pie. It goes beyond that by separating the immediate combatants, those responsible for social disorder, from the rest of the Community. The Community's interest is in social co-operation. The interest of the Public is in social order and social control. The implications of this analysis become plain when King attempts to show how 'impersonal attitudes' are to be overcome.

King begins with a point that has become familiar in Mavor's work and in his own writings on the structure of the union movement, the notion that large-scale organization, whether labour or of capital, creates the danger of unprincipled leaders becoming tyrants. 'Labor and Capital in their mutual relations have everything to gain from character in their representatives,' he writes [p. 120], and goes on to discuss at some length the necessity of institutionalizing the spirit of fair play through such 'human relations' techniques as company newsletters, management shaking hands with the workers, and various techniques of remuneration, from piece-work to profit-sharing. Labour and Capital ought to be represented by men who see in Industry the opportunity of social service and who understand their essential mutuality of interest, in the Community sense. This is the context in which King's extensive discussion of industrial joint councils and representation plans – Industrial Democracy – and of such welfare state reforms as a national health insurance scheme, unemployment insurance, the 'national minimum' and so on must be understood. This discussion has led at least one commentator to celebrate *Industry and Humanity* as a plan for the basic restructuring of society along social democratic lines.[7] But King makes it clear that he considers these proposals to be 'forms' which have no meaning in the absence of 'faith' – although, admittedly, he is occasionally inconsistent on this point as on so many others. His general attitude is summed up in this statement [p.128]:

Confidence, being faith in fair intentions and just dealings, constitutes a first line of defence against the distrust and suspicion that breed fears. Whilst confidence is inseparable from character, which finds no adequate substitute in forms or devices of any kind, both confidence and good-will may be fostered by methods and measures which beget a right attitude, and keep human nature true to its better self.

But what if human nature proves insufficiently true to its better self? What if workers and capitalists persist in their irrational attachment to opposed

7 Hutchison, *The Incredible Canadian*.

instead of common interests? The lengthy catalogue of social reforms and managerial possibilities is presented in order to give human nature its chance. King would prefer voluntarism to compulsion, for 'to apply Force in seeking to prevent and settle industrial differences ... is to destroy the very spirit it is desired to create and maintain, namely, confidence and good-will' [p. 144]. But in the final analysis, force may be necessary. It is at this point in the argument that the notion of Community is replaced by the notion of the Public, and both of them are clearly represented by the social 'form' of Government.

King recognizes that compulsion will be necessary where voluntarism has failed. If the parties refuse to acknowledge their fundamental common interest, then the dictates of that interest must be imposed. The Community – the common interest in maintaining production – provides the rationale for compulsion. The Public – everybody who is not engaged in a particular strike or lock-out – is the population on whose behalf compulsion must be exercised. When it comes to this, the Public has as its agent Government.

But King has some hesitations about the use of naked force, which destroys 'the very spirit it is desired to create and maintain.' While it may be in the interest of the Public, it is not so clearly for the good of the Community, inasmuch as the participants in the strike remain part of the latter. Moreover, the use of force negates the very notion of Community. But there is a middle way:

Were Force the only power to be relied upon for the adoption of a course of conduct obviously in the interests of all the parties to a dispute, there would be a dilemma indeed. Fortunately in human relations there is a power superior even to Force, and that is Reason. [p. 144]

This constitutes the justification for King's argument in favour of compulsory investigation of industrial disputes, the principle underlying his Industrial Disputes Investigation Act of 1907. The policy prohibited strikes and lock-outs pending the completion of an investigation of the matters in dispute and attempts at conciliation by a tripartite board. The board's findings were not binding on the parties, but King anticipated that the combined forces of public opinion and Reason would persuade them to settle:

As a means of effecting the application of Reason to industrial disputes, Publicity has merits quite the equal of penalties imposed by process of law. Reason can be exercised properly only in the light of knowledge. Through the knowledge of facts it discloses, Compulsory Investigation coupled with Publicity gives Reason its chance.

Exercised prior to the severance of industrial relations, Compulsory Investigation tends wholly toward the exercise of Reason. [p. 148]

It should replace the strike as the principle weapon in labour's arsenal:

The right of public investigation in matters of labor controversy is a very far-reaching and potent right. Compared with it, as a means of securing justice, the strike and lockout fade into insignificance. I know of no instrument so powerful to put a stop to arbitrary conduct. There is no direction in which the right of investigation cannot be employed with the utmost advantage to Labor and to the Community. It is worth any concession Labor is able to make. [p. 327]

But King makes it plain that if this opportunity is not embraced, if Reason gives way to irrationality, Force remains in reserve. For while investigation looks at the matters in dispute, it is the dispute itself which is intolerable. The basic interest of the Public lies in the preservation of order, and disorder, in the shape of industrial conflict, is anathema. Force must be met with Force:

Let there be no mistake. The method of the strike and the lockout is not distinguishable from the method of Force ... All industrial strife is a form of anarchy. [pp.312–13]

And again:

Strikes and lockouts do not help make the world safe for Democracy. Viewed from the standpoint of Democracy, what are they but 'a combination of men not elected by the people and not accountable to the people, to prevent other citizens from exercising their rights'? [pp. 313–14]

This element in *Industry and Humanity* has not been sufficiently recognized. Most commentators tend to stress the welfare-state elements, or the appeal to transcendental faith, or the inherent 'corporatism' of King's industrial representation schemes. But to fully understand King and his role, it is necessary to penetrate to the threat veiled thinly in these words:

Private rights must cease when they become public wrongs. Is not this the principle underlying law and order in all civilized communities? Is it a principle from which communities can depart without inviting anarchy? It cannot be contended that what is a matter of grave concern to the public is a matter of exclusive concern to private parties. There is no right superior to that of the community as a whole. [p. 329][8]

And the right of the community as a whole is to have industry continuously operating at peak efficiency, on a solid basis of law and order.

III

Industry was for King an amoral force, and scale of organization played an important part in his thinking. In the case of the International Typographical Union, large and complex organization created the danger of tyranny, but at the same time permitted wide scope for the exercise of conservative reason. With appropriate constitutional safeguards, the former could be avoided and the advantages of the latter be experienced unalloyed. In the case of the clothing industry, the problems of 'sweating' were abuses whose persistence could be explained by the incompleteness of the transition to large-scale factory production. Government intervention was necessary to remove these abuses, principally by removing the obstacles that lay in the way of this transformation. Industrial conflict is another abuse that results from problems in the development of large-scale organization of industry, and the material agent for curing this disease, the beneficial element that emerges in the same causal process as the breakdown of the social relations of industry, is Management. Government intervention to protect the public interest here has the same function as it had in the case of sweating: it is to clear away the abuses and create the preconditions for rational elements in the situation to flourish. Anti-sweating contracts would create a situation in which the beneficial aspects of factory production could develop unhampered by throwbacks to earlier stages. Government intervention to impose rationality on industrial relations would permit Management to assume its proper function and ensure future harmony.

Management, like Industry, is amoral: but as is true of King's metaphysic as a whole, the superior strength and ultimate victory of good is unquestioned from the outset. Management is organizing genius and executive ability: the manager is an 'expert' in much the same way as King considered himself to be. The manager is dedicated to finding the best possible solutions to practical problems, and King is highly ambivalent as to what, if any,

---

8 Cf. F.R. Scott, 'Mr. King and the King Makers,' *Canadian Forum*, Dec. 1950, reprinted in J.L. Granatstein and Peter Stevens, eds., *Forum: Canadian Life and Letters 1920–1970* (Toronto: University of Toronto Press, 1972), 268–70.

restrictions ought to be placed upon him. Indeed, there are hints in *Industry and Humanity* that some sort of technocracy will be necessary to co-ordinate industry and government as both these fields become increasingly complex and interdependent. Thus Management never becomes fully integrated into the analysis of the four parties to industry, and King's prescription remains ambiguous: managerial authority must not be diminished in the area of general administration, although some control over immediate concerns should be delegated, through the principle of 'Representation,' to the other three parties [p. 236]. He draws an analogy between industrial government and the government of a state:

Management need not be robbed of any of its necessary measure of control. Its function in Industry would continue to correspond with that of the Executive in the State. As in the case of the State, the distinction in Industry between legislative and executive powers would become more and more clearly marked. The executive would be rendered more and more responsible to the body which has to do with the shaping of policies. In the case of Industry, this body would be the Directorate representative of Labor, Capital, Management, and the Community, with Management advising, *and often dictating to*, the other constituent elements, just as under the British constitution, the Prime Minister and his Cabinet, ... notwithstanding that their primary function is executive, advise, and, within bounds, dictate to Parliament. [pp. 271–2; emphasis supplied]

King believed that, as it developed, the large-scale organization of industry would become coextensive with the community, and hence with the state. Seen in this light, his proposals for a rational government of industry are more than mere analogues to national government: they amount to forecasts of its replacement. This is to some extent a consequence of the reconstruction theme in *Industry and Humanity*, and King's insistence on the equation of industrial and international conflict. But the view of rational government expressed, in more or less comprehensive form, in *Industry and Humanity* raises questions about King's political theory that go beyond the problem of state intervention in industrial relations, and beyond the scope of this study. Specifically, his advocacy of tripartite representation leads along the path to a corporatist polity, while his emphasis on the role of the manager, the expert, seems to point in the direction of plebiscitarianism. Where did these ideas come from, and are they reconcilable with each other or with King's practice in the labour department? The source for either might be seen in the new political economy: Mavor, for example, seemed to exhibit some leaning in the corporatist direction, and Ashley, with his emphasis on the role of the expert, in the other. But these are only the most slender of inclinations, and if we are to bring these questions to our project of understanding King's labour policy, it is necessary to move beyond the realm of ideas. It is time for the intellectual constellation of King's 'formation' to be brought into contact with the material world which both shaped it and was shaped by it. The hypothesis of chapter 1 spoke of King's task as forming a 'superstructural' complement to changes in the structure of production in the Canada of his day. It follows that, the political economists having been examined, the political economy must have its turn.

4

The large-scale organization
of industry

What chance will the small man have in the industrial contest that is to come?
[*Industrial Canada*, January 1908]

The labour policy initiatives of the turn of the century must be understood in part in the context of Mackenzie King's ideological inheritance. But both of these – the labour policy and King's ideology – must be understood in their Canadian context. And the Canada of the turn of the century was, as one recent book has put it, 'a nation transformed.'[1] The Laurier years encompassed a period of rapid and qualitative economic and social change. Between the turn of the century and the Great War, Canada experienced its first extended economic boom since Confederation. A huge surge of capital investment in railways, housing, mining, manufacturing, and service facilities was associated with the growth of the wheat staple and the emergence of the new mineral and pulp staples. The value of manufacturing output more than doubled in a decade, while the adult population grew by more than 35 per cent. Despite the rapid growth of the western wheat economy, the proportion of the labour force engaged in agriculture declined from about 40 per cent in 1901 to 34 per cent a decade later, and notwithstanding the rush to take up rural homesteads Canada became increasingly urbanized in the course of the decade. Accompanying this rapid growth, moreover, was a continuous price inflation and a continuous lag of wages behind prices.

Before this boom period, manufacturing had been limited in size and scope, oriented for the most part to local markets, with the small, owner-operated workshop or factory the basic unit of production. The growth of the

1 R.C. Brown and Ramsay Cook, *Canada 1896–1921: A Nation Transformed* (Toronto: McClelland and Stewart, 1974)

wheat economy, with its captive consumer population and its efficient transportation infrastructure, signalled the emergence of a national market, and the industrial structure changed to meet the new situation. The product range was broadened, more sophisticated production and managerial techniques were introduced, and the scale of industrial organization increased to the point that quantitative became qualitative change with the emergence of the modern corporation. The growth of American direct investment provided one channel along which advanced technique could flow into the Canadian manufacturing and mining sectors.

Notwithstanding this appearance of diversified growth, the staples-based economy remained highly vulnerable to exogenous factors. Some aspects of the growth were more apparent than real: the great 'merger movement' that peaked after 1908, for example, seems to have amounted more to a scramble for paper profits in stock manipulation than to a fundamental restructuring of industrial production to achieve real economies of scale.[2] The motor of Canadian development remained metropolitan demand, and with the shift from a British to an American metropolis the integrity of the national market came under attack. In an immediate sense, what was most vulnerable was the exorbitantly expensive infrastructure of transcontinental transportation, the old thorn in the side of the Laurentian economy. The unusually active role of the Canadian state in economic development had focused since colonial days on putting this infrastructure into place and protecting it from the continental threat, and when the state came to intervene in industrial disputes in a new way after 1900, it was to the infrastructure that most of the original initiatives were directed. They turned out, in the somewhat longer run, to be appropriate to other important sectors as well.

The emergence of large-scale business brought with it managerial reorganization. In the traditional businesses of an earlier era, owners were managers and managers owners. There were exceptions to this rule, of course, prominent among them the railway companies. In most sectors of the economy, however, the work force had been sufficiently small, and the production and distribution processes sufficiently unsophisticated, that they could come under the direct personal supervision of the owner. But by the beginning of the twentieth century, Canadian businessmen had begun to discover the

2 For the flight from competition, see Michael Bliss, *A Living Profit* (Toronto: McClelland and Stewart, 1974), chap. 2: for the merger movement see, *inter alia*, A.E. Epp, 'Cooperation Among Capitalists: the Canadian Merger Movement 1909–13' (unpublished PHD dissertation, Johns Hopkins, 1973), and J.C. Weldon, 'Consolidations in Canadian Industry 1900–1948,' in L.A. Skeoch, ed., *Restrictive Trade Practices in Canada: Selected Readings* (Toronto: McClelland and Stewart, 1966).

advantages of bigness, 'system,' and 'efficiency.' Business began to become bureaucratically organized, and, often influenced by American know-how, hierarchies of professional managers emerged. They were not usually owners of the firms they ran: their stake in the success of their companies lay in their own job security, their prestige, and their ability to progress along a professional career path. To some extent, these developments in business were parallelled by similar developments in government organization.

Yet the managerial reorganization of the Canadian economy proceeded in an extremely uneven fashion in the first decade of the century. As quantitative research reported in the Appendix indicates, Canadian industry's performance on an index of the proliferation of management functions reveals an aggregate increase similar to that of American industry. When Canadian industry is disaggregated, however, large and significant differences between the experiences of different sectors emerge. The over-all increase masks the fact that more individual industries experienced a *decline* in the ratio of administrative to productive employees than experienced growth. Thus industries on the leading edge of the new industrialism – the highly integrated textile industry, railway suppliers, high-technology manufacturing, and industries associated with the new staples, smelting and pulp and paper – participated fully and rapidly in the managerial revolution, while other industries, including much of the clothing industry, food and beverage manufacturing, and highly specialized manufacturing firms, experienced relative declines in administrative overhead. At the same time, as much of the qualitative evidence to be discussed in this chapter suggests, the ideological concomitants of large-scale bureaucratic industry tended to diffuse far more broadly within the Canadian business class than one might expect on the basis of the quantitative investigation of managerial structure alone. But as we shall suggest later on, this mismatch of the material and the ideological helps to explain some of the problems in the reception of King's labour policy.

For businessmen encountering the new managerial organizational problems that came with bigness (and, one suspects, with the fashionability of the new techniques), the 'labour problem' took on a new poignancy. The advocates of 'system' and 'scientific management' called for a fundamental reorientation in the organization of the work process and in methods of payment. Simultaneously, employers sought to increase the loyalty of their work forces, diminished in their view by the increasing depersonalization of industrial relations, through profit sharing, pension and insurance schemes and by the whole host of work-place reforms that went under the rubric of 'welfare work.' As employers crossed the watershed to modern business practices, they dragged their workers over with them.

It is all too easy to emphasize the extent of change during this dramatic expansion of the economy, at the expense of the continuities. The first decade of the century saw, as well, the reweaving of old patterns that had long been characteristic of Canadian development. In great measure the burst of business activity following the turn of the century was a response to the new opportunities created by the incipient shift away from staples-based dependency on Britain to staples-based dependency on the United States. This shift brought change and growth, but it also reproduced the familiar patterns of vulnerability and exaggerated unevenness of development. Canadian manufacturers were well aware of this, as their insistence on the maintenance of tariff protection throughout the period illustrates. In 1911 this perception was to result in the dismissal of the government which had taken responsibility for the good times. But in 1904, the businessmen had no difficulty in accepting that the twentieth century was theirs, and Laurier's.

I

Recent works by two American scholars have made significant contributions to our understanding of the nature and origins of modern business management. In his magisterial study, *The Visible Hand*, Alfred Dupont Chandler interprets the history of United States business in terms of a managerial revolution. Modern business enterprise replaces the determination of the market, Adam Smith's 'invisible hand,' with managerial controls: 'Modern multiunit business enterprise replaced small traditional enterprise when administrative coordination permitted greater productivity, lower costs, and higher profits than coordination by market mechanisms,' and these advantages could only be realized with the creation of a managerial hierarchy.[3] The impact of the managerial revolution on the organization of the work process itself is the major theme of Harry Braverman's *Labor and Monopoly Capital*.[4] The development of 'scientific management' techniques after the turn of the century involved the separation of planning and control functions from productive tasks, with managers responsible for the former and the latter delegated on an increasingly detailed basis to unskilled and semi-skilled workers. These changes all took place in the context of technological changes permitting mass production and distribution, and the development of a mass

3 *The Visible Hand: The Managerial Revolution in American Business* (Cambridge, Mass.: Harvard University Press, 1977), 6.
4 *Labor and Monopoly Capital: The Degradation of Work in the Twentieth Century* (New York: Monthly Review Press, 1974)

market for consumer goods. Modern management emerged first in those industries characterized by technological innovation and expanding markets.

In Canada, the turn of the century saw the beginnings of changes in the organization of enterprise that were essentially similar to those characteristic of US business. In this, Canada reaped one of the 'advantages' of backwardness. The reliance on imported technique characteristic of the staples economy extended to techniques of business organization as well. Canada's managerial revolution, in a word, was imported from the United States. This importation was accomplished in three basic ways.

Some management technique was imported along with American direct investment: whatever the nationality of the branch plants' managers, these firms' organizational structures were dictated from outside the country.[5] For example, when Quaker Oats established its mill at Peterborough, Ontario, in 1902 in order to ensure access to the British market, the decision to locate in Canada rather than in Britain was based on the realization that 'a Canadian plant could be supervised by U.S. technicians without great expense.' The president of INCO from its incorporation in 1902, Ambrose Monell, came to the company from Carnegie Steel. When the United States Rubber Company acquired control of Canadian Consolidated Rubber, a holding company organized by Canadian financiers to acquire control of the rubber industry, 'much of the experience and skills of the vast United States Rubber Company were now passed on to its new Canadian interests.'[6]

A second method by which US managerial technique was imported to Canada was the tendency of some Canadian companies to employ managers with American experience, or to hire American management consultants. Both variants were used by the Canadian railways, for example. Van Horne had worked his way up the management ladder in a number of US railways,

---

5 Cf. Mira Wilkins, *The Emergence of Multinational Enterprise* (Cambridge, Mass.: Harvard University Press, 1970), 147f
6 For Quaker, see A.F. Marquette, *Brands, Trademarks and Good Will: The Story of the Quaker Oats Company* (New York: McGraw-Hill, 1967), 218f. For Inco, see H.E. Main, *The Canadian Nickel Industry* (Toronto: University of Toronto Press, 1955), 146 n164, where the United States origins and associations of the company's directors are identified. For the rubber industry example, see Leslie Roberts, *From Three Men* (n.p.: Dominion Rubber Company, n.d.), 33. Many other examples might have been cited: it is curious that this aspect of United States direct investment in Canada has been neglected in the secondary literature. For numerous examples in particular sectors, see W.J.A. Donald, *The Canadian Iron and Steel Industry* (Boston: Houghton, 1915), and E.S. Moore, *American Influence in Canadian Mining* (Toronto: University of Toronto Press, 1941), as well as H. Marshall, F. Southard Jr., and K.W. Taylor, *Canadian-American Industry* [1936] (Toronto: McClelland & Stewart, 1976).

during the period of great managerial innovation in that industry,[7] before becoming General Manager of the Canadian Pacific in 1882. His influence became more generalized thereafter through his participation on the boards of directors of a long list of large Canadian companies and branch plants. The Grand Trunk Railway furnishes an even more interesting case: the company was Britain's largest overseas investment, and had originally been run on British railway management principles. The great success of the CPR under Van Horne convinced the Grand Trunk's London board of directors that American methods were better suited to Canadian conditions than English ones, and they hired their own experienced American railwayman, Charles Melville Hays, to oversee competition with Van Horne's CPR.[8] The Grand Trunk is perhaps the great transitional enterprise in this age of transition: a railway with both ends in the United States, owned by British finance capital, and run by an expatriate American manager, was Canada's second largest employer (after the CPR). But the railways did not limit their imports of American managerial technique to providing permanent employment for US managers. They were also in the lead in hiring the American management consultants who flourished in the era of 'system' and scientific management. Thus the Canadian Pacific received the assistance of one of the pioneers of the new movement, H.L. Gantt, in organizing production at its giant locomotive repair facilities, the Angus Shops, in Montreal. The system developed there was to be introduced in the company's shops across Canada.[9] There appear to have been attempts at reorganization of the work process along similar lines at the St Thomas, Ontario, shops of the Michigan Central Railway as early as 1902.[10] The Canadian Composing Company in Montreal implemented the Taylor shop management system, perhaps under the guidance of US management consultant Kenneth Falconer.[11]

Beyond these direct imports of American managerial technique in the shape of American managers, Canadian businessmen were exposed to the new

7 Cf. Chandler, *Visible Hand*, chaps. 3–5.
8 G.R. Stevens, *Canadian National Railways* (Toronto: Clarke, Irwin, 1962), vol. II, 231f, and *passim*. See also chap. 10 below.
9 'Scheduling Locomotive Repair Work on the Canadian Pacific Railway,' *Industrial Engineering and Engineering Digest*, vol. VIII (1910), 380–3; 'Canadian Pacific Shop Management,' *American Machinist*, 21 Dec. 1911
10 Canada, *Labour Gazette* (henceforth *LG*), Dec. 1901, 338; June 1902, 729; and *passim*. See chap. 5 below.
11 Kenneth Falconer, 'Cost-Finding Methods for Moderate-Sized Shops: The Shop System of the Canadian Composing Company,' *Engineering Magazine*, April 1903, 89f. For the example of a Toronto bearing factory, see 'Efficiency in Production Methods,' *Industrial Canada* (henceforth *IC*), May 1911, 1073f.

methods through their trade organizations and journals. *Industrial Canada*, organ of the Canadian Manufacturers' Association, devoted increasing amounts of space throughout the decade to discussions of cost accounting and shop practices, the two essential elements of scientific management: some of these were reprinted from American publications, while others reported on local developments. Before discussing this literature, it will be useful to review what scientific management, broadly conceived, entailed.[12]

The new management was concerned, first and foremost, with cost accounting techniques. While the old Italian system of double-entry book-keeping had served the purposes of small traditional business reasonably well, given the ability of the owner-manager to maintain constant personal supervision over a simple operation, with the increasing scale of the enterprise, the rapid proliferation of transactions in the mass market, and the new technological ability to increase output vastly, the ability of the owner or manager to maintain control of the activities of his firm was threatened. Cost accounting systems were devised to generate information about the day-to-day operations of the firm, organize it for easy access, and channel its flow into the hands of responsible managers. Chandler has argued that before the 1850s in the United States, even relatively large-scale factories like the New England textile mills were managed without reference to detailed information about costs: 'The treasurer's accounts show clearly that these factories were run by merchants for merchants ... This lack of interest in accounting suggests that textile executives were not using their accounts to assist them in the management of their enterprises. As in the case of commercial firms, accounting remained merely a recording of past transactions. It was not until the 1850's that the owners and managers began to use their accounts to determine unit costs.'[13] With the emergence of modern cost accounting practices, efficiency became the by-word of business. Now that the new record-keeping techniques made it possible, managers sought to account for every scrap of material, every unit of machine capacity, every moment of labour time. In pursuing this goal, they found it necessary to accumulate and organize a body of knowledge about industrial practices and procedures, and to define levels of utilization and output that were truly 'efficient.'

In his analysis of the writings of Frederick Winslow Taylor, the pioneer of scientific management, Braverman establishes three principles of the new

---

12 Although the term 'scientific management' was not coined until towards the end of our period, we use it here, for simplicity's sake, to cover the whole range of managerial innovations later identified with it.

13 *Visible Hand*, 69f

technique which underpinned the evolving practices of labour management. The first he calls 'the dissociation of the labor process from the skills of the workers.' Shop practice in the first instance is the possession of the craft workers, and is rooted in traditional procedures and levels of output, customary notions of a fair day's work, and the workers' own experience and innovations. The first task of scientific management is to make this body of knowledge the property of the manager. The second principle is 'the separation of conception from execution.' The functions of planning the work process, scheduling production, deciding what materials and equipment are to be used, and so forth, are separated from the process of work itself. The former become management's responsibility; the latter remains the worker's. The outcome is a substantial monopoly of knowledge in the hands of management. The third principle is 'the use of this monopoly over knowledge to control each step of the labor process and its mode of execution.'[14] Thus cost accounting and efficiency meant control. The innovations loosely associated under the rubric of scientific management afforded the executives in charge of production and distribution a degree of control over these activities which far exceeded the organizational capacity of custom, tradition, or the market.

The Canadian Manufacturers' Association supplied its members with information about the new management techniques through its journal, *Industrial Canada*. These articles are of interest both because they illustrate the growing sophistication of managerial expertise and because they afford occasional examples of the implementation of the techniques in Canadian industry. As early as May 1902, *Industrial Canada* informed its readers of the introduction of a new time clock which 'has come into general use in the best factories in the States,' and which enabled each employee to 'record his own time and make a record from which there is no appeal.' The emphasis was on the accumulation of records in usable form, and indicated some familiarity with cost accounting principles. A few months later cost accounting itself received specific mention: 'Mr. W.C. Eddis, F.C.A., the Auditor of the Canadian Manufacturers' Association, and Mr. W.B. Tindall, A.C.A., of the Parry Sound Lumber Co., have published a book dealing with Manufacturers' Accounts drawing special attention to the importance of Cost Accounts and showing how these may best be kept in practice.'[15]

In December 1902, the Montreal branch of the CMA sponsored an address by Principal Miller of the Philadelphia Textile School. He emphasized the role of the professional manager, the detailed division of labour, and the

14 Braverman, *Labor and Monopoly Capital*, chap. 4 and *passim*
15 *IC*, Sept. 1902, 43

emphasis on minutiae which characterized the efficiency approach: 'The tele-
scope was very well, and is very well, but the age in which we are dwelling is
the age more of the microscope. It is the attention to small things, it is the
respect for details that makes success in modern manufacturing. (Applause)
... The introduction of the trained method, of the educated man, into industry, means an economy which makes the difference between success and
failure ...'[16]

An article by Kenneth Falconer, 'The Practical Value of Cost Accounting,' which appeared in February 1905, was the first in a long series of
special treatments of this topic in *Industrial Canada*. Under titles like 'Factory Costs,' 'Ascertaining the Cost of Production,' 'Cost Accounting,'
'Economy in Manufacturing,' and 'The Model Factory,' Canadian manufacturers were treated both to enthusiastic propaganda for the new techniques
and to detailed instructions about how to implement them. Some of these
articles were written by American management consultants or reprinted
from American trade journals, while others were home-grown products. The
development of a cadre of Canadian management experts can be traced in
the pages of the journal: the Eddis and Tindall book was followed in 1907 by
Samuel Sparling's *Business Organization*, which contained lengthy discussions of 'system' (a scientific management buzz-word) and cost accounting
principles. In a full-page advertisement in December 1906, the Toronto
printing firm Copeland-Chatterson announced itself as 'Devisers and Manufacturers of Systems for Business,' while an article on 'System Applied to
Factories' a year later identified its author, C.R. Stevenson, as a member of
the firm of 'Miller & Franklin Co., Business Engineers.'

In an editorial introducing its first article on cost accounting, *Industrial
Canada* promised that 'the series will be continued only so long as seems
justified by the interest with which these articles are received.'[17] The interest must have been maintained, for the journal's proselytizing continued
unabated throughout the period. Thus a descriptive feature on the Grand
Trunk Railway's Toronto freight yards was subtitled 'In the big Freight
Sheds of the G.T.R. in Toronto System prevents Chaos,' and as late as 1911
the editor could both celebrate the advantages of 'system' and berate his
readers for their backwardness in applying the new techniques:

'Intensive' management discovers and eliminates waste of energy in the performance
of various operations, it hunts out the weak spots in the work of machines, it obviates

16 *Ibid*., Jan. 1903, 283
17 *Ibid*., Feb. 1905, 420

delay in feeding and in handling materials, it consists in an infinite capacity for taking pains. Its aim is the maintenance of the plant in a state of the highest efficiency. That the success of a business depends on the small details which enter into every stage of operations is not generally appreciated. These are passed over; they are left to someone else who may or may not be attending to them. As a matter of fact, nothing can be taken for granted.[18]

II

With the increasing importance of big business, a split developed within the ranks of the CMA. On the one side were ranged the more traditionally-oriented small owner-operators: on the other were the new managers in charge of the big factories and the branch plants. It was a conflict between members subject to cut-throat competition in the market and those seeking to exploit the non-market controls inherent in oligopoly.[19] In January 1908, *Industrial Canada* contributed to this debate an article on 'The Future of the Small Manufacturer.' The anonymous author sought to establish grounds for hope, and listed a number of factors operating in favour of the survival of small business. Among these, he thought he could discern a *managerial* make-weight on the side of the small owner-manager: 'He superintends the work himself, which constitutes an inestimable advantage in securing consistent results and honest workmanship. No factory system, necessary as it is in the case of the big establishment, can compensate for the lack of personal supervision of the manufacturer, which is possible alone in the less pretentious factory.'

When businessmen crossed the watershed to efficiency, they had to rethink their perceptions of labour relations. Under the rubric of the 'labour problem,' as it now presented itself to them, they grouped a number of interlocking concerns. At the most immediate level was the problem of work-place efficiency which the new managerial techniques were designed to solve. The separation of conception from execution, the introduction of pay incentives, and systematic hiring, supervision, and promotion were all called into service here. At a somewhat more abstract level was the problem of retaining work-force loyalty under the new conditions. The quasi-feudal relations of master and man were incompatible with the new emphasis on sys-

18 *Ibid.*, March 1911, 832. This was an editorial introduction to the reprint of an article by H.L. Gantt.
19 Cf S.D. Clark, *The Canadian Manufacturers Association* (Toronto: University of Toronto Press, 1939), 40ff.

tem and efficiency. The social relations of employer and employee were becoming increasingly depersonalized, especially in the growing industrial cities with their wealth of alternative employments and their sophisticated labour markets. Moreover, the burgeoning trade-union movement was both supplying an alternative focus for the worker's loyalty and training him in the logic of the market. At the same time, employers were coming to realize that a well-fed, well-housed, and healthy work force was likely to be a hard-working one. The general solution to this second problem was variously described as 'welfare work' or 'industrial betterment.' It sought to retain the loyalty of the worker by providing him with a range of benefits, from profit-sharing through hot lunches to pension schemes. These benefits met most of the difficulties, from the employer's point of view. They reproduced the old dependent relationship of master and man within a new bureaucratic context. In competing with benefit packages offered by trade unions, they counterbalanced some of the unions' claims on workers' loyalty. Moreover, they went part of the way towards guaranteeing a fit and rested work force ready for the rigours of intensive production and supervision. Finally, they no doubt helped to salve the sometimes troubled consciences of employers who were aware that in introducing system and efficiency they were making the work process infinitely more onerous for their employees and removing what intrinsic satisfactions it had once provided. At a third, and still more abstract level, the 'labour problem' resolved itself into the problem of class relations. Businessmen worried about trade unionism and socialism, and sought to demonstrate that workers and employers shared a common interest more fundamental than their differences.

The first of these components has been touched on in the discussion of scientific management, and we must return to it in chapter 5. Here, we turn our attention to 'industrial betterment,' and, in the next section, to the problem of class relations as the manufacturers saw it.

The notion that increased labour efficiency could not be obtained simply by speed-up was central to scientific management's emphasis on 'system.' One of *Industrial Canada*'s authorities on the new techniques stressed that this was likely to be counter-productive: 'Now, please understand at once, and right at the start, that there is nothing in what I shall say which is to be construed as advice to crowd or rush your workmen. That cannot be done with any degree of success. Even the most ignorant of foreign-born workmen will resent such tactics, and will take from you in ways you cannot detect much more than you can possibly force out of them by the most strenuous driving.'[20] Managerial organization and control of the work process, coupled with a system of incentive payment, was the answer. Incentives had been used for some time before the introduction of the new management techniques, and although pioneers like Taylor insisted that incentive payments alone were inadequate, various piece-work and bonus arrangements invariably entered into the holistic reorganization of factory practices that 'system' entailed. It was not a very great leap from the idea of incentive payment to motivate greater labour efficiency, to the idea of bonuses and profit-sharing plans as a means of cementing the loyalty of the whole work force to the firm.

Profit-sharing was in most cases a variant of the old paternalistic practice of the Christmas bonus. A Hamilton cigar company 'continued a long established practice of presenting five of its employees who were with the firm for 21 years with a deed for a building lot and $225 each,' at Christmas, 1903. Brantford's Cockshutt Plough Company distributed the traditional turkeys, while the Waterous Engine Works gave a day's wages for Christmas day: 'Friendly relations between employers and employees continued.' The bonus was sometimes tied to length of service or to the amount earned during the preceding year, thus being a reward for continued loyalty or, in the latter case, a move in the direction of incentive payment. 'The Winnipeg Street Railway Company decided, as a mark of their appreciation of faithful service, to give a bonus as a Christmas gift to all employees who have been six months or more in their employ, such bonus to consist of 5 per cent on all moneys received by each employee during the year ended November 30, 1903.' Or, even more clearly an incentive: 'The Ottawa Electric Railway Company followed the custom of previous years and gave some of the older men, and those who merited it by faithful service, a bonus.' The New Brunswick confectioners, Ganong Brothers, developed a complicated Christmas bonus *cum* incentive scheme in order to 'maintain the supply of labour' during the pre-Christmas rush: 'During the Christmas season each year amounts varying from $2 to $10 are distributed to the employees, without regard to the wages received, but based solely on the number of years each employee has been in the service of the company ... the minimum bonus ($2) being paid to those who have for two years been in the service of the company. One dollar is added to the bonus for each year's service up to $10 ... On September 1, this year, a printed slip was placed in each pay envelope stating, that if the employee were present every working day during the balance of the year, an additional $10 bonus would be granted, but that for every day's absence $1.00 would be deducted from this extra amount. The result was stated by the company to have been most satisfactory ...'[21]

From this sort of thing to formal profit-sharing schemes was no great leap. For many such schemes, it is not even clear that a precise statement was made of the proportion of profits to be distributed among employees, so profit-sharing in these cases was merely the incentive bonus in fancy dress. 'In fulfillment of a promise made last year that their employees should share in the profits of the business, the firm of Williamson and J.G. Greey, mill machine manufacturers, Church Street, have divided $4,000 among the men. The division was in proportion to the number of years the employee had worked with the firm.' Brantford's Ham and Nott 'shared profits' partly on the basis of length of service, and partly on age and marital status. A more formal system was introduced in 1902 by the British Columbia Electric Railway Company: 'Hereafter all regular employees will receive as their share of the profits one-third of the amount available for dividends after the ordinary shareholder has received four per cent on his shares; that is, two-thirds to the shareholders and one-third to the regular employees.' Other firms used the term to cover a much more casual practice: Holt, Renfrew gave a bonus of one week's salary in 1903, 'owing to the firm desiring their men to share in the exceptional prosperity of the year just closed.' Stratford's White Packing Company issued a cash bonus to its workers when it was faced with a labour shortage. Some companies tried to use profit-sharing techniques and keep the money in the capitalization of the firm, all at once. A London firm distributed 'profits' on the basis of service, and offered six per cent interest to those employees 'wishing to leave their share with the firm.' The Henry Morgan department stores, reorganized as a limited liability corporation in 1906, inaugurated an employee share-purchasing plan to supplement an earlier scheme of profit sharing among department heads. The general intent of all these plans was summed up by an officer of the John Morrow Machine Screw Company, who described his company's profit-sharing arrangement as 'a very satisfactory method of securing the good-will and best services of the employees through giving them an interest in the welfare of the business.'[22]

Besides profit-sharing, industrial betterment involved a number of other schemes and arrangements. *Industrial Canada* provided a partial list in 1907: 'Mutual Benefit Societies to aid employees in cases of sickness, disability or death are often to be found and work satisfactorily. Monthly magazines are

21 *LG*, Jan. 1904, 629, 633, 639; Jan. 1907, 724; Nov. 1906, 458
22 *Ibid.*, Aug. 1901, 78, 80; Sept. 1902, 148; March 1903, 614, 657; Feb. 1904, 761; Nov. 1906, 458; Sept. 1906, 225

sometimes carried on to aid in advertising and to encourage the employees to learn more about the theoretical side of their work. Christmas remembrances occur in the form of a stuffed turkey and a quart of cranberries to each family represented in the establishment. Some manufacturers, to encourage the spirit of long and loyal service make a rule of presenting an honorarium of value to every employee who serves twenty-five years in his factory,' and these were in addition to the provision of hot meals, toilets, club rooms, and annual picnics: 'The cost of carrying out these improvement schemes has often been considerable, yet many a manufacturer has found that care for the physical, intellectual and moral welfare of his employees has a direct return in increased output and better work. Even when applied on very advanced lines it has resulted profitably to the factory owner.'[23]

The same point was made in the title of an article on National Cash Register's innovations at its Dayton, Ohio plant: 'A Twentieth Century Factory Treats Its Employees Well, Because "It Pays".' Canadian General Electric, at Peterborough, donated $1000 as the basis for a mutual benefit society for its employees. The Montreal Street Railway Company initiated a similar scheme, and announced its intention to consult with its employees on the matter. Its object 'was asserted to be the bringing of the men into closer touch with the management and the creation of a fund for the relief of the sick and injured, for the assistance of widows and children, and for pensioning those who had grown old in the service.' The company requested its employees not to move towards organizing their own scheme for sixty days following this announcement: it was likely intended to forestall employee action, perhaps in the form of a trade union. The Waterous Engine Works had an Employees' Sick Benefit Society. The British Columbia Electric Railway proposed a pension scheme, bu the employees turned it down.[24] The Grand Trunk Railway had a particularly pernicious benefits plan, used to discipline its work force and, in the wake of the 1910 strike, withdrawn punitively.[25] After 1909, the Canadian Government Annuities plan offered 'every employer convenient and trustworthy machinery for the establishment of a pension fund whereby old or disabled employees may be retired without suffering to themselves or imposing a heavy financial burden on the employer.'[26]

23 *IC*, Jan. 1907, 506
24 *LG*, Oct. 1902, 265f; July 1903, 8; Feb. 1904, 759; Aug. 1906, 154
25 See chapter 10, below.
26 *LG*, Sept. 1909, 339

The McClary Stove Company, in London, provided a cafeteria and reading room for its employees. 'The dishes are thoroughly sterilized after each meal.' The Frost Fence Company provided recreational facilities and a playing field. But the big winner in the 'welfare work' sweeps must have been the CPR, which issued a 32-page illustrated brochure in 1909 to publicize its efforts in this field. Apart from benefit and pension plans, the railway included under the rubric of welfare work its apprentice training programme, a scholarship programme at McGill University, evening and correspondence classes, a first aid programme, The 'Railway Y.M.C.A.'s' built by the company and administered as boarding houses and recreation centres by the charity organization, provision of meals, bunk houses, a 'Safety League,' recreational facilities, and more. 'Now, this railroad company does not claim that its motive in this work is purely philanthropic,' the brochure confided. 'The management frankly confesses that considerate treatment towards its employees is a paying business.'[27]

Some employers – notably S.J. Williams of the Greene and Rome shirt company in Berlin, Ontario – confidently asserted that welfare work would be the cure for all labour troubles. *Industrial Canada* commented: 'Those who listened to his words of hope and optimism at the recent luncheon of the Toronto manufacturers could not but feel that the millennium was at hand when such conditions as he outlines could exist ... Welfare work pays, he reiterates again and again. It is as a financial investment that he urges the general adoption of methods similar to those which he has found so successful in his own business.'[28] Some staunch advocates of the scientific management hard line were not convinced. 'It is not at all necessary to be a business pirate to be a business success,' wrote H.L.C. Hall, 'but it is necessary to get what you pay for, and as a consequence there must be no mixture of business and philanthropy. Be philanthropic if you can afford it, but do not delude yourself by making it at the expense of your business. If you use your business as a vehicle for charity, you will some day find that there is but little save the charity left, and you may do your best to live on that.'[29]

27 *Ibid.*, July 1909, 9; *IC*, Dec. 1904, 327; Canadian Pacific Railway Company, *Welfare Work* (n.p., n.d.), copy in National Library, Ottawa. The date, 1909, is attributed on the basis of a review of this brochure, *LG*, Oct. 1909, 488.
28 *IC*, May 1907, 778
29 *Ibid.*, Sept. 1906, 103ff. Hall did concede, at the end of this article, that 'Certain wise ones have discovered that it pays to spend a little something on the comfort of the worker. It is a cold business proposition. You get more out of them.'

III

Canadian manufacturers were well aware that capitalism was under attack in some quarters, and their organization occasionally found it necessary to issue a 'rebuke.' But as the period developed, they came to realize that socialism and trade unionism were not necessarily the same thing. *Industrial Canada* used the occasion of the publication of the *Communist Manifesto* in Esperanto to underscore this point and meditate on its problems:

It is well to bear in mind that trade unionism is in theory opposed to socialism. But nowadays, one cannot overlook, unionists are often far from informed on the true basis of their own organization. Trade unionism is based on the system of wage-payments, and the idea that by union workingmen are in a position to secure the best possible wage – that is all. It is not subversive of society – which is more than can be said of many of the labour agitators who, as far as the real interests of workingmen are concerned, are wolves in sheep's clothing.[30]

If trade unionism pure and simple was a sheep – one is tempted to add, to be led to the slaughter – the CMA was not in principle opposed. But as the unions grew, strikes multiplied, and 'labor agitators' acquired an ever-increasing following after the turn of the century, it did seem to put in question the simple market analysis implicit in the quote. The CMA had a particular need to demonstrate that the interest of workers and employers was one. Beyond the general usefulness of showing that industrial conflict was self-defeating, the common interest argument was used to try and enlist the support of the labour movement for the CMA's political *raison d'être* – the maintenance and extension of the protective tariff. This meant that the organization itself was unwilling to take up arms against the unions in the manner of its US counterpart, the National Association of Manufacturers. It was not above pointing out the futility of union action, however, and waging battle against union-sponsored legislation through parliamentary lobbying.

The growing split within the CMA, between big business and small, caused problems in this area. Small employers wanted to use the association to carry out a range of interventions that would, in effect, confer on them some of the freedom from market constraints enjoyed by their oligopolistic big brothers. Big businessmen wanted to store up the association's ammunition for the tariff fight alone, for they could manage the other things better by

30 *Ibid.*, Dec. 1907, 421 ('A Rebuke to Haters of Capital'), Feb. 1908, 556

themselves. Perhaps the symbolic turning-point came in 1905, when C.C. Ballantyne, manager of the sprawling Canadian operations of the Sherwin-Williams Company, became president of the CMA. Denied direct association action in the labour field, Canadian businessmen set up separate employers' organizations to battle the unions on their home ground.

The CMA's basic argument for the unity of interest of capital and labour was a simple one. *Industrial Canada* had reprinted an article from the *American Economist* in January 1904: 'Labor and capital are, and must be, one. They are necessary to each other. Without the use of labour capital would be idle. Without the use of capital labor would be idle ... Any antagonism of labor toward capital that is employed in honest enterprise ... is absolutely wrong. Any antagonism of capital towards the labor it employs and which it needs is also absolutely wrong. These two units, labor and capital, are so wrapped together, and so involved with one another, that they must work together, and in harmony, in order [to] acquire mutual success.' But this was all too simple. Canadian manufacturers realized that the introduction of machine production and systematic management was displacing workers even if it did 'make work easier,' and that this might be thought to involve some measure of injustice.

The efficiency experts had an answer: 'This is a false view, and one which the spirit of progress cannot countenance for a moment. No man who is worth a cent to the country wants to stay for a minute in a place where he is useless ... He cannot expect to stay where he is and be a drag on the wheels of progress.' The language of Social Darwinism was brought in here to legitimate the consequences of the business revolution. But if this did not put an end to objections, *Industrial Canada* could summon up the words of 'an observant and sympathetic' American businessman, John Thayer Lincoln: '[M]achinery, while it does the work of many men, has not degraded labor. Rather it has placed it on a pinnacle never reached before its introduction. The finer and more complicated are the operations which it performs, the higher is the intellectual effort represented by it and the better the work required from the workman who directs it.'[31]

Perhaps this was of some comfort. But system and efficiency brought with them other problems as well. Now that businessmen had access to an accurate method of determining their costs, they found that their workers' apparent inability to grasp the principles of cost accounting was the source of much misunderstanding. 'The average workman fails utterly to appreciate the expense under which a manufacturing business is conducted,' com-

31 *Ibid.*, Feb. 1907, 586; Nov. 1906, 355f

plained one writer. 'He does not see things from the office end. He has not the proper perspective.' The worker persists in believing that the price of a product ought to bear some relation to the cost of labour and materials, and this is the source of much unrest. It is not that he is stupid, but he is too easily influenced by agitators. Moreover, he 'is not made of the same heroic stuff out of which investors are made,' so he does not really understand capital.[32]

As conception was separated from execution, and as managers appropriated the knowledge of the work process that had previously been the province of the craftsmen, manufacturers began to concern themselves more and more with the problem of technical education. In some cases, this meant setting up company apprenticeship programmes to replace those earlier administered by unions, or to supply such training where none had existed before. The Toronto Employers' Association drew up a complicated contract of indenture for the use of its members: it also prepared 'a codified set of shop rules' and employee record cards and time sheets. The Grand Trunk Railway shops had a very sophisticated apprenticeship programme, whose textbook demonstrates that the scientific management technique of intensive experimentation with materials and processes had passed into at least one major Canadian company by 1906. It included a detailed table for ascertaining the correct speeds for drilling different metals with various types of drills.[33] As the 'welfare work' brochure discussed above shows, the CPR had a similar programme.

Many businessmen, however, wanted the cost of training workers in the new methods of machine production to be borne by the public generally, and the CMA agitated for the establishment of technical schools. The demand was to be recognized in 1910, when Mackenzie King introduced a Royal Commission on the question. In this area, the CMA found it could ally itself with the labour movement. *Industrial Canada* reviewed the demands made by the Trades and Labour Congress in its 1908 cap-in-hand session with the Prime Minister, and prophesied that most of them would 'go on the shelf.' An alternative strategy would have been more successful: 'If, instead of going up with a whole string of demands, these gentlemen concentrated their energy on some one worthy object, they would be doing something in the interests of the people they profess to represent. For instance, they ask for a commission on technical education. If, instead of mixing this up with a lot of other impossible demands, they concentrated their energies on it alone, they

---

32 *Ibid.*, April 1905, 538f; Dec. 1907, 407f
33 *Ibid.*, March 1904, 410f; May 1905, 618f; Dec. 1906, 433

would have the support of the manufacturers and employers, and their united action would be sure to produce the desired result.'[34]

But the great field for co-operation between manufacturers and workers was the tariff question.[35] 'For every million dollars worth of goods we import we are supporting in a foreign country an industrial army of workmen and officers.' An increased tariff would force American industrialists to locate branch plants in Canada, creating jobs for Canadian workers. 'A 25 per cent. duty does more to establish factories on Canadian soil, furnish employment for Canadian workingmen, and create a market at home for Canadian farmers, than a million tons of sentiment could do in as many years.' But the Canadian worker (and farmer) refuses to realize this. He must be brought to understand 'that when the pinch comes the only friend he has is the man who risks his capital in establishing the industries of the country ... If he were taught to realize his helplessness without the aid of capital, and the folly of listening to self-interested agitators who seek at every opportunity to injure, and even to destroy, the industries that give value to labor, it would be better for him and for the country in which he lives.'[36]

If the country's businessmen were willing to rely on the 'Made in Canada' label, the country's workers ought to do likewise, and abjure the solicitations of foreign agitators. During the recession of 1907-8, unemployed Americans flocked into Canada and competed with Canadian workers for jobs. 'It is no worse however to have these men coming in to make things harder for our own men than it is to have labor unions, with headquarters in the United States, sending agitators over here in times when labor is scarce to make trouble for the employer. The workingman is really only getting a little of his own medicine, and it is not the employer who is responsible for it, either.'[37]

Canadian businessmen after the turn of the century hailed the long-awaited emergence of an age of prosperity. In seeking to preserve what they saw as the preconditions for Canada's triumphant entry into the ranks of the industrial nations – pre-eminently the tariff – they sought to win the allegiance of other classes in the community. At the same time, the very conditions which created such hope, the emergence of big business and the implementation of the new managerial techniques, created as well a heightening of the conflict between worker and employer. The businessmen interpreted this conflict as self-defeating and sought to contain, prevent, and, if

34 *Ibid.*, March 1908, 621
35 See chapter 6 below.
36 *IC*, Aug. 1907, 13; June 1908, 878; Dec. 1907, 407f
37 *Ibid.*, Dec. 1907, 411

necessary, win it in the name of progress. The ideology of the Canadian businessman rampant was more than adequately expressed by *Industrial Canada* in a January 1908 editorial entitled 'Misleading the Masses':

We are told that this century belongs to Canada as the last century belonged to the United States. If the prophets are right, and everything at present indicates that they are, the next twenty-five years will see remarkable strides made in the industrial life of this country. We are now just at the beginning of an era of rapid development, both in agricultural pursuits and in manufacturing. It is, therfore, important that we should begin with a proper understanding. Labor should know at the outset that its hope lies in capital, that its future, as its present, depends upon the man who has money to invest and the courage to invest it in some line of production which will create employment. Let him understand, too, that the more money the employer makes through his first venture, the better able he will be to enlarge his plant and provide more work for more people. Get away from the false idea that the employer's success means the oppression of the employed. What his success really means is the development of Canada into a manufacturing country, where every kind of labor will be in constant demand, at fair wages and under reasonable conditions. If the false idea that labor and capital are antagonistic and should go about constantly armed against each other holds sway, industrial progress will be retarded and labor will be made to suffer. Let us understand at the beginning that labor and capital are depen-dent upon each other for profitable employment, and that the country in which they work together in the greatest harmony is the country in which each will find its richest reward.

5
The labour movement and industrial relations

Les idéologies véhiculées par le mouvement ouvrier ont entretenu de multiples illusions sur le caractère 'global' de la classe ouvrière ... Chaque période, chaque âge de l'organisation du travail tend, en effet, à créer une structure relativement stable de la classe opératrice des moyens de production ... Ainsi les représentations sociales prennent-elles un caractère totalisateur qui ne reflète pas la complexité des phénomènes réels. [Serge Mallet, *La nouvelle classe ouvrière*]

Discussing the development of worker and employer attitudes in nineteenth-century Britain, Eric Hobsbawm points to two important 'watersheds' in the long process of learning the 'rules of the game' in market society. By about 1850, workers had come to regard their labour as a commodity, but persisted in fixing its price, quantity, and quality according to customary, rather than economic criteria. Employers by this time had 'learned the value of intensive rather than extensive labour utilization and to a lesser degree of incentives, but still measured the degree of labour utilization by custom or empirically – if at all.' The second watershed occurred in the mid-1890s, towards the end of the long depression, when 'workers began to demand what the traffic would bear and, ... to measure effort by payment. Employers discovered genuinely efficient ways of utilizing ... labour time,' culminating in the formalization of scientific management after the turn of the century.[1]

Much of the recent work in nineteenth-century Canadian working-class history may be interpreted to confirm not only that a similar sequence occurred in this country, but that there was a roughly similar periodization as

1 Eric Hobsbawm, 'Custom, Wages and Workload in Nineteenth Century Industry,' in Asa Briggs and John Saville, eds., *Essays in Labour History* (London: Macmillan, 1960), 113–39

well. The long depression, coupled with the introduction of new technologies, undercut the position of the traditional artisan in many trades. Even for those trades in which unions were successful in adapting to the new situation, traditions of workshop control came under concerted employer attack.[2] Canadian workers found themselves engaged on two fronts. On the one hand, they were fighting against the attrition of custom and against the new prerogatives of 'management's rights.' On the other, as they crossed the second watershed to a sophisticated understanding of the 'rules of the game,' they began to experiment with various methods of meeting their employers in the market-place and arriving at a high valuation on their commodity, labour. This was a complex process, complicated as well by the regional and sectoral fragmentation of the labour movement precisely when a national market, for labour almost as much as for other commodities, was developing. Canadian employers were learning the new managerial techniques from the United States, and as American managerial expertise moved into Canada along various channels, so did the American trade movement.

This was not the first time that American labour organizations had made an impact on Canadian workers: the Knights of Labor had done the same thing in the wake of the first 'watershed' which seems to have occurred in Canada in the 1870s. Other US unions, which had arisen in radical opposition to the American Federation of Labor, organized in the mining camps and railroad towns of British Columbia. But when the AFL managed to seize control of the Canadian Trades and Labour Congress in 1902, it marked the turning point for the Canadian labour movement. Continental trade unionism – termed, somewhat misleadingly, 'international' unionism – had come to stay. By 1911 almost 120,000 of the slightly more than 133,000 trade unionists in Canada were members of organizations domiciled in the United States, and the AFL had quite successfully asserted its claim to determine the direction of the labour movements' development in both countries. Fragmentation and disarray persisted, as much because of AFL policy as in spite of it, but the transition to market attitudes had reached its major formal expression. As Canadian industrial relations policy was developed in this period, it operated both to smooth this process of transition and to modify in some respects the practice of the American unions. It operated, too, to impose a degree of standardization on a very unsystematic range of practices

2 See, for example, Greg Kealey's analysis of the fortunes of three craft groups in Toronto during the last third of the century, '"The Honest Workingman" and Workers' Control: The Experience of Toronto Skilled Workers, 1860–1892,' *Labour/Le Travailleur* 1 (1976), 32–68; and, for yet another case, his 'Artisans Respond to Industrialism: Shoemakers, Shoe Factories and the Knights of St. Crispin in Toronto,' CHA Papers (1973).

and experiments. But at the same time, its emphasis was not on implement-ing collective bargaining relations, or on attempting to over-rule the market in assigning rates and working conditions; its emphasis, in the main, was on the prevention of strikes, particularly in the infrastructure industries.

And strikes there were. The Department of Labour, established in 1900, collected data on more than 1300 strikes, against more than 7100 different employers, between 1901 and 1911.[3] Although corresponding series for earlier years are not available, there is enough qualitative evidence to suggest that the years of rapid economic growth and social change that ushered in the new century were years, as well, of unprecedented tensions in industrial relations, 'a classic period of widespread unrest and violence,' as Jamieson has put it.[4] This unrest was not unique to Canada: it was experienced in the United States, Australia, New Zealand, Britain, and Western Europe as well. But what was done about it in Canada was in no small measure unique, and the reasons for that uniqueness are to be found in the meeting of a particular way of interpreting the world with the real tensions and strains inherent in the Canadian situation.

The staples-dependency interpretation of the Canadian political economy in this period suggests one line of approach to this problem. It implies that the industrial unrest of turn-of-the-century Canada, and the state's responses to it, cannot be adequately analysed in simple class-conflict terms. The confron-tation of American managerial technique with American trade-union tech-nique on Canadian soil was not just a re-enactment on the periphery of a play scripted in the metropolitan centre and performed *ad nauseam* by a road-show cast, although some facets of its *mise-en-scène* must be understood in these terms. In several ways, the historic vulnerability of the Canadian eco-nomy, with the special roles it created not only for the state but for social classes as well, in their relations both to it and to one another, confounded the original script and made a new reading necessary, forcing variant atti-tudes and postures upon the main characters. The metaphor of the provincial road show will not do: were we to seek for a better one, the modern 'adapta-tion' of a classic drama might be as good a one as we could hope to find. The basic outlines of the plot remain, though they may have been bowdlerized here and there; the text is for the most part intact, barring some excisions and the introduction of a little new matter designed to underline the rele-vance of the performance for its modern participants; the characters play

3 For annual data, see M.C. Urquhart and K.A.H. Buckley, *Historical Statistics of Canada* (Toronto: Macmillan, 1965), tables D426–433.
4 Jamieson, 62

their parts according to new theories of stagecraft; and while the essential structure of plot and text is still clearly visible, the subtext has been altered, subtly, perhaps, but unmistakeably. Text, context, and subtext mutually interact, so that our ability to understand the burden of the play rests in large part on our grasp of their intersections and linkages, their reinforcements and estrangements.

I

'It will be clear, however, that the advantages of international affiliations are bought at a certain price. Nevertheless, their attractions may easily be thought irresistible.'[5] Thus Canada's first labour historian, and as good a statement as any of the ambivalent response international unionism has called forth from successive generations of observers. On the one hand, Canadian workers joined American unions because they offered a degree of financial and organizational support unobtainable, for the most part, from what shards of Canadian unionism had survived the contortions of the late nineteenth-century business cycle. Once the period of sustained growth was under way, of course, there was no reason why, all other things being equal, Canadian workers should not have been able to reorganize their own trade union movement on firmer foundations. But all other things were not equal: the AFL unions were there, and eager to expand into Canada at their president's behest. They could offer a number of benefits to Canadian workers, not least among which were healthy strike funds and travelling cards to admit emigrating Canadians to employment in American cities. But if there were benefits to be reaped from the international connection, there were drawbacks as well. The deal offered Canadian workers by the AFL had some strings attached, as Robert Babcock, in his *Gompers in Canada*, has unequivocally demonstrated.[6]

Babcock argues that US commercial expansion in the 1890s laid the groundwork, both economic and ideological, for international unionism: 'branch plant factories begat "branch plant" unionism.' The 'business unionist' stance of Samuel Gompers and the AFL insisted that labour could make real gains within the system of American capitalism. What Gompers

---

5 R.H. Coats, 'The Labour Movement in Canada,' in Adam Shortt and Arthur G.
   Doughty, eds., *Canada and Its Provinces* (Toronto: Glasgow, Brook & Co., 1914), vol. 9,
   335
6 *Gompers in Canada: A Study in American Continentalism before the First World War*
   (Toronto: University of Toronto Press, 1974). The following four paragraphs summarize
   Babcock's major thesis.

chose to consider the *bona fide* trade union movement in the US accepted the prevailing business ideology of Social Darwinism and manifest destiny. In the early 'nineties, Gompers was interested in building a worldwide trade-union movement on the AFL model, partly in order to create an alternative to the Socialist International, and this led to the first exchanges of fraternal delegates between the AFL and the Trades and Labor Congress of Canada, and to small-scale financial support from the AFL for TLC legislative lobbying. During this period, the international craft unions grew slowly in Canada. There was no great urgency to their expansion, and they seemed more concerned to retain the allegiance of their current membership in Canada – for example, by approving a $100 annual grant to the TLC to forestall local breakaways occasioned by disputes over the destination of dues paid by Canadian members – than to escalate their growth rates.

By the turn of the century, however, this had begun to change. The large-scale movement of American branch plants across the Canadian tariff wall was foreshadowing the development of a continental economy wherein employers could shift production from areas where labour was organized and militant to others where the labour problem was less acute. 'It is clear,' writes Babcock, 'that Gompers and other American union leaders were anxious to devote resources to the Canadian labour field because they feared that American employers would take too many jobs across the boundary if Canadian labour was poorly organized. As one of them put it, "International bosses have made the welfare of a trade in one country of vital importance to the welfare of the same trade in another country."' Suddenly, organizing Canadian workers was high on the list of AFL priorities.

The Canadian labour movement, as represented in the TLC, was an uneven amalgam of international craft unions affiliated to the AFL, internationals in the railway running trades and outside the AFL, Canadian unions, and Knights of Labor assemblies. While the TLC had just begun to organize on its own behalf, issuing charters to a number of Federal Labor Unions, lack of funds restricted this activity. By contrast, the AFL was relatively affluent. Following successful efforts by volunteer Canadian organizers in the late 'nineties, Gompers was satisfied that Canadian dues payments would justify the cost of a full-time paid organizer. By December 1899, the AFL claimed to have more than ten thousand members in Canada. It began to compete with the TLC in issuing charters to Canadian labour councils and, in 1900, Hamilton trade unionist John A. Flett was appointed AFL general organizer for Canada.

Gompers' project of continental labour unity under the AFL banner spelled the end of formal labour unity in Canada. As the power of the international crafts within the TLC grew, the American labour leaders began to press for the expulsion of non-AFL unions from the Congress: the bitter infighting of American labour was exported to Canada. The climax came in 1902, at the TLC's Berlin Convention, when the Congress constitution was amended to provide that 'no National Union be recognized, where an International Union exists,' and that 'in no case shall there be more than one Central Body in any City or Town, said Central Body to be chartered by the Trades and Labor Congress of Canada.'[7] About one-fifth of the Congress membership, largely Knights' assemblies, was expelled and AFL organizer Flett was elected Congress president. Moreover, in the ensuing years, AFL policies designed for American conditions were imposed on the Canadian Congress. These included the doctrine of craft autonomy, opposition to independent labour politics, and an interdict on compulsory arbitration, once an element in the Congress programme.[8] Gompers repeatedly attempted to reduce the TLC to the equivalent of a state federation in the AFL. The AFL came to Canada, not in the disinterested spirit of internationalism, but in order to safeguard the position of American craft workers in an expanding imperial system founded on the continental extension of American business.

Babcock's book may be read as a detailed indictment of international unionism's origins: he estimates that the AFL made a net profit of some $16,000 on its Canadian operations between 1901 and 1914. At the same time it must be recognized, as Coats first pointed out and as other writers have not tired of repeating, that the attractions of the AFL may have seemed well-nigh irresistible to many Canadian workers. Coats cited 'such tangible considerations as large strike funds, cheap insurance, out-of-work pay, sick and old age benefits, the financing of which is possible only to a union of large membership,' as well as the travelling card. But there was that 'certain price,' and Babcock is probably best read as an accounting of the hidden and unforeseen costs acquired by Canadian workers along with these benefits. Innis seems to have thought that international unionism was a more or less inevitable consequence of the reorientation of the Canadian economy on north-south lines and the import of technique:[9] inevitable or not, it is certain that the nature and role of the Canadian labour movement after 1902 was to a significant extent subject to exogenous constraints.

7 TLC 1902, 78
8 The TLC's position on compulsory arbitration and on government intervention in industrial relations generally is discussed later in this chapter.
9 H.A. Innis, 'Editor's Introduction' to H.A. Logan and N.J. Ware, *Labor in Canadian-American Relations* [The Relations of Canada and the United States, 1937] (New York: Russell & Russell, 1970); see also Ware's essay, 'The History of Labor Interaction,' in that volume.

II

But it would be a mistake to assume that the Canadian labour movement after 1902 was simply a miniature replica of the AFL. There remained a somewhat distinctive character to the TLC and, outside the Congress, there were significant movements in opposition to the AFL/TLC. These included radical opponents of the AFL like the Western Federation of Miners and the United Brotherhood of Railway Employees, which briefly flourished on the CPR in western Canada in 1903. They included, as well, more or less business-unionist organizations striving to maintain national unions independent of the American Federation, like the National Trades and Labour Congress, formed from the TLC membership outlawed at Berlin. In Quebec, shortly after the turn of the century, the first moves in the direction of Church-directed confessional unionism were made,[10] while in Nova Scotia the Provincial Workmen's Association long remained aloof from national and international organizations.[11] The Canadian Brotherhood of Railroad Employees, founded in 1908, organized the government-owned Intercolonial Railway.[12] The international brotherhoods organizing in the railway running trades remained outside the AFL and, for the most part, the TLC after 1902, although they sometimes co-operated with the latter in legislative lobbying.[13]

The Canadian labour movement was also divided on regional lines. Unions in western Canada, within or without the TLC, tended to be more radical, more interested in independent labour politics, and more militant than their eastern and central Canadian counterparts. It was in the west that the syndicalist affiliates of the American Labor Union and, later, the Industrial Workers of the World, made the most headway, as did socialist politics. Several competing explanations for western radicalism and militancy have

10 Esdras Minville, *Labour Legislation and Social Services in the Province of Quebec*, App. 5 to Royal Commission on Dominion-Provincial Relations (Ottawa, 1939), 14ff; Jacques Rouillard, *Les syndicats nationaux au Québec de 1900 à 1930* (Quebec: Les Presses de l'Université Laval, 1979)

11 For the Provincial Workmen's Association see, *inter alia*, J.M. Cameron, *The Pictonian Colliers* (Halifax: The Nova Scotia Museum, 1974), and, although with a strong international unionist viewpoint, Paul MacEwan, *Miners and Steelworkers: Labour in Cape Breton* (Toronto: Hakkert, 1976).

12 There is a fine discussion of the organization of the CBRE in an unpublished paper on Aaron Mosher, by Stephen Bingham, Carleton University.

13 For the international brotherhoods in Canada, J.H. Tuck, 'Canadian Railways and the International Brotherhoods: Labour Organization in the Railway Running Trades in Canada, 1865–1914,' unpublished PHD dissertation, University of Western Ontario, 1975

been advanced.[14] (It is perhaps noteworthy that most Canadian labour historians have considered western radicalism, rather than the relative conservatism of unions in central Canada, to be in need of an explanation; Pentland is the interesting exception.) While these interpretations have varied significantly, most of them focus on the 'frontier' character of western industrialism. 'Frontier' is meant, not in the Turner sense, but to indicate the peripheral character of western industry. The coal and metal mines, the logging camps and the railway towns which furnished the constituency for radical unionism were a far cry from the relatively diversified indusrial cities of Ontario. Western Canada was to no small extent a land of company towns, where the theory of class conflict received daily confirmation in practice. The mining companies were among the most uncompromising of Canadian employers, and while welfare work and industrial betterment could make some headway in the effeminate East, the mine bosses would brook no nonsense of the kind. They had at their disposal an enormous reserve army of labour, in the form of Chinese, Japanese, and Indians imported on contract at extremely low wages, and they did not hesitate to use it to break unions. This translated into a second reason for western militancy. When the western workers were able to force their local governments to ban Oriental immigration, the federal government time after time disallowed the legislation, inviting regional conflict and an intense mistrust of the central government. Labour market conditions in the west translated into militant racism, and Vancouver was on more than one occasion torn by race riots.[15]

In striking contrast to the militant unions of the western miners were the railway brotherhoods. The railway unions furnished by far the largest proportion of union locals in Canada: 36 per cent in 1902, and 25 per cent as late as 1914. The brotherhoods organized the aristocrats of the labour movements in Canada and the United States, the highly skilled men in the 'running trades': engineers, conductors, firemen and trainmen, and the equally skilled telegraphers. Trackmen, yardmen, and other semi- and unskilled labourers

14 See, inter alia, A. Ross McCormack, Reformers, Rebels, and Revolutionaries: The Western Canadian Radical Movement, 1899-1919 (Toronto: University of Toronto Press, 1977); Paul Phillips, No Power Greater: A Century of Labour in B.C. (Vancouver: BC Federation of Labour and Boag Foundation, 1967); D.J. Bercuson, 'Labour Radicalism and the Western Industrial Frontier: 1897-1919,' CHR, vol. 58 (June 1977); Innis' introduction to Logan and Ware; and H.C. Pentland, 'The Western Canadian Labour Movement, 1867-1919,' Can. J. Pol. Soc. Theory 3, Spring-Summer 1979.

15 There were serious anti-Oriental riots in 1887 (Phillips, No Power Greater, 14) and in 1907. A Royal Commission was appointed to investigate compensation claims after the 1907 riot: King was appointed commissioner, and he played an important role in negotiating restricted immigration with the Chinese, Japanese, and Indian governments.

were left to fend for themselves. (Machinists, carpenters, and other skilled workers in the railway shops were organized, for the most part, by the craft unions in their trades.) When the UBRE attempted to organize unskilled railway workers in an industrial union in 1902–3, the brotherhoods joined the CPR management in breaking their strike. The high skill level of the brotherhoods' members was one important factor in their highly developed bargaining power: another was their commitment to co-operation with management. Particularly in the United States, the brotherhoods assisted the railway owners in fighting against public regulation of freight rates, and generally acquiesced in railway policy, in the belief that, in the long run at least, the interests of the railway and its skilled employees were identical.[16]

This policy was expressed, among other ways, in the traditional reluctance of the brotherhoods to take strike action. They had a history of accepting wage cuts and temporary lay-offs, and attempted to dissociate themselves from what they saw as the strike-happy tendencies of other unions. This was a factor in the brotherhoods' aloofness from the AFL. For many years the Order of Railway Conductors, for example, prohibited its members from going on strike on pain of expulsion. During this period, members of the ORC acted as strikebreakers against the other brotherhoods, with the predictable consequence, as an early historian of the union put it, that 'engineers, firemen, switchmen and brakemen vied with each other in placing obstacles in the way of the Order, which was nearly wiped out of existence by their continued opposition.'[17] Many conductors refused to join, partly because of the hostility of the other brotherhoods, and partly because the ORC was able to offer so little in improved wages and conditons. Finally, the order had to change its policy and pay more attention to basic trade-union concerns but, like the other brotherhoods, it sought when possible to work through co-

16 For union-management co-operation, especially after the First World War, see L.A. Wood, *Union-Management Co-Operation on the Railroads* (New Haven: Yale University Press, 1931). Tuck, 'International Brotherhoods,' gives some anecdotal evidence for union-management relations in Canada: e.g., 18: 'Generally speaking, the management of Canadian railways approved of the [Brotherhood of Locomotive Engineers] ... The Great Western became so impressed with the positive virtues of the Brotherhood, in fact, that it supplied London Division Number 68 with a fully furnished meeting hall in 1872 ... [the railway's mechanical superintendent] encouraged the engineers on the Western to become members ...' But there is in general little secondary material on union-management relations in Canada – a surprising lack considering the importance of railways and railway rates in the Canadian political economy.

17 E.C. Robbins, *Railway Conductors: A Study in Organized Labor* (New York: n.p., 1914), 22. See also W.F. McCaleb's *Brotherhood of Railroad Trainmen, With Special Reference to the Life of Alexander F. Whitney* (New York: Boni, 1936).

operation rather than confrontation. This is not to say that the brotherhoods never went on strike. In Canada, the Engineers won a particularly difficult battle against the Grand Trunk in 1876;[18] in 1910, the Conductors and Trainmen lost what was evidently a more difficult one against the same railway. It was made more difficult by the intervention of Mackenzie King, as chapter 10 argues.

Second only to the railway brotherhoods in the proportion of locals they organized were the building trades unions. These were almost exclusively locals of AFL crafts: the United Brotherhood of Carpenters and Joiners, the Bricklayers' and Masons' International Union, the United Association of Plumbers and Steamfitters, and the rest. Coats counted 328 locals in the building trades, basing his figures on 1912 statistics.[19] Craft autonomy in the building trades led to the interminable jurisdictional squabbles still familiar in the construction industry today; at the same time, though, the crafts sometimes united in industry-wide bargaining at the local level with construction employers' associations.[20] Jurisdictional disputes would normally be referred to the American Federation of Labor; for example, a time-honoured conflict between electrical workers and plumbers over who had the right to install wires within conduit pipes was so referred by the Toronto locals in 1903. Failing this, recourse might be made to another body. In 1902, the Ontario Bureau of Labour mediated a jurisdictional dispute between Thorold and St Catharines carpenters. The local in the former town was chartered by the International Brotherhood, while the other was directly chartered by the AFL: the settlement arrived at was a merger of the two locals.[21]

While collective bargaining was carried on between individual locals and employers and, occasionally, union councils and employers' associations, locals came together at the municipal, provincial, and federal levels for legislative lobbying and mutual support. In the major central Canadian cities, local trades and labour councils had long been familiar institutions: Toronto's enjoyed a continuous existence from the early 1880s, and local councils in other Ontario industrial towns were also established in that decade. The existence of two competing councils in Montreal, one composed of international crafts locals and the other of Knights' assemblies and national unions,

18 Desmond Morton, 'Taking on the Grand Trunk: The Locomotive Engineers Strike of 1876–7,' *Labour/Le Travailleur*, vol. 2, (1977)
19 Coats, 'Labour Movement,' 321. He counted 447 locals 'in the railway service.'
20 See A.G. Gruchy, 'Collective Bargaining in the Building, Coal Mining, and Transportation Industries of Canada, 1900–1927,' unpublished MA thesis, McGill, 1929
21 *LG*, May 1903, 842; Dec. 1902, 479

helped to spark the AFL's purge of the TLC in 1902.[22] By 1909, when the TLC met at Quebec City, trades and labour councils from Berlin, Brantford, Fort William, Guelph, Halifax, Hamilton, Kingston, London, Moose Jaw, Moncton, Montreal, Ottawa, Port Arthur, Quebec and Levis, Regina, Revelstoke, Sherbrooke, Sydney, Toronto and district, Vancouver, and Winnipeg were all represented. In 1911, at Brandon, Calgary, Edmonton, Medicine Hat, New Westminster, and Saskatoon all sent trades and labour council delegates, in addition to many of the cities represented at Quebec. Before 1910, lobbying the provincial governments was the responsibility of TLC provincial executive committees. In that year, the British Columbia Federation of Labour was formed and the TLC constitution amended to provide for provincial federations, which would replace executive committees where they were established. British Columbia was still the only province with a federation in 1911.[23]

Outside the post-1902 TLC, other legislative bodies existed. The railway brotherhoods had a common parliamentary representative. The unions which had been exiled from the TLC at Berlin formed their own lobbying and organizing centre, the National Trades and Labour Congress, later to be renamed the Canadian Federation of Labour. At the outset, this organization's affiliates were heavily concentrated in Quebec. In 1904, it gave its membership as 10,435 organized in 47 locals. About five thousand of its members were in Quebec City alone, while a total of approximately nine thousand were in Quebec; most of the remainder seem to have been in Ottawa.[24] The beginnings of confessional unionism – organizations supervised by Catholic priests, in open opposition to the secular unionism of the AFL – following Archbishop Bégin's intervention in a boot and shoe lockout in 1901 took place within the NTLC, so that Quebec and Montreal shoe workers furnished the largest group in the federation. Shortly after its organization the NTLC sought to win the affiliation of the large and independent Provincial Workmen's Association of Nova Scotia: the pre-1902 TLC had always been interested, unsuccessfully, in this.[25] In 1910, the PWA finally linked itself to the NTLC, and this event may well have had some bearing on

22 Jacques Rouillard, 'Le Québec et le congrès de Berlin, 1902,' *Labour/Le Travailleur*, vol. 1, (1976)
23 *TLC* 1909, 5f; 1911, 6f; 1910, 79; 1911, 24, which indicates the imminent formation of an Alberta Federation of Labour.
24 H.A. Logan, *Trade Unions in Canada: Their Development and Functioning* (Toronto: Macmillan, 1948), 370ff
25 E.g., *TLC* 1898, 10. Similarly unsuccessful attempts were made after 1902: e.g., *TLC* 1904, 25.

the decision by the United Mine Workers, an AFL affiliate, to move into the Nova Scotia coalfields in what was to be, after a long battle, a successful attempt to destroy the PWA and replace it with international unionism.

Not surprisingly, the TLC and the NTLC were bitter enemies. The TLC claimed that the national organization was a pawn of the Canadian Manufacturers' Association, organized solely to weaken true trade unionism.[26] The NTLC returned the compliment, charging that the TLC was being used to destroy Canadian industry, and hence the jobs of Canadian workers, to the competitive advantage of American business and the AFL.[27] The AFL's long unwillingness to place a French-speaking organizer in Quebec, despite the frequent pleadings of the TLC,[28] was a factor in the NTLC's success in winning both the allegiance of Québécois workers and the support of the Church: the AFL, and by extension the TLC, could be painted as a threat to the cultural survival of the Quebec majority. Such a picture would not be wholly false. The propaganda of both TLC and NTLC has effectively obscured objective evaluations of the claims of the two rival bodies. Some labour historians, perhaps in their zeal to support what turned out to be the winning side, have denigrated the NTLC in favour of the spread of international unionism.

III

This raises the more general question of attitudes towards international and national unionism. The positions of the TLC and NTLC have been briefly

26 E.g., President's address to *TLC* 1905, 10: 'As the members are probably well aware, the so-called National Movement has practically faded from sight since we last met ... As usual, a number of requests were presented to the Dominion Government on behalf of this body, the requests giving general evidence of inspiration from the Canadian Manufacturers' Association. It is confidently expected that the next year will witness the disappearance of this body altogether ...' But 1905 marked 'the high-water mark in point of attendance' at NTLC conventions. Coats, 'Labour Movement,' 309

27 Cf. Logan, *Trade Unions*, 375–6: the major assumption of the NTLC/CFL was that 'the threat to the Canadian labourer comes not only from the capitalist in Canada, but also from the foreign capitalist and the foreign labourer, who respectively seek to exploit and to replace him in the production activities which should be his.' The constitution of the Canadian Federation of Labour (1908) had a preamble beginning, 'In studying the history of the present time, Canadian workers cannot fail to be impressed with the imperative necessity of protection, both in their relationship to capital in the hands of the organized employing class, and in the autocratic domination of trade unionism and its policy exercised by the present system of internationalism.'

28 E.g., *TLC* 1904, Report of Quebec Executive, 23: 'We cannot too forcibly impress upon the Congress the necessity of renewing its request to the American Federation of Labor for a permanent organizer, speaking both languages ...'

sketched in, as has the ambivalence of Canada's first labour historian. The attitudes of Canadian employers, of political leaders, and of Mackenzie King should also be noted.

Canadian employers, in the aggregate, were hostile to trade unionism. This was particularly marked in the western resource industries, where men like James Dunsmuir, colliery operator, sometime BC premier, and later lieutenant-governor of the province, developed a simple and for a long time effective policy: anybody who joined a union would be fired, and if a strike took place Chinese labour would be brought in to replace the white miners. In central Canada, as we have seen, the Canadian Manufacturers' Association was reluctant to engage in direct confrontation with the unions, leaving this to the employers' associations, but it would be a mistake to conclude that the CMA was indifferent to the spread of unionism. Largely, one imagines, because of the strength of the AFL unions, and also because of its opportunity to reflect on the experience of American employers, the CMA was particularly hostile to international unionism. It occasionally took pains to distinguish between Gompersism and revolutionary syndicalism, but this was by no means always the case. The CMA warmly supported legislation that was from time to time introduced in the Canadian Senate to ban the international unions or their organizers and officers.

The Canadian Manufacturers' Association made several attempts to define its relationship to the trade union movement and the labour problem in the early years of the century. At its 1901 convention, president P.W. Ellis pointed out that the Association's position was quite different from that of its counterparts in the United States. 'At the outset let me say that our Association has never had any connection with labor questions as such, that we have no organization for industrial warfare, and that in the past our relations with labor organizations have been most cordial.' He went on, however, to specify 'one or two features in connection with Trade Unionism ... that we must deplore today.' 'One is the policy of some international trade unions, which have declared industrial strife in Canada at the incentive of organizations whose headquarters are situated in the United States, and whose interests are entirely opposed to the furtherance of the industrial progress of Canada. The other is the growing tendency of certain unions to claim privileges relating to the government of business which practically mean handing over of the management by those who have responsibility to those who have not.'[29] Ellis ended by affirming that, while the CMA would always try to help the furtherance of good relations between employers and workers, 'the labor question is

29 IC, Nov. 1901

at present no part of our work.' He warned, though, that 'should any occasion arise ... that might check Canadian industrial development, we could not stand aloof.' The two issues singled out by Ellis – international unionism and management's rights – were to recur frequently in the manufacturers' musings on the labour question. Both, of course, were to a substantial extent artifacts of the new industrialism. American unions had come to Canada in the wake of American business, while management's rights became a major bone of contention only when, guided by the new techniques and information, management asserted its right to control every facet of the work process.

The CMA's 1902 convention adopted a resolution appointing a special committee 'to enquire into the whole question of labor organizations and their effect on our manufacturing industries.'[30] which was to report the following year. In the interim, some new moves were made. In May 1903, a special meeting of the Montreal Branch executive committee was called to discuss a sympathy strike by the city's teamsters, who had gone out to support a longshoremen's strike. Two resolutions were adopted. The first condemned 'foreign professional agitators,' and proposed that 'all organizations or unions of workingmen should be local in composition, and in all cases so organized as to be amenable to civil law.' The second condemned the practice of sympathy strikes. When the Montreal Branch held its Annual Meeting a few months later, the chairman, Hon. J.D. Rolland (a banker and paper manufacturer, who was to become CMA president in 1907), repeated the sense of these resolutions in his address: 'we need ... reasonable and enlightened men who are thoroughly Canadian at the head of the workingmen's organizations.' This came, of course, barely a year after the American Federation of Labor had established its title to the leadership of the Canadian labour movement. The executive committee's report to this meeting echoed Ellis's comments at the convention: 'Our Association has, up to the present, made it a rule to touch these labour troubles only on points of legislation. But it may be that conditions could become so acute that they would call for further action.' This had seemed to be in the offing earlier in the year, during the longshoremen's and teamsters' strikes, 'but happily the evil worked its own cure.' The committee set out the principles by which direct intervention might be justified: 'As an organized body we cannot deny the workingmen the right to organize, but it must be the duty of the manufacturers, both individually and collectively, to protect the rights of free [i.e., unorganized] labor, to retain shop government in the hands of those on whom rests the

30 See chap. 6 below.

responsibility of the success of our industrial enterprises, and to see that the union officers do not injure our industrial well-being.'[31]

When the CMA's annual convention met again in October 1903, the new president expanded on this idea. Trade unions are free to organize, he said, and employers must be willing to listen to the 'legitimate grievances' of their workers. But the fundamental rights, 'which are sacred to every British citizen,' admit of no compromise: 'The workingman of Canada must never forfeit his right to sell his labor where he desires. The employer of Canada must correspondingly be free to purchase without interference such labor as he requires. The value of labor must be fixed by the capability of the seller. In justice to our best workingmen, capability must not be handicapped by incapacity. It is our duty as citizens not only to defend our own rights, but to defend the rights of our workingmen. On these principles we must stand or fall together.' He 'regretted' the fact of international unionism, which he hinted had worked to the detriment of Canadian, and the advantage of American, business.

At this convention the report of the Special Committee on Labour was presented. It covered the now-familiar ground, and ended by proposing a 'Declaration of Principles' for the Association:

(1) The Canadian Manufacturers' Association is not opposed to organized labor as such, but is unalterably opposed to illegal acts of interference with the personal liberty of employer or employee.
(2) The Canadian Manufacturers' Association disapproves of strikes and lockouts and favors an equitable adjustment of all differences between employers and employees by any amicable method which will preserve the rights of both parties.
(3) No person should be refused employment in Canada, or in any way discriminated against on account of membership or non-membership in any labor organization, and there should be no interference with any employee who is not a member of a labor organization by members of such organization.
(4) With due regard to contracts, it is the right of the employee to leave his employment whenever he desires, and it is the right of the employer to discharge any employee when he sees fit.
(5) Employers must be free to employ their work people at wages mutually satisfactory without interference or dictation on the part of individuals or organizations not directly parties to such contracts.
(6) Employers must be unmolested and unhampered in the management of their business in determining the amount and quality of their product, and in the use of any methods or systems of factory management which are just and equitable.

31 *IC*, June 1903, 182; Sept. 1903, 57, 59

(7) In the interest of employees and employers of the country, no limitation should be placed upon the opportunities of any person to learn any trade to which he or she may be adapted.

(8) The Canadian Manufacturers' Association believes that Canadian labor unions should be incorporated national organizations, governed by Canadian officials and free from foreign control.[32]

The debate which followed the introduction of this report was enlivened only by the spectacle of Mr J.M. Fortier, the celebrated beater of small girls in his Montreal cigar factory,[33] posing as a moralist. The committee report had condemned the 'vilest epithets' visited on 'innocent women and children' by picketers, presumably when the innocents were strike-breakers or scabs. One member of the Association wished the language of this section to be moderated; Fortier insisted that the original wording be retained. The report was adopted without specific discussion of the declaration of principles. The only substantive point was raised by P.H. Burton, a Toronto textile manufacturer, who asked whether the committee had considered the use of CMA funds to assist members in the legal costs of fighting unions. The president replied: 'Up to the present time the policy of the Association has been not to take up, as an association, work of that kind. I question whether the time is opportune for introducing work of that kind yet.' The CMA remained aloof from any direct fight with labour, although, as its president noted, other organizations were developing with that end in view.

The adoption of the Special Committee's report in 1903 did not mark the end of the CMA's concern with defining its relation to the labour movement. In November of that year, only a month after the convention, the executive decided to begin publishing a labour column in *Industrial Canada*. Its purpose 'would not be to discuss controversial phases of the labor question, but to publish for the information of the members such important labor items as might be useful and interesting to manufacturers generally.'[34] In fact, the column was used to crow over trade unions' reversals in the courts, to condemn the 'unreasonable demands' and tactics of strikers, and to trumpet the defeat of unions whenever circumstances permitted.

The president's address to the 1904 convention repeated in essence the principles established a year earlier, but there was one new note. 'There can

32 *Ibid.*, Oct. 1903, 111, 133ff
33 The scandal was publicized by the Royal Commission on the Relations of Labour and Capital, 1889. See Kealey, *Canada Investigates Industrialism*, xv, xix, 215f., and *passim*.
34 *IC*, Dec. 1903, 274

be no objection to the organization of employers, as well as the organization of labour.' G.E. Drummond announced, 'and I believe that such organizations of capital and labor, if carried on in a proper spirit, can be made to work in the best interest of all.'[35] The organizations to which Drummond was referring were those mentioned a year earlier in connection with the direct fight against unionism. When the CMA refused to get involved because of its broader political programme of tariff protection, alternative employer organizations sprang up to carry on the fight.

In December 1901, the *Labour Gazette* had reported the organization of an association of employers of loggers in the Vancouver area. 'The rules and regulations are founded on those of the Loggers' Association of the State of Washington.' It is not clear whether this association was intended primarily to deal with the 'labour question.' But a year later, on 7 October 1902, the Employers' Association of Toronto was established with the explicit purpose of fighting workers' organizations. The *Gazette* printed what appears to have been a manifesto:

– The unions are for the most part branches of alien institutions and have aliens for leaders. – Their organization and strength causes them to be catered to by both the highest authorities and insignificant ward heelers. – Present prosperity has caused the coming dangers to be overlooked. – Having taken our place in the world's markets, ability to preserve our position must be assured. – Unstable prices, unreliable deliveries and imperfect goods must be guarded against. The excuse of labor troubles does not find willing listeners. – No body of men has the right to interfere with an individual for selling his labor to and for what price he chooses. – The individual manufacturer must protect himself against the united workmen and the allied unions. – The aim of the organization is not to wage war on labor unions, but to provide an organized body of manufacturers to treat with organized labor. – When the demands made by unions are reasonable and fair the Employers' Association will assist in having them complied with.[36]

The members believed 'there was a place for such an organization in Toronto and the labor unions should consider it as a further step to assist in the proper adjusting of disputes that will arise from time to time.' In 1903, a similar organization, 'to resist unfair demands that may be made by the labor unions,' was formed at Kingston; its founding meeting was addressed by a Cincinnati manufacturer, among others. The Vancouver Employers' Asso-

35 *Ibid.*, Oct. 1904, 127
36 *LG*, Nov. 1902, 197

ciation was formed a month or two later, and issued a statement roughly similar in its essentials to that of the Toronto organization.[37]

Whether or not American influence was decisive in these events, it is clear that Canadian employers looked to the example set by their US brethren. In May 1903, while the CMA was preparing its 'Declaration of Principles,' *Industrial Canada* published a long account of the convention held by the National Association of Manufacturers at New Orleans. Here, another declaration had been adopted, and, while it was not identical to that brought before the CMA some months later, it appears to have furnished an example both in form and content. 'If the [U.S.] Convention had done nothing more than adopt the "Declaration of Principles",' *Industrial Canada* enthused, 'it has rendered all important services to every employer of labor on this continent, and let us hope, has marked the beginning of a new era which shall not be the domination of any one class over any other, but the happy unity of all.' Two months later, the magazine reprinted an editorial, 'Employers Must Organize,' from the *New York Commercial*. A year later, it published an enthusiastic story about the American Anti-Boycott Association, and, in the same issue, a report on the annual convention, in Philadelphia, of the National Metal Trades' Association, perhaps the most virulently anti-union of all US organizations. The writer compared the stands of the CMA and NMTA regarding unions and came up with an analysis that, in light of the turn Canadian disputes policy was soon to take, is extremely interesting:

In the first place, the battle between labor and capital is being fought more generally in the United States than in Canada. In the second place, one hundred per cent. of the members of the National Metal Trades Association are deeply interested in the labor problem, and prepared to take an out and out stand, while only a comparatively small percentage of the members of our Association have suffered through strikes. The problem of employers in the United States at the present time is largely *how to fight* organized labor, and to a certain extent this must be the problem of Canadian employers also, but with us there must be also the element *how to prevent* labor crises, and the prevention doctrine will no doubt appeal strongest to the majority of Canadian employers under the present conditions.[38]

He went on to predict 'a great movement ... which will result in the federation of all employers' organizations in the United States, which will make it practicable to marshal the forces of the employers upon lines similar to those used by labor in the American Federation.'

37 *Ibid.*, April 1903, 739; July 1903, 8
38 *Ibid.*, May 1903, 445f; July 1903, 526; May 1905, 501, 489

By early 1904, the employers' association movement was growing apace in Canada.[39] Four such organizations were established in one month in Windsor alone. The Master Bricklayers Association in Hamilton signed an agreement with the local union. A Builders' Exchange was organized in Winnipeg. The Vancouver Engineering Works posted NMTA shop rules in April 1904, and a strike resulted. When the Toronto Builders' Exchange proved unable to settle a major strike, a Master Carpenters' Association was organized to replace it. The Windsor Exchange 'declared for the "open shop",' and the union carpenters quit work as a result.[40] In 1905, the *Labour Gazette* was able to publish a list of two hundred such organizations.

If the Canadian Manufacturers' Association decided to abdicate the battle on the shop floors to the employers' associations, it kept up the good fight on the legislative lobbying front. The CMA's Parliamentary Committee kept a careful eye on the dominion and provincial legislatures, and was always ready to intervene against trade-union-inspired attempts at social legislation. It denounced the Eight-Hour Bill and the attempt to give union labels the status of trademarks. It called for the banning of American union organizers from Canada, but argued against the Alien Labour Bill, a retaliatory measure designed to limit the movement of workers across the border. Always the message was the same: legislation in favour of the unions was 'class legislation' which hampered the harmonious march to national prosperity. And the greatest evil, the most pernicious threat to harmony, was personified by the 'foreign agitator.'

As early as 1901, *Industrial Canada* lamented the case of the Toronto manufacturer who had once enjoyed a wonderful relationship with his employees. Then, one day, 'a gathering of labor delegates from the United States was held in Toronto, and the result has been the agitation of labor unions here by the outside representatives who were present.' The good manufacturer's workers came to him, demanding 'he sign documents restricting himself permanently with reference to the management of his own factory,' and a strike resulted. CMA president Ellis's remarks to the 1901 convention, charging that international unions in Canada were 'entirely opposed to the furtherance of the industrial progress of Canada,' have

39 Both employer organizations and trade associations have had a long history in Canada. But before the turn of the century, the former were mostly *ad hoc* affairs organized to wage a particular battle and becoming inactive thereafter: George Brown's Master Printers' Association is probably the best-known example. Permanently organized employer associations were a feature of early twentieth-century industrialism, a product both of increased trade-union activity and of the employers' new-found aggressiveness in the service of 'efficiency.'

40 *LG*, April 1904, 995, 988, 997, 1002; Sept. 1906, 299; Oct. 1906, 366

already been quoted. In 1902, *Industrial Canada* praised Montreal cigar manufacturers, who had defeated a strike, for demonstrating that employers, 'by taking united action, and by clinging firmly to their determination, can successfully resist the unreasonable assaults of the strongest international unions.'[41] The strike was broken when the manufacturers imported non-union workers from New York; so much for the CMA's economic nationalism and 'made in Canada by Canadian workers.'

The CMA was particularly hostile to the paid professional organizers, the 'roadmen' or 'walking delegates,' who worked for the internationals. The Montreal longshoremen's strike was the work of 'foreign professional agitators, whose interest and aims are antagonistic to the best interests of the port of Montreal and therefore of the Dominion of Canada.' This theme, that American unions worked to harm Canadian industry's competitive position vis-à-vis the United States, was developed by both the CMA and the NTLC. 'Instances are not rare where, through this affiliation, Canadian industries have suffered to the advantage of the employers and workingmen of the United States,' the CMA's president warned its 1903 convention. The Special Committee on Labour advised the same convention that international unionism lay behind many of the 'labour problems' manufacturers had to face:

... these conditions are due in a measure to the unhappy influence of United States labor officials and Associations over our Canadian Unions. We are informed by the Department of Labor that there are in Canada 1400 Labor unions of which they have cognizance and that 1275 of these are affiliated with alien organizations. Why is this? Does the Canadian workman require the assistance of this foreign competitor? Surely this is not the day of brute force.

Let us have reason; and the Canadian workingmen themselves can secure better terms from their employers than through the medium of a foreign agitator or walking delegate.

What is the actual effect of the evil upon Canada? A whole report might be made on this subject alone. Industries are paralyzed, contracts are broken, homes and families are broken up and thrown into poverty, and the mutual friendship and confidence which should be preserved between employer and employee, and also between employees themselves is inevitably destroyed.[42]

Similarly, when Senator Lougheed introduced his bill to 'prohibit the foreign agitator from inciting Canadian workmen to strike,' the CMA 'placed

41 *IC*, July 1901, 310; May 1902, 314
42 *Ibid.*, June 1903, 182; Oct. 1903, 111, 134

before the Senate at Ottawa specified instances showing that unjust and unreasonable strikes have occurred in Canada through the interference of walking delegates from the United States, resulting often in paralyzing industry for the time being, and proving nothing short of a disaster to Canadian workmen.' When the CMA began planning to meet with the TLC to discuss the tariff late in 1904, *Industrial Canada* explained to its readers that 'The average Canadian workman ... is opposed to strikes which are thrust upon him through foreign influences and agitators.' But in the same issue, the labour column decried 'the absurd extreme to which labor men are sometimes carried by a strict adherence to union principle,' and, in another column, the continuing friction in the Quebec shoe industry was blamed on conflict between national and international unions. When the 1905 convention met, delegates were informed by the Parliamentary Committee that 'were it not for the too frequent appearance of the United States business agent or agitator, we believe that conditions in Canada between the workmen and employers would be generally satisfactory.' Later that year, discussing a strike by Montreal leather cutters, *Industrial Canada* remarked that 'this strike was declared not at the request of the men, but under instructions from officers of the International Union, and is a typical case of the unreasonable methods which labor agitators sometimes adopt to carry out their ends.' The 'sometimes' may be significant here – it is one of the few *qualified* attacks on 'agitators' to be found in the journal. But by the summer of 1908, it had recovered sufficiently to publish a cautionary tale about a Montreal bricklayers' strike which occurred when the international union, 'rather than accept any but their own dictatorial terms ... ordered a strike, assuring its dupes that they would be looked after.' Strike pay was not forthcoming, 'driving home the truth that unionism was, after all, only a rotten reed, and could not be relied upon to support them over the crisis ... It was a hard lesson, sternly taught, but if they have learned it their time and efforts will not be wholly lost.'[43]

The CMA opposed international unionism largely because it used the strike weapon, and it deplored the influence of the roadmen because it saw in them the carriers of strikes. By shifting the responsibility for strike action to foreign agitators, the CMA could maintain its view that Canadian workers, were they to be freed from this sinister influence, would come to their senses and support the manufacturers' programme. The CMA's nationalist rhetoric was perhaps nine-tenths simple opposition to effective unionism, but the other tenth was bound up with the grand design of getting working-class support for the tariff.

43 *Ibid.*, Oct. 1903, 131; Dec. 1904, 326; Oct. 1905, 141; Dec. 1905, 331; July 1908, 1091

So far as politicians' attitudes to international unionism are concerned, it must be stated at the outset that there was a broad spectrum of views. The Senate, of course, was the bulwark of anti-unionism in general and anti-international unionism in particular. But none of the Senate's attempts at legislating these unions out of Canada made much headway in the Commons. On the other hand, a number of bills in the interest of labour passed by the Commons were halted in the Senate. Most significant among these were bills to give union labels trade-mark status and attempts to legislate the eight-hour working day. As numerous reports by the CMA's Parliamentary Committee indicate, lobbying by manufacturers was most successful in the Upper House. But too much weight should not be placed on conflict between the Commons and the 'other place.' Members of the Commons were mindful of the working-class franchise, of course, and may well have assented to labour legislation in the expectation that its progress would be stopped short in the Senate. For years, the TLC placed abolition of the Senate in its urgent lobbying programme, but the House never moved to acquiesce in this constitutional change. The labour members of the Commons – Smith, Puttee, Verville – were fairly effective in having pro-labour measures introduced, but were rarely able to overcome the barrier of the Senate.

So far as government leaders are concerned, the evidence for their attitudes is patchy at best. The most important figures were Prime Minister Sir Wilfrid Laurier and Sir William Mulock, the Postmaster-General who was responsible for the Labour Department from its inception in 1900 until 1905, when the dual portfolio passed to A.B. Aylesworth. (Aylesworth held it for about eight months, when it was taken over by Rodolphe Lemieux. Mackenzie King became Canada's first full-time Minister of Labour in June 1909.) Laurier and Mulock appear to have deplored the consequences of the Berlin Convention, although they played no public part in the debate. It must be considered that they were both amenable to CMA and other employer pressure, although for electoral reasons they could not afford to swing their wholehearted support behind the anti-international union drive. In this connection, Pentland noted that the TLC's practice of presenting its legislative demands to Cabinet was established before the Berlin Convention (although he is wrong in asserting that this occurred for the first time in 1901[44]) and argued that 'it may be doubted whether such meetings could have been initiated so easily

44 The TLC had been sending its legislative demands to the government since as early as 1895. In 1898 three executive members 'waited on the Government and laid before it the subjects of most vital importance to the interest of labor.' They met with four members of the Government, although not with the Prime Minister (TLC 1898). This experience was repeated in the following years and took place at both the federal and provincial levels.

after the labour split of 1902, which was bound to complicate the Laurier government's policy of cultivating labour. However, as the years went on, this government increasingly accepted the A.F. of L.-oriented Trades and Labour Congress as the authentic voice of Canadian labour, presumably finding it easier to do so because of its own American or "continental" orientation.'[45] This shift was very much the work of Mackenzie King.

While evidence for King's attitude towards international unionism is far more plentiful than that for Laurier's or Mulock's, it is far from consistent. Mention has already been made of King's claim that AFL-style unionism was the highest form of labour organization, in the discussion of his articles in the *Journal of Political Economy*. But this was to be complicated by King's dislike, in common with but probably differently motivated than that of the CMA, for the 'agitator.' King's views on the importance of moderate leadership have already been discussed. Since the representatives of the American unions in Canada could often be labelled 'agitators,' King was sometimes disposed to reproach the internationals. Thus in 1901 King described John Flett, who at that time was the AFL's full-time organizer in Canada and vice-president of the TLC, as 'a worthless troublesome mischief maker and agitator of the worst sort.'[46]

As American syndicalism spread into the Canadian west, the government failed to distinguish between the American Labor Union affiliates and the AFL unions, and favoured the project of Ralph Smith, TLC president and Lib-Lab MP, to form an independent Canadian Federation of Labour. Smith, of course, had firmly allied himself with the Liberals in Ottawa. 'The Ministers are all down on American Union leaders,' King noted in his diary during a 1901 Western Federation of Miners strike, '& wd. favour a Canadian Federation.' The following day one of these ministers, Tarte, 'spoke against American Unions, but favoured a Canadian Federation & men belonging to unions.' This apparent consensus in Cabinet seems to have made some impression on King, for he raised the matter with Daniel O'Donoghue, perhaps the most prominent of Canadian labour leaders to have found employment with the Department of Labour: 'In a talk with O'Donaghue [sic] today he pointed out that the danger of severance with American union wd. be the loss to Canadian wkgn. in not having their cards recognized in U.S. & so having to pay large fees to join union there, that 10 go to U.S. for one who comes here. I think tho' that an interchange of cards cld. be arranged, the Fed'n is sure to come within a year or two.'[47]

45 Pentland, 151n
46 Diary, 4 March 1901
47 *Ibid.*, 2 and 3 Oct. 1901

When the 1902 split came, King's reaction seems to have been influenced strongly by his developing friendship with Ralph Smith, who was deposed as TLC president by Flett, and by the example of his Cabinet masters. But this is not a total explanation: his reaction was conditioned as well by his judgement of the importance of 'character' in trade union leaders and by a genuine concern for the unity of the 'legitimate' trade union movement: 'Had a talk with O'Donaghue [sic] & Williams about the last meeting of the Trades & Labour Congress. The way Ralph Smith has been treated shews how little the support of the working classes is to be relied on by their friends, and the action of the Congress in electing the pd. organizer of the American Federat'n of Labour as Presdt. shews to what extent corruption prevails among the so-called 'leaders' themselves. The Congress has been put under American dictation and the step is a backward one in the labour movement of this country. At present all the head bodies are struggling amongt themselves for the affiliation with them of subordinate unions, and not for the unity or progress of the movement as a whole.'[48]

In 1904, King was invited to address a convention of the National Trades and Labour Congress. He noted in his diary that it had 'made great strides, especially among the French,' and projected an 'increase in strength in that direction,' but not west of Quebec. King evidently accepted the standard TLC attack on the national organization: 'I think it was inspired in the first instance by Canadian Manufacturers, & I believe some of them have a controlling hand in its affairs at present.' He approved of most of the NTLC leadership, but he disliked the organization's emphasis on attacking the TLC: 'I thought [one speaker] went too far in denouncing international unions, being led away by his audience being in favour of national unions. There was no talk against Capital, but much against Intern'l labour unions.'[49]

King's attitude towards international and national unionism, it is clear, was a complex one. He was not particularly swayed by the NTLC's rhetoric, although he conceded that it 'gave scope for fine displays of patriotism.' He was most concerned with the aims of particular unions, and with the character of their leaders. Thus he strongly defended the United Mine Workers, an AFL affiliate, in the western coalfields, and just as strongly opposed the Western Federation. While he continued to dislike Flett, he was quite friendly with Patrick Draper, secretary of the TLC, and used Draper to further some of his own *desiderata* within the Congress. Of course, the events of 1902 really offered King no choice but to foster good relations with the

48 *Ibid.*, 22 Sept. 1902
49 *Ibid.*, 29 Sept. 1904

internationals, given his conviction that workers ought to be permitted to join the organizations of their choice, so long as these were *bona fide* trade unions. The AFL affiliates certainly fell within this category.

But there was more to King's position than the recognition of necessity. He continued to believe that the unionism of the AFL was the model of what trade unionism ought to be, and be counted some of the leaders of the internationals among his warmest correspondents. And there was an additional complexity. King did not discourage nationalist attacks on AFL unionism; not because he necessarily agreed with them, but because he could use this 'public opinion' to put pressure on the American union leaders to settle disputes in Canada as quickly and hygienically as possible. This was particularly the case in his relations with John Mitchell, with whom he had an agreement covering such incidents.[50] Finally, King was fully capable of attacking international unionism – when he found his own efforts thwarted by American labour leaders. King sometimes railed against the undemocratic practices of US headquarters in calling Canadian strikes without, he felt, appropriate authority from the local membership. On the other hand, he praised American labour leaders who ordered an end to Canadian strikes against the will of the local membership. For King, labour nationalism was a weapon to be used to bring the internationals into line, but never to ban them from the country. What is perhaps the most sweeping outburst against international unions to be found in the diaries was written in November 1905, immediately after King had intervened in a strike at the Stratford shops of the Grand Trunk. It should be read, not as a statement of King's general position, but as a measure of his frustration in seeing a settlement he had been instrumental in arranging rejected by the local rank and file:

I was shewn a telegram from Stratford to an Ottawa paper, announcing that the Stratford Union had repudiated the agreement they had come to at their meeting on Saturday night last. The presence of officers of the Union from the U.S. & other points and the opposition of the few men out at other places caused them to do this, – how easily led [,] how easily deceived by their leaders men of this sort are. They will never get as much as they got at the time I was in Stratford. Their strike is an utter failure, their remaining out only means added loss and distress with worse defeat in the end. Perhaps a bitter experience may help their faith in honest advice albeit it is not as agreeable to listen to as the false. I dictated an interview for 'the Journal' with just enough suggestion in what was said to shew the danger of American Leaders coming to this country, and the danger of American influence in our affairs. I am

50 This agreement and King's action on it are discussed in chapter 8 below.

becoming more & more convinced that both in the field of Labour & Capital the influence is in large measure pernicious. We must seek to have the influence extend horizontally across the map toward British affiliations and not vertically towards American, – the British ideals being the higher and stronger, and ideals being a potent factor in shaping character & consequently the lives and destiny of a people.[51]

This emphasis on character is largely what determined King's attitude towards trade unions. After all, they were made up of a rank and file which he had no hesitation in describing, in terms similar to those employed by the CMA, as impressionable dupes, and of leaders who could be either good or bad. The worth of the leaders would be determined by two criteria: the proclaimed ends of their organizations ('socialistic' or legitimate) and King's appraisal of the force of their character, their 'manliness.' These considerations overshadowed in most instances the nationality of the organization: when he criticized American unions *per se*, as in this quote, it was because they had foiled one of this schemes. He had described a group of labour leaders in 1901 (in a similarly disappointing context) as having 'a sort of slow vengeance in their natures.' Mackenzie King was not entirely free of this quality himself, as the little morality tale quoted above – similar in many respects to the occasional labour parable broadcast by *Industrial Canada* – makes plain.

IV

Writing just after the Great War, Thorstein Veblen made a contribution to the reconstruction debate that differed radically from King's. In *The Vested Interests and the Common Man*, he described 'the vested interests and the kept classes' which were ranged in support of 'the old order,' liberal capitalism, and found he had to include the AFL in those ranks:

Beyond [those], whose life-interests are, after all, closely bound up with the kept classes, there are other vested interests of a more doubtful and perplexing kind; classes and occupations which would seem to belong with the common lot, but which range themselves at least provisionally with the vested interests and can scarcely be denied standing as such. Such, as an illustrative instance, is the A.F. of L. ... The rank and file assuredly are not of the kept classes ... Yet they stand on the defensive in

51 Diary, 4 Nov. 1905

maintaining a vested interest in the prerogatives and perquisites of their organisation. They are apparently moved by a feeling that so long as the established arrangements are maintained they will come in for a little something over and above what would come to them if they were to make common cause with the undistinguished common lot. In other words, they have a vested interest in a narrow margin of preference over and above what goes to the common man.[52]

Veblen's preference was for revolutionary syndicalism and the Industrial Workers of the World. His critique of the AFL – and he pointed out that the 'narrow margin of preference' that it defended was narrow indeed – was founded on the insight that its defensive posture entailed a defence of American capitalism, and that its margin of preference entailed the defence of structured inequalities in the labour force. This analysis needs to be placed beside the unhappy alarums of Canadian businessmen and politicians concerned about 'foreign agitators' and the proliferation of strikes. King, of course, shared Veblen's view that the mainstream labour movement was not philosophically opposed to capitalism – his articles on the American trade-union movement and the typographical union make this plain – although for him this was cause for celebration rather than chagrin. Gompers' dictum, that 'the American trade union movement should fit into the American system,' was but one of a number of expressions of this view that emanated from the centre of the AFL.

Alongside Gompers' insistence that a *bona fide* trade-union movement ought not to challenge the basic precepts of industrial capitalism was the related policy of craft autonomy. This had been an important ideological weapon wielded by the AFL in its earlier battles with the comprehensive unionism of the Knights of Labor, and it was reaffirmed at the Federation's convention in December 1901. The question had arisen there because, as the TLC's fraternal delegate reported to the Berlin convention, 'changes following upon the introduction of improved and labor saving machinery' caused 'friction' between workers in various trades when new processes cut across craft lines. Delegates to the AFL convention were confronted with a choice between maintaining traditional craft jurisdictions or opting for industrial unionism, uniting all the workers in a given plant or industry in a single union, irrespective of trade or skill level. The convention was faced with seven resolutions seeking to clarify or alter the section of the AFL constitution which invoked the 'strict recognition of the autonomy of each trade,' and a Special Committee on Autonomy, numbering Gompers and John

52 [1919] (New York: Capricorn, 1969), 164f

Mitchell among its members, was established to deal with the question. While the Special Committee's report recognized the need to amalgamate some fragmented crafts, it reaffirmed the old position of craft autonomy in opposition to industrial unionism, and recommended that the AFL serve as arbiter of the many jurisdictional disputes that this decision, in the context of widespread changes in production methods, necessarily produced. 'As the magnificent growth of the American Federation of Labor is conceded by all students of economic thought to be the result of organization on trade lines, and believing it neither necessary nor expedient to make any radical departure from this fundamental principle,' the Special Committee declared, 'as a general proposition, the interests of the workers will be best conserved by adhering as closely to that doctrine as the recent great changes in methods of production and employment make practicable.'[53]

This decision, jealously guarded for decades to follow, meant that the AFL and by extension its Canadian subsidiary, the TLC, would be unable and unwilling to adapt the mainstream of the labour movement to the radical changes that the growth of large-scale production and the spread of scientific management effected. Defence of the old craft jurisdictions entailed the failure of AFL-style unionism either to draw in the masses of unskilled and semi-skilled labour in the new factories, or to really come to terms with the industrialists' assault on traditional work practices. When employers crossed the watershed to truly efficient labour utilization they did drag their workers across with them but, at least so far as the North American mainstream was concerned, the unions were dragged extremely reluctantly, and with faces firmly turned towards the past. The labour movement's response was less to defend the interests of the workers in mass-production industries than to defend the old aristocracy of craft, to defend the minimally exalted status of a relatively small group of skilled workers as much against the aspirations of the rest of the working class as against the new exactions of twentieth-century industrial capitalism.

There has recently been a great flowering of interest in nineteenth-century Canadian working-class history, and much of the new work has turned on an analysis of the 'culture' of the autonomous craftsman and its emphasis on control of the work process. Drawing on the seminal American work of David Montgomery, Kealey and Palmer, to name only two of the leading Canadian writers in this field, have placed the skilled worker's efforts to retain a substantial measure of shop-floor control in the face of employer

53 Quoted in *TLC* 1902, 50

attack at the centre of the labour historical stage.[54] This research has been invaluable in dispelling the myths of technological determinism and the primacy of residual work attitudes that permeated much of the earlier literature, by demonstrating that some groups of craftsmen were able to extend a significant degree of control over mechanization and that many aspects of the 'culture' of job control emerged within the context of industrialism itself. But at the same time, by giving the artisan pride of place in working-class history, it may have failed to recognize that the skilled workers' strategy for resisting employer attacks on control of the work process became increasingly irrelevant as the reliance of employers on craftworkers declined. By the turn of the century, the craftworkers' resistance had crystallized in dogmatic adherence to a principle of exclusion, of which the Gompers doctrine of craft autonomy was the major institutional expression. One's sympathy for the plight of the once-proud artisan cannot be permitted to obscure the fact that early twentieth-century craft unionism in its AFL manifestation was becoming incongruent with the concerns of the industrial working class as a whole.

One consequence was the failure of the unions to come decisively to terms with scientific management. In Canada, the TLC attempted to retain time payment as against the plethora of incentive and piece-work payment schemes that flourished on the threshold of scientific management proper. Thus in 1899 it endorsed a resolution opposing the introduction of piece-work in the Intercolonial Railway shops.[55] The TLC did not deal with scientific management practices *per se* until 1911, when a delegate from the International Association of Machinists moved the following resolution:

Whereas, a system of so-called 'scientific shop management,' commonly known as the 'Taylor System' is being introduced in some of our large manufacturing centres, and, whereas, the said system upon investigation can be shown to be nothing more or less than a speeding up process where none but the very strong can survive, and they being crowded constantly to the extreme point of physical endurance, and whereas the said Taylor system is of such a character and nature as to be detrimental to the best interests of the Canadian working man. And whereas, the highest func-

---

54 David Montgomery, 'Workers' Control of Machine Production in the Nineteenth Century,' in his *Workers' Control in America* (London: Cambridge University Press, 1979); Bryan Palmer, *A Culture in Conflict: Skilled Workers and Industrial Capitalism in Hamilton, Ontario, 1860–1914* (Montreal: McGill-Queen's University Press, 1979); Greg Kealey, *Toronto Workers Respond to Industrial Capitalism* (Toronto: University of Toronto Press, 1980).
55 *TLC* 1899, 10

tion of any government should be to guard with zealous care the happiness and welfare of its great army of workers. And, whereas, the partial or complete installation of the said Taylor system into any of our factories or workshops is a matter of grave importance to the people of Canada and may create consequences of a far-reaching character both to capital and labor. And, whereas, the declared purpose of the so-called inventor is to extend the system to all branches of industry. And, whereas, any and all attempts of introducing the aforesaid system in Canada, will surely lead to industrial disputes, therefore be it resolved, that the Trades and Labor Congress of Canada instruct its executive to assist any body of workers so involved to secure government investigation and protection.[56]

The same convention also endorsed a resolution 'to suppress the piece-work system now in existence in many of the large concerns in Eastern Canada.' The IAM, whose delegate introduced the anti-Taylorism resolution to the TLC in 1911, had opposed scientific management and its progenitors in the US since 1903. The TLC resolution was cast in terms similar to those used by Gompers earlier in 1911, and the American trade union movement did not mount a full-scale attack against scientific management until the second decade of the century.[57] But, as we have earlier suggested, the new managerial techniques predated their formalization under the rubric of scientific management, and some groups of Canadian workers had come up against the new system early on.

In December 1901, the *Labour Gazette*'s St Thomas correspondent reported that the Michigan Central Railway was planning to change 'the whole mechanical system' of its shops in that town from day work to piece-work. 'Although no definite time has been set for the change,' he wrote, 'the preparatory steps have been taken for the introduction of the new system. The company's piece work inspector or organizer has commenced work on the undertaking, and the schedules of prices have been adopted.' The mechanical superintendent insisted that although the company would benefit greatly from the change, there would be no detriment to 'the earning capacity of the men individually'; all the same, the workers reacted 'with a considerable amount of disfavour.' The MCR set about implementing the scheme in March, but when the workers strongly objected the company rather ominously decided 'to give the men time for reflection before pressing

56 *TLC* 1911, 72f
57 M.J. Nadworny, *Scientific Management and the Unions, 1900–1932* (Cambridge, Mass.: Harvard University Press, 1955), 25, 51ff; and R.F. Hoxie, *Scientific Management and Labor* [1915] (New York: Kelley, 1966)

the matter.' The following month the correspondent reported that 'the most noteworthy feature in labour circles is the agitation among the employees of the M.C.R. locomotive and car-shops over the proposed introduction of the piece-work system. No new phase of the situation has developed over the month. The question continues to agitate the employees and many of the men are leaving to take other situations ...' In May, the shop workers demanded a 10 per cent pay increase and the company laid off 42 men in the car department: implementation of the piece-work scheme was still undecided, and still 'agitated' the men. The company offered a compromise: it would grant the 10 per cent increase if the men waived their objection to piece-work. A strike followed, and was settled with 'a verbal understanding that the piece work system will not be applied for at least one year.' Then, it appears, the company dropped its original scheme in favour of a more radical systematization of the work process. 'It is claimed that as a result of the new system,' the correspondent wrote in the November 1902 issue, 'cars are now being built at a less labour cost than was offered the men in the piece work proposal of the early spring.' The following May, the *Labour Gazette* published an epilogue to the story: 'The output of the local locomotive and car shops is reported to be increasing in volume, without any increase in the number of workmen employed, as a result of progressive systematizing in method of shop management.'[58]

Other examples might be cited. The Toronto typographers formulated a new wage scale in 1902, 'changing the basis from the "bonus" or piece system to a time system.' Guelph iron moulders successfully resisted the introduction of piece-work in the same year. Toronto carpet weavers went on strike to protest the introduction of a time clock, unsuccessfully. The women employees of Hamilton's Eagle Knitting Mill went on strike against 'a new system of cutting and work classification.' The company claimed that the system would not reduce wages, but the strikers 'gave the new system a trial before quitting,' and decided that it cut wages almost in half. Another strike against a time clock occurred at Union Point, New Brunswick, in 1903. This one had an interesting twist: the workers objected to the clock because they found it inefficient to have to register four times a day.[59] Some of these examples seem to have involved fairly sophisticated reorganizations of the work process; others much less so. But they all demonstrate the existence of

58 *LG*, Dec. 1901, 338; April 1902, 583; May 1902, 653; June 1902, 729; July 1902, 23f; Aug. 1902, 87; Nov. 1902, 312; May 1903, 851
59 *Ibid.*, April 1902, 576, 580; Aug. 1902, 109f; Sept. 1902, 211; Oct. 1902, 271f; Dec. 1902, 479; April 1903, 731

worker opposition to such changes early in the century. This opposition, and these changes, were not the focus of initiatives at the level of the TLC, at least partly due to the conservatism of craft unionism's defensive posture, and to its unwillingness to act on behalf of those most directly affected by the new managerial techniques, the unskilled and semi-skilled workers in the growing factories.

V

The Canadian labour movement's orientation towards government intervention also changed following the events of 1902. Under the influence of the AFL, the TLC abandoned its long-standing advocacy of compulsory arbitration much as it abandoned its *de facto* commitment to being the legislative centre of a unified Canadian labour movement. Gompers' reassertion of craft autonomy in 1901 had much to do with the latter; his attack on compulsory arbitration at the AFL's 1900 convention is a good part of the explanation of the former. Yet even with its formal abandonment of compulsory arbitration from 1902 on, the TLC retained a much stronger commitment to government intervention in industrial relations than the AFL. To some extent this was mirrored in the TLC's continuing, if frequently lukewarm support of independent labour politics. In a later chapter, we shall have to take up the TLC's position vis-à-vis King's industrial peace legislation. Here we sketch in the background of its general orientation towards the role of the state in industrial disputes.

Compulsory arbitration of labour disputes was a key plank in the programme of the Knights of Labor in the 1880s. Many of the workers who gave evidence before the Royal Commission on the Relations of Labour and Capital in the late 'eighties supported arbitration, and several of these thought it ought to be made compulsory by statute. There is some uncertainty, however, as to whether they all meant the same thing by the term. It is used today to denote a method of disputes settlement in which a third party is involved (whether or not in concert with representatives of the employer and employees) in drawing up a settlement which then becomes binding. In several of the cases described to the commission, however, arbitration seems to have meant collective bargaining between appointed representatives of the two principals. Item 10 of the Knights' declaration of principles declared for 'the enactment of laws providing for arbitration between employers and employed, and to enforce the decision of the arbitrators,' while item 22 committed the Knights 'to persuade employers to agree to arbitrate all differences which may arise between them and their employés, in order that the bonds of sympathy between them may be strengthened and that strikes may be rendered unnecessary.'[60] Neither of these, it is clear, prescribes the form which arbitration is to take. The interpretation favoured by the Provincial Workmen's Association was more nearly that which the term is nowadays understood to imply. The PWA managed to get an arbitration bill through the Nova Scotia legislature. As its secretary told the Commission, 'It provides for the appointment of two arbitrators by the workmen and one by the managers, these three to select a fourth ... and the arbitration is to be compulsory. There can be no arbitration unless it is compulsory.'[61]

The founding convention of the TLC in 1886 had passed a resolution requesting 'that a law be passed making it binding that in all cases where disputes arise, each party must proceed to arbitrate, and making the decision of such arbitration in all cases binding.'[62] There are difficulties of interpretation here; 'arbitration' may just mean collective bargaining. But by the 1890s, at least, the Congress's position was clarified. The 1892 convention recommended the appointment by government of a Board of Conciliation and Arbitration, and in 1894 the TLC endorsed the (voluntary) board established by Ontario legislation. The 1898 convention authorized a sixteen-point platform, of which 'Compulsory arbitration of labor disputes' was number thirteen. Some writers have explained the abandonment of this plank in favour of voluntarism in 1902 as the consequence of a bill introduced in that year which would make arbitration compulsory in railway disputes. Forsey, for example, writes that the plank was dropped 'when an actual bill for compulsory arbitration on the railways caused the delegates to recoil in horror!'[63] The railway arbitration bill is discussed elsewhere in this study; here, it must be pointed out that the groundwork for the TLC's rejection of compulsory arbitration had been laid before the proposed legislation had seen the light of day, while significant elements in the TLC continued to favour compulsory arbitration in 'public interest' disputes even after the Berlin Convention.

The TLC's 1901 convention heard a report on the previous year's AFL meeting, where Gompers had issued a stern rebuke to those 'who, playing upon the credulity of the uninformed, seek to divert the principle of arbitra-

---

60 Kealey, ed., *Canada Investigates Industrialism*, 164f
61 *Ibid.*, 439. See, however, *The Miners' Arbitration Act*, R.S.N.S. 1900, c.21, where equal representation for both parties is specified. By 'compulsory,' the PWA spokesman meant 'binding.'
62 Quoted in Jack Williams, *The Story of Unions in Canada* (n.p.: Dent, 1975), 70
63 Eugene Forsey, 'The Canadian Labour Movement 1812–1902,' Canadian Historical Association historical booklet #27 (1974), 15

tion into the coercive policy of so-called compulsory arbitration ... Observers have for years noted that those inclined to this policy have devised many schemes to deny the workers the right to quit their employments; and the scheme of so-called compulsory arbitration is the latest design of the well-intentioned, but uninformed, as well as faddists and schemers.' Compulsory abritration, he urged – in terms identical to those he would use against King's Industrial Disputes Investigation Act during the Walsh Commission hearings – was 'not one scintilla of distinction, not one jot removed from slavery.'[64] In his address to the TLC that year, president Ralph Smith begged to differ with the AFL president:

I must admit that, looking at his arguments from the standpoint of an American leader and American politics, there is some reason to fear that owing to the control of political power by the different authorities, who would be likely to be the arbitrators in any case, Mr. Gompers' conclusion is worthy of consideration: but considering our situation in Canada I am convinced that the compulsory principle of settling these grievances is worth a trial. Both capital and labor have a legal right to insist on what each considers its due; but when the enforcement of these claims brings stagnation and danger to the public, they ought to be compelled to submit to the decision of impartial arbitrators appointed by the Government. I am convinced this would be a great advantage to this country, and I am persuaded that there is not any single question that labor unions ought to concentrate their energies to bring about of so vast importance as this.[65]

Smith ended his speech with his famous appeal for a Canadian Federation equal in status to the AFL: neither of his goals was to be achieved.

After the delegates had heard Smith's address and the report of the AFL convention, delegate Alfred Gossel of the Winnipeg Trades and Labour Council rose to move 'That in view of the recent disastrous Trackmen's strike, the time has arrived when the Dominion Trades Congress should formulate some practical scheme of compulsory arbitration, and press the Government for its adoption.' The motion was passed. But the following day, the Committee on President's Address reported itself 'not prepared to recommend a dogmatic pronouncement by your body in favor of the principle of Compulsory Arbitration ... but submit as an alternative that your body approve of a trial of Compulsory Conciliation.'[66] This was concurred in.

64 *TLC* 1901, 57, 58
65 *Ibid.*, 8
66 *Ibid.*, 62, 77

Thus the TLC was left, after its 1901 convention, with a contradictory policy. It had not removed compulsory arbitration from its programme, and it had endorsed a resolution calling for the translation of that principle into a 'practical scheme.' At the same time, it had adopted a report opposing any such 'dogmatic pronouncement.' The stage was set for the Berlin Convention.

At Berlin, the normal order of business at TLC conventions was significantly altered. Instead of the president's address being the first major item of business, the constitutional changes that were to result in the expulsion of dual unions came first. Smith did not have his say until he had been, to all intents and purposes, drummed out. And before Smith gave his address, Joseph Marks, editor of the London (Ontario) *Industrial Banner*, rose to give notice 'that I will move, on Friday next, to strike out Plank 13, referring to Compulsory Arbitration, of the Platform of Principles of the Trades and Labor Congress of Canada.'

Smith's address, when it finally came, gave distressing evidence of having been written before the constitutional changes and, probably, in expectation of their having taken another direction entirely. 'We have today before us,' he said, 'a foundation of what is destined to become the great National Federation of Canada.' Coming to compulsory arbitration, Smith admitted that the railway unions were opposed to the draft bill, but he insisted that the government was merely seeking the opinion of various labour organizations: 'I think it is absolutely important that this Congress should express itself very plainly on this question,' he said, but refrained from suggesting what position that expression should take. The General Executive Committee reported in similar fashion, but the Quebec Executive thought the railway bill to be 'a measure conducive to happy results and tending to avoid strikes and their nefarious consequences, that is – if the clauses of the Bill were made to extend to the other branches of labor.' Then Ben Tillett, fraternal delegate from the British Trades Union Congress, gave his whole-hearted support for compulsory arbitration. But on the last day of the convention, plank 13 was amended to read 'voluntary arbitration.'[67] The disagreement over the railway disputes act had played its part, but the principal factors in the rejection of compulsory arbitration had been Gompers' influence and the repudiation of Ralph Smith's programme for an independent Canadian federation of labour. 'What concerned Gompers,' writes Irving Abella, 'was that some TLC leaders and unions seemed to be making approving sounds towards socialism, industrial unionism ... and compulsory arbitration, all three of which were anathema to the AFL president ... Thus to protect Ameri-

67 *TLC* 1902, 13, 14, 36, 69

can labour from these insidious Canadian influences, Gompers ordered all
international union affiliates in Canada ... to vote to strip the Congress of its
nationalist pretensions and to make it subordinate in every way to the AFL'[68]

The official rejection of compulsory arbitration in 1902 did not put an end
to the TLC's historic interest in attempting to turn the state to its own ends.
The TLC remained far more committed to state intervention in industrial
relations and to independent labour politics than did its American counterpart. But the 1902 decision did signify that the American trade union model
was replacing that of Britain and Australasia for the Canadian labour movement. The TLC's earlier advocacy of compulsory arbitration had not been a
weak-kneed repudiation of the strike, nor had it been a confession of weakness on the part of Canadian unions. It had been based on the experience in
New Zealand and Australia, where powerful labour movements active in
politics had been able, in the wake of disastrous strikes, to use their political
strength to force arbitration on recalcitrant employers.

The first compulsory arbitration legislation was passed in New Zealand in
1894 by a pro-labour Liberal government. It was supported by the labour
movement and opposed by employers. In Australia, a Labour party had
become one of the two major political parties. A compulsory arbitration bill
became law in New South Wales in 1901, the year of Gompers' repudiation
of this strategy, and a Commonwealth compulsory arbitration law was
enacted three years later.[69] Thus compulsory arbitration was inextricably
linked with labour politics in Australasia – the New Zealand Liberal party had
the express support of the unions – and it was to this model that the Canadian
labour movement looked for inspiration. In these countries, labour benefitted
from compulsory arbitration, especially since it exercised a *de facto* right to
strike when it disagreed with the awards. Commons suggests that compulsory
arbitration was not suited to the American context as it was to Australasia,
but whether this was true for Canada surely depended on the ability of the
unions to engage in truly independent labour politics, or, as seemed to be the
case under the leadership of Ralph Smith, on their commitment to turn the
ruling Liberal party in favour of moderate labour demands. Whether or not
compulsory arbitration in the labour interest was suited to Canadian conditions, the Trades and Labour Congress at the turn of the century had before
it the example of one of the most powerful and militant labour movements
in the world, and, taken together with the recent successes of 'labourism' in

68 'The Canadian Labour Movement, 1902–1960,' Canadian Historical Association
historical booklet #28 (1975), 4
69 This legislation is discussed in J.R. Commons and J.B. Andrews, *Principles of Labor
Legislation* [4th ed., 1936] (New York: Kelley, 1967), 439ff.

Britain, the path of labour politics and state intervention was at least as attractive, and rightly so, as the 'pure and simple' unionism of the AFL.

These traditions remained part of the Canadian movement after 1902, although they were subject to constraints emanating from the American centre. For instance, Canadian labour's pacifism and opposition to conscription during the First World War were to be savagely attacked by Gompers once the United States abandoned neutrality. Before 1902, the Canadian movement's orientation to politics was more similar to that of New Zealand than Australia. The most prominent labour politician, Ralph Smith, worked closely with the Liberal party, and other influential figures, like Daniel O'Donoghue and Chris Foley, did the same. At the same time, and especially in British Columbia, there was much agitation for an independent labour party on socialist principles. But a Canadian variant of 'Lib-Lab' politics remained the rule and, as the next chapter suggests, it was fairly effective in winning concessions from the Laurier government.

Martin Robin has rather ambivalently interpreted the Berlin decision as a rejection of Smith's Liberal party labourism and a move leftwards on the part of the TLC: 'The ousting of the Knights, the defeat of the cause of Liberal National unionism, the replacement of Ralph Smith by John Flett as president, Smith's attempted repudiation of partyism during his presidential address, the reconstruction of the Congress as an effective lobby, and the endorsement of independent representation, all testified to a move "left" by the Congress.' But as he makes clear in his subsequent paragraphs, the new political philosophy of the TLC was the Gompers principle of 'rewarding friends and punishing enemies in the major parties.'[70] While some socialists retained influence in the TLC after 1902, notably James Simpson, it would be difficult to maintain that the TLC was any more 'left' after 1902 than before. The pressure for socialist politics came from the West, particularly from BC, and the more radical unions and leaders were as often outside the TLC as within it. Nor is there much evidence that the post-1902 TLC was any more effective as a lobby than it had been in the immediate past.[71] In any event,

---

70 *Radical Politics and Canadian Labour* (Kingston: Queen's University Industrial Relations Centre, 1968), 68, 69

71 In fact, Robin himself states that 'the T.L.C. could lobby Ottawa ... effectively only if it campaigned as the "national legislative mouthpiece" of organized labour. But insofar as the industrial union socialists fostered dual unionism and weakened the Congress in the second most highly industrialized and unionized province in the Dominion, [i.e., B.C.] there developed an opposition of interest which blocked a rapprochement at the political level.' (69). This is just one of a host of examples of Robin's ambivalence about the Berlin decision. The effectiveness of the TLC, and of the labour movement in general, as a lobbying or political organization, was diminished by the post-1902 fragmentation, and by the acceptance of craft autonomy by the Congress.

the organization's Ottawa lobbyist, J.G. O'Donoghue, Daniel's lawyer son, found that Smith remained one of the labour movement's best friends in Ottawa even after Berlin.[72] Ralph Smith and Lib-Lab politicians in general have been summarily dismissed by historians as collaborationist 'fakirs,' but this evaluation has been partly conditioned by the rush to celebrate the victor; a re-examination, while it cannot be attempted here, would not be out of order.

Moreover, there is persuasive evidence that the official abandonment of the compulsory arbitration plank at Berlin did not mean that trade unionists unequivocally turned their backs on the old policy, or that they blithely accepted Gompers' equation of it with slavery. T.W. Banton, the Toronto *Star*'s labour columnist and himself a strong supporter of international unionism, wrote an article defending the New Zealand law a month after the convention. 'The people of New Zealand have long enjoyed industrial peace,' he wrote, and quoted a former member of the New Zealand Parliament to underscore the point: '"They have ceased to enjoy the privilege of engaging in civil war." It's not such a precious boon, after all, the liberty to fight!'[73]

Banton's views were not idiosyncratic, as he proceeded to demonstrate. In November 1902 he published the results of a mail survey of approximately one hundred trade union officers in Ontario. Three questions were asked:

1. Are you in favor of compulsory arbitration in the settlement of all labor disputes?
2. Are you in favor of compulsory arbitration in respect merely to services of a public or semi-public character?
3. Are you in favor of purely voluntary arbitration?

While only 30 per cent of Banton's respondents answered 'yes' to the first question, 76 per cent answered 'yes' to questions two and three: about a third of the labour leadership in Ontario supported universal compulsory arbitration.[74] It must be remembered, first, that Ontario was the province in which AFL-style international unionism had made the most headway and, second, that local officers were probably more likely than the rank and file to understand and to support the AFL line. The large majority supporting com-

---

72 E.g., *TLC* 1904, 35, Synopsis of Solicitor's Report: 'He particularly thanks Mr. Ralph Smith for his labors in connection with the Union Label Bill'; and *TLC* 1906, 38ff, Report of Pariamentary Solicitor, where it is evident that Smith was the prime mover on behalf of numerous TLC legislative concerns.
73 18 Oct. 1902
74 *Ibid.*, 29 Nov. 1902

pulsory arbitration in 'services of a public or semi-public character' indicates that a simple-minded rejection of this form of state intervention along the lines Gompers had laid down was not the ruling factor in the Berlin decision.

Thus while its offical advocacy of compulsory arbitration was effectively undermined by the Berlin decision, the Canadian labour movement remained open to the possibility of state intervention in industrial disputes, and the TLC was to show more faith than its American counterpart in the ability of government to act in the labour interest. The reasons for this were complex: they had partly to do with Canadian labour's experience with a variety of disputes settlement practices, and partly with the special nature of the Canadian state and the labour movement's perception of its role. The latter is examined in the next chapter, while this one concludes with some discussion of the former.

VI

It remains here to survey the range of disputes settlement practices in Canadian industrial relations at the turn of the century. These were many and varied, and no discussion of the institutionalization of certain practices in certain industries by the Canadian state can afford to ignore them. The Conciliation, Railway Labour Disputes, and Industrial Disputes Investigation Acts did not suddenly appear in a vacuum. On the contrary, Canadian workers, unions, and employers experimented with a variety of practices at the turn of the century. While data for the period before 1900 are fairly scant and widely dispersed, the *Labour Gazette*, which began publication in mid-1900, is a rich source of information. Local correspondents sent monthly reports to the *Gazette*, concentrating in part on disputes settlement. The discussion which follows is based on this source, emphasizing the first few years of publication, and leaving government intervention to be discussed elsewhere.

Once again, the term 'arbitration' was used somewhat indiscriminately. Sometimes it denoted collective bargaining by nominated representatives of workers and employers; sometimes it meant third-party intervention to assist negotiations; and sometimes it had its present connotation of third-party intervention with a view to drawing up a form of settlement binding on the parties. Similarly, non-binding intervention by a third party, when it was not called arbitration, was apparently indiscriminately labelled mediation or conciliation. In the language of modern industrial relations, conciliation usually means third-party assistance at the bargaining table, designed to foster 'good faith' bargaining by the two principal parties, while mediation is reserved for the more active intervention of a third party, often after negotiations have broken down, involving the mediator as go-between in formulating a mutually satisfactory settlement. The conciliator's role, in other words, is to assist the two parties to engage in productive negotiation; the mediator's role is to attempt to bring them to a settlement. Thus in attempting to fit the language of the *Labour Gazette* to the more specific language current today, we find:

MODERN TERMINOLOGY	*Labour Gazette*, 1900–5
Collective bargaining	Arbitration (sometimes)
Conciliation	Conciliation, mediation, arbitration
Mediation	Conciliation, mediation, arbitration
Arbitration	Arbitration[75]

The appropriate modern term to apply in any specific case can often be determined by the context, but this is not always the case. When we are told, for example, that several grievances between the City of Hamilton and the Teamsters' Association 'were settled by arbitration,' the meaning must remain obscure. This problem of industrial relations terminology will have to be raised again when we consider the federal legislation. For the time being, we should recall that 'compulsory arbitration' had a narrow meaning for Gompers and the TLC: it was binding third-party intervention imposed by statute and involving both an imposed settlement and a prohibition on strikes.

One complicated set of negotiations occurred between the Canadian Pacific Railway and unions representing machinists, blacksmiths, and related trades on the railway's Pacific and Western divisions in the fall of 1900. About 800 men, half of them union members, went out on strike for new wage rates. In May, three separate unions presented new wage schedules to management, none of them in concert with the others, but when the company responded by laying off a number of machinists, including those most active in the unions, a committee was formed representing all the men affected, which called a general strike for 3 August. Settlement negotiations began four days after the inception of the strike, 'through the mediation of Mr. Hoare, manager of the Imperial Bank, and Mr. J.A. McKercher, a prominent local tradesman.' These 'mediators' seem to have been concilia-

---

75 This point about the flexibility of the term, arbitration, as used at the turn of the century has been carried by some authors to the opposite extreme: that it always meant collective bargaining and nothing more. This point is discussed with reference to the language of the statutes in chapter 7. It should also be mentioned that the distinction between 'conciliation' and 'mediation' is not always preserved in present-day practice.

tors; their principal role was to assure 'the men that the general manager ... would receive and treat with them.' A 'sub-committee of the general committee' then met with the general manager and negotiated a new collective agreement, but the wage schedules for machinists were 'submitted to arbitration, the outcome of which was a slight general advance in wages.' Arbitration in this case meant binding arbitration: each party appointed a board member, and a third party 'was called in'; the board's decision was binding upon both parties. Beyond this, the collective agreement provided that wage rates would be decided by arbitration, and promised that the company would not discriminate 'against any machinist who may from time to time represent any of his fellow workmen on committees of investigation,' although the nature and role of such committees was not specified in the Labour Gazette's account.[76]

The CPR negotiations, then, involved the following practices: group bargaining, conciliation, collective bargaining, voluntary arbitration, and, somewhat obscurely, provision for committees of investigation. They terminated with the signing of a contract, providing not only for wages and conditions, but for renewal and disputes settlement procedures. It was signed by a company representative and a representative of the workers, in his capacity as a union officer: the agreement, therefore, involved union recognition, and in the machinists' arbitration the men were represented by the international president of their union.

In 1901, the maintenance-of-way men struck the CPR. The Railroad Employees Protective Board, the running trades brotherhoods' joint committee, approached the company's vice-president with an offer to conciliate the dispute, but it was turned down. The following year, the maintenance-of-way men again sought to open negotiations with the company, and this time the CPR president agreed to negotiate with the Joint Protective Board and to refer any items on which agreement could not be reached 'to arbitration for final determination, one of the arbitrators to be selected by the company, one by the men, and these two to select the third.' Following this, 'numerous conferences' took place and all items except the new wage rates were settled, these to be sent to 'arbitration.' The company and men appointed their arbitrators and for five days these two sought to reach an agreement: up to this point, it was not arbitration but collective bargaining that was taking place. Finally, failing to agree, the two appointed the Chancellor of the Ontario High Court of Justice as the third party. The company and men presented long statements to the arbitration board, and finally an award was made. 'Too great significance cannot be attached to this adoption of the principle of voluntary conciliation and arbitration by one of the largest corporations and one of the largest labour organizations on the continent,' King's *Gazette* commented. 'It is an indication of a decided advance in the movement which, through these agencies, is making for industrial peace.'[77]

Another 'agency of industrial peace' was the outcome of a lock-out by Quebec City boot and shoe manufacturers in 1900: the agency was clerical intervention and the eventual institutional outcome was confessional unionism. Workers in the Quebec boot and shoe industry had been organized by three international trade unions. Following strikes at two factories, the employers formed a manufacturers' association and decided to break the unions; on 27 October they declared a general lock-out, and by the end of the month twenty-two of the city's twenty-six boot and shoe factories had been closed, throwing some five thousand employees out of work. 'The manufacturers are decided not to reopen their doors until they have checked the intervention of foreign labour unions in carrying on of their business,' the employers' association announced and it drew up a 'Solemn Declaration' to be signed by returning workers, which provided that the supplicant belonged to no union, had withdrawn from any union to which he or she might previously have belonged, and declared that he or she 'will take no part in any difficulty that may arise between my employer and one or more of his employees.' Workers were further required to sign a contract providing for arbitration of disputes by a board composed solely of shoe manufacturers. While a few foremen signed these documents, the majority of the locked-out workers refused to, and the shut-down continued. On 24 November the manufacturers' association applied to Archbishop Bégin to intervene, and he signified his willingness to do so provided that the workers agreed. They did, and the employers announced that they would reopen the factories pending the Archbishop's award so long as the workers signed the two documents, on the understanding that if the award went against the manufacturers the documents would become void. The workers, through the joint committee of their three unions, refused to accept the declaration and contract, and the lock-out continued until 5 December when the Archbishop prevailed on the manufacturers to reopen their factories and on the workers to take no part in their unions' affairs during the arbitration.

The award was brought down on January 14, 1901. The Archbishop quoted copiously from the encyclical *Rerum Novarum* concerning the right of workers to form associations, but not just any associations they pleased, and

77 *Ibid*., Aug. 1901, 85; June 1902, 746ff, 701f

he demanded changes in the union constitutions that would ensure that the organizations complied with Papal views of the proper relations of workers and employers. He then set up permanent disputes settlement machinery. The workers would elect from their number a three-member 'Board of Complaint,' and the manufacturers an equivalent 'Board of Conciliation.' A permanent Board of Arbitration would be constituted of one member to be chosen by each of these boards, and a third by these two or, failing that, by the Archbishop. Grievances would be referred to the arbitration board, and no strike or lock-out could take place pending its award. 'By means of such a proceeding,' Archbishop Bégin proclaimed, 'the rights of each party will be respected, and the relations between employers and employees will never cease to be friendly. In effect, it is from the spirit of justice and of Christian charity that we must chiefly expect the peace and welfare of society.'[78] This then was compulsory arbitration backed up, not by the temporal power of the state, but by the normative power of the Catholic Church. Mackenzie King considered the award 'a victory for the men and conciliation.' 'If the Boards to be formed work at all successfully,' he noted in his diary, 'the lockout will have borne good fruit.'[79]

But there were still problems by the anniversary of the lock-out. The machinists refused to amend their local union by-laws along the lines desired by the Archbishop, and only the threat of another industry-wide lock-out persuaded them to do so. And the lasters were faced with a new threat: the introduction of labour-saving machinery. An arbitration award granting slightly higher wages had disappointed the lasters who thought they ought to get more, but in January 1902, with machines displacing hand work, they offered to take a substantial wage cut if the manufacturers discontinued the use of the new technology. 'Some of the shops have accepted this offer, others have refrained from doing so as yet, the latter holding out for a five-year contract with the men at this price.'[80] Compulsory arbitration in the Quebec boot and shoe trades meant the destruction of effective unionism and, in the wake of the Berlin Convention, the rise of Church-dominated workers' associations.

But voluntary arbitration remained a popular method of disputes settlement elsewhere. In June 1902, members of the International Brotherhood of Electrical Workers struck the Cataract Power Company for higher wages. They agreed after two weeks to refer the dispute to arbitration and each side

78 *Ibid.*, Dec. 1900, 153ff; Jan. 1901, 229f; Feb. 1901, 294ff
79 16 Jan. 1901
80 *LG*, Nov. 1901, 259; Feb. 1902, 436f. See also *ibid.*, July 1901, 3f; Aug. 1901, 72

appointed one arbitrator. When these two were unable to agree on a third, they resigned and a new strike commenced. This was finally settled by a new three-party board. None of the members of either of these boards, under this form of arbitration, were directly interested in the outcome of the dispute; they included a minister, two lawyers, a manufacturers' agent, and a wholesale grocer. Carpenters in Winnipeg approved an agreement with the city's contractors providing that if a permanent joint committee of six employers and six workers should fail to settle any dispute, it should be empowered to appoint a 'disinterested party' whose decision would be binding. The Hamilton Trades and Labour Council requested City Council to write a compulsory arbitration clause into the city's franchise contracts to settle 'all disputes arising between such companies and their employees that cannot be arranged in any other way' – this was a period of bitter street railway strikes. During a Toronto carpenters' strike, the men applied to the architect, J.E. Lennox (the designer of the City Hall), to arbitrate or mediate – the context is not clear – but the Builders' Exchange declined. Toronto brass workers set up a collective bargaining conference with their employers and agreed, if no settlement could be made, to submit the dispute to arbitration. Halifax carpenters went on strike when their employers refused to adopt an arbitration award. A strike of piano and organ makers in Hamilton was settled 'on the following basis: – Each side had an arbitrator and the two chose a third ...' The Toronto Building Trades Council asked the Toronto Chapter of the Ontario Association of Architects to insert an arbitration clause in agreements with contractors, but the application was refused; when the Ontario Association held its annual meeting that year, however, it approved of 'the labour legislation of New Zealand and New South Wales ... as having created an atmosphere of confidence between workers and the employers.' Some Hamilton piano makers, unwilling to accept an arbitration award, set up their own factory.[81]

Municipal councils and boards of trade frequently offered to assist disputes settlement by conciliation or mediation. The Quebec Board of Trade set up a special committee to intervene in a longshoremen's strike and to prevail on the parties, 'in their own interest and that of the city of Quebec,' to end the strike. When the President of the Ottawa Board of Trade offered to 'arbitrate' between striking woodworkers and their employers, the latter refused, whereupon the Mayor announced that he would ask city council 'to make some effort to settle the strikes.' A conciliation committee of the Toronto

81 *Ibid.*, Oct. 1902, 260f; March 1902, 511; Aug. 1902, 81; July 1903, 20; Aug. 1903, 162; Dec. 1903, 511; Jan. 1904, 613f; Feb. 1904, 734; March 1904, 869

Board of Trade intervened in the street railway strike of 1902. The Mayor and Council of Shawinigan Falls helped settle a strike against the Belgo-Canadian Pulp Company. When the Canadian Locomotive Works in Kingston imported German machinists to break a strike, City Council and the Board of Trade intervened, to no avail. The Hamilton Trades and Labour Council asked the local Board of Trade to appoint members to a joint committee 'to act as a conciliation board in times of labour troubles so as to avoid strikes.' Labour councils themselves became involved in attempts at conciliation and mediation. The Toronto Trades and Labour Council negotiated with the Adamson Moulding Company, but failed to end a strike, and the matter passed to Gompers for investigation. A committee of the Victoria TLC intervened in a longshoremen's strike, again unsuccessfully.[82]

'Employers Associations,' President Flett told the 1904 TLC convention, 'as now constituted, may be divided roughly into two classes, – First, – Those which propose to fight the unions. Their leaders emphasize the fact that industry is war. Second, – Those which seek to deal with the unions. Their leaders emphasize the fact that industry is business.[83] Unions in Canada, as they went about their business, quite frequently entered into agreements with employers' associations, presumably those of the second order. The Toronto Employers' Association 'arbitrated' a dispute over piano rubbers' wages: the board consisted of two representatives of the employers and two of the men. The Vancouver Typographical Association negotiated an increase in wage rates with the Master Printers' Association, and the publishers announced an increase in the price of newspapers in consequence. In Halifax, builders' labourers dealt with the Master Builders' Association when they attempted to win increased wages, and in Toronto the tailors' union dealt with the master tailors' section of the Retail Merchants' Association. A Stevedores' Association determined wage rates for longshoremen in Vancouver. In Ottawa, the International Plumbers and Steamfitters' Union called for higher pay and shorter hours from the Master Plumbers' Association, but no reply came and, perhaps in consequence, a number of members left the international to organize a national union.[84]

Then there are many cases of two-party 'arbitration,' which probably amount to collective bargaining. Guelph iron moulders demanded an increased minimum wage, and 'the matter was referred to an arbitration board

82 *Ibid.*, Feb. 1904, 742; July 1901, 7; July 1902, 1, 35ff; Sept. 1902, 128; March 1903, 650; April 1903, 739; Dec. 1903, 510; Aug. 1901, 78; Oct. 1901, 209
83 *TLC* 1904, 11; Flett was quoting Ray Stannard Baker.
84 *LG*, Jan. 1904, 614, 644; Feb. 1904, 739; March 1904, 864, 886; May 1904, 1095

of equal numbers from the [US-based] National Foundrymen's Association and from the Iron Moulders' Union of America.' The board failed to come to an agreement, and a strike ensued. Montreal boot and shoe manufacturers 'adopted rules and regulations by which the employer and employee may come together and adjust their differences, by an arbitration board, appointed jointly by the two sides of the controversy,' but it is not certain whether this plan was ever carried out. On the union side, the annual conference of the bricklayers' and masons' unions in Ontario decided to set up 'an arbitration committee for the settlement of grievances that may occur in Canada.'[85]

Of course, there were many other methods of dealing with industrial disputes, some of them, like replacing strikers with non-union workers, peculiar to employers. But the point here is not to provide an exhaustive catalogue of practices – to do so would likely be impossible, given that not everything was reported in the *Gazette*, and what was reported was often ambiguous – but merely to indicate the context within which state intervention in disputes settlement occurred. The great variety of techniques made use of from time to time was in part a consequence of the heterogeneity of the trade union movement in Canada, and while the official policy of the AFL came to dominate the TLC after 1902 its preferences in disputes settlement practices likely had more effect on the content of the Congress' legislative lobbying than on the choice of methods made by particular locals and their employers when faced with a conflict. Besides, as we have seen, Gompers' notions of what was permissible were only imperfectly assimilated by the Canadian movement. There was a degree of vitality and experimentation in disputes settlement procedures at the local level that received only defective expression in the pronouncements of the central body. But even there, as we shall see when we come to examine the TLC's reception of King's disputes policy, the Canadian unionists showed greater flexibility than their American counterparts. Part of the difference may be traced to the Canadians' view of the state and its role, and it is to that topic that we now turn.

85 *Ibid.*, Oct. 1902, 216f; Nov. 1902, 298; July 1903, 73

6
The labour problem and the Canadian state

If we add to this rule, which we have laid down for the practical guidance of the State, those laws which are imposed on it by the theory we previously developed, we shall conclude that its activity should always be left to be determined by necessity. [Wilhelm von Humboldt, *The Limits of State Action*, 1792]

Canadian labour policy after 1900, as it was crafted by the expert hand of Mackenzie King, constituted a response to the leading edge of industrial development and its associated changes in the trade-union movement and other institutions. As these changes were filtered through the categories of King's thought, and as they met with the exigencies of a still vulnerable economy, they were resolved into a new framework of policy designed in the first instance to provide for 'industrial peace' and used to foster what were regarded as beneficial aspects in the newly emerging political economy. To this extent at least – to the extent that the new policy was devised and used to smooth the way for change, and not to obstruct its possibility – King's labour policy was progressive. It rested – for the most part, but not entirely, implicitly – on the anticipation that the leading edge of change in industry was the shape of things to come throughout the economy and society as a whole. This anticipation, of course, was fostered by comparisons with other more advanced economies whose pasts resembled Canada's present and whose presents were therefore taken to be Canada's future, by general optimism regarding the proprietorship of the new century, and, indeed, by the whole bent of the Liberal creed.

But it would be a mistake to see King's innovations in labour policy as emerging fully formed from a complex alchemy of industrial development and personal ideology thrown into the stewpot in 1900. The history of state involvement with the 'labour problem' antedates the turn of the century in Canada and owes much to precedents established elsewhere. To a degree, the existing body of policy lightened King's task: to a degree, especially in so far as judicial interpretation or executive neglect weakened the force of the early statutes, it may have hindered it. Furthermore, many of King's innovations were administrative rather than substantive in nature. The work of the Department of Labour turned out to be less the invention of new approaches to old problems than the selection of certain aspects of the established pattern and their elevation to the status of general formulae. Finally, the interventionism that characterized King's policy, for all the comment that it excited in, for example, the United States, was not outside the mainstream of Canadian state activity as it had developed since long before Confederation. There is, therefore, the danger that, in focusing attention on the activities of the Department of Labour after its formation in 1900, new departures, significant though they were, be stressed at the expense of continuities. The progressive side of the new policies and practices stands out so as to obscure what was equally, and profoundly, conservative in them. In seeking to adapt the institutional framework of industrial relations to a changing political economy, no violence was done to the most fundamental postulates of liberal society.

I

Two quite different lodes of scholarship might be mined to produce a framework for interpreting the Canadian state's response to the 'labour problem.' On the one hand is the general model of the structure and function of the state in liberal capitalist society that has emerged from the recent renewal of interest in this subject among writers with a broadly Marxian approach, and inspired by Ralph Miliband's path-breaking analysis. On the other is the somewhat older but none the less rich vein worked by Canadian political economists and economic historians in the liberal tradition, concerned with explaining the apparent absence of a *laissez-faire* tradition in Canada, as opposed to Britain or the United States. That these two approaches are not wholly incompatible has been recognized by others; and there exists at least one superbly crafted example of what may be gained by integrating the two.[1]

1 On the former point see Mel Watkins, 'The State in a Staples Economy,' paper presented to 'The American Empire and Dependent States' conference, University of Toronto, 19 November 1977. For the latter, H.V. Nelles, *The Politics of Development: Forests, Mines and Hydro-Electric Power in Ontario, 1849–1941* (Toronto: Macmillan, 1974). Nelles makes no explicit claim to undertake this task of integration, but he performs it, silently, beyond the professedly empirical limits of his subject.

This section attempts a partial synthesis and examines its bearing on the 'labour problem.'

Modern descriptions of the structure of the capitalist state generally hold to the view that the state is a complex of institutions across which state power is distributed in a relatively flexible way and which may develop internally compelling vested interests and imperatives of their own. Miliband views the state as a system of such institutions which, taken as a whole, maintains a degree of autonomy from civil society and, taken severally, reveal some degree of autonomy within and among themselves. These institutions and the interactions among them constitute what he calls the 'state system.' He lists six institutions or sets of institutions as typical constituents: the government (i.e., 'of the day'); the state bureaucracy or administrative apparatus; the military and police forces which make up the coercive or repressive apparatus and embody the liberal state's monopoly of the legitimate use of violence; the judiciary; parliament; and the 'sub-central governments,' with which may be associated sub-central versions of some or all of the other institutions in the system.[2] Miliband distinguishes these institutions of state power from the range of institutions – political parties, business, farmer and labour organizations, protest movements, and so on – which operate within the sphere of politics but outside the state proper.[3] That social power of a special nature should be vested in and reserved to this complex of institutions, and that the state system's continuing ability to reserve this authority is guaranteed in the last instance by its monopoly over the legitimate use of force, are due to the ultimate responsibility of the state for, minimally, two broad functions, accumulation and legitimation.[4] The first of these requires at least the maintenance and protection of capitalist property relations in the society as a whole and may ramify into extensive state involvement in economic activity. The second requires at least that the state be able to supply a convincing *negative* justification for popular allegiance – 'King or Chaos!' as the 1935 election slogan had it – and inasmuch as the capitalist state is a liberal state, it must do for the most part something better than this.

2 Ralph Miliband, *The State in Capitalist Society* (London: Weidenfeld and Nicholson, 1972), esp. chap. 3
3 Miliband's argument here has been criticized – in my view, unsuccessfully – by Nicos Poulantzas in a widely known debate conducted in *New Left Review* and reprinted in part in Robin Blackburn, ed., *Ideology and Social Science* (London: Fontana, 1972). See also Poulantzas, *Political Power and Social Classes* (London: New Left Books, 1973).
4 Panitch's recent attempt to add a third 'function,' coercion, seems to confuse the functions of the state with the means available to it to achieve those ends. See his 'The Role and Nature of the Canadian State,' in Leo Panitch, ed., *The Canadian State: Political Economy and Political Power* (Toronto: University of Toronto Press, 1977), 8.

These two functions, accumulation and legitimation, while they may not be necessarily contradictory, will ordinarily exhibit a greater or lesser amount of tension. The successful exercise of the accumulation function under certain conditions may be such that economic growth furnishes its own legitimation. This is the concept, by now familiar, of the ever-expanding pie, and there may have been periods in Canadian history when the rapid expansion of economic opportunity has been sufficient in itself to secure a measure of class or regional reconciliation, although it would be easy to overestimate the extent to which this has been true. The first great period of economic growth after Confederation, the Laurier boom, did not fall into this category: on the contrary, as we have seen, conflict was exacerbated. New ventures in legitimation had to be initiated in response, and we shall argue that the creation of the Department of Labour was among these.

Perhaps no better example of the endemic tension between accumulation and legitimation might be found than the 'labour problem.' Under the rubric of accumulation, labour constitutes an indispensable factor of production with whose general availability, quality, discipline, and price the state may have to concern itself in the service of economic efficiency and growth. But the 'labour problem' is a problem of legitimation in so far as class conflict threatens the justificatory foundations of the liberal state in equity and community. Whole-hearted pursuit of accumulation might imply the most ruthless 'manpower planning' and controls on the price and mobility of labour, utilizing a spectrum of means from eugenics to the relentless suppression of collective protest. Whole-hearted pursuit of legitimation might imply the redefinition of property rights to include, first, property in work and, second, property in an array of equitable social relations.[5] Both pursuits have been attempted, but one thing is clear: either is incompatible with liberal capitalism. In the first case, capitalist society ceases to be liberal; in the second, liberal society ceases to be capitalist. These cessations may be taken as absolute ones, and it is obvious that within any liberal capitalist society properly so designated there will be a broad trade-off zone between the two. But if the whole-hearted pursuit of either of these ends is incompatible with the other, within the confines of liberal capitalism, and if the instances in which the pursuit of one may incorporate the other are limited and rare, then the tensions between them must furnish some of the dynamic for change. It is tempting, then, to take the hypothetically possible case of rapid growth furnishing its own legitimation (to some appreciable extent) less as the har-

5 See C.B. Macpherson, 'A Political Theory of Property,' in his *Democratic Theory*, for the argument behind this assertion.

monious norm than as an uneasy dynamic equilibrium between two incongruent forces. Moreover, to the extent that the functions of accumulation and legitimation are unequally distributed over the various components of the state system, this tension will be imported into the structure of the state itself, and may help to account for the relative autonomy and competing interests and imperatives both within the state and between the state and civil society.

Notwithstanding the deep-seated tension between the functions of accumulation and legitimation, it would be an error to view the state system as instrumentally bifurcated to the extent that it cannot be considered a single system at all. The special functions of accumulation and legitimation are subsumed within a larger function that characterizes the state system as a whole and sets it apart from other institutional complexes in liberal society, and it is to this that Poulantzas seems to be speaking when he claims that the state 'constitutes the factor of cohesion between the levels of a social formation,' or that it is 'the regulating factor of the society's global equilibrium.'[6] To make sense of these very abstract formulations, it will be useful to consider them in the context of the emerging Canadian political economy in the late nineteenth and early twentieth centuries.

Industrial Canada was a tissue of conflicts and contradictions. To begin with, there was the industrial impulse within what was still predominantly an agrarian political economy, albeit agriculture was embedded in capitalist commercialism. The advent of industrialism created tensions between the requirements of those sectors of the society and its economy which were more or less fully industrialized, and those still rooted in preindustrial conditions. Industrialism created new social classes with divergent interests and consequent conflicts and tensions. Its uneven development within Canada, and Canada's continuing location within an international imperialist system, generated a complex web of regional interests and tensions ranging from conflicts between city and countryside to the dominance of central geographic regions over dependent peripheral ones within the nation state, and to problems of dependency for Canada as a whole when confronted with its position in the international political economy. These tensions, conflicts, and contradictions were expressed in a host of ideological and institutional responses to industrialism, with very different images of the society and man's place within it being promulgated by the various groups that industrialism created, defined, and set in opposition, and these tensions were overlaid by the alternative nationalisms of Canadian and *Canadien*.

6 *Political Power and Social Classes*, 44f

To say that the state constitutes the factor of cohesion between the levels of a social formation, or that it is the regulating factor of the society's global equilibrium, is to say that the broad function of the state is to subordinate these competing and conflicting interests and images to an overarching definition of the society as a unitary entity, to elicit or impose social order and national unity, from this chaos of contradiction. This is not to say that the state *resolves* in any permanent way the conflict of classes or regions or competing ideologies: it cannot do this, precisely because the process of industrialism is continually reproducing all of these tensions and because, as we have argued, the specific instrumentalities of the state are correspondingly in tension. The role of the state is not to resolve endemic conflicts of class, nation and region, but to subordinate them to a single dominant ordering of the society. In an industrial capitalist society, that ordering is capitalist industrialism. The state orders the society, organizes, regulates, equilibrates it, in the general interest of capitalist industrialism: that this role can be played at all is explained by the state's ultimate monopoly on legitimate violence, but it is not a role that can be played to completion. Later in this study, we shall have to return to the implications of the state's role in subordinating social tension to national unity in light of Mackenzie King's labour policy: here it will be sufficient to suggest that one consequence is that the problem of the legitimacy of the capitalist social order is reinterpreted in terms of the legitimacy of the capitalist state itself.

We turn now to a second approach to the problem of the state: the approach from the traditional preoccupation in Canadian political economy with explaining the unusually extensive role of the state in economic development. Innis's well-known words set out this commonplace: 'the relation of the government of Canada to general economic growth has been unique ... The Canadian government has a closer relation to economic activities than most governments.'[7] Several competing or complementary explanations are offered in the literature; they may be broadly classed into two general groups. One of them focuses attention on the special characteristics of the population or of some significant group within it, while the other emphasizes the structural imperatives of economic activity in the rugged Canadian environment. Into the first group, then, goes Horowitz's adaptation of Louis Hartz's fragment theory: Canada was peopled by a Tory fragment of European civilization, and retained the statist orientation brought to it by the Loyalists and similar groups.[8] Naylor's distinction between commercially and industrially

7 H.A. Innis, *The Fur Trade in Canada: An Introduction to Canadian Economic History* (Toronto: University of Toronto Press, 1970), 400, 401
8 Gad Horowitz, *Canadian Labour in Politics*, chap. 1

oriented strata of the Canadian business class seems to combine some elements of this cultural trait argument with the 'staples trap' thesis discussed in an earlier chapter.[9] The second group is larger and more intellectually respectable. Aitken's notion of 'defensive expansion'[10] – the proliferation of state activities in order to ward off the threat of economic assimilation by the United States – fits in here, as does the argument that originated with Innis and has enjoyed a long and varied career, that the heavy infrastructure costs of the staples economy made the socialization of entrepreneurial risk imperative. Corry, following the Mackintosh variant of the staples approach, generalized this to incorporate all economic activities in 'new societies,' although staples development was the *sine qua non* of economic development in these societies for Mackintosh, Lower, and their followers: 'In a new country, the state is saddled with positive duties of helping people to help themselves. Even though its ultimate function is only that of a referee, it must turn in and help to build the playing field before the game can begin.'[11]

The Canadian state certainly helped 'people' – the Hudson's Bay Company, the Canadian Pacific Railway – to 'help themselves' to whatever might be available, but Corry's words are doubly interesting in that they look forward in true whig-staples fashion to an end of the necessity for state intervention, and make delightfully zestful use of the umpire metaphor that King found suited his purposes just as well – and just as speciously. In the narrower sense, however, this view has been restricted in the first instance to state involvement in establishing the transportation infrastructure associated with the staples trades: canals before 1850, railways after, and, by extension, highways and air transport later still. The involvement of the state took the form either of bond guarantees, bonuses, or direct subsidies to private entrepreneurs, or state ownership *ab initio*. The extension of state involvement, assistance, and regulation beyond the imperatives of the staples trades has frequently been 'explained' as a relict of the nasty, if necessary, habit acquired during the days of nation-building. This, it is to be presumed, allowed the whig-staples purveyors to have everything their own way: Canada *had* become an advanced, modern, diversified, industrial economy with full national independence, and if the state had not reverted to that

9 R.T. Naylor, 'The Rise and Fall of the Third Commercial Empire of the St. Lawrence,' in Gary Teeple, ed., *Capitalism and the National Question in Canada* (Toronto: University of Toronto Press, 1972)

10 H.G.J. Aitken, 'Defensive Expansionism: The State and Economic Growth in Canada,' in W.T. Easterbrook and M.H. Watkins, eds., *Approaches to Canadian Economic History* (Toronto: McClelland and Stewart, 1967)

11 J.A. Corry, 'The Growth of Government Activities since Confederation,' study prepared for Royal Commission on Dominion-Provincial Relations (Ottawa, 1939), 4

function of simple referee which properly belongs to the end of history, but persisted in mucking about with the playing field, it was because old habits die hard. This overstates the case to the point of parody, of course, but it does point up the danger of substituting description for explanation and it provides us with the critical wedge to break into the perfect circle of a related usage, the notion of the paternalistic state.

Briefly, some writers, recognizing that the Canadian state involved itself in a range of activities unusually extensive for its time, cast about for an adjectival qualifier to set it off from other sorts of states. Recognizing an apparent analogy with European government activity before the rise of *laissez-faire*, they settled on the term 'paternalistic' to describe the nature of Canadian state activities. Corry may serve as an example once more: 'This kind of grandfatherly paternalism which distributes sweetmeats and is sparing of restraint has been a striking feature of Canadian government since Confederation.'[12]

It must be noted that 'paternalism' was not taken at the outset to be an *explanation* of the Canadian state's extensive activity: this was to be explained in terms of the material imperatives of staples production in the northern landscape. Paternalism described the state's response to these imperatives, but then it was extended to name the 'habit' so acquired, and, finally, to serve as explanation for later extensions of the state's role. Why is the Canadian state such a persistent meddler in business affairs? Because it is a paternalistic state, of course. This, obviously, is an explanation that explains nothing, and it is unfortunate that it should have become entangled with explanations that attempt to do a great deal more. Pentland's use of the term, for example, derives from his attempt to draw together the two principal themes in this literature, fragment cultures and economic exigency.

Pentland's argument is about *attitudes*, and he traces the Canadian response to early twentieth-century industrialism to the prevalence of rural, small-town, and commercial outlooks, tempered by the moral reform movement centred upon 'efficiency,' and by a 'predilection' for 'Tory Radicalism': 'piecemeal reform that avoids challenging the essential structure and is for the general purpose of preserving it.'[13] These general attitudes amounted at the political level to widespread acceptance of the concept of a 'father state,' inasmuch as 'Canadians have been traditionally conscious that their society did not run by itself, that its good operation required government intervention, and their frequent fear has been that the state would *not* act, or not act sufficiently':

12 *Ibid.*, 5
13 Pentland, 20–35

Whereas the American hope for justice, or at least order, has rested on a conflict of interests, re-stated more recently as a concept of countervailing power, the Canadian's experience – of the relation of his country with other countries, of the relationships of Canadian regions and provinces, of large versus small business, of farmers and their predators, and of employers and workers – denies that there is any natural or automatic balance of forces. Rather, justice or even order are only attainable by action of the father state. His parliamentary system was designed precisely to overcome centrifugal forces and centralize authority so that the state could apply the necessary correctives and, whatever the defects of practice, he inherited from Britain a strong tradition of the moral obligation of those clothed with state power to intervene in an even-handed manner.[14]

Pentland's argument here complements an important insight of Corry's, 'the view that Canadians have never had any fear of or prejudice against state action as such. Great numbers of them have always been able, thus far [1939], to recall the origin of the state. Having seen it constructed and having watched it grow, they had that familiarity which at least dispels fear. An authority which gives away homesteads and timber limits is not likely to arouse contempt while its benevolence is worth cultivating. Thus the state has lacked the awe and mystery with which age and ceremonial surrounded it in older countries and it has never had the record of bad behaviour which made men fear it in England.'[15] While the last clause is almost impossibly naive – homesteads and timber limits have figured prominently among the scandals whose infinite variety Canadian custom has hardly staled – the general point is well taken.

Concepts like 'paternalism' and 'habit,' then, are most useful as *post hoc* descriptions, not as explanations in their own right. In the latter use they run away with the argument and plunge it into the disputatious whirlpool of 'national character,' whence it is not easily retrieved. What these writers have noticed, though, is that significant groups in the Canadian political economy have not hesitated to approach the state with their particular demands, albeit those demands are couched in the rhetoric of national or public interest, and that the state has frequently responded; more frequently, at least in the later nineteenth and early twentieth centuries, than was the rule elsewhere. Presumably, these groups continued to apply to the state both because it was in their interests to do so and – what is in some respects the same thing – because the state could usually be counted upon to respond. The paternalism of the state and the predilection for such groups to apply to

14 *Ibid.*, 163f
15 Corry, 'Growth of Government Activities,' 4

it – the habit, in short – are reconstructed from observations of this pattern: the terms name, but do not explain, the pattern.

The analysis may then proceed in two directions: it may seek to account for the supposedly unusual readiness of the state to respond to such applications, calling on the vulnerability of the staples economy and the heavy overhead costs associated with it, among other explanations, or it may attempt to explain Canadians' attitudes towards state intervention, government behaviour, political programmes and so forth in terms of this historic pattern. These approaches escape the whirlpool's – perhaps a more appropriate metaphor would be the muskeg's – embrace, at least at the outset. Both of them may be necessary to explain the persistence of the pattern: it would be reinforced by the prevalence of attitudes it itself had spawned, but only to the extent, one hypothesizes, that the pay-off is still forthcoming, that the interests are somehow served.

And these interests may well be served indirectly. Take, for example, Nelles's analysis of the persistence of Crown property rights in Ontario in the age of industrialism. Preindustrial land tenure furnished the legal matrix for extensive state involvement in developing the resource sector of the economy, to the manifest advantage of the industrialists who were the supplicants. But the maintenance of Crown property in the forests was also to the advantage of another much larger group of Ontarians, the politically influential farmers who had no direct interest in the development of the Shield timberlands. Given the limited taxing powers granted to the provinces in the British North America Act, Crown revenues from resource exploitation could offset the need for higher direct taxation on agricultural land. For all the traditional rhetoric about the individualistic *laissez-faire* yeoman farmer, Ontario agrarians had much to gain from 'the maintenance of the old, imperial habit of authority into the industrial age,'[16] at least in the short run. Nelles goes on to show, of course, that the state in Ontario increasingly became the client of the resource industries and that the historic agrarian programme of responsible government was undermined in consequence.

The most conspicuous claimants for the federal state's largesse were the manufacturers, who achieved their grandest victory with Macdonald's National Policy in the late 1870s and even after lobbied to retain the spoils in the form of the protective tariff. But organized labour was not an insignificant member of the queue and, as we suggested in the last chapter, made persistent demands for intervention in its favour. Labour's proclaimed interests were served, after a fashion, although as we shall see what one element in

16 Nelles, *Politics of Development*, 46f

the state system gave another as often as not took away. Labour's first real victory, the decriminalization of trade-union membership, was contemporaneous with the manufacturers' acquisition of the tariff, and this fact has led to speculation that the two were linked by more than just temporal association. This point is important, as it sets the stage for the reciprocal interrelations of business, labour, and government after the turn of the century, and permits us to introduce, as well, the tariff question as it emerged after 1902, when the possibility of collaboration between business and labour was canvassed and found wanting.

II

The Trade Union Act of 1872 relieved workers of the charge of criminal conspiracy for merely forming a combination in restraint of trade. This Act, subject to the restrictions imposed in the Criminal Law Amendment Acts which accompanied and followed it, was designed to rescue members of trade unions from the common law doctrine of criminal conspiracy; however, as will be seen, it did not by any means constitute complete relief from the legal barriers to effective defence of wages and working conditions. It is necessary to deal with the legal principles involved here at some length, before turning to the political implications of the Act itself.

In liberal society, transactions in the labour market are taken, in the first instance, to be an undifferentiated subset of transactions in the general commodity market and, to that extent, are completely and sufficiently governed by the law of contract and by other relevant sections of commercial law. Commercial relations at law are considered to be relations in the nature of contract between natural persons or, following the invention of the corporation, between natural and artificial persons or between artificial persons. Thus the legal personality of the parties to such a relationship is paramount in deciding whether their contract is enforceable at law. Trade unions faced a serious legal disability inasmuch as, not being legal persons, their contracts were unenforceable at law. This disability must be clearly distinguished from a second one, the susceptibility of the members of a trade union to the charge of criminal conspiracy. In the first case, the trade union is an association that has no existence in the eyes of the law: in the second case, it is an unlawful association in the sense that its members are subject to prosecution on account of their membership. It was to the remedy of this second disability alone that the provisions of the 1872 Act were directed.

At the base of this criminal disability lay the common law doctrines of public policy and conspiracy. Under the first of these, judges could declare invalid contracts or agreements which, while they were not criminal, offended against 'public policy.' In the *laissez-faire* environment of early industrial Britain, judges proved willing to declare any form of commercial restraint – for example, an agreement among workers not to accept less than a certain wage – to be against public policy and hence invalid. The burden of such a ruling, in the example given, would be to prohibit any of the workers involved from enforcing the agreement on any of the others, and was therefore akin to the first disability discussed above. Far more serious was the linking of the public policy doctrine to the doctrine of conspiracy. In its simplest form the conspiracy doctrine provides that an agreement among two or more persons to perform a criminal act is itself a separate criminal act and one that may carry a far more serious penalty than the first. The damage was done when the doctrine of conspiracy was extended to cover not only agreements to perform crimes but agreements to act against public policy as well. With this extension, the workers in our example have not only negotiated an unenforceable contract as among themselves but in so doing have committed a serious crime. Pritt summarizes the implications of this doctrine: 'the crime of conspiracy is committed by all who agree to commit a crime, even if they make no move whatever to carry out their agreement, and ... it is also committed by all who agree to do something objectionable, even if they make no move to carry it out, and even if none of them would be guilty of any crime at all if he just did that something all by himself, without combination or previous agreement with others.'[17]

When the repeal of the Combination Acts in England in the 1820s removed the principal statutory barriers to trade unionism, the extended doctrine of criminal conspiracy in common law stepped in to fill the gap. It was not until the passage of the 1871 Trade Union Act in England that the liability of union members to prosecution for criminal conspiracy on account of their organizations being in restraint of trade, and thus contrary to public policy, was relieved. But the English statute had no bearing in Canada, and common law conspiracy could still apply.

There are fragmentary records of criminal conspiracy charges having been brought against Toronto printers and tailors in the 1850s but, perhaps because the penalties upon conviction had been token fines, the law seems not to have been seriously challenged. This was not the case in 1872, however, when the Master Printers' Association, under the zealous leadership of

---

17 D.N. Pritt, *Employers, Workers and Trade Unions* (London: Lawrence and Wishart, 1970), 21

George Brown, obtained the indictment of twenty-four Toronto printers on a criminal conspiracy charge. The story of the Toronto printers' strike and the nine-hour agitation is well known: the massive demonstrations in Queen's Park; the widespread public sentiment against Brown's use of an outdated law; the magistrate's refusal to hear counter-charges that the Master Printers' Association itself constituted an illegal conspiracy; Macdonald's gleeful introduction of a Bill similar to that passed in England the year before, on the eve of an election campaign; his arch-enemy Brown hoist with his own Gladstonian petard.[18] This much is not in doubt, and there is a general consensus, too, that Macdonald seized upon this double opportunity of embarrassing Brown and the Liberals and capitalizing on popular indignation with the state of the law, with an eye to the main chance in the coming campaign. It is at this point that consensus seems to break down and the accounts become especially interesting, with the attempts of some writers to link the passage of the Trade Union Act to Macdonald's National Policy tariff.

The National Policy, that three-cornered developmental strategy embracing railway construction, western agricultural settlement, and a protective tariff for central Canada's 'infant industries,' was the keynote of the Conservative campaign in 1878 and the party's principal claim to popular support for decades thereafter. But, as Creighton pointed out in 1943, the new programme had been tried on for the first time by the Tories, not in 1878, but in 1872, when it was overshadowed by the Liberals' successful exploitation of the Pacific Scandal. There were, then, two new achievements for the Conservatives to display on the hustings in 1872: the Trade Union Act, and their new-found commitment to the principle of (at least) incidental protection. Were these just separate planks in an election platform, their simultaneous appearance merely coincidental, or was there some more profound connection between them? Three writers in particular have argued for the latter, although they have not all argued it in the same way.[19]

Creighton was the first to stake the general claim. Macdonald, looking to the coming election, had been 'anxiously debating' commercial policy and addressing himself, for the first time, to the social and political significance of the 'growing manufacturing system of the country.' He became aware that

18 For the background to the strike see, *inter alia*, Sally Zerker, 'George Brown and the Printers' Union,' *Journal of Canadian Studies*, vol. x, 1 (Feb. 1975), 42ff.

19 Donald Creighton, 'George Brown, Sir John Macdonald, and the "Workingman,"' *CHR* (Dec. 1943), 362ff; Bernard Ostry, 'Conservatives, Liberals and Labour in the 1870's,' *CHR* (June 1960), 93ff; Steven W. Langdon, 'The Political Economy of Capitalist Transformation: Central Canada from the 1840's to the 1870's,' unpublished MA thesis, Carleton University, 1972

'he must also devote himself to labour,' and on the very heels of this realization came Brown's precipitate action in Toronto. This, of course, gave him his opening: he could present the Conservative party as the workingman's friend at the same time as his new commercial policy was introduced to the public. The Trade Union Act, Creighton stressed, was 'not the only, nor perhaps the most important, inducement, in the new Conservative appeal to the industrial population of Canada.' Protection of home industry was to be the main drawing-card, the incentive that would attract industrial interests, workers and employers, to the Tory ranks. Before the Pacific Scandal stole the show, Creighton claimed, the 1872 campaign had another, equally unprecedented, fascination for the electorate: 'For them it was the first election in which the industrial classes of Canada had been the chief centre of interest and the industrial future of the Dominion the main question at issue. In their eyes it had been made memorable by working-men candidates and great labour rallies; and it had been won by the party which most successfully united in its own favour the twin interests of labour and capital.'

For Creighton, then, protection of home industries was the plank which would win the support of labour and manufacturers to the Tories. To make this appeal wholly credible to the workers, and to win them away from the Reform traditions of the Liberals, Macdonald had to portray himself as the workingman's friend in some sphere distinct from the tariff policy itself. The printers' strike gave him this opportunity: with one stroke he could discredit Brown and pose as the champion of trade unionism. The two planks were linked, somewhat tenuously, by Macdonald's need to wean labour support away from the Grits.

Ostry elaborated the argument by attempting to strengthen the link. While for Creighton the Trade Union Act had been merely a political manoeuvre designed to ensure the broadest possible support for the tariff, for Ostry it became a sort of codicil to the National Policy itself. Ostry argued that Creighton's analysis of the trade union legislation as an election ploy overlooked the limitations of the Canadian franchise at the time. All the provinces except Ontario retained their pre-Confederation franchises for dominion elections, while Ontario retained its 1869 law. All of these were householders' franchises and, Ostry claimed, it was unlikely that a very large proportion of wage workers, even of skilled artisans, possessed the vote. Moreover, he continued, it was surely not necessary for Macdonald to take positive action in order to win what few working-class votes might have been available. Brown's own actions were sufficient to alienate Grit supporters among the working class, and all Macdonald had to do was sit tight and reap what Brown had sown. This was all the more true inasmuch as there was little agreement within the Conservative party about the trade unions, and for Macdonald to introduce the Act merely in order to capture an insignificant handful of ballots in a few constituencies was to risk a rift in a party already uneasy over the implications of the Red River Rebellion and the Washington Treaty. But Macdonald had pressed forward with the Trade Union Act, so he must have had good reason for it. If vote-gathering was not reason enough, Ostry argued, Macdonald must have had a better one.

Before examining Ostry's proposed alternative explanation, it may be useful to look a little more closely at his main reason for rejecting Creighton's: the limited number of votes that could be commanded by the labour movement and by unorganized workers influenced by it. While Ostry does adduce a little evidence on this point, it is too little to be convincing: 'The figures of the results of the 1872 election in three urban centres suggest how limited the voting strength of this class must have been. If James Beaty [a Toronto Tory M.P. who had supported the printers against Brown through the columns of his newspaper] could not muster more than 872 votes in Toronto East which was certainly not Toronto's wealthiest constituency at a time when there must have been nearly a thousand organized and aroused trade unionists in Toronto, one is frankly hard put to accept the thesis that all Macdonald was interested in was the industrial worker's vote ... In 1872 the artisan obviously was not in a position to wield much political influence at the polling station.'

Ostry's argument here may be more or less persuasive, but his conclusion is not quite 'obvious.' It is, unfortunately, one of the more astonishing lacunae in late nineteenth-century Canadian historiography that no detailed study of the range of the franchise has been carried out. We possess a useful account of the *nature* of the pre-Confederation franchises in Garner's work,[20] but even here there is no attempt to decide who actually had the vote – what proportion of the male population, in what occupations or localities – under the various enactments that are discussed. Perhaps with the current interest in quantitative social history, the cliometricians will unleash their computers on this problem. In the meantime, judgment on Ostry's negative claim must be suspended.

But all this is really by the way so far as Ostry's positive argument is concerned. Perhaps his suspicions about Creighton's attribution of the Act to Macdonald's desire for working-class votes prompted him to delve more deeply into the question, but for all that the answer he comes up with is not

20 John Garner, *The Franchise and Politics in British North America, 1755–1867* (Toronto: University of Toronto Press, 1969)

incompatible with Creighton's. Ostry argues that the Trade Union Act was a necessary (although certainly not a sufficient) condition for the success of the National Policy. The National Policy was a strategy for developing the manufacturing base of central Canada. One of the ingredients in such a strategy must be the provision and maintenance of an adequate skilled labour force. Canadian artisans must be retained, and this pool must be enlarged by immigration from Great Britain. But Canadian artisans would emigrate – *were* emigrating – to the United States in search of higher wages, and so long as unionization was prohibited in Canada, with no effective check on employer attempts to reduce wage rates, this flow would continue. Moreover, skilled British artisans would not be likely to come to Canada so long as they were denied the right to unionize, a right they had won themselves after years of struggle only a year before. Already, the Canadian unionists were in touch with their British counterparts, seeking support for the nine-hour and trade union movements and propagandizing against immigration. Ostry is able to show, through Macdonald's correspondence and speeches, that he had these considerations in mind. It was 'the realities of Canadian economic and political life' that persuaded Macdonald to remove the criminal liability from trade unionism: the Trade Union Act was an imperative precondition for the success of the National Policy. The development of an industrial economy required a skilled labour force; the development of a skilled labour force required, at the least, that Canada's trade union law be brought into line with England's. To oversimplify, where Creighton saw legitimation, Ostry saw accumulation.

Another, more recent contribution to the debate over the link between the Trade Union Act and the National Policy is made by Langdon, who sees the National Policy as 'a political reflection of the rise of industrial capitalism in central Canada,' and a 'critical triumph' for industrial capitalists over agrarian and commercial interests. In his view, part of the impetus both for collective action by industrial capitalists and for tariff protection came from the emergent working-class movement. These two interests – the labour interest and the organized manufacturers – grew up side by side and reinforced each other in pressuring the government to support their ends over those of other, traditionally more potent, groups in the economy. In this view, the Trade Union Act would be a partial recognition of the emergence of a labour movement with political power, while the National Policy recognized the manufacturing interest in general and placed it at the centre of economic development strategy. Langdon argues that there were electoral gains to be made from the Trade Union Act in 1872 and that there was room for political collaboration between manufacturers and the labour movement on the tariff question, but he claims that the most significant consequence of the working-class movement in the 1870s was the effect it had on employers, 'stimulating' the 'class-conscious cohesion' that was necessary for them to consolidate the position of industrial capitalism in both the state and civil society. Langdon, then, draws together the accumulation and legitimation functions, and stresses the partial capture of the state by the forces of industrial capitalism rather than the implicit trade-off between worker and employer interests within that mode of production. The significance of both the Trade Union Act and the National Policy is that they 'reflect' the victory of this new mode, at least at the level of the state. While this analysis broadens the context within which these issues may be discussed, it would seem to depend, at least in part, on Langdon's ability to show that manufacturers and workers did perceive some community of interest as against other economic groups: a common interest in the protective tariff.

Unfortunately, Langdon does not present evidence of this for the critical years, 1872 and before. At the same time, he recognizes that the fact that the National Policy received its first airing in 1872, rather than 1878, is 'the best evidence' for his view that it reflected the triumph of a new mode of production, because the alternative explanations that could be entertained for 1878 – anti-Americanism, the effects of the depression – will not hold for the earlier date. He is able to show, however, that the labour movement, or part of it, supported the tariff from 1874 on. In that year, the Canadian Labour Union, the trade union centre organized by the Toronto Trades Assembly after the events of 1872, called for measures to 'let our struggling industries become once established ... We claim the right to get a foothold upon our own soil without being pulled down by foreigners.' In 1877, it 'demanded protection,' complained 'that the closed market of the United States and the open market of Canada were unfair to the latter,' and protested 'the excessive importation of foreign manufactured goods.'

Canadian manufacturers may have found an ally in the labour movement when it came to demanding protection, but they soon found that there were limits to collaboration over the National Policy. If the Trade Union Act and state toleration for union organization were indispensable codicils to the National Policy, as Ostry suggested, it was to the immigration requirements of that policy that these were directed. But Canadian workers, not surprisingly, resisted the competition of imported labour as strongly as manufacturers resisted the competition of imported commodities. The CLU, Langdon reports, attacked the Canadian immigration service's efforts 'to import large numbers of skilled workers' in 1875, and the following year the labour organization denounced it as an 'artificial means to maintain an excess supply in the labour market.'[21]

That the tariff question was still the hub of the manufacturers' collective programme a quarter century later – when the ideology of efficiency led to demands to 'take the tariff out of politics' – has already been argued. We have seen, too, that unrestricted immigration, especially but by no means exclusively the importation of Orientals under contract, was an outstanding grievance of the labour movement. In the first decade of the century, as the Liberal government's economic continentalism took shape, Canadian manufacturers fretted constantly if, until 1911, for the most part unnecessarily, at the prospect of a tariff-free future. Now, as perhaps not in the 'seventies, they realized the necessity for a political alliance with other classes in the community, and while they appealed rather hopelessly to agrarian opinion from time to time, it was to the labour movement that their thoughts most often strayed. We have already argued that this was the imperative underlying the difference between the CMA and its American counterparts when it came to action against trade unions: unsavoury though it must have seemed to many of the organization's members, an alliance with the labour movement for the purpose of a strengthened and secure protective tariff was among the CMA's main priorities, the promise that kept both large and small businesses, whose interests otherwise were diverging widely, in a single organization. This attempt was to run on the rocks of immigration.

The TLC had consistently opposed unrestricted immigration of wage workers from its foundation, but not until the turn of the century did the labour central as consistently link this to the tariff question. As it emerged, the TLC position took the form of opposition to protection for manufacturers without protection for workers: it was not a whole-hearted free trade policy but, if the speculations of Ostry and Langdon are correct, and if the conditions of 1872 still held thirty years later, as the manufacturers claimed they did, it nevertheless constituted an attack on the centre of the National Policy strategy. The trade unionists might have denied this, arguing instead that there was already sufficient labour available in Canada to serve the cause of industrial progress, but no matter whose claim on this point was more nearly correct, neither manufacturers nor workers were willing to give in. And as the tariff question and the immigration question merged in the labour question, the prospect for collaboration between organized manufacturers and organized labour in legislative lobbying became ever more remote.

21 For these quotations, see Langdon, 'Political Economy,' 370–2.

III

For all that the Liberals in opposition had condemned the National Policy tariff as a 'servile copy' of the American system,[22] their commercial policy as a government after 1896 bore an equally remarkable similarity to that of their predecessors. Despite the rhetoric of a 'tariff for revenue only,' and taking into account the British preference that was the Liberals' principal innovation in trade policy before 1911, by 1903 the average Liberal impost on dutiable goods was about 27 per cent, only two points below the average in 1887, and the free list had actually shrunk as a proportion of all imports. The Liberals had introduced a 25 per cent British preference in 1898, and two years later increased this to 33.3 per cent, but neither Canadian nor British manufacturers were satisfied with the innovation. The Canadians decried it as a first step in the dismemberment of the tariff, the more so when the British refused to reciprocate, arguing that the Canadian rates were still inequitably high. Then, at the height of Colonial Secretary Joseph Chamberlain's campaign for imperial federation, a movement that had its influential counterpart in Canada,[23] came the 1902 Colonial Conference. In his keynote address, Chamberlain called for a system of thorough-going free trade. The Canadian delegates, with the backing of the CMA, replied with a request for exemption from the British revenue duties and the erection of a British tariff wall against 'foreign' – non-Empire – exporters. When the British spokesmen countered with a call for more Canadian concessions, the conference broke up with no formal agreement, but a symbolic victory for the Canadians in Britain's apparent modification of its free-trade hard line. Canadian manufacturers continued to lobby for a tariff wall around the Empire including, as Canada's loyal contribution, more protection for themselves, and in 1903 Fielding, the Minister of Finance, began to move in the direction of a stronger tariff. A trade war erupted with Germany over that country's dissatisfaction with the preferential features of Canadian policy; new duties were introduced on heavy steel rails; and, in 1904, an effective anti-dumping clause was made part of Canadian commercial policy for the first time. The CMA had continued to attack the British preference as one-sided so long as

22 Quoted in O.J. McDiarmid, *Commercial Policy in the Canadian Economy* (Cambridge, Mass.: Harvard University Press, 1946), 204, from the Report of the 1893 Liberal convention
23 See, *inter alia*, Carl Berger, *The Sense of Power: Studies in the Ideas of Canadian Imperialism, 1867–1914* (Toronto: University of Toronto Press, 1970), and James A. Colvin, 'Sir Wilfrid Laurier and the British Preferential Tariff System,' in Carl Berger, ed., *Imperial Relations in the Age of Laurier* (Toronto: University of Toronto Press, 1969).

the British refused to reciprocate, and in 1903 and the following year Fielding made some tentative moves to restrict the scope of its operation. At the same time, he pledged his support for Chamberlain's general scheme of an Empire preference, but his attempts to implement the first stage in this by imposing a penalty tariff to match the Americans' was foiled by farmer pressure. Several things were happening, then, between 1902 and 1904. Imperial free trade was in the air, but it brought as its corollary, from the Canadian manufacturers' point of view, higher protection against 'foreign' imports and the exemption of Canadians from British revenue tariffs as a show of good metropolitan faith. Under the tutelage of the CMA, Fielding had moved on both fronts but had encountered, in 1904, the first signs of effectively organized agrarian protest, a fact of commercial life that was to achieve its full significance a year or two later. The manufacturers were slowly gaining their higher tariff, but they were also quite aware that misguided elements in the population failed to understand that the CMA programme was in the national interest. 'If the manufacturers would educate the people to believe in higher protection,' Fielding had told the Association in 1901, 'they might get what they wanted from the government.' The CMA propaganda campaign had opened at the 1902 Colonial Conference and was gathering momentum.[24]

The labour movement did not respond immediately to the manufacturers' offensive, but its response was not long in coming. While the TLC had passed an anti-tariff resolution at its 1902 convention, it was couched in Single Tax language and had little bearing on the events just set in train. But in 1903, the TLC convention embarked for the first time on extended discussions of commercial policy in the climate of increasing protection. The Executive Committee had submitted to the government, in line with the Single Tax resolution of the previous year, 'that no increase be made in the tariff, as urged by the Manufacturers Association,' and Laurier had replied, declining 'to discuss the tariff question, declaring that the government's views were well known.' When the responsible committee reported on this exchange to the convention, it changed the terms of the anti-tariff protest significantly, linking it to a resolution opposing unrestricted immigration to Canada: 'the present Dominion immigration policy is inimical to the best interests of the Canadian wage-earners,' it proclaimed, 'applying the policy of free trade in labor while at the same time employers enjoy special legislation for their protection.' A second anti-immigration resolution before the convention made the same point in its preamble: 'While this assistance to immigration

---

24 The general account of tariff developments presented here is based on McDiarmid, *Commercial Policy*, chap. IX, and J. Castell Hopkins, *Canadian Annual Review* (henceforth, *CAR*) for the appropriate years.

compels the laborer to sell his labor at the lowest price in competition with the whole world, the employers are protected from foreign competition by a tariff often exceeding fifty per cent.'[25]

Neither of these statements necessarily implied an attack on the tariff, of course: either might be interpreted to mean whole-hearted support for the protection of manufacturers so long as the interests of workers received equivalent safeguards. The ambiguity was no doubt intentional, but the drift of opinion in the Congress was visible in the Executive Committee's submission to Laurier. The convention reserved its only unambiguous expression of opinion about the tariff for a resolution on the Colonial Conference proposals, and even here it was put in terms of the international, or at least intra-imperial, solidarity of the working class:

Whereas it has been represented to the British people by the British press, through Canadian manufacturers and employers, that Canada approves of the policy recently outlined by the Hon. Jos. Chamberlain to the British people, calling for the substitution of a protective tariff for the free trade policy which has been the bulwark of British commercial institutions; and whereas the policy outlined by Mr. Chamberlain has been pronounced inimical to the best interests of the British working class by the recent convention of the British Trades Congress; therefore be it resolved by this convention of the Canadian Trades Congress now assembled, representing the organized workers of this Dominion, that we endorse the action taken by the British Trades Congress, and place ourselves on record as disapproving of any capitalistic policy intended to benefit the Colonies to the detriment of the proletariat of the British Isles.

The resolution, which had been proposed by James Simpson of the Toronto Typographical Union, passed narrowly after lengthy debate.[26] Perhaps it was imperial federationist sentiment among the opposition that accounted for the closeness of the vote, or perhaps the dissidents could not bring themselves to be so selfless as to agree to the ultimate clause. What was clear, however, was that Simpson's resolution, in proclaiming solidarity with the British worker, was posing a direct and conscious challenge to the strategy of the Canadian manufacturers.

In January 1904, the new Minister of Inland Revenue, Louis-Philippe Brodeur, promised in the most general terms that changes in the tariff were shortly to be made. The CMA's proselytizing apparatus immediately swung into high gear and an official of the Association, Watson Griffith, inaugu-

25 *TLC* 1902, 70; 1903, 12f, 43f, 56
26 *TLC* 1903, 65. The vote on the resolution was 35 in favour, 30 against.

rated its front organization to win broad popular support for stronger protection, the Canadian Industrial League. At the same time, the CMA managed to enrage the labour movement over its actions in an area which the manufacturers insisted had no, and the unions insisted had every, relation to the tariff question – immigration. The CMA had sponsored the establishment of an employment recruiting agency in London and had embarked on an active propaganda throughout England about what it claimed was a serious labour shortage in Canada. In May, the Toronto and District Labor Council debated a resolution to send a representative to England, 'for the purpose of offsetting the adgitation [sic] of the Manufacturers Assoc. that mechanics were wanted in Canada,' and to collect funds for that purpose, and it decided to take the matter to the TLC convention in the fall.[27] At the same time, the newly reactivated farmers' organizations were reaching out to the labour movement for support. The TDLC meeting immediately following that in which the sending of a representative to England had been debated recorded the following in its minutes: 'The Report of Legislative Committee was read by Del. Reeks, as provided for at the previous meeting. The Report also contained the address presented to Premier Ross by the Committee, cooperating with Secy. of Farmers Association, re the abuses of the Bonus System especially in the matter of Railroads.'[28]

We come now to an episode whose all-important origins remain faintly obscure: the attempt in 1904 to find common ground between the CMA and the TLC, through the institution of a joint committee. Both organizations, by a convenient coincidence, were holding their annual conventions simultaneously at Montreal. The TLC's convention had opened with its president's reiteration of what had quickly become a common theme, the linking of immigration and the tariff. 'The manufacturing interests are protected by an increase in the tariff,' he complained, 'while labor is placed on the free list.' But then, as the first order of business on the morning of the fourth day, the Congress secretary rose to read a letter from his counterpart in the Manufacturers' Association:

DEAR SIR, – A letter addressed to this Association by the President and Secretary of the Toronto District Labor Council under date of August 29th, 1904, has just come to hand to-day. This letter suggests that a conference should be held between the representatives of the organizations of employees and this Association.

27 Toronto and District Labor Council, *Minute Books* (PAC mfm C-4588; henceforth, *TDLC*), 19 May 1904
28 *Ibid.*, 26 May 1904

This Association accepts with pleasure the suggestion of a conference as above mentioned believing that there are many questions involving our common interests which can be discussed with mutual profit to both the employers and employees and to the general benefit of our common country.

We shall be pleased to have you suggest the day and place for the proposed interview, also the number of representatives to be in attendance.[29]

The Labor Council letter of 29 August, unfortunately, seems not to have survived. We do not know why it was that the Council wished to arrange a conference with manufacturers, although it certainly had a large backlog of grievances, from the Toronto Employers' Association through the CMA's 1903 labour policy to the CMA's London employment bureau, and it cannot be assumed that it wished to discuss tariff policy. We do know, however, that there was a good deal of disagreement on the Council over the proposal to contact the CMA, and here may lie the explanation for a letter of 29 August failing to 'come to hand' until 20 September, the date of CMA secretary Younge's letter to the TLC. There is no mention of correspondence with the manufacturers in the minutes of the TDLC's August meetings, but the minutes of the 15 September meeting recorded this debate:

Report of Executive Comm. was read, which advised the reading of letter from Peace association and Letter from Delegate Douglas ... Letter from Delegate Douglas was read and not Concurred in. Executive Report was adopted except letter from Delegate Douglas. It was immediately moved to re-consider Executive report. Carried. It was then moved that the Executive Report be adopted as read. Moved in amendment that report be adopted, except Concurrence in letter of Delegate Douglas. Amendment lost and motion carried. The Said Letter to be Sent to meeting of Manufacturers Assoc. in City of Montreal.[30]

It seems very probable that this was the letter of 29 August, and the floor fight indicates something less than total unanimity about the matter. The TDLC's newspaper, the *Toiler*, did not record this debate in its report of the meeting; nor, in reporting the TLC's decision to meet with the manufacturers, did it give credit to its own sponsor as *primum mobile*.

At any rate, one Younge's letter had been read to the TLC convention delegates, two Toronto unionists rose to support a conference 'for the purpose of arriving at a better understanding between capital and labor,' moving

29 *TLC* 1904, 9, 36
30 *TDLC*, 15 Sept. 1904

that a committee of seven be appointed to meet with the CMA. Their motion was concurred in, and a letter was sent inviting the manufacturers to meet with the TLC committee at a time and place of their choosing on the following day. The Congress selected a committee of its notables and it was perhaps ironic that the next item of business was a resolution moved by one of that number, James Simpson, 'that the only way for the working class to obtain the full benefit of their labor is the substitution of the co-operative for the competitive system of industry by the common ownership by the people of the means of production and distribution.' After lengthy debate, Simpson's resolution was defeated.[31]

There was nothing in the TLC's deliberations on the question of a conference with the CMA to suggest that the tariff was uppermost in the labour delegates' minds. Over at the CMA convention, on the other hand, the manufacturers were thinking of little else. Former president P.W. Ellis made an expansive speech suggesting that the trade union movement be reorganized into two congresses, 'unions representing that one class of employees who are competing with each other only within the limits of this Dominion; unions representing that other and more numerous class of employees who compete with the foreign workman, and who are as vitally interested in having a proper tariff to protect the industries of this country as we, the employers of Canada are.' By getting together with the latter and discussing the tariff 'thoroughly and practically, as business men,' the manufacturers could arrive at 'a mutual understanding of our joint interests' with their employees:

Now, gentlemen, these are not idle words. It is a conclusion that is, in my judgement, strictly accurate, and I am of opinion that if our employees can be brought to see this matter in its proper light, instead of engaging in ruinous strikes that prevent the employer giving them a proper return for their labor, we will have instead of opposition their most earnest co-operation. It is my earnest desire, and I am sure it must be of each member of this Association – and perhaps it can be arranged before the close of this convention – that the representatives of that important labor organization now meeting in this city, will meet with the representatives of our organization, that we confer together dispassionately and prudently with a sincere desire to arrive at the best results and endeavor to agree upon those fundamental principles which mean so much for the success of the industries of Canada and equally for the success of all our employees. (Applause.)[32]

31 *TLC* 1904, 37
32 *IC*, Oct. 1904, 153

But somehow the two conventions got their wires crossed, and the meeting did not take place at once. The CMA convention adjourned before the two committees could meet, and secretary Younge telephoned his counterpart in the TLC to suggest a Toronto meeting for the following month.[33] Before their meeting broke up, though, the manufacturers passed their strongest motion yet on political action for a higher tariff: 'to support in coming elections only those candidates who favoured "an immediate general review of the tariff upon lines which will more effectively transfer to the workshops of our Dominion the manufactures of many of the goods which we now import from other countries".'[34]

Once again, the meeting was postponed. It had been scheduled for October, but in December 1904 *Industrial Canada* editorialized about 'the approaching conference with labor,' to take place that month. And in the long sermon the CMA journal preached, there was not a mention of the tariff issue. It was to be a meeting to discuss 'ways and means for the prevention and settlement of labor disputes,' and the article was fulsome in its goodwill to workers: 'The average Canadian workman is fair and manly,' and so on, while the conference was intended 'to bring about the larger union between the hearts and minds of citizens of a common progressive country.'[35] The reason for this change in emphasis is likely to be found in the CMA's change of tactics, its decision to take the tariff out of politics – a rather dramatic about-face from its convention resolution! – and seek a 'scientific practical tariff.'[36]

Industrial Canada never reported the outcome of the conference. But in September 1905, the TLC's committee gave the convention delegates its account of what had taken place:

the representatives sent by this Congress to that Conference have, as was sincerely desired by this body, endeavoured to remove some of the differences between the manufacturer and the workingmen by mutual understanding and agreement.

The subjects brought forward by both parties, viz., The Tariff, Civic Federation, Group Bargaining, Immigration, Minimum Wage, Collective Bargaining, and Permanent Board of Arbitration and Conciliation, were well worthy of consideration, but we regret that nothing was accomplished.[37]

33 *TLC* 1904, 52
34 *CAR* 1904, 40
35 *IC*, Dec. 1904, 326
36 *CAR* 1904, 149
37 *TLC* 1905, 43f

The committee blamed the CMA for continually postponing the meeting and failing to request a continuation of negotiations, and the report ended anticlimactically with a recommendation to keep the TLC committee in existence, but to place the onus for calling further meetings on the manufacturers.

The attempt at winning labour support had been something less than a triumph for the CMA, but its larger strategy paid off handsomely. The political action resolution had won results, for on 6 July, Fielding announced a special ministerial commission of inquiry into tariff revision. The TLC's response to this announcement at its 1905 convention effectively terminated, for the time being at least, any hope of co-operation with the manufacturers. Whether or not Fielding's announcement had led to the CMA's abandonment of the conferences, the TLC was now to embark on a strategy of attacking the manufacturers' tariff programme not only on the grounds of equal protection for labour, but also with the explicit intent of wreaking retribution upon the businessmen for a multitude of sins.

But even had Fielding not established his commission, it was likely that the attempt at joint conferences would have come to grief on the shoals of immigration policy. The manufacturers continued to insist that there was a serious labour shortage in Canada and that every means must be embraced to secure the immigration of skilled workmen; the unions were no less emphatic in their denunciation of these schemes as attempts to lower the price of labour and weaken working-class organization. If the National Policy political strategy had been to unite the 'industrial classes' against the rest of the community, it contained within itself the seeds of its own destruction. If immigration and the tariff were inextricably interrelated, class collaboration by workers and manufacturers seemed impossible of achievement. But as the TLC was to find to its chagrin, certain of its member unions found more to gain by supporting the cause of their employers than that of their central organization.

When the TLC convention met in September 1905, the month of the first sittings of the new tariff commission, a good part of its time was devoted to the Congress' relationship with both the manufacturers and protection. The president, as usual, led off the attack in his address, denouncing the recent mission of a CMA group to England. It was P.W. Ellis's absence in England that had been the Association's reason for postponing the joint conference, and while there he and his fellow envoys had repeatedly assured the British that Canada warmly approved of Chamberlain's imperial free trade scheme. 'This purely selfish organization cannot express the sympathetic support of Canadians in a propaganda of the kind,' the TLC delegates were told, 'and organized labor will oppose any movement of that character.' James Simpson moved a slightly revised version of his 1903 resolution, supporting the British labour movement's opposition to Chamberlain, and adding 'that we believe that an injustice done to the wageworkers of the Motherland is a blow, either directly or indirectly, at the wageworkers of Canada, and would ultimately attach added burdens to an already overburdened Canadian working class.'[38]

Having agreed to support the British worker, although this time with a slightly more selfish rhetoric than two years before, the convention moved on to consider domestic commercial policy. Sam Landers, a delegate from the United Garment Workers, moved that unions in trades affected by imports appear before the tariff commission 'with statistical evidence and endeavour to have the tariff increased on those goods to protect the Canadian wage earner from idleness while those abroad are in employment.' His resolution, explicitly calling for higher tariffs, was referred to the Committee on Solicitor's Report, which replaced it with a far blander one, recommending 'that this Congress appoint a Special Committee to meet the Commission and also instruct the Local Labor Councils in cities in which the Commission sits to appoint committees to place before the Commission on Revision of the Tariff the views of the wage earners.'[39]

It looked as though the convention would not have to come to terms with any particular stance towards the tariff: that could be left to the Special Committee. But then, once the committee had been appointed, John Flett rose to propose a resolution which managed to combine an attack on the CMA and a restatement of the tariff-immigration trade-off with a suitably feeble conclusion, given the evident differences of opinion among convention delegates:

Whereas, the Trades and Labor Congress of Canada has time and again put itself on record by resolutions as well as by active participation in measures having for their purpose the advancement of the interests of manufacturers and employers of labor generally; and, whereas, in pursuing this course we have accepted as correct the representations of employers that there is a common, mutual bond of material interests between Capital and Labor; and, whereas, this oneness of interest has not been manifest to Labor by reciprocal co-operation from Capital in measures calculated to promote the material welfare of Labor through their organizations, but on the contrary Labor has been met by hostile action from employers, and particularly from associations of employers; therefore, be it resolved, That while free trade in labor is held by employers to be necessary for the promotion of their interests, we hold that

38 *Ibid.*, 15, 35f
39 *Ibid.*, 37f, 45

free trade in the products of labor is equally logical and necessary for our well being; therefore, the mutuality of interests between Capital and Labor can only be established when they operate to their interest through protection, reciprocity, or free trade in labor and its products at one and the same time, as either one or the other becomes an economic necessity for the welfare of our country; resolved, That all possible effort be put forth, and all opportunities be embraced to bring about an equality before the law, as between the buyers and sellers of Labor, which can best be secured at this time by the advocacy of such changes in our Trade policy, as will result in more equitable protection.[40]

But this, of course, was no policy. It merely stated that to the extent manufacturers might receive protection in the form of a tariff, so too, to that extent, should labour be protected by restrictions on immigration. It hardly amounted to a position that might be presented to the Fielding Commission as the reasoned conclusions of the organized workers about Canada's future commercial policy. But it was not intended to do this, in no small part because there was no unanimity among the unions on the tariff question. It served instead to castigate the CMA for its handling of the joint conference and to warn the organized manufacturers that the TLC would use vague opposition to their tariff demands as a bargaining counter in its attempt to win concessions in other areas. If collaboration in legislative lobbying was impossible, then each would lobby on its own in a three-cornered fight for special advantage.

The CMA lost ground before the Fielding Commission. The credit for this partial reversal was due, however, not to the labour movement but to the organized farmers who, for the first time, presented a determined and united front for more liberal commercial policy.[41] The labour movement, by contrast, was in total disarray before the Commission.

The TLC tariff committee – James Simpson, D.A. Carey, John Flett, E.W.A. O'Dell, and J.G. O'Donoghue – circulated a position paper to 'advise' member organizations about the case they should make to the commission. The document, which Simpson and O'Donoghue read as part of their formal presentation to the Commission, heavily stressed the view that opposing protection would be just retribution on the CMA:

---

40 *Ibid.*, 63
41 For an account of the farm organizations' anti-tariff campaign, see L.A. Wood, *A History of Farmers' Movements in Canada* [1924] (Toronto: University of Toronto Press, 1975), chap. xx.

1. The Canadian Manufacturers' Association will be clamouring for more protection. That organization has set itself out to oppose every demand made by organized labor. For the time being, therefore, organized labor will sink its individual opinions and give special heed to the 'class' legislation sought by the Canadian Manufacturers' Association in tariff matters.

2. The Canadian Manufacturers' Association will seek an increase in the tariff. We will oppose any increase. It is not desirable, at the present time, to make any pronouncement upon the relative merits of Free Trade and protection. Our position simply is that *the tariff is now high enough*.

...

5. There is free trade in labor, and protection for the products of labor. *If protection were a good thing for the workman, the Canadian Manufacturers' Association would not be in favor of it*.

6. The Canadian Manufacturers' Association opposed the change in the law that assured to workmen the right of trial by jury.[42]

Item 3 of the statement outlined some reasons for asserting the general position that 'the tariff is now high enough,' while item 4 outlined one or two tactical suggestions for conduct at the commission hearings. It was clear that the committee, unable to find any common ground for a commercial policy proposal, intended to use labour participation in the hearings for a vendetta against the CMA. Most member organizations seem to have responded to the leaflet by staying severely away from the Fielding Commission. Those that did make presentations hardly bolstered the TLC case.

Simpson and O'Donoghue made an heroic attempt to argue their position for no changes of any kind in the tariff, and O'Donoghue in particular made a strong case for the view that the tariff reduced working Canadians' standard of living, although the question of whether there would be work to be found in the absence of protection was left hanging. But their position was, in the final analysis, an untenable one on principle. As a matter of expediency, it might have served the Commission very well to be able to decide that no changes were desirable or necessary, given the antipodal stances of farmers and manufacturers – and, indeed, Fielding did eventually split the difference and introduce an 'intermediate' tariff schedule in 1907. The TLC position was almost explicitly an expedient one, for no other construction could really be

---

42 The proceedings of the Fielding Tariff Inquiry Commission, 1905–6, are preserved in transcript form in the first ten volumes of [PAC] RG36, ser. 17; henceforth, *Fielding transcripts*. The *TLC* presentation is in vol. 3, 433–64.

placed on the contention in its circular that 'it is not desirable, at the present time, to make any pronouncement upon the relative merits of Free Trade and protection.' But while this position did not amount to a declaration of principle by the TLC – and any such declaration would unquestionably have split the organization, perhaps into the 'two congresses' which Ellis had so desired – it did amount to something that could be perhaps equally effective in uniting the labour forces, a declaration of war on the CMA.

If the manufacturers lost ground in the face of concerted farm opposition, it was because their own organizational coherence was weakened by diffuse self-interests. Each manufacturer wanted more protection for his end-products and lower tariffs on his raw materials, semi-manufactured inputs, and capital items. The problem was that one Canadian manufacturer's input was not infrequently another Canadian manufacturer's output, so that while all could agree to lower tariffs on items which could not be produced or substituted for in Canada there was a wide range of disagreement on what commodities ought to receive more protection. The few TLC member organizations which did appear before the commission took stands very similar to those of the manufacturers. They wanted more protection for the products of their labour and less for both items of consumption and raw materials and tools. Thus the Cigarmakers International Union seconded its members' employers and opposed the farmers in protesting against a higher tariff on American leaf tobacco, arguing that Canadian tobacco was of such low quality that nobody would buy cigars made from it, so that a tariff increase would mean that the industry would have to keep importing US leaf at higher cost, and unemployment and depressed wages would result. Besides, some pointed out, workers smoked a lot of cigars. The Cigarmakers was the only union to pull its locals out in force, but scattered locals and labour councils elsewhere also made presentations.

A group of carpet weavers in Guelph called for more protection against imported carpets as this would make for steady work, and they were supported by the local labour council. The Guelph TLC also called for lower duties on mechanics' tools, the raising of the duty on cream separators – a local product – to the same level as other agricultural implements, and higher duties on cut and dressed building stone since imports had 'throwed all our stone-cutters out of an awful lot of employment.' It wanted the 'absolute necessaries of life' put on the free list. Fielding exploited the discrepancy between this presentation and that of the TLC, and in response the leader of the delegation quoted the TLC circular in his defence! 'I beg to state to you

Honorable Gentlemen, all these articles may be in opposition to what I or somebody else may think, but this is the consenssus [sic] of opinion from a general vote of the eight hundred union members in the city of Guelph. We have to sink our personal feelings on this matter. This is the order that this committee got from the Head Body.'

The supreme irony came, however, in Toronto, where James Simpson's own union, the Typographical, came out for a higher tariff on typeset work. Once again the Commissioners exploited the divergence from the official TLC position, and John Armstrong, representing the TTU, told them that 'If the Dominion Trade Congress had taken a referendum of the working class in the great centres of industry they would have been in the interests of an increased tariff.' He went on, in effect, to disown Simpson: 'A great many of those in these labor organizations represent only themselves, not the bodies that sent them here ... We can speak for the Body to which we belong, the Typographical Union.'[43]

The TLC's strategy for the tariff commission had not been an unqualified success, so it is not surprising that when the 1906 convention received a formal request from the Farmers' Association to endorse a resolution condemning protectionism as 'a prolific source of political corruption and moral degradation of our national life, as well as unjust to the great masses of the Canadian people,' it chose not to act.[44] The TLC never again used an attack on the tariff to press its opposition to unrestricted immigration. In 1907, it complained about the highly protected steel industry's refusal to tender on civic contracts which included 'fair wage' clauses, but it did not attack the steel tariffs or bounties per se.[45] In 1909 and again in 1910 the stone-cutters requested Congress support for a higher tariff on cut stone, but the TLC first refused them, and then merely instructed its Executive to 'take early notice of the stone-cutters' complaint with a view of suggesting to the Government an appropriate remedy for the evils complained of.'[46] The TLC would not – in all likelihood, could not – take a firm position on the tariff.

In 1911, an enraged J.B. McLachlan, faced with organizing for the United Mine Workers in Nova Scotia against the opposition of both the Dominion Iron and Steel Company and the Provincial Workmen's Association, managed to get a resolution through protesting the renewal of Dosco's bounties

---

43 *Fielding transcripts*, vol. 7, 140f, and *infra*; vol. 4, 567ff, 676ff, 685; vol. 2, 756ff, 762
44 *TLC* 1906, 53
45 *Ibid.*, 1907, 10
46 *Ibid.*, 1909, 92; 1910, 80f. A similar resolution presented in 1911 was referred to the Executive Committee: *TLC* 1911, 84.

pending an investigation of conditions at the company, but this was as far as the TLC was willing to go. The Congress refused to adopt any position on reciprocity that year, 'on account of the fact that the acceptance or rejection of this clause would mean an endorsation of either the Liberal or Conservative parties, and in our opinion such action would not be in the best interests of this Congress, as the question at present is not one of principles, but a political party issue.'[47] Faced with internal dissension and the weaknesses of a position based purely on retaliation, the TLC had abdicated its claim to speak for the working-class interest in economic policy.

IV

Conflicts between the TLC and the CMA over a number of issues told against their collaboration on the tariff. Both organizations represented *industrial* interests, but at the same time they were *class* organizations, and in the specific conjuncture of turn-of-the-century commercial policy the parties to industry found more to set them apart than to bring them together. At the same time it must be noted that the issues agitating the CMA and the TLC were to some extent removed from the unceasing quotidian struggles of particular employers and groups of workers over wages, conditions of work, and union recognition. The TLC confronted the CMA most frequently not as its antagonist in the day-to-day conflict of capital and labour, but as a competitor for the favours of the state. The TLC seemed usually to view the state – by which it more often than not meant the government – as being properly an honest broker operating on a principle of 'fairness,' while the CMA conceived of it as the guardian and promoter of the community's larger interests. Thus the TLC's repeated requests for the establishment of government labour bureaux at the provincial and federal levels were predicated on the argument that other groups in the economy had their Departments of Agriculture and Bureaux of Industry, so that it was only fair that labour should receive equivalent recognition. Similarly, the argument that whatever protection manufacturers might receive in commercial policy should be extended to labour in immigration policy flowed from this same perception of the state's role as the guarantor of equitable treatment to all groups in the economy.

The CMA, on the other hand, supported its claim for a higher tariff with the argument that a prosperous manufacturing sector was in the greater national interest, and it attacked those policies which it disliked with the label

47 *Ibid.*, 1911, 86, 91

'class legislation.'[48] The CMA could afford to condemn special-interest legislation only so long as it could successfully maintain the identification of its own special interests with those of the nation as a whole. While these two models of the state could overlap considerably they were clearly not identical. To stretch a point, the bias of the first was towards legitimation, and of the second towards accumulation. The first reflected the lingering presence of pre-market values in the labour movement, while the second marked to some degree the confidence of a business class which had crossed the watershed to 'modernity.'

The bias towards legitimation inherent in the TLC's model of the state flowed from the conservative implications of the notion of fairness. Of course, fairness *per se* need not amount to the silent acknowledgment of the justice or inevitability of existing social arrangements. A broad conception of equitable social relations would imply a radical restructuring of society, but only a tiny minority of the Canadian labour movement at the turn of the century placed this construction upon the term. When workers crossed the first watershed, the democratic egalitarianism of the 'rights of man' paled before the distinction they came increasingly to make between their labour power and their existence as citizens; with the second watershed, market valuations of that commodity replaced customary criteria of a fair day's work and a fair day's pay. The first transition had been to acquiescence in the permanence of their status as wage workers, and this implied significant constraints on the range of meanings 'fairness' could bear. It implied acceptance of an employment hierarchy, so that equity came to mean not the equality of worker and employer – this was reserved for the rights of citizenship, equality before the law, the 'rights of every free-born British subject' – but fair treatment *within* the fundamentally inegalitarian social structure. As the new managerial practices reverberated within the labour movement, the AFL and, by extension, the TLC looked first to safeguard the positions of their members within the employment hierarchy, by reaffirming craft principles. The

---

48 The use of this term was for the most part restricted to businessmen. When labour organizations like the TLC used it, it was usually to satirize the CMA. The range of its applicability as an invidious epithet was wider than one might think. For example, retail merchants attacked the introduction of cheap parcel post in 1910 as 'class legislation' because 'the system of government parcels post will allow the large department stores to send their parcels all over the country at a uniform low rate as letters are now sent, the government standing sponsor and footing the deficit ... Ostensibly the reason is given out that this parcels post movement is for the benefit of the public, but a little consideration will show that it is rather a benefit for the few against the many – the few department stores in the large cities against the many merchants in the smaller centres scattered throughout the country.' *Bookseller and Stationer*, XXVI, 12 (Dec. 1910) 5f

market model involved a new burden for the notion of fairness, but this amounted for the most part to a change in the method of computing the constituents of a fair day's work for a fair day's pay, rather than a challenge to the basic principle of structured inequality. Indeed, an emphasis on making a fair bargain in the market place reaffirmed the legitimacy of the existing economic order, without raising complementary questions about distinctions between employer and worker.

This analysis may be clarified by relating it to the question of 'fair wages,' a question that in any case deserves investigation for its importance to the Canadian labour movement at the turn of the century and its implications for the development of federal labour policy. The distinction between fairness and equity as it arises in this context was illuminated by G.D.H. Cole:

The whole intrusion of the concept of 'equity' into the determination of wages gives rise to very difficult problems. There is a clear and admitted case in equity for the abolition of sweating, and therefore in sweated trades no great difficulty arises; but as soon as any attempt is made to apply the principle of equity to the whole of industry we are absolutely without a common standard ... That some labour is robbed everyone will admit; but any attempt to regulate wages as a whole raises the pertinent and searching question whether *all* labour is robbed. It stands, in fact, at the parting of the ways of revolution and reform.[49]

We know that Mackenzie King, in directing attention to abuses of the industrial system rather than to the question whether that system was itself abusive, chose the road of reform in this matter. But so did the labour movement. The fair-wages policy which it endorsed was one that provided for the inclusion in contracts let out by governments to private firms of a clause insisting that employees be paid the prevailing or union rates of wages in the vicinity. For the labour movement, this had several implications. As an attack on the sweating system and on substandard wage rates it might benefit the working class as a whole. It was of specific benefit to trade unions which would no longer have to fear the competition of underpaid non-union workers on these jobs. It harked back, as well, to the craft unions' pre-market emphasis on the 'standard rate.'[50] But at the same time, it affirmed what Hyman and Brough, following Lockwood, call the 'conservative'

49 Quoted in Richard Hyman and Ian Brough, *Social Values and Industrial Relations* (Oxford: Blackwell, 1975), 10n
50 Cf. Sidney and Beatrice Webb, *Industrial Democracy* [1897, 1920] (New York: Kelley, 1965), chap. v.

notion of fair wages: 'those wages are considered fair which "maintain a group's position within the hierarchy and the hierarchy's position within the wider society."'[51] Employees performing a given kind of work on government contract ought, in fairness, to receive wages equivalent to those being paid for the same kind of work in the private sector. Moreover, the provision for comparisons within the local vicinity further curtailed the scope of equity, reflecting the market emphasis in labour's developing ideology. What is fair for these workers in this area is what other workers in the area have been able to achieve in the local labour market; and the partial removal of government contract work from market constraints ought not to affect this equivalence of wage rates.

Thus the notion of fairness implicit in demands of this sort embraced the essential legitimacy of the capitalist social order, and in meeting them the state would be both reaffirming that legitimacy and fostering the image of itself as umpire. For manufacturers, King had interpreted the anti-sweating initiative as the removal of obstacles to the fuller development of an industrial economy. Moreover, unionized employers in the clothing industry would no longer be at a competitive disadvantage in bidding for government contracts, and the impetus to factory industry that would follow from the prohibition of sweating reinforced the CMA's conception of progress and the place of the modern manufacturer in its van. Government spokesmen played on these themes when they introduced the reform.

Shortly after his conversation with King in the summer of 1897, Postmaster-General Mulock announced the introduction of an anti-sweating clause in post office uniform and mail bag contracts. He characterized his action as a measure 'to protect the wage-earner and the honest employer,' and argued that 'if there is a basic condition that the wages to be paid to the workmen under the contract shall not be less than the current wages paid in the district to the competent workmen it appears to me that that condition both protects the workmen and also enables the honest, fair-minded tenderer to compete ...' He added, as a final justification if one were needed, that the British House of Commons had already taken similar steps. A week later, the Prime Minister turned to this theme in a speech at the Toronto Board of Trade's annual banquet, emphasizing the 'citizenship' aspects of the question to loud applause:

Fair work deserves fair wages, and a fair wage for fair work is the birthright of every Canadian. (Hear, hear.) Unfortunately, there has grown up in some of our cities a

51 Hyman and Brough, *Social Values*, 10

system called the sweating system, which is an injury and a shame and a blot on the fair name of Canada ... I do not want to see that system of white slavery to which I have referred prevail in Canada. (Hear, hear.) We want every man in Canada to work, and certainly it is the birthright of every Canadian to receive fair wages for honest work. But you will ask what has this question to do in such an audience as this? It has everything to do in such an audience as this, because there is a solidarity in all class [sic] of our community, and I am glad to have the opportunity of enlisting the sympathies of the business men of the City of Toronto in this question, and that is the reason why I bring it before you.[52]

He went on to state 'that there is no class of men who can give such valuable advice to the Government as the business men of the country ... They know how to advance, and they know when advancing how to avoid the dangers which always beset the path of change and reform,' but it is worth noting that Laurier, too, went out of his way to assure his audience that 'we have not acted on our own initiative' in introducing the fair wages reform: 'We have acted on the example of the mother land.'

After testing the waters with the Post Office and then the Militia Department, and finding few unfavourable eddies, the government proceeded to broaden the application of its new-found principle. In 1900, an election year, Mulock introduced a resolution in the House, 'that all government contracts should contain such conditions as will prevent abuses' such as sweating.[53] His argument was instructive: he began by insisting that 'the principles enunciated in this resolution are ... eminently fair and just,' and 'have already received sanction and adoption by the English House of Commons.' He went on to provide a hard-nosed economic analysis based in the theory of common interest: 'It is the best policy, leaving aside the humanitarian view of it altogether. It is better for the workmen, for high wages enable him to supply himself with more of the necessaries, more of the comforts, more of the luxuries of life. This is better for the country also, as it stimulates the consumption of manufactured goods of all kinds. Higher wages benefit not only him who receives but him who gives, and they benefit not only the parties directly concerned, but the whole community.'[54]

The labour movement was highly pleased with the passage of this resolution, the more so when a prominent trade unionist, Daniel O'Donoghue, was appointed to enforce it. In the years that followed, the TLC attempted with varying success to widen the range of the policy to provincial and

52 Toronto *Globe*, 30 Sept. 1897, 7 Oct. 1897
53 *LG*, Sept. 1900, 15
54 *Debates* (1900), 2469

municipal governments and to work done by companies receiving government aid of one kind or another, but it did not seek to amend the fundamental principles involved.[55] The state had acted in the interests of fairness, albeit narrowly conceived, and that was all that was expected of it.

The demand for fair wages and an end to sweating was a limited demand, and one that could be conceded without transgressing market relations – it was 'abuses,' after all, that were to be removed – or disconcerting 'responsible' employers. Laurier's government sought to deal with other labour demands in a similar fashion, although not always so successfully. For example, the long-standing grievance over low-wage immigration was met with the passage of the Alien Labour Act in 1897, prohibiting the importation of foreign workers under contract. The operation of the Act, however, was restricted so as 'to apply only to such foreign countries as have enacted and retained in force laws or ordinances applying to Canada of a character similar to it.'[56] 'Fairness' of a sort was involved here, but of course it did not meet labour's demand for protection equivalent to that afforded manufacturers. The oriental countries which supplied the great bulk of the contract labour to which Canadian trade unionists objected were hardly likely to legislate against the importation of Canadians on contract, so what the TLC viewed as the greatest evil went unremedied. The Act was designed to retaliate against US legislation, which in turn had originally been enacted to keep Orientals imported into Canada out of the American labour market; even given this limited and retaliatory intent, the TLC had continually to complain that the statute was inadequately enforced.[57] In the Alien Labour Act, two principles of equity came into conflict. Equitable conditions in the international labour market were assured, in the government's view, by providing for equivalent terms of trade between countries. The TLC remained dissatisfied because for it equity meant according the same treatment to the commodity labour as to other commodities in the general context of commercial policy. If labour was a commodity like any other, then it should receive the protection accorded to others.[58]

55 *TLC* 1900, 9; 1901, 13, 17f, 37, 38ff, 51, 78; 1902, 23, 26; 1904, 19, 33; 1905, 63f; 1906, 54, 78; 1907, 51, 65, 72f; 1908, 13, 20, 70f, 74, 86f, 87; 1909, 20, 22, 71, 93; 1910, 81; 1911, 18

56 *LG*, Sept. 1900, 26

57 *TLC* 1897, 7, 8, 21; 1898, 29; 1899, 7, 9; 1900, 7, 10; 1901, 7, 37, 15; 1902, 22, 26, 28, 29, 67; 1903, 12, 17, 58; 1904, 8, 34, 42f, 54; 1905, 12, 44, 47; 1906, 9, 43, 45, 57f; 1908, 24, 69, 84f; 1909, 10, 53f; 1910, 51, 73 (where the Act is described as a 'farce'); 1911, 57, 87

58 For the extent to which European immigrants entered the industrial labour market, see Donald Avery, 'Continental European Immigrant Workers in Canada 1896–1919: From "Stalwart Peasants" to Radical Proletariat,' *CRSA*, vol. 12, 1 (Feb. 1975)

The demand for a government bureau of labour statistics was based on similar grounds. There were departments of industry and of agriculture; the third great economic interest should, in justice, be granted equivalent recognition. Early experience with a labour bureau in British Columbia suggested that the usefulness of such an agency would depend on the sympathies of its staff. In 1895, Vancouver's labour council complained to the TLC convention that 'the department of British Columbia has not proved a success, because the people have not faith in it. If this kind of legislation is to benefit workingmen the government must be in sympathy with the masses.' 'The fact being that "all laws do not bear equally upon capital and labour," we are constrained to suggest as an expedient two separate sections be created in the government department of labor statistics – one in the interest of employers, and the other the employed. Because, as it is now, both parties have not confidence in each other.'[59] But this was carrying equity to unreasonable lengths, so when the TLC urged the formation of a federal bureau in the following year, it recommended that 'it be placed under a competent person having the confidence of the working people.' The federal Tories had prefaced the election of 1891 with the passage of 'An Act to provide for the collection and publishing of Labour Statistics' (1890, c.15), but after their victory its usefulness was no longer evident to the government. Following the Laurier victory in 1896, the labour movement began to bring renewed pressure to bear for its implementation. 'The great value of reliable data of this character is beyond computation,' president Carey told the 1897 TLC convention, 'and in the matter of securing and publishing such statistics as were contemplated in the schedule to that Act, Canada is far behind most other civilized countries.' The following year, the convention reaffirmed this demand, making it 'an imperative order' to the officers of the Congress that they press it upon the dominion government.[60]

This, again, was something the Liberals could concede, the more so since the collection of adequate wage statistics was a necessary concomitant to the enforcement of the Fair Wages Resolution. 'Fair wages schedules' had to be inserted in government contracts, and these required a knowledge of prevailing wage rates for various occupations in numerous localities. Shortly after O'Donoghue's appointment as Fair Wages Officer, the government introduced the Conciliation Act, 'to aid in the prevention and settlement of trade disputes and the publication of statistical industrial information.'[61] This was

---

59 A list of labour bureaux published in the *Second Report* of the Ontario Bureau of Labor (1901, 15) does not include a BC department.
60 *TLC* 1896, 6; 1897, 7; 1898, 27
61 *Debates* (1900), 8399

to kill two birds with a single, originally rather modest, stone. It would meet labour's long-standing demand for a representative department, now rendered necessary by the government's fair wages policy, and it would go part of the way towards meeting that other even more frequently pressed demand, compulsory arbitration. Some form of state intervention in strikes was necessitated by their increasing frequency and severity, and a policy of voluntary conciliation could be safely introduced in the wake of a British precedent of 1896.[62] In introducing the Act, Mulock harped monotonously on the English experience, and quoted copiously from respected authorities in that country. In practice, Canadian conciliation was to differ substantially from its imperial parent, but at the time of its introduction that could not be foretold. The development of conciliation is discussed in the next chapter; what is important here is that labour's demand for a department of its own at the federal level was granted. But even this was not enough; no sooner had the Act been passed than the TLC decided to lobby the government to make it a separate department with its own responsible minister.[63] This goal was finally achieved in 1909.

The TLC achieved at least partial success in the majority of its demands on the Laurier government. It did not win compulsory arbitration but, as we have seen, it abandoned that plank in 1902. Some important measures, like the Union Label Bill, were defeated by active CMA lobbying in the Senate after having passed through the Commons, but the TLC was not inclined to blame the government for these reverses. It won the fair wages policy on government contracts, although not on bonused industries or public employment. Its demand for restricted immigration was inadequately served by the Alien Labour Act, but the rate of oriental immigration was later slowed when Laurier sent King to negotiate restrictions with the Chinese, Japanese, and Indian governments, although it took race riots in Vancouver to convince the government of the advisability of this course.[64] It achieved a Royal Commission on technical education in 1910, although here its lobbying was complemented by that of the CMA. It acquired its 'own' department of government whose responsible Minister and staff were men both 'competent' and 'having the confidence of the working people,' at least so far as the TLC could see. On these issues, and on others, the government may have moved

---

62 For the English Act and its application in various industries, see Elizabeth Brunner, 'The Origins of Industrial Peace: The Case of the British Boot and Shoe Industry,' *Oxford Economic Papers*, new series, vol. 1 (1949), and A.J. Odber, 'The Origins of Industrial Peace: The Manufactured Iron Trade of the North of England,' *ibid.*, vol. 3 (1951).
63 *TLC* 1901, 81; 1906, 55; 1907, 55; 1908, 18
64 See Dawson, 151ff.

slowly and not quite as decisively as might have been wished, but it had moved. This success rate was due as much to the moderation of labour's demands, founded in its principle of equity and its conception of the role of the state, as to the eagerness of the government to gain and hold labour support. But the government was eager to do this, especially since so much could be accomplished with so little, and Mackenzie King in particular grasped the importance of this point.

V

So long as the labour movement identified the state with the government and made demands which the government for the most part was willing to concede, the legitimacy of the state was hardly threatened. There were revolutionary socialists in the labour movement, to be sure, and they viewed the state in larger terms as an instrument of oppression in the hands of the capitalist class, but they were a small and ineffective minority within the TLC, and it was to the Congress that the government looked for an expression of labour's views. Other institutions in the state system also had importance for the labour movement, but the movement did not identify them as part of the state – except, of course, the Senate. The TLC never abandoned its commitment to winning the abolition of that body. But it had made its mark on the administrative apparatus in acquiring its own department, and it persisted in seeing it as a department that could and would operate in labour's interest. The coercive apparatus, the militia and the RNWMP, only received the TLC's attention when the question of their intervention in labour disputes arose, and it tended to accept their exercise of the police power in the majority of instances. Labour's experience with the provincial and municipal governments is a subject too large to be adequately treated here, but the most common grievance was that while provincial governments were frequently willing to put parts of labour's programme on the statute books, they were far less interested in enforcing the legislation. 'Of the scores of laws now on the Statute Books of Ontario,' the provincial executive told the TLC in 1897, 'many of them are dead to those in whose interests they were passed. Your Committee would urge the Congress to see to the carrying out of laws already in existence instead of asking for new ones,' and this complaint was to be echoed in subsequent years.[65] Aside from the Senate, the institution in the state system which posed the greatest stumbling block to the labour

65 *TLC* 1897, 10

movement in the first decade of the century was the one which appeared most independent of the government, the judiciary.

Apart from the Trade Union Act and the criminal code amendments of the 1870s, trade union law in Canada had been largely neglected by the legislatures. In the absence of statute law, the judge-made common law held the field, and even where statutory provisions existed, as in the area of picketing, their terms were often so vague as to leave ample scope for the most various judicial interpretations. For all the governmental recognition the labour movement had achieved in the formation of labour bureaux and departments, the courts still viewed trade-union law as an undifferentiated form of the law of contract, and trade unions remained associations unrecognized by law. The consequence was an apparent contradiction between legislative intent and judicial interpretation, an inconsistency within the state system between progressive reforms and conservative doctrine. In effect, public policy in the labour field was far from coextensive with legislative pronouncements, so that there was a wide discrepancy between the position the unions were able to occupy in their lobbying efforts and that in which they found themselves before the courts.

In general, such poorness of fit follows from the uneven development of institutions in a changing society, and to the extent that the transformation is rapid and relatively abrupt the fit will be particularly poor. This, of course, explains why social revolutions are typically accompanied by codification of the law on new principles, and why statutory activity in particular institutional areas tends to come in bursts. Industrial growth and trade union development at the turn of the century yielded unprecedented legislative returns in a number of areas of importance to the labour movement, but trade-union law itself was scarcely affected. Ironically, the constitutional safeguard of judicial independence provided a justification for the maintenance of reactionary doctrine at this level of the state structure. To the extent that the courts were not identified with the state in the trade unions' ideology, the discrepancy between the apparent attitude of the government and the all too real one of the judiciary as a whole did not threaten the legitimacy of the state. But every major attack on the labour movement by the courts increased the potential for such a crisis. It finally came, as we shall see, in 1911, when an unfavourable and in all likelihood unwarranted interpretation of the Industrial Disputes Investigation Act in a Nova Scotia court convinced the TLC, at least hesitantly, that legislature and judiciary bore some organic connection, and it responded by demanding the repeal of the Act, thus repudiating, in effect, the legitimacy of Liberal labour policy.

Before 1911, governments in Canada sought to tinker as little as possible with the machinery of trade-union law, but in attempting to postpone the crisis of legitimacy some minor tinkering proved necessary.[66]

One interesting case which occurred early in our period might serve as an illustration of some of these points. The facts are somewhat obscure, and no official court report has been located, but the story can be pieced together from discussions in the TLC *Proceedings*. It appears that in 1899 the notorious Montreal cigar manufacturer, J.M. Fortier, was annoyed by the publication in a local newspaper of a story on his use of child labour at substandard wages. Fortier had been burned once before by a scandal of this sort, and he had no intention of permitting the old tales to be told once more. He laid criminal libel charges against four members of the Cigarmakers Union and the publisher of the newspaper, and they were duly arrested. In court, the five sought to defend their case by proving the truth of their allegations, but the prosecution countered with the claim that this plea could not stand since the matter was not in the public interest. A plea of justification in a libel suit may only be heard if it is ruled that the matter of the alleged libel is one of public interest; if not, the truth of the allegation is held to be irrelevant to the question whether a libel has been committed. When the TLC met in convention in 1899, the case was still in progress, and when a motion was put supporting the defendants on the grounds that 'when an employer of child labor does not pay wages enough in return for the labor given him, it is of public interest that the community of large be made acquainted with the methods employed by him in the running of his business,' it was defeated. But when the convention reassembled the following year, the case had progressed further. This time the TLC adopted a resolution which explicitly pointed to the discrepancy between judicial interpretation and broad legislative intent:

Whereas, in the J.M. Fortier libel case, Judge Wurtell, in his address to the jury, devoted the greater part of his remarks to showing that labor difficulties such as existed between J.M. Fortier and the Cigar Makers Union, 58, of Montreal, were not matters of public interest under the law, and that therefore the criticism of Fortier's conduct complained of were, even if true, unjustifiable; and whereas the Federal Government has since passed a Conciliation and Arbitration Act which practically affirms to labor difficulties being matters of public interest; therefore be it resolved,

66 Some of the problems surrounding 'the politics of the judiciary' were the subject of an interesting and extended controversy in the *Times Literary Supplement*, 6 Jan. 1978, and subsequent issues.

That this Congress instruct its executive to ask the Government to amend the libel Act so as to embody this principle and thus prevent the possibility of hostile judges arguing that no plea of justification by public interest cannot [sic] be admitted in the criticism of a person's conduct in industrial affairs.[67]

There is no indication that the government complied with this request, but notice had been served that legislative action in one area of labour's concerns would be taken to have ramifications for others.

Canadian trade unionists considered their situation with one eye on the United States, the homeland of their unions, and another on Britain, the homeland of their law. They sought to anticipate the application of legal strategies devised by employers in those countries to Canada, and their record of success in this was mixed. Three new developments in particular worried the Canadians. In the United States, the anti-trust law was being used to harass unions on the old grounds that they were in restraint of trade, and the use of *ex parte* injunctions to prohibit picketing, boycotts, and other union tactics was increasing rapidly.[68] In Britain, the Taff Vale judgment meant that while for most purposes trade unions had no legal personality and therefore could neither sue nor be sued, their assets might still be vulnerable in damage suits.[69]

In 1900, when the anti-trust issue arose, Canada had no legislation comparable to the Sherman Act. There was a provision in the criminal code outlawing conspiracies in restraint of trade although, as Bliss has pointed out, it amounted to nothing more than a restatement of existing common law.[70] The common law provisions which were restated in the codification were those against which the 1872 Act had granted protection to the unions, so that the statute effectively if unintentionally repealed the Trade Union Act. Through the Winnipeg labour member, A.W. Puttee, the TLC managed to have the code amended to provide that 'nothing in this section shall be construed to apply to combinations of workmen or employees for their own reasonable protection as such workmen or employees.' Once the

---

67 *TLC* 1899, 21; 1900, 26
68 For trade union law in the United States, see, *inter alia*, Commons and Andrews, *Principles of Labor Legislation*, and Nicholas S. Falcone, *Labor Law* (New York: Wiley, 1962).
69 For trade union law in Britain, see, *inter alia*, Pritt, *Employers, Workers and Trade Unions*, and K.W. Wedderburn, *The Worker and the Law* (Harmondsworth: Penguin, 1965)
70 Michael Bliss, 'Another Anti-Trust Tradition: Canadian Anti-Combines Policy, 1889–1910,' in Glenn Porter and R.D. Cuff, eds., *Enterprise and National Development: Essays in Canadian Business and Economic History* (Toronto: Hakkert, 1973)

problem had been pointed out the labour movement encountered stiff opposition from the usual place: '[Puttee's subsection] was introduced and adopted by the Commons, three times rejected by the Senate, and was only finally concurred in by that body when it became apparent that there [sic] own bill would fail to get the sanction of the Commons and be killed by non-concurrence.'[71] Ten years later, when King introduced his Combines Investigation Act, he 'cordially assented' to a TLC request that a clause protecting unions from its provisions be inserted.[72] The labour movement won its demand for exemption from anti-trust legislation, but what it really achieved was nothing more than the reaffirmation of the law of 1872.

The labour movement's first encounters with the problem of injunctions were connected with the Trade Union Act's companion legislation, the law on picketing contained in the Criminal Code Amendment Acts. In 1900, the TLC executive was instructed by the convention to seek federal legislation clarifying the intent of the law on picketing, 'inasmuch as the judges of Canadian courts differ very much in their interpretation of the terms "watching and besetting".' When this demand was presented to the government, Puttee explained 'that an alteration was wanted in the law so that there could be no reason for the issue of injunctions under it forbidding men on strike or lockout for [sic] doing perfectly legal acts.' In 1902, the BC unions reported to the TLC that they had been successful in having a provincial law passed restricting the issue of injunctions and the granting of damages in civil suits against trade unions. The following year, the Ontario Executive Committee presented a report to the TLC which illustrates the anticipatory character of much of this concern:

The past year has amply demonstrated the necessity for legislation restraining the granting of injunctions. In the United States the powers of the Courts, with respect to injunctions, have been so exercised as to make the administration of justice in this regard a farce. Unless some restraining influence be imposed at once in Ontario, the same wretched conditions will soon prevail here. The Courts during the past year have been flooded with cases involving disputes between capital and labor, and while the unions and working people involved have been very successful, at the same time the conditions are abnormal and tend to unduly accentuate the unfortunate differences existing between capital and labor. Your Committee recommend a strong

71 *TLC* 1900, 11
72 *Ibid.*, 1910, 54

effort for the enactment of anti-injunction legislation on the lines of that in force in British Columbia.[73]

The convention considered the establishment of a 'National Law Bureau and Defense Fund' to combat 'the growing disposition on the part of the employers of labor in Canada to use the aid of the law courts and the injunction to crush and defeat the honest efforts of individual workingmen and trade unions to better their conditions,' and decided to hold a referendum on the matter. In 1904, when the convention met to discuss the outcome of the canvass, it learned that the Gurney Foundry Company of Toronto had acquired an injunction against the Metal Polishers' Union, the Toronto District Labor Council, and the latter's newspaper, the *Toiler*, and was seeking $60,000 in damages. President Flett reported that the referendum had been almost unanimously in favour of the establishment of a law fund and the retention of a permanent solicitor. The following year, the convention complained again about the vagueness of trade-union law, and in 1906 the age of the injunction was declared arrived:

The evil of government by injunction has become so great and so oppressive that the strongest efforts should be made to secure anti-injunction legislation. In Winnipeg, Toronto and elsewhere this instrument of oppression has been particularly in evidence, and if working men are to be cautioned and urged to respect the law, the Judges must be placed by legislation, if they will not do it of themselves, in a position where they must recognize that working men have rights as well as employers. The judges are rapidly losing the respect of the public in this matter, and it is time our legislators pointed out by positive enactments what the rights and duties of the public are. Nothing is so much needed as a categorical determination of the rights and duties of labor and capital in connection with trade disputes.[74]

This new, if still incipient, crisis of legitimacy was fostered by two additional areas of grievance. One, the implications of the Taff Vale ruling, will be discussed presently, but first another must be canvassed: the occurrence of one or two instances of flagrant judicial prejudice against workers that necessarily offended the TLC's acute, if limited, sense of fair play. The first took place in Toronto, where police magistrate Denison, true to his practice of dispensing quick and 'common sense' justice in the court over which he

---

73 *Ibid.*, 1900, 26, 13; 1902, 40, 55; 1903, 26
74 *TLC* 1903, 43, 64f; 1904, 52, 10; 1905, 16; 1906, 9f

was to preside until the age of 82,[75] refused to allow some trade unionists to elect trial by jury. The 1905 TLC convention complimented Denison warmly on his general performance as a magistrate by way of preface to the rebuke that, in taking advantage of a 'so-called ambiguity in the law,' 'he was depriving citizens of one of their greatest rights.'[76] The moderation of this comment was due, first, to the fact that the unions had received welcome justice from Denison's hands on other occasions, when he had convicted delinquent members of charges brought against them by their unions, and, second, because the TLC had managed, against stiff opposition from the CMA, to have its complaint rectified by Act of Parliament. The second instance took place at Stratford, also in 1905, when in criminal and civil charges laid against strikers by the Grand Trunk, the same lawyer was permitted to act as Crown Prosecutor in the criminal trials and as the company's solicitor in the civil ones. The convention requested a change in the Ontario law to make such situations impossible.[77] Events like these threatened to impair the image of the courts a impartial dispensers of justice under the law, and could contribute to a challenge to the legitimacy of the state were the government to fail to respond adequately to such self-evidently justified grievances. The government, as the guardian of equitable treatment, did respond, in the first instance at least, and it is noteworthy that the TLC then redirected its indignation towards its competitor in the lobbies, the CMA. The Congress's anti-tariff indictment, it will be recalled, was to condemn the manufacturers for their opposition to this legal reform in its final particular.

But more important by far were the implications of the Taff Vale decision of 1902 which threatened, as Ralph Smith told the Berlin convention, to make 'the trade unions subject to actions by employers, and placed the funds of the unions in a very dangerous position, especially if these actions came before special juries, which were selected from a class of the community higher than the class from which the common juries were selected.'[78] Two issues had arisen in the case brought by the Taff Vale Railway Company against the Amalgamated Society of Railway Servants for an injunction against picketing. The first was whether a trade union could be sued for tort so as to make its assets liable, and the second was whether a trade union, still devoid of legal personality, could be sued in its own name. The trial judge ruled in favour of the company; his decision was reversed by a Court of Appeal; the

75 Cf. David Gagan, *The Denison Family of Toronto, 1792–1925* (Toronto: University of Toronto Press, 1973), 64f
76 *TLC* 1905, 14
77 *Ibid.*, 58f
78 *Ibid* 1902, 16

House of Lords then restored the first judgment, and henceforth the position of the law was, first, that unions could be enjoined against the performance by their members of many of the actions necessary to the successful prosecution of strikes, and, second, that their assets were liable to seizure in civil suits by employers. This amounted to the reinstatement of the legal vulnerability that the Trade Union Act had been designed to alleviate, and the Webbs criticized the decision as an instance of class domination:

There has seldom been an instance in which a judicial decision has so completely and extensively reversed the previous legal opinions, and – we do not hesitate to say – the conscious intention, thirty years before, of Parliament itself ... The real grievance of the Trade Unions, and the serious danger to their continued usefulness and improvement, lies in the uncertainty of the English law, and its liability to be used as a means of oppression. This danger is increased, and the grievance aggravated, by the dislike of Trades Unionism and strikes which nearly all judges and juries share with the rest of the upper and middle classes ... Under the influence of this adverse bias the courts of law have, for the last ten years, been gradually limiting what were supposed to be the legal rights of Trade Unions ... a clear majority of our judges evidently believe, quite honestly, that Trade Unionism ... is anomalous, objectionable, detrimental to English industry, and even a wicked infringement of individual liberty, which Parliament has been foolishly persuaded to take out of the category of crimes ... The result is that Trade Unions must expect to find practically every incident of a strike, and possibly every refusal to work with non-unionists, treated as actionable, and made the subject of suits for damages, which the Trade Union will have to pay from its corporate funds.[79]

The Webbs' indignation was matched by a broadly based popular protest against the decision, and in 1906 the English Parliament responded with the passage of the Trade Disputes Act, largely relieving the unions of their newfound liabilities. The furor over the decision had extremely significant consequences for the state's legitimation problem, and contributed materially to the unions' decision to ally themselves with the nucleus of the Labour party and to the defeat of the government in 1906.[80]

Ralph Smith drew the attention of his TLC colleagues to the British decision in 1902, and indicated that the Congress was already working for a law which would prevent its application in Canada. He suggested that the British Columbia anti-injunction legislation served the purpose, but events were to

---

79 *Industrial Democracy*, xxvi–xxxii
80 Pritt, *Employers, Workers and Trade Unions*, 57

prove this judgment too sanguine. The following year, the Ontario Executive Committee told the convention that it had prepared a draft bill for presentation to the provincial government, 'which provided that no trade union shall be liable for damages for any act of omission or commission, during any labor trouble, unless the union is a consenting party.' Among its purposes, according to Congress solicitor O'Donoghue, was the protection of unions 'from the danger of a decision such as was reached in the Taff Vale case in England.'[81]

Canadian employers were not slow to realize the implications of the British decision. The Gurney case of 1904 has already been mentioned, and the Congress in that year learned of another, one which underlined the limitations of the British Columbia law. President Flett quoted from a newspaper clipping:

Rossland, July 23 – In the action of the Centre Star Company against the Rossland Miners' Union for damages for loss sustained through the strike of 1901, the jury returned a verdict sustaining the suit and assessing the damages at the sum of $12,500 ... The jury found that the Union entered into a conspiracy to prevent men working in the company's mines. The case was heard before Judge Duff and a special jury.[82]

The following year, in the course of its complaint about the inadequate legal definition of the rights and duties of the unions, the TLC's executive climaxed its list of liabilities under the law by pointing out that 'when we surmount all these difficulties we are confronted with that bogey known as conspiracy which is ever-present, all-inclusive, and whose confines are beyond mortal ken.'[83] By 1906, the issues of injunctions, civil liability, and the status of trade unions before the law had culminated in a single case, the litigation brought by the Metallic Roofing Company of Toronto against the Amalgamated Sheet Metal Workers International Alliance, local 30. Unsuccessful in its efforts to gain statutory clarification of trade union law, hampered by the fragmented provincial jurisdictions in civil cases, and heartened by the success of the British labour movement, the TLC decided to tackle a test case of Taff Vale's applicability to Canada, using the common resources of all its affiliates.

The Metallic Roofing Company had taken action against the local union for an injunction to cease picketing and for damages in 1902, hard on the

81 *TLC* 1903, 25
82 *Ibid.*, 1904, 10. The strike is discussed in chapter 7 below.
83 *Ibid.*, 1905, 16

heels of the Taff Vale decision. When the case was heard on appeal in 1905, the Ontario court held that an action against the union in its own name could not be heard, since the union had no personality. But it also ruled that the plaintiff could proceed in a representative action naming the officers of the union as representatives of the whole membership. Moreover, while the trial judge had ruled in 1903 that his court had jurisdiction over the local union but not over the parent international union to which it belonged, the appeal court held that there was jurisdiction as to both bodies. After it assessed the costs of the appeal action against the union, complicated litigation ensued over the vulnerability of the union's various assets to seizure for payment of the judgment.[84] The position which faced the TLC convention in 1906, then, was a complicated one. It had been held that a trade union could be sued in a representative action for the acts of one or more of its members, and it had been held similarly that an international union was liable for the actions of one of its locals. Costs had been assessed, and the question of the exigibility of union funds and property was now before the courts.

The convention established a Special Committee, assisted by the solicitor, to consider the situation and report back at once. It came back with a recommendation that 'an appeal should be carried, if necessary, to the Privy Council. For this purpose your committee recommends a special assessment of 10 cents per head should be levied on the membership of every body affiliated with the Congress.' The convention rejected the proposed compulsory levy, instructing the executive, instead, 'to take the most effective means available to aid the Sheet Metal Workers, financially, in reaching the Privy Council.' The following year, the convention heard a report that voluntary contributions totalling $1492.90 had been collected from labour organizations in amounts ranging from two dollars to three hundred.[85] With Congress solicitor O'Donoghue acting for the union, the case was fought through the Canadian appeal courts to the Judicial Committee of the Privy Council, which ordered a re-trial on procedural grounds without suggesting that the original action had been improperly constituted.[86] The 1908 TLC convention celebrated the 'success' of the appeal and congratulated the 'victors,' but the executive was constrained by the circum-

84 Margaret Mackintosh, *Trade Union Law in Canada* (Ottawa: Department of Labour, January 1935), 35ff
85 *TLC* 1906, 49, 75–6; 1907, 28ff
86 Mackintosh, *Trade Union Law*, 37. The Privy Council ruled that the trial judge had misdirected the jury in stating that 'the calling out of the men on strike by resolutions of the union was an actionable wrong, without regard to motive.' *Jose* vs. *Metallic Roofing* (1908) A.C. 514.

stances of the ruling to add a recommendation 'that local unions throughout Canada be urged to assist the Sheet Metal Workers both morally and financially in the event of it being necessary to continue the fight against the Metallic Roofing Company. Your Executive Council have been advised that the company have taken the necessary procedure to fight the case through to the Privy Council again, if necessary.'[87] In the event, the case was settled out of court and the unions were denied a final judicial determination of their position before the law.

Then, in 1909, a similar case developed in an action taken by the Master Plumbers' Association of Winnipeg against the plumbers' union in that city. Once again, the TLC issued an appeal for funds to carry the case to the Privy Council, and the following year, when leave to appeal had been denied, it issued its strongest condemnation of the law to date:

Whereas, the Courts of Canada do by the misuse of the power of injunction during trades disputes, restraining workmen from doing that which it is lawful for them to do; and whereas, the Plumbers' Union of Winnipeg was forced to disband by the application of the said rule of injunction; and whereas, said Union was denied the right to appeal their case to the Privy Council of Great Britain; and, whereas, such application of the power of injunction deprives citizens of the right of trial by jury; therefore be it resolved, That the Dominion Trades and Labor Congress go on record as being opposed to the system of government by injunction which is being rapidly developed by the employers, and do instruct its Executive to endeavor to have the law amended so as to eliminate this accursed system, or enact a Bill similar to the Trades Disputes Bill of Great Britain.[88]

The TLC had firmly identified its legal disabilities with the class orientation of the courts, a view that the victorious chortling of the CMA in all of these cases did nothing to dispel. Perhaps more dangerously, it had decided to abandon the court system in its search for justice and had now turned unequivocally to government. The federal government did not act, taking refuge behind the civil law provisions of the BNA Act.

By 1911, then, unfavourable judicial decisions had convinced the TLC that the courts could not automatically be expected to rule impartially in labour cases, and the rights of trade unions which, it had believed, were firmly guaranteed by the 1872 legislation were now very much in doubt. The courts were seen to be aligning themselves with employers against the working-

87 *TLC* 1908, 13
88 *Ibid.*, 1909, 88; 1910, 70

class interest, and the government refused to intervene in the interests of fairness. The legitimacy of the state was in question. It is impossible to say whether or to what extent this played a part in the outcome of the 1911 election, but it would be ironic indeed if the Liberals met defeat then for the same failing that had lost them the election in 1872. In that year, the Tories had united the 'industrial classes' under the banner of protection and promised fair treatment to the labour movement in its relation to the criminal law. In 1911, the Liberals once again embraced Reciprocity and failed to extend the Trade Union Act with corresponding guarantees regarding the law of tort. The 'industrial classes' had failed to find common ground during the Laurier regime, as the tariff battle had shown, but those class antagonisms might well have been muted in the election results of 1911 by a peculiar conjunction of circumstances. Manufacturers voted against the Liberals because they appeared to have abandoned the principle of protection. Some trade unionists may have voted against them for the same reason; but the unionists had another reason for opposing the Liberals. In refusing to remedy the legal disabilities of the trade unions, the government had allied itself with what the unions saw as an employer-dominated judicial system. Labour may have voted against the Liberals as a vote against the employers: class collaboration at the polls may have been the consequence of a deeper antagonism of classes than had heretofore been seen. If history repeated itself in 1911, the repetition was a farce indeed.[89]

89 Other, complementary, reasons for the unions' loss of faith in Liberal labour policy by 1911 are developed in chapters 9 and 10.

7
The making of the labour department

The *corporations* are the materialism of the bureaucracy, and the bureaucracy is the *spiritualism* of the corporations ... The same spirit which creates the corporation in society creates the bureaucracy in the state. Hence, the attack on the spirit of the corporations is an attack on the spirit of the bureaucracy; and if earlier the bureaucracy combated the existence of the corporations in order to make room for its own existence, so now it tries forcibly to keep them in existence in order to preserve the spirit of the corporations, which is its own spirit. [Karl Marx, 'Contribution to the Critique of Hegel's Philosophy of Law,' 1843]

Early in the year 1900, Mackenzie King was in Europe making a desultory pursuit of further study and awaiting his summons to a teaching job at Harvard. He had gone armed with letters of introduction to the greats of the day, among them a letter from Daniel O'Donoghue recommending him to British labour leaders as one who, 'besides being "to the manor [*sic*!] born," ' is, naturally, well thought of and deservedly respected in Labor circles throughout Canada.'[1] In London, King lectured on 'State & Labour' and 'Christianity & Labour,' stressing in the latter that without the 'law of love,' social changes must necessarily fail, while 'with this social condit'ns wd. soon adjust themselves.'[2] He crossed to the Continent, and was in Rome on 26 June:

This morning I went first thing to the P.O. after breakfast and was rather startled by receiving a telegram. I opened it with some alarm, not knowing why a cable should come to me in Rome unless something ill had befallen, but what I read was the following, 'Confidential, Will you accept the editorship and management of new Government Labour Gazette, Ottawa begin duties early in July. Salary Fifteen hundred dollars

1 King correspondence, O'Donoghue to King and enclosure, 11 Sept. 1899
2 Diary, 19 and 22 Feb. 1900

may increase if yes come. (sd.) Wm. Mulock.' This was a great surprise but I experienced little elation because of it. I was disappointed in not getting any word from Harvard without which it is impossible for me to arrive at a decision. All day I have been reflecting on this offer and confess that I am unable to see my way clear to an acceptance of it. What holds me back is the breaking away from an academic career ...[3]

An offer from Harvard shortly came, an instructorship paying perhaps $600 a year, and King decided to accept it. But in the meantime John King was bestirring himself. He wrote to Taussig at Harvard, and obtained his advice that King would be better off taking the government job. A cable from his father was awaiting King at London on 5 July: he went to ask Cunningham's opinion and, on 9 July, wired his acceptance to Mulock.

King arrived at New York on 21 July and two days later he was closeted with Mulock in Toronto. They discussed the proposed *Gazette*, and then Mulock asked King to write him 'a small labor speech.' King's views on the separation of politics and civil service were somewhat idealistic this early in his career: he agreed to prepare the speech, but did so during office hours only because he had worked at departmental affairs in the evenings at home – or so he excused this conduct to his friend and colleague Albert Harper. 'I have given him a good speech,' King wrote of this first piece of government business. 'It is good for the working classes. Here my greatest power will [lie] & I can be a power behind the throne[:] what matter the credit so long as the end is achieved?'[4]

I

King was the making of the Labour Department as much as the Labour Department was the making of King. From the outset, he realized that his plans for the new agency differed materially from Mulock's. 'I don't believe Mr Mulock thought he was organizing a new Gov't deprtmt.,' he wrote on his first day in Ottawa, and he was undoubtedly right. What Mulock seems to have had in mind was a relatively ineffective sop to labour pressure, an appendage to the Post Office just as the Ontario Bureau of Labor was to the provincial Department of Agriculture. An election was to come in November, and a labour bureau would both meet the trade unions' demand for a labour statistics agency and provide a nice little machine for working-class patronage. For King, on the other hand, the Department of Labour was the germ of a great agency of industrial peace, the institutionalized form of the

3 *Ibid.*, 26 June 1900
4 *Ibid.*, 23 July, 3 Aug. 1900

'gospel of duty.' From the beginning, he wanted it to become a real department of government with its own minister, run on professional lines. And perhaps from the beginning, too, he saw himself as that minister. On that first day in Ottawa, he realized the magnitude of the task, were his conception to overcome Mulock's. 'I find myself at present the whole thing,' he wrote, 'department, Editor of Gazette, staff & all, and have to begin at the base with the finding of suitable quarters.'[5]

Of course, these two conceptions of the nature and role of the Department came into conflict almost immediately. When the drafts for the first issue of the *Gazette* had been prepared, King received 'a pretty good revelation as to the attitude of politicians towards govt. work': 'Mr. Mulock went thro' my articles & everything wh. in any way cld. count for a Conservative he scored out. He wd. not have even a reference to reports begun by them, e.g. statistical year book, tho' mentioned only as a source of information. When I spoke of publishing legal decisions he was opposed to this because in a recent decision made in favor of labor, the judge had been a Conservative.'[6]

But the major conflict was to come, not over the content of the *Gazette*, but over the appointment of departmental staff and the journal's local correspondents. When Mulock had finished blue-pencilling King's articles, he informed him 'that all the apptmts. wd. have to be political, and that the govt. wd. have to make them. I will not have a say ...' Daniel O'Donoghue had already been appointed Fair Wages Officer, and now Mulock proposed to make Phillips Thompson, the old socialist journalist whose invitation to campus had helped spark the University of Toronto student strike, Toronto correspondent to the *Gazette*. This was all right with King – once Thompson had approved his plan for the *Gazette*, King wrote that he liked 'the old man,' and believed him to be earnest and honest – although when he discovered that Thompson had pseudonymously authored an election pamphlet entitled 'What the Laurier Government Has Done for Labour,' he remarked, 'how these fellows sell themselves.' 'The thought comes,' he continued, 'that perhaps I am doing the same but this I don't believe, for I am expressing no opinion which I do not feel convinced to be true & right.' It would be some years yet before King would author an election pamphlet entitled 'What the Laurier Government Has Done for Labour.'[7]

The Thompson appointment may have been mutually agreeable, but others were not. Later that month, King was called to Mulock's office, where

5 *Ibid.*, 24 July 1900
6 *Ibid.*, 5 Aug. 1900
7 *Ibid.*, and 20 Aug. 1900. King prepared a pamphlet with this title for the 1908 election. *Ibid.*, 29 Aug. 1908

the Postmaster-General was sitting with James Sutherland, minister without portfolio. Mulock dictated two letters in King's presence:

... one to Williams, a man in Hamilton appointing him a Govt. officer to see to the enforcement of the Alien Labor Law, and one to Plant, an alderman or ex-alderman in London, a labor leader there telling him that he had been appt'd to the staff of the Labor Deprtmt. These men both got their positions because of political necessity or expediency. Mr. S. was there to see that they got them. Mr. M. in writing privately to another gentleman, told him to see that Plant's apptmt. got favorable notices in the press, etc. etc. This is the sort of thing I abhor. It is not right, men should receive apptmts. on ground of merit & worth primarily.[8]

King had his own candidates for departmental positions, of course. The most important of these, to his mind, was his old friend Albert Harper. Harper became second in command in the Department, more or less taking over the *Gazette* once King became heavily involved in conciliation work. They roomed together in Ottawa and spent pleasant Sunday afternoons lying, one's head in the other's bosom, reading Tennyson and Matthew Arnold aloud. Harper was drowned in 1901, and King replaced him with R.H. Coats and F.A. Acland. During the first few weeks when the Department was being organized, King also lobbied for the appointment of John Appleton, president of the Winnipeg labour council, to the Ottawa staff.[9] In this he was unsuccessful, although Appleton soon became Winnipeg correspondent for the *Gazette*.

But the matter of staff was only part of King's programme to make the Labour Department a real ministry, in both senses of the term. In the first place, he tried to persuade Mulock to style himself 'Minister of Labour.' He linked his initial approaches to the coming election campaign, and by August 17 he had so far prevailed that Mulock consented to have letterhead printed with 'Minister of Labour' on it. King also wanted his superior to make a major labour speech in his new capacity. But Mulock was unable to take his new-found distinction quite so seriously as King; he could hardly mention the title, Minister of Labour, without breaking into laughter. 'He is tickled over the title,' King complained to his diary, 'but what pains me is that he does not rejoice in it because of its nobility etc.'[10] Nevertheless, by the end of the year King had been successful not only in getting Mulock to take his title at

8 *Ibid.*, 18 Aug. 1900
9 *Ibid.*, 16 Aug. 1900. See King correspondence, Appleton to King, 12 Aug. 1900.
10 Diary, 18 Aug. 1900

least as seriously as might reasonably be expected, but in having himself made Deputy Minister as well. 'I can feel I have largely created a Department of Labour here,' he noted in his customary annual inventory. But if the foundation had been laid in those first few months, there was still much to be done.

One of King's early successes in conciliating a strike was the occasion for his next approach. When Mulock congratulated him, King 'took advantage of the occasion to try & secure an addition to the staff ... I pointed out that with these duties etc. it was impossible to watch the Gazette as it shld. be watched.' When a new appointment came, however, it was the same old story: 'This is a case of a man getting a position purely because of his supposed pull with the workingmen of Montreal prior to election, a case of the division of the spoils.' A couple of days later, he had recommended to him 'a young fellow named Giddens,' and decided to try to hire him as clerk. King realized that he could have no control over his staff if the Labour Department was to remain the place where Liberal labour leaders found their just rewards, and he determined to do something about it. 'Am going to try to get an Act thro' establishing Dept. of Labour on Civil Service List & if possible will get Auditor Gen'l to recommend this in writing tomorrow.'[11]

While Canada did not have a Civil Service Commission until 1908, its predecessor, the Civil Service Board of Examiners, did provide a slight bulwark against unmitigated patronage, at least in comparison to straight ministerial control of departments.[12] Mulock's main portfolio was second only to the Public Works Department in its opportunities for political rewards, although Customs and Excise was surely not far behind. Postmasters and customs collectors came and went like flies with every change of government. While having the Labour Department put on the civil service list could not entirely save it from a similar fate – the Civil Service Board of Examiners was wholly subordinate to Cabinet – it would at least establish it as a full-fledged department of government and give its Deputy Minister some control over the staff. 'I saw the Auditor General,' King wrote, '... got him to recommend introduct'n of an Act putting Department on same basis as others. This is something I am going to try and get thro' this session, an Act establishing the Department in a regular manner, & outlining its work. I believe the Minister will consent to it & will let me draft a bill.' But when

11 *Ibid.*, 26 Jan., 9 Feb., 11 Feb., 18 Feb. 1901
12 For the antecedents of the Civil Service Commission, see J.E. Hodgetts, *The Canadian Public Service: A Physiology of Government 1867–1970* (Toronto: University of Toronto Press, 1973) and J.E. Hodgetts *et al.*, *The Biography of an Institution: The Civil Service Commission of Canada 1908–1967* (Montreal: McGill-Queen's University Press, 1972). The latter contains a useful discussion of patronage, pp. 8ff.

King ventured to broach the matter with Mulock, he was told that the government had no wish to prolong the session.[13]

King, of course, wished to persevere, but for the time little could be done. It was not until a year later, on the appointment of R.H. Coats as Harper's successor, that he forcibly brought the matter up again. He linked the demand to his contention that, as he had the rank of deputy minister, he should receive a deputy minister's salary as well. Mulock and the Cabinet gave in, and the Minister advised King to save his money. This was enough to set King thinking about his long-term prospects: 'I seemed to see some day in the future when I may be or rather will be Minister of the Department of which I am now Deputy. This seems to be the direction in which my steps are being led. The one obstacle, before seeming impossible, has been the "means of livelihood which would enable one to be independent." If I can save enough to draw an income from saving I may be able to take the step into active public life for which my whole nature & ambition longs.'[14]

Several months before this, however, King had become aware that there was a rival for the position of Minister of Labour. So long as Mulock remained in charge there would be no difficulty, for not only was he merely amused at the greatness King had thrust upon him, but he was also evidently eager to see his young client make a name for himself in the department. The labour movement was pressing for the early appointment of a full-time minister though, and it was pressing, too, for the appointment of a labour leader to that position. As early as December 1900, King became aware of the existence of his rival in the person of Ralph Smith. As King and Mulock went over the annual estimates for the department, King gathered this much by what seems to have been osmosis: 'He gave no hint of a new Minister but I feel Ralph Smith is sure to be appointed.' Early in the new year, King was having trouble with O'Donoghue, who continued to play the part of labour spokesman despite his civil service job. 'I fear there may be trouble yet,' King wrote, 'especially if Ralph Smith don't [sic] or does get what he wants.' Two days later, he had the pleasure of meeting the competition for the first time. King was not impressed: 'He came into the office with a cigar in the corner of his mouth & looking decidedly tough.' King suspected Smith of fishing for information about the Department preparatory to taking it over, and accused him, at least in his diary, of being a liar. 'He is playing for the posit'n of Min. of Labour & the Govt. are going to have a time in dealing with him ... One thing is certain if he is appointed Minister I will resign. He wd. be sure to

13 Diary, 19 and 23 Feb. 1901
14 *Ibid.*, 10 Feb. 1902

bring embarrassment on any govt. I believe him to be first & foremost a "politician" and this is not the part I am serving in the labour cause.'[15]

The stronger were the rumours that Smith would become minister, the stronger was King's antipathy. 'Ralph Smith came into the office awhile today,' he wrote a few days after their first meeting. 'He was saying that by doing one or two things the Govt. could carry the whole labour element with them – the one thing is to make him Minister. I do not believe the Govt. can do or will do this.' King's first opportunity for revenge came a few weeks later, when Smith wanted him to have a certain conciliator intervene in a British Columbia coal mining dispute. King refused: 'I went to the House at 4.30 & waited till 5 to see Mr. S. Ralph Smith was very angry. I could see that he was so. It may do him no harm to know he does not control the Gov't even in Labour matters. The more I see of Labour leaders from the ranks, the more I distrust their motives.' A little later, King elaborated on this last statement: 'The truth is he is a politician, an office seeker, no true leader of a cause, all the views behind the scenes shew him to be using position etc. for political purposes & that he has practically sold himself to the Liberal Party.'[16]

Smith could hardly have been unaware of King's animosity, and he soon set himself to be of service to the young deputy. The Conservatives accused King of political campaigning during his conciliation of a strike at Valleyfield, and Smith undertook to defend him in the House. By the fall of 1901, when Smith came to Ottawa to discuss compulsory arbitration, King had softened a little: 'He is looking very well, & as one talks with him & hears him talk impresses one as [having] a shrewd & rather sound judgement in dealing with men, but biassed from one point of view.' King called on Smith's wife, and then invited the two to have dinner with Harper and him: 'They both enjoyed the evening very much & we all became better known to each other & strong friends. I see where Ralph Smith's future is made for him, he is sure to remain at the front & rise. This woman wd. make any man ...' After Berlin, of course, and the defeat of his programme to make the TLC the Canadian equivalent of the American Federation, there could be little question of Smith's becoming Labour Minister. Still, as late as 1907 and although he was on far better terms with Smith, King was still worried about competition for the cabinet post. 'I thought I was entitled to it ... I knew Smith wd. like it ...' and Smith would be better off in the Yukon or the Senate.[17]

At the time King was in receipt of the official deputy minister's salary, though, there were few clouds on his horizon. But at the same time, as he soon

15 *Ibid.*, 9 Dec. 1900, 28 and 30 Jan. 1901
16 *Ibid.*, 2 Feb., 13 and 22 March 1901
17 *Ibid.*, 11 April, 30 Sept., 1 Oct. 1901, 9 Jan. 1907

came to realize, the department was not on as sound a basis as Mulock had led him to believe. Two years later, he was again 'drafting an Act ... to put the Dept. of Labour on a proper footing with the other Depts. in the Civil Service':

We have not been established in a regular manner. If the truth were known, even the Minister himself did not contemplate a separate Dept. of the Govt., till the thing grew up under & in spite of him. I think I can take credit or blame for this, & I know that had I never lived the Dept. of Labour wd. not exist today, or the legis'n which has been passed to date in the interests of labour, been on the Statute books. I suggested to the Minister first to interest himself in labour, suggested the fair wages condit'ns in gov't clothing contracts, suggested he shd. take the title of Minister of Labour, put this crest on the paper and got out the Gazette etc. in form of regular Dept. did everything I think in the way of construct'n save suggest that actual measure be introduced, or the apptmt. of myself to office, or any position. The last two years, in fact since the first few months, he has hardly been inside of the Dept.[18]

Self-serving as this evaluation might be, it was not entirely without foundation. King was, at any rate, more responsible than anyone else for the creation of the department and its activities. And it seemed as though the government agreed with him. After Mulock's departure for the greener pastures of the Ontario bench, the department remained in the caretaker hands of successive Postmasters-General until King was ready to run for Parliament and take it over himself. Until that day it was not set 'on a proper footing,' and indeed, had it been, King would likely not have become Minister. After a good deal of uncertainty about a riding, King ran in the 1908 election and persuaded Laurier to make the creation of an independent Labour Department one of the planks in the Liberal platform. King gained his seat, and not long afterwards became a member of the Privy Council. Only then was the department put 'on a proper footing' – but its foundations had been well laid in the preceding years.

II

At the beginning the Department of Labour had four principal tasks: the administration of the Fair Wages Resolution and of the Alien Labour Act, the publication of the *Labour Gazette*, and the provision of voluntary conciliation services.[19] King had little to do with the first two of these. Daniel

18 *Ibid.*, 24 Feb. 1904
19 Cf. J.J. Atherton, 'The Department of Labour and Industrial Relations, 1900–1911,' unpublished MA thesis, Carleton University, 1972.

O'Donoghue was Fair Wages Officer, and while King supervised his work he seems not to have taken much interest in it. He had little favour for the Alien Labour law and did as little to ensure its enforcement. Until the pressure of conciliation requests came to absorb much of his time, he put a great deal of effort into the *Gazette*, but as his other duties became more pressing the day-to-day responsibilities of the journal were delegated to others. King was also in charge of preparing the department's annual reports, and he took on sundry additional tasks. He was secretary to one Royal Commission in 1903, and served as commissioner in his own right on several occasions thereafter. He negotiated immigration restrictions with the Chinese, Japanese, and Indian authorities on behalf of the Canadian government, and he put time into drafting new legislation. Beyond these duties, of course, he was responsible for drafting speeches and preparing answers to questions in the House, and he was *de facto* minister plenipotentiary to the Canadian labour movement. Mackenzie King earned his deputy minister's salary.

The first issue of the *Labour Gazette* was timed to appear at the TLC's Ottawa convention in September 1900. Laurier and Mulock both attended the opening ceremonies of the convention, where the Postmaster-General presented President Smith with the first copy of the *Gazette* and with the fair wages resolution. The TLC president, in his annual address, told the delegates that the journal would contain 'matters of supreme importance to the labor movement.' The *Gazette* was well launched among trade unionists and the triumph was secured the following January when the CMA, at King's suggestion, sent a bulk subscription covering its entire membership.[20] There was to be trouble with both the TLC and the CMA over the *Labour Gazette*, but that was in the future and unforeseen. For the time being, it had been inaugurated most successfully.

The first few numbers of the *Gazette* set the pattern for future issues. It would begin with a brief editorial and a general review of economic conditions during the month. These would be followed by the reports of local correspondents across the country, most if not all of them labour activists in their districts. Then would come a review of 'trade disputes' – strikes and lockouts – during the month, with special articles on any of them that might be particularly significant. There would be reports on the various activities of the department, and one or two longer articles, frequently part of a series, on wages and conditions in particular trades, on the extent of labour organization, on labour legislation in the various provinces, and so on. The *Gazette* also printed summaries of the department's annual reports and official reports of departmental interventions in labour disputes. Then would come a brief anno-

20 Diary, 10 Jan. 1901

tated list of recent publications bearing on labour, and a review of legal decisions affecting labour. This pattern was not unalterable – Royal Commission reports, for example, often rated special articles – but for the most part each number of the *Gazette* followed the general scheme. Only once during King's tenure in the Labour Department were many of the regular features displaced from an issue by a major article: this occasion was the United Mine Workers' strike which shut down anthracite production in Pennsylvania in 1902.[21]

The first, and by far the most serious, attack on the *Gazette* came from the Canadian Manufacturers' Association. When its convention met in October 1901, it appointed a special committee to reconsider its bulk subscription to the journal, 'having regard to numerous complaints on the part of members as to the management and influence of the Gazette.' The committee listed three objections. It took issue with the 'definition of labor implied in the general character of the Gazette': 'Labor, we venture to believe, conceived in its proper sense, is not limited to the employee, but embraces the whole field of industrial and commercial life. Industrial interests are essentially one; and this narrow definition of labor is calculated to militate against the recognition of this community of interests, which is at the basis of the relations between an employer and employee.' The second objection had to do with the reports of local correspondents, which were 'not such as to guarantee to the country at large the most reliable and serviceable reports,' and finally the committee reported that the monthly *Gazette* was open to too much ephemeral material; a quarterly would be more likely to contain 'matter of more permanent value.'[22] King wrote to the association secretary requesting more detailed information on these objections, and the reply revealed quite clearly that what the CMA objected to most was the fact that the local correspondents were trade unionists.[23] In marshalling his arguments, the secretary wrote that he did 'not know to what extent you have made efforts to secure information from the employers' standpoint, but it has appeared to our members that practically everything published from your correspondents has been written from the standpoint of employees only.' Perhaps he would have been somewhat more forthright had he recalled an exchange on the floor of the CMA

21 *LG*, Nov. 1902, 321–74. There were shorter reports in subsequent issues.
22 *IC*, Nov. 1901, 137. The dispute was still alive five years later: *ibid.*, Oct. 1906, 191.
23 *Ibid.*, April 1902, 285f; Diary, 19 Feb. 1902 Cf. *ibid.*: 'A good part of the time I talked with Tony Russell of the Canadian Mffrs. Association. He confessed to me that the criticism of the Assoc'n vs. the Gazetee [*sic*], was meant in reality as a protest against giving so much recognition to labour – Could there be a more direct acknowledgement that slavery exists[,] Industrial servitude[,] and that a large body of men – those with power in their hands[–]seek to maintain that power at the expense of large bodies of their fellow men[?] There is no alternative explanation. To aid even most remotely in sweeping away this state of affairs is not to live in vain.'

convention immediately after the presentation of the special committee's report:

Mr. J.R. Shaw. – I would like to ask whether the labor department sends out to the various manufacturers a form to be filled out. I have never gone to the trouble of filling it out myself, but have put it in the wastepaper basket, and I would like to know if that is the course that manufacturers are usually pursuing.

The President. – Mr. Shaw wishes to know if the form is generally filled up, or consigned to the wastepaper basket.

Chorus of Voices. – The waste-paper basket.[24]

The labour movement, so far as it was represented by the TLC, also had its differences with the *Gazette*, although these were never as far reaching as the CMA's. The TLC, like the CMA, recognized that the *Gazette* was a significant mouthpiece for local labour leaders, but of course it was unwilling to draw the manufacturers' conclusions from this self-evident fact. Indeed, what the TLC most often objected to was editorial interference with the local correspondents' reports. In 1904, the TLC president objected to the *Gazette*'s report of the outcome of the Berlin convention as the disbarring of purely Canadian organizations from the Congress:

I considered it my duty to correct this statement, as untruthful and misleading, no such resolution having been passed, and wrote accordingly to the Editor. Some of our organizations have seen fit to condemn the Department of Labor, and ask to discontinue the publication of the *Labor Gazette* as being unduly influenced by the Manufacturers' Association. This, I think, is a most serious mistake on the part of those who would resort to this extreme measure. It is just as necessary to have a Department of Labor as a Department of Commerce or Agriculture, and it can be made of great value to the toilers of Canada, if men peculiarly fitted for, and in sympathy with the work, are selected to carry on the work of the Department, and removed from the influence and impertinent interference of the Manufacturers' Association.

By 'the influence of the Manufacturers' Association' Flett probably intended a swipe at the Department of Labour's willingness to listen to the NTLC as well as the TLC. But the real objection, beyond the supposedly misleading account of what happened at Berlin, was brought down to the level of the local correspondence columns by the committee on the president's report: 'We concur with the President in recommending unions to furnish the

24 *IC*, Nov. 1901, 137

necessary information to the *Labor Gazette*, but would recommend that representation be made to the Minister of Labor to have the correspondents instructed to get their information, officially, from the officers of the unions in their districts ...'[25]

In 1906, the TLC rejected a resolution endorsing the *Labour Gazette* because a new disagreement had arisen. The *Gazette* had decided against reporting the existence or continuation of strikes in cases where 'information has been received on reliable authority to the effect that the business interests of the firms affected are no longer seriously embarrassed in consequence of the strike,'[26] normally because the firm was maintaining operations with strike-breakers or scabs. This decision, or at any rate its consequences, seems to have been behind Delegate Trotter's resolution to the 1906 TLC convention:

Whereas, it frequently happens that much harm is done to organized labor engaged in industrial disputes in Canada by reason of the only partial truth contained in reports appearing from time to time in the Dominion Labor *Gazette* concerning the continuance or discontinuance of such disputes; – be it resolved, that this Congress present this complaint to the Minister of Labor with a request that greater attention and notice be given in the *Labor Gazette* to the statements of the workmen involved in such disputes, so that disputes will not henceforth be reported as settled, when as a matter of fact, they are still in existence.[27]

Again in 1908, the TLC passed a resolution bearing on the local correspondents' reports. This time it urged that the department only appoint correspondents who had been 'endorsed by Central Labor Bodies' and that 'the manuscript supplied ... by such correspondents be published exactly as it is submitted, that is that the sense and meaning which the said correspondence is intended to convey, be not changed, as is now the custom.'[28]

It might appear a little paradoxical that the patronage features of the Labour Department, leading as they did to the appointment of labour leaders as *Gazette* correspondents, accounted for much of its usefulness to the labour movement. Had King been successful in insisting that the best qualified got the jobs, or had he interpreted fairness as meaning disinterestedness in an immediate sense, it is unlikely that labour leaders would have been the principal contributors to the month-by-month accounts of the labour market and industrial disputes. Perhaps local journalists would have been appointed instead. As it was, the character of the *Gazette* was affected in a number of ways

25 *TLC* 1904, 12, 54
26 *Ibid.*, 1906, 54; *LG*, Feb. 1903, 627
27 *TLC* 1906, 77
28 *Ibid.*, 1908, 75

by the nature of these appointments. Apart from the points of view expressed, directly and indirectly, in the correspondents' reports, the unwillingness of many businessmen to furnish information was contingent on the perceived labour bias of the local staff. No matter how much King might have wanted 'fair' reportage, his ability to provide it was limited by the information available. So long as most unions were eager to provide material and most employers were not, the *Labour Gazette* possessed a definite union flavour. This was no doubt in part due to King's sympathies, but at least as big a part was played by Mulock's insistence on using the journal as a pork barrel. Thus the CMA denounced the whole enterprise almost at the outset, while the TLC, which of course had lobbied for the establishment of such a journal for years, had only occasional and specific objections relating mainly to the editorial restrictions placed on recipients of patronage appointments. This is not to say that the TLC's objections were insignificant, but merely to point out that in its view even the refusal of the *Gazette* to publicize the maintenance of ineffective strikes was more bathwater than baby.

III

The *Labour Gazette* was an important aspect of the department's work but, at least in King's view, conciliation was more important. That this view was not at first shared is indicated by the initial reaction of the TLC to the Conciliation Act. President Smith told the Congress that 'whilst it does not go the distance that many would desire, it is our duty as honest men to appreciate the step taken,' and the Manitoba Executive elaborated:

The passage of the Conciliation bill is important because it provides the necessary authority for the establishment of a labor bureau and the publication of a labor gazette, two matters that have long been neglected ... The Conciliation bill as such cannot, of course, be acceptable to our Congress, it being a purely voluntary measure ... The Conciliation Act provides for the registration of boards of conciliation constituted for the purpose of settling disputes between employers and workmen by conciliation or arbitration. It would doubtless be a good thing to get these boards organized wherever possible and steps should be taken by the various organizations to invite the employers to join them in erecting conciliation boards to be registered under the new Act.[29]

What was most promising to the labour movement was the *Gazette* and little, it seemed, was to be hoped for from the conciliation provision in the act. King himself recognized that 'the Conciliat'n Act was the least important

29 *Ibid.*, 1900, 7, 11

part of the business, what the working people cared most about was the department of Labour & the Fair Wages Clause,' and he took Mulock to task for the fact that 'his mind & that of practically all in the debate was focused on the conciliat'n part of the bill.' But from the first, King volunteered to take over conciliation work,[30] and in his hands it became not only an increasingly important part of the department's work, but something quite different from what had been envisaged by Parliament.

The latter point needs to be stressed, because there has been a tendency on the part of some authors, unconsciously parallelling the TLC's initial reaction, to dismiss conciliation on the grounds of the Act and the Commons debate. This is quite misleading, as it is clear on examination of King's practice that 'conciliation' as it was contemplated in the Act and as it was carried on by King meant two different things. Thus Williams argues, on the basis of the Commons debates on the Conciliation Act and the parallel with British legislation and practice, that 'the conciliation referred to by Muloch [sic] involved the bringing together of the parties to discuss, argue, debate and hence try to reach consent among themselves ... Little emphasis, if any, is placed on the role of the third party as a participant in formulating the terms of settlement. It is suggested that the conciliation referred to in the above law, and envisaged on the part of the legislators, was not more that [sic] what we today call collective bargaining, in the sense of bringing parties together to discuss and work out their dispute differences. The role of the third party was not so much to partake of discussions and suggest possible areas of settlement (to mediate) as it was to bring the parties together for purposes of collective bargaining (to conciliate).'[31]

This is fine so far as it is intended merely to elucidate the language of the debate, but it is clear that Williams intends this description to extend over the actual practice of conciliation under the Act as well, since he wishes to explain the development of Canadian industrial disputes policy. From the outset, however, King placed far more stress on the role of the third party than seems to have been intended by the legislators. His version of conciliation far more closely resembled what Williams describes as mediation, and on some occasions he went beyond even that. Moreover, the machinery of registration for boards of conciliation and arbitration contemplated in the Act was completely disregarded by King. He favoured – in practice if not in theory – *ad hoc* interventions with a view to ending strikes or lock-outs. This did not entail collective bargaining in any strong sense, since in practice the intent was not so much

30 Diary, 16 and 17 Aug. 1900
31 C.B. Williams, 'Notes on the Evolution of Compulsory Conciliation in Canada,' *Relations Industrielles* 19 (1964) 305

to reach a mutually agreeable settlement, or to realize some standard of equitable treatment, as to get the men back to work as quickly as possible.

If, in evaluating the evolution of Canadian industrial peace policy, more weight is assigned to practice than to legislative debate, there seems to be much more continuity from Conciliation Act to Industrial Disputes Investigation Act than would otherwise appear. This continuity may be very simply explained. King was responsible for administering the Conciliation Act and for both drafting and administering later legislation, and his view of the third party's role underwent no significant change. Later legislation was introduced for two principal reasons: to guarantee that King's brand of third-party intervention could be enforced in difficult situations, and to lessen his own increasingly heavy workload in this area. Thus the Railway Labour Disputes Act and the Industrial Disputes Investigation Act both made intervention mandatory in some of the instances in which it was not mandatory under the Conciliation Act, while the IDIA also provided for the appointment of tripartite boards, freeing King to intervene only in cases where his personal touch seemed to him really essential. In fact, King on occasion intervened in disputes even while a board was being constituted, and he also sometimes intervened once a board had finished its proceedings. Examples of both of these will be furnished later on. For the time being, it is important to recognize that King's interpretation of the third-party role was not coextensive with legislative pronouncement, and that a description of the development of Canadian labour policy which focuses exclusively on the language of the legislation and on the parliamentary debates will be an inadequate one.

Our present ability to describe King's practice and to identify its divergence from the letter of the legislation is founded in part on the view that official reports of interventions in the *Labour Gazette*, the annual reports of the department, and similar sources must be regarded as in themselves aspects of King's practice. The virtues of 'publicity' in the armamentarium of industrial peace were not spelled out until the IDI Act, but it is apparent that from the beginning these reports served a special purpose. That they were not taken by King to be *complete* accounts of the methods used to arrive at settlements is demonstrated by the existence of other, 'confidential,' accounts by his hand. This is not to say that the published versions need always, or even occasionally, to be thought of as dishonest, although we shall see that they were sometimes disingenuous. Nor need we conclude that King felt he had something to hide, although this, too, seems sometimes to have been the case. A general explanation that is both more generous and more comprehensive would be that the confidential reports and the official reports were written for different purposes. This is equally the case when there exists, as sometimes there does, a third 'layer' of reportage, the private account of an intervention in King's diary existing alongside a confidential report to the government and an official report for publication. We might in general say of both private and confidential accounts that their purpose, beyond merely describing events and motivations, was to protect King in particular or the government in general from later accusations concerning the method of disputes settlement. Perhaps there was a secondary purpose in providing a confidential cook-book for Department of Labour investigations, since occasionally King included in his reports to the government a commentary on intervention techniques,[32] and even where such comments were not made explicitly the detailed account of King's activities might serve the purpose.

The intent of the official published reports was different. While there were probably various purposes which these were designed to meet, ranging from propaganda for the Liberal party (which in its wisdom had created both conciliation and the *Gazette* in which the reports were printed) to singling out a particular union or employer for praise or obloquy, and while, like the other layers, the official reports attempted to describe events, they generally had the additional purpose of presenting simple parables about the proper relations of labour and capital. In this, they often played down the role of the conciliator to the extent of portraying suggestions, initiatives, or even decisions that he had made as the autonomous and often spontaneous productions of one or the other of the principal parties. Of course, one can imagine several reasons why this might have been done, including a desire to cement the commitment of the parties to a decision by portraying it as completely their own; but in any event the net effect is that interventions as portrayed in the *Labour Gazette* often seem more like conciliation in Williams' sense than do the same interventions when non-public documentation is examined. This is probably not so much because King was anxious that it should seem that he was obeying the letter of the conciliation law, as because the non-obvious purpose of the published reports, the intervention as parable, necessitated that his own role should be downplayed. Here we give one rather straightforward example of this as illustration: other more complex cases will be found later on.

The case to be described here is chosen because it is both simple and unexceptionable. It has none of the special difficulties of King's numerous Conciliation Act interventions in western coal mining disputes, which require a chapter of their own, or the additional technicalities of intervention under later legislation. It involves one of the early triumphs of the department: a strike which had gone on for months was settled in a couple of days through King's intervention. In its own right, this particular intervention is insignifi-

32 An instance of this is quoted in chapter 8, section IV, with reference to the Lethbridge strike of 1906.

cant – as an uncomplicated example of general practice, it is invaluable. There are three accounts of it, all of them short: King's diary, the *Labour Gazette*, and the department's annual report.

On 8 October 1900, some fifty journeymen and apprentice machinists struck the machine tool factory of John Bertram and Sons in Dundas, Ontario. They wanted recognition of their union, the International Association of Machinists, a guaranteed minimum hourly wage, and restrictions on the employment of apprentices. By January 1901, many of the strikers had drifted away and their places had been filled by strikebreakers. On 22 January, on receipt of a letter from the union secretary, King was authorized to conciliate the dispute. He arrived at Dundas on 24 January, and the following day a verbal settlement was arranged.

The report in the *Labour Gazette* consists of three paragraphs. The first two give the background to the strike, summarized above, while the third is quoted here in its entirety:

On January 22, the Honourable the Minister of Labour received a communication on behalf of the strikers requesting that action be taken under the Conciliation Act to bring about an adjustment of the existing difficulties. On the day following, the deputy Minister of Labour left Ottawa for Dundas for the purpose of interviewing both parties and of effecting, if possible, an amicable settlement of the points at issue. On his arrival in Dundas, on the 24th instant, both parties expressed a willingness to avail themselves of the good offices of the government under the Act for the purpose of bringing to an end the long standing differences between them, and each showed a disposition to lend every assistance to effect this end. The firm permitted the Deputy Minister to examine its books in order that he might form a correct judgement as to the wages being paid and the numbers employed. Mr. Arthur W. Holmes of the executive of the International Machinists' Association came to Dundas from Toronto to assist the local union in the settlement negotiations, and after a few conferences an understanding was reached which was satisfactory to both parties concerned. The union declared the strike to be at an end and the firm re-employed such of the men as had not, in the interval, secured employment elsewhere.[33]

The account of the settlement in the Annual Report of the Department of Labour was even more curt:

The third strike settled under the Conciliation Act was that of certain employees of the Bertram Tool Works at Dundas, Ont. The men, originally 55 in number, had gone on strike because of the refusal of the company to grant certain requests as to

33 *LG*, Feb. 1901, 287

rates of wages to be paid, the number of apprentices to be employed, and other matters. The strike had been in progress for nearly three months before the intervention of the Department of Labour was asked for in the month of January. The day following this request, the Deputy Minister of Labour visited Dundas, and after interviews with both parties, effected a settlement, the terms of which, at the request of the interested parties, were not made public. That these terms were satisfactory to both sides, however, was evidenced by the fact that the men returned to work the following morning, and have continued at work without making further complaint, and that a communication was sent by the firm to the Minister thanking the government for its friendly offices in securing an adjustment of this long-standing dispute.[34]

Before turning to the account of this intervention in King's diary and comparing it to the two published accounts, it will be useful to examine these official versions both separately and together. Both accounts are parables, to continue that analogy, but they are parables for different audiences and therefore with different lessons. The *Labour Gazette* version is directed first and foremost to trade unionists and employers. It is the story of how satisfactory results may be obtained from the exercise of good faith and co-operative negotiation. The Annual Report version is directed to the members of Parliament, first and foremost. It is a story about the marvellous efficacy of an agency of government in healing a long-open wound in civil society. In the first version, the emphasis is on the goodwill of the parties: in the second, it is on the intervention and on the satisfaction which that intervention afforded the parties to the dispute.

The *Labour Gazette* version abounds in phrases evocative of the goodwill of the parties to the settlement and reminiscent of King's ideas about the significance of character: 'amicable settlement,' 'a willingness to avail themselves of the good offices,' 'a disposition to lend every assistance,' the opening of the books, the arrival of the IAM executive member to 'assist,' 'conferences,' and 'understanding,' 'satisfactory to both parties.' It is noteworthy that not only does this version fail to indicate the disposition of the matters in dispute, but it does not even mention the allegation in the second version that the parties agreed to keep the terms of the settlement secret. Perhaps it

34 Canada, *Sessional Papers*, 36 (1902), 36; King correspondence, Bertram to Mulock, 29 Jan. 1901: 'We have the honor to acknowledge receipt of your courteous favor of the 26th inst. [Mulock wrote to thank the Bertrams for their hospitality to King] and in reply we desire to express our pleasure in meeting your Deputy, Mr. King, and also to say that there is is [sic] no doubt but that owing to his good judgement the slight difficulty which existed between a few of our employees and ourselves was adjusted to the satisfaction of all parties concerned. We would ask you to kindly accept our very best thanks for your interest on our behalf.'

would not be going too far to state that these considerations are really irrelevant to the real burden of the story, the moral of peace on earth to men of goodwill. This version, then, is a parable about how two opponents, unable to reconcile themselves one to the other, may call upon a third party in whom both are able to repose their trust, and how, if both are really intent upon fair and amicable dealing, his efforts may be crowned with success.

The Annual Report version, on the other hand, does not so much as mention the good faith or co-operative spirit of the parties to the dispute. Instead, it is burdened with intimations that the situation was a very difficult one, with little to be hoped for. The strike had gone on for three months and the settlement, once it was arranged, could not be made public. The impression this account leaves with the reader is that of a situation abounding in danger, which only the efforts of a true diplomat could bring to a successful close. There is no suggestion of 'conferences' here; instead there were only 'interviews with both parties.' The stress in on the activity of the Deputy Minister, not so much because he is frequently mentioned (he is not), but because no other factors explaining the settlement are adduced. Perhaps it was this atmosphere of difficulty and diplomatic intrigue which induced King to provide 'proofs' of the satisfactory nature of the settlement. It must be noted, of course, that in neither account are these 'proofs' very satisfactory, and so far as the union side is concerned they are wholly inconclusive, inasmuch as several reasons besides real 'satisfaction' could easily be proposed for the fact that the men returned to work. Finally, mention should be made of a further discrepancy between the two accounts, for reasons that will shortly become evident: this is that the *Labour Gazette* version names all three issues in contention in the dispute, while the Annual Report version names two and leaves the issue of union recognition buried under the phrase, 'other matters.'

Let us now turn to a third version of the intervention in the Bertram strike, a version pieced together from King's diary. The first mention of the strike appears in the entry for 22 January 1901, although King had received a letter about it from the local MP in December.[35] King showed Mulock a letter from the IAM secretary in January, 'inviting intervention under the Conciliat'n Act. He asked me if I wanted to go. I told him I wd. & he sd. I had better write to that effect. I think he feels it is a mere chance, or he wd. have wished to write a line himself.' The following day King replied offering the department's services, and Mulock approved the letter and wished him a safe journey to Dundas. King arrived there late the following afternoon and immediately had a talk with the machinists' secretary. 'Heard his story & felt the men's case to be weak at the start, then went to the Bertram Works &

35 King correspondence, J.R. Brown to King, 15 Dec. 1900

had a talk with Henry Bertram, the chief manager of the firm, found him very decent & approachable, but firm in not being willing to yield much or anything yet desirous of having an end to the dispute. Impressed on him the harm the dispute was doing to the firm & its business. Went back & saw Dickinson [the union secretary, Dickson] & later took a car back into Hamilton where I stayed the night at the new Royal Hotel.' The following morning King returned to Dundas:

A.W. Holmes, the organizer of the Machinists Union was the first man I met, & we talked together on the way out. I got off at the Bertram Works and had a talk with Henry Bertram & his brother. He said in regard to the men, that they were willing to take back all still out of employment in Dundas except the two named last night (one a foreman, the other an apprentice). They were willing to let me see their books, & said that every journeyman was receiving 16 cents per hour or over and that it would not pay them to have one in their employ who was not. I tried to get him to give me an assurance that for the next year he wd. not employ anyone at less, but he said, while this was a fact, he was unwilling to make any agreement. As to the apprentices he took the same attitude, was willing to shew the books, and sd. that the no. of apprentices was less now than before the strike, and that the proportion wd. not be increased but wd. not give this assurance in the form of an agreement. I saw that the firm was determined not to yield, also that the men had acted too hastily, & so sought to patch up a settlement with Holmes & Dickson, on the basis of their weakness and that the choice for them was one of settlement with some advantage, as [vs.] continuance of strike with total loss to the Union. They saw this & after a conference with them for an hour or so I had lunch with Holmes & went back to the firm, looked thro their books, & pointed out the large no. of labourers, under neither head, which was chief object'n of men. Took back figures to men, & advised them accepting a form of settlement, to take the two objectionable men & find places for them elsewhere & with this understood have the firm agree to take all back. I left them to themselves & later they told me they had agreed to the terms. I told the firm & they were greatly pleased. Both the Bertram Bros. thanked me for coming & sd. to tell Mr Mulock they wd. have 'to vote Grit next time'. The men were I think thankful to get off without total defeat. Henry Bertram took me thro' their works & at 4 I left for Toronto, Holmes & I together. We had a pleasant talk on the way ... This has been a good day, a settlement effected which means some six or 8 more men at work tomorrow & much friction ended ...

Back in Ottawa the following day, King 'went over to see the Minister and have a talk with him, he was greatly pleased with the result of the settlement effected. He told me to sit down and tell him how it was done, & listened attentively and approvingly. He said when my telegram came he was at a meeting of Council. He stopped proceedings and read it aloud, explaining the nature of this victory, etc. He dictated a letter to the Bertrams thanking them for their kindness to his deputy, etc.'[36] Thereupon King made his appeal for more staff, quoted above.

King's diary has been quoted extensively in order to present everything even marginally relevant to the intervention. It is evident immediately that there are great discrepancies of ommision and implication between this and the two official accounts. Neither of the official accounts mentions the firm's absolute refusal to compromise on any of the men's demands. This may be a discrepancy of implication as well as one of omission, considering the stress in the *Labour Gazette* version on the willingness of both parties to arrive at a settlement. What is certainly a discrepancy of implication is the use of the term 'conferences' in the *Gazette* version which would seem to imply, especially when 'interviews' are separately mentioned, that the two parties were brought face to face, something which the diary version indicates did not happen. Similarly, when the Annual Report version states that 55 men went on strike and 'the men returned to work the following morning,' the implication is that many more than the 'six or 8' were involved in the settlement. Again, the fact that the men made no further complaint seems, in light of the diary, to be even less conclusive a demonstration of their satisfaction with the result. A handful of them got their jobs back with no concessions, and to achieve even this they had to jettison two 'objectionable men.'

There is what may perhaps be termed an epistemological problem here, or at least a methodological one, which bears on the reliability of the diary account, and about which one or two considerations might be advanced, the more so since we shall be making use of testimony of this sort in later chapters. It might be objected that the diary version has no better claim to objective truth than the other two versions. Our treatment of this claim must first of all rest on what it is that the objective truth is to be about, namely, whether it is to be considered a true account of King's perceptions of the intervention, or else a true account of the intervention *per se*. For the former, which is the less interesting of the two for our broad purposes, it might at least be argued that King had less reason not to be honest about his perceptions in the diary than in the official versions, that the account was written closer to the date and therefore his impressions were more readily available, and that the wealth of incidental detail in the diary version – much of it of a circumstantial nature in contrast to the other versions – lends it some credibility. Of course, King may have had psychological blocks preventing him from revealing his true perceptions to himself; his memory may have been more or less at fault; there may have been other factual data

36 Diary, 23, 24, 25, 26 Jan. 1901

which would have lent a rather different slant to the account had they not been forgotten or otherwise suppressed. But the other versions are at least as susceptible, and on several counts more so, than the diary to these errors. On balance, then, while the absolute validity of the diary account cannot be guaranteed, it appears to be more reliable than the other versions and, so far as King's perceptions are concerned, the most reliable account available.

On the other and more important question, the validity of the diary as an account of the intervention *per se*, it is clear at the outset that there is a problem in possessing only one such account from one point of view, particularly when we expect that King had biases and perspectives of his own. But we do not have alternative accounts from Henry Bertram or from A.W. Holmes or from any of the other participants. Once again, and since all of the considerations applying to our first question apply here also, King's diary is the best account we have of the intervention. We can probably accept it, at least tentatively, so far as it bears on reportage of events, leaving open the possibility that some fairly significant events may have occurred without being reported, for the reasons suggested above as well as because events may have taken place without King's knowledge. But there is no warrant for accepting King's evaluative statements as part of the account of the intervention *per se* except in the sense that they may help to explain King's role. Thus when King writes in the diary, 'Heard his story and felt the men's case to be weak at the start,' we are justified in accepting, for want of contrary evidence, that the meeting with Dickson took place when and where King said it did, that it covered at least the topics King mentioned, and that King felt the men's case was weak. We are not, however, warranted in concluding that their case was in fact weak, by any independent criterion of weakness we might like to justify. In the absence of direct evidence about the strength of their case, we must suspend judgment about it. We must, therefore, both accept that our case for the validity and reliability of this account is relatively weak, and at the same time accept it, subject to the cautions mentioned, as the best account available and therefore as evidentially prior to the official versions, at least in so far as there is no indication that King received additional data about the situation between the writing of this diary account and the preparation of the official reports. In the case of the Bertram strike there is one datum evinced of the latter sort in the statement in the Annual Report that the men 'have continued at work without making further complaint,'[37] but, as we have seen, this is subject to varying interpretations and does not necessarily support the *use* King wants to make of it.

The burden of this discussion, then, may be summarized briefly. Private accounts, where they exist, are to be considered superior to confidential, and these to public, versions. Moreover, the various accounts are to be taken as whole versions in their own right, and therefore not susceptible to composite treatment, for to do otherwise would lead to contradictions of connotation or of denotation. Thus there is a hierarchy of interpretation assumed, by which confidential accounts may be measured against private ones, and public accounts against both of the other two types. These, at any rate, are the assumptions underlying the interpretations which follow.

IV

Between 1900 and 1907, when the Conciliation Act was to all practical purposes replaced by the IDI Act,[37] there were forty-two interventions by the Department of Labour into industrial disputes under its provisions. These ranged from disputes involving a mere handful of men, for example the strike of twenty-two employees against the Cornwall street railway company in 1905, to much larger ones. The very first time the Conciliation act was invoked some three thousand labourers at the Montreal Cotton Company were involved in the dispute. A general strike of Halifax longshoremen in 1901 involved twelve hundred men, nine steamship companies, and sixteen merchant houses. Fifteen hundred miners were involved in one strike in 1903, and in the same year the Act was invoked in a strike by all the Grand Trunk Railway's trackmen. The mean number of workers involved in the thirty-four cases for which numbers are available for disputes involving single companies over the eight years is approximately 456. Excluding railway systems (but including railway shops), the mean is still 453. Evidently King was correct when he wrote in the Department's Annual Report for 1901 that 'the industrial establishments immediately interested were ... the largest and most important industrial concerns in this country ...'[38] The establishments involved ranged over the whole spectrum of the Canadian economy, from primary resource extraction (mining, lumbering, pulp and paper), through railways, to iron and steel, construction, secondary manufacturing, and the service sector (Bell Telephone). They took place in every province except Prince Edward Island or, if the railway systems are excluded, Saskatchewan and New Brunswick as well.

Accounts other than official reports are not available for all of these interventions. There are enough, however, to venture on some generalizations about King's procedure under the Conciliation Act. Several further examples of interventions in the western mining industry are presented in the next

37 The term, Conciliation Act, is used here throughout, although in 1906 it was consolidated with the Railway Labour Disputes Act, as the *Conciliation and Labour Act, 1906.*
38 Canada, *Sessional Papers*, 36 (1901) 34: similar statements were made in subsequent Annual Reports.

chapter, and these, together with the Bertram case discussed above, may serve as illustrations. All the cases available have been examined, and the following generalizations apply across the vast majority of them.

It may be useful to discuss King's procedure within the framework of the statute. In its original form – amendments will be discussed below – the Conciliation Act consisted of 12 sections. Sections 3, 8, and 9 referred exclusively to conciliation boards and their registration. The sections directly applicable to the case of a single government-appointed conciliation officer are 4 through 7. Section 4 begins by setting out the powers of the minister 'where a difference exists or is apprehended between an employer or any class of employers and workmen, or between different classes of workmen.' He may inquire into the causes of the dispute (4.1a), appoint a chairman for a negotiating or arbitration committee if jointly requested by both parties to the dispute (4.1b), appoint a conciliation officer on the request of one of the parties (4.1c), or, on the application of both parties, appoint an arbitrator (4.1d). The remainder of this section deals with proceedings under (4.1c). The conciliator so appointed 'shall inquire into the causes and circumstances of the difference by communication with the parties, and otherwise shall endeavour to bring about a settlement of the difference, and shall report his proceedings to the Minister' (4.2), and, if a settlement is effected either by conciliation or arbitration, 'a memorandum of the terms thereof shall be drawn up and signed by the parties or their representatives, and a copy thereof shall be delivered to and kept by the Minister' (4.3).

Section 5 deals with the duties of the conciliator in general: 'It shall be the duty of the conciliator to promote conditions favourable to a settlement by endeavouring to allay distrust, to remove causes of friction, to promote good feeling, to restore confidence, and to encourage the parties to come together and themselves effect a settlement, and also to promote agreements between employers and employees with a view to the submission of differences to conciliation or arbitration before resorting to strikes or lock-outs.' The remaining sections (6 and 7) provide for assistance to the conciliator and for the appointment of the conciliator as a commissioner under the Inquiries Act on cabinet approval and the written consent of both parties to the dispute.[39]

So far as government intervention, as opposed to purely secular boards, was concerned, then, the Act permitted the minister, at his discretion, to inquire into a dispute on his own initiative, appoint a conciliator on the request of one of the parties, or appoint an arbitrator on the request of both. In practice, the majority of interventions under the Act involved the second of these options, although on occasion King used the first of them to

39 63–64 Vict., chap. 24

bring about the second: he would, in the course of inquiring into a dispute, persuade one of the parties to apply for a conciliator. The duties of the conciliator, while rather vague in the Act, were clearly limited to the creation of friendly or co-operative attitudes and to the encouragement of the parties 'to come together and themselves effect a settlement.'

In many of the cases for which adequate data are available, and as we have seen in the Bertram case, King's interventions were more active than this clause seems to have required. Rather than limiting his efforts to persuading the parties to meet together, King frequently took it upon himself to serve as messenger between the two, apparently with little or no interest in bringing about a joint conference. Moreover, the messages that he carried back and forth were often ones that he had suggested himself, and occasionally it appears that a message of King's creation was spuriously presented as having originated with one of the parties even when that party had no knowledge of it. There is no need to provide illustrations here; all of these are shown in one or another of the cases discussed elsewhere in this study. The point, though, is one that has been made earlier in connection with Williams' characterization of the Act. King was the very active mediator, not merely the conciliator lending his good offices to bringing the parties together for productive consultations.

Many reasons may be adduced for King's stress, in his practice, on this mediation function. Three seem particularly significant. The first is King's conception of his role as an *interested* third party to the dispute. The conciliator was not a neutral friend, but represented the interests of the public in the dispute, and had therefore an active role to play. This conception was institutionalized in the IDI Act, and will be discussed at length in that connection.

The second reason was King's stress on a rapid settlement of the dispute. This language is somewhat tendentious, of course, since it was not so much the matters in dispute which were to be settled as the disruption of work which was to be terminated. When these two goals came into conflict – where it might have seemed, for instance, that the issues in dispute could be resolved only by a protracted trial of strength resulting in a willingness on both sides to negotiate in good faith – King quite consistently opted for an end to the work stoppage as an alternative to the resolution of the issues. The history of King's mediation is a history of aborted situations of this kind. On the face of it, this might appear to mean that King had no real sympathy for the issues which motivated workers to go on strike, inasmuch as his efforts were directed not to the resolution of these issues but to the termination of strikes. King, however, rationalized this interpretation away with his stress on the 'personal factor':

Read over an article by Miss MacMurchy on The Labour Problem, the best points in it are those in which stress is laid on the personal equation, and the matter of personality. It lies at the root of all. This being so talk of the 'solution' of the Labour problem, apart from the 'solution' of 'restoring humanity' is to speak of an impossible thing. People mean only a solution of some of the present day difficulties which appear incident to relationships between employers and employees as they frequently are.[40]

Since strikes or lock-outs tend only to exacerbate ill-feeling, their continuance must necessarily lead away from the restoration of humanity. To bring about a resumption of work, then, is to help recreate the preconditions for proper relations. Attention to particular grievances, if it is misplaced from an attempt to bring about an end to the work stoppage, is incorrect on this interpretation as it deals only with what is 'incident to relationships,' rather than the all-important relationships themselves. Of course, as suggested above, this line of reasoning was at least partly a rationalization. The equation of a settlement with an end to hostilities also flowed from the dictates of economic development and, less abstractly, from the ever-present fact that the Department of Labour's success or worth would be measured in government eyes much more in terms of its ability to put an end to strikes than in terms of its record of improving wages, working conditions, or the long-term prospects for industrial relations in a particular industry. This emphasis on the short term has led some commentators to criticize King's policy, particularly the IDI Act, as merely postponing strikes inasmuch as the resolution of issues in dispute was postponed to another, and perhaps more bloody, day. This critique is discussed in Chapter 9, below.

The third reason for King's mediation is related to the second. King was extremely reluctant to grant legitimacy to some typical demands made by unions – in particular, recognition – and he was, at the same time, surprisingly willing in many instances to accept the contention of employers, reluctant to deal with a union, that the strike was ineffective. This, of course, was related to the ease of finding strikebreakers in a period when the pace of economic development, no matter how rapid, was outrun by the pace of immigration. We have seen some indication of both of these tendencies already: we have noted the *Labour Gazette* decision, resented by the TLC, to refrain from publishing accounts of strikes when employers claimed they were no longer 'embarrassed,' and in the Bertram case we have seen King's willingness – justified perhaps by the small number of strikers remaining – to

40 Diary, 2 Jan. 1903

accept the employers' estimate of the situation. One further brief example may help to clarify what is involved: this is King's diary account of his intervention in a strike at the Gurney Foundry Company, Toronto, in 1902:

I met the committee of the stove mounters at 9.30 and got a statement of their case from them. It seemed to me they had acted hastily, and that the dispute was a poor affair at best. Two apprentices had asked at the demand of the Union to receive journeymen's pay, and were told their time as apprentices was up that they must leave the Union or the Co's employ. The union decided to back them up & with small funds at their disposal they came out. When I went to see Mr. Guerney [*sic*] about it, his reply in brief was that it was convenient to work with fewer men just now, & that there were no places to fill. My feeling is that the men were in the right, that the so-called apprentices were really more than entitled to be classed as journeymen & to receive journeymen's wages, but that the Co. adopts this plan to squeeze more gain into its own coffers at the expense of those who help to produce its wealth. I think, too, the Co. is endeavouring to crush out the unionism in its employ, for the same reason – to prevent any parity between itself & those in its employ in the matter of making a bargain. The situation, certainly, gave no opportunity of settlement, & means only defeat for the men, as the Co. can replace them & knows it. A lying foreman, is, I think, too, responsible for much.[41]

The 'nature of settlement' in this affair, as reported in the Annual Report, was that 'Company claimed to have reduced its working staff and filled vacancies caused by strike with outside men.'[42] Now King clearly had little sympathy for the employer in this case, but his judgment that there was 'no opportunity for settlement, & means only defeat for the men,' could only have been favourable to the employer. Employers in general seem to have recognized this, for a few months after the 'settlement' of the Gurney strike another Toronto foundryman active in that industry's warfare approached King. 'Had talk with Mr. Polson, re offer from National Metal Trades Association of position $6000 & expenses, wished & urged me to apply for it.'[43]

Of course, King's assessment of the situation may have been correct, and the fact that there were many similar assessments in his career may simply mean that there were many similar situations. Perhaps unions only turned to the Department of Labour when all else was lost; in the absence of independent evidence we must either accept King's view or suspend judgment. But what is interesting here is that King made no move to provide or support

41 *Ibid.*, 20 Feb. 1902
42 Canada, *Sessional Papers*, 36 (1902), 41
43 Diary, 8 June 1902

statutory assistance to unions or workers in situations like these. Apprentices denied their due had no recourse, and unions faced with extinction by reactionary employers were in a similar situation. If strikes could not win the day for the forces of righteousness – and King leaves us in no doubt about who constituted the armies of light in the Gurney situation – conciliation seemed to be no better. Moreover, in many instances where strikes were waged at least partly for recognition – for the commitment of the employer to dealing with the union as the representative of his employees – conciliation proved to be one of the causes for defeat.

King's position on recognition disputes is, on the face of it, paradoxical. If he believed in trade unions and in fair dealing between employer and employee, why should he have been so hostile to attempts by unions to institutionalize a bargaining relationship? We noted in an earlier chapter King's youthful (and wholly erroneous) judgment that the development of the union movement in the United States was commendable because 'the struggle for existence and subsequent recognition ... has been almost entirely wanting.' One of the principal features of the western coal mining interventions was his resistance to the recognition demand. There seem to have been two reasons for this hostility.

The first, a practical one, was that recognition was a no-compromise demand. It arose when employers refused to deal with a union and posed an often insurmountable stumbling block to settlement, the more so when King's intervention cut short the struggle. It is suggested in Chapter 8 that King's well-known, if miscalled, 'company union' strategy was devised to deal with situations like these. The second reason, also mentioned there, was an ideological one founded in the emphasis on the personal equation. This was set out in the *Report* of the Royal Commission on Industrial Disputes in British Columbia, where the argument was made, in effect, that unions which deserved recognition would get it because they would convince management of their reasonableness and of the indispensability of a good working relationship. This sort of argument, of course, is quite beneath contempt and may only be excused by noting that King was not the sole author of that chapter of the report. But it is clear that King resented the recognition demand because he saw in it both the machinations of unprincipled 'agitators' and a stumbling block to settlement, and could fall back on the argument that while recognition in general might be a good thing, any given employer might have good reason for not wanting to recognize a particular union. The significance of this, of course, is that it made it even more unlikely that King's interventions would result in the establishment of a lasting bargaining relationship between company and union. True 'conciliation' was impossible under such circumstances; hence King had to substitute his brand of mediation.

V

King's apprenticeship – a sorcerer's apprenticeship, Ferns and Ostry would have it – was served under the Conciliation Act. The lessons he learned then were translated, somewhat abortively, into the Railway Labour Disputes Act and, much more successfully, the IDI Act. One final aspect of that apprenticeship might be examined: King's developing relationship with the trade union movement, particularly the post-Berlin TLC. Such an examination is all the more important because King's interventions in industrial disputes usually appear, in retrospect, to have been of far greater value to the employers than to the workers involved. This, naturally enough, has led to some rather severe and often penetrating judgments by later commentators about the effects of King's policy and practice, although it ought to be clear by now that there can be no easy translation from effect to intent. This being so, it is essential to note that King and his policy retained the favour of the official voice of the labour movement. Much of that policy, however reactionary its effects may appear in hindsight, was the belated if usually partial realization of demands that the labour movement had been making for some time. Moreover, King managed to gain some personal influence in the TLC through one of its two principal leaders, Patrick Draper, although the other, John Flett, quite reciprocated King's hostility.

The TLC was in general favourable to the Conciliation Act, although vestiges of its disappointment that the Act did not amount to a compulsory arbitration measure were still in evidence even after the Berlin convention. In 1901 the TLC Executive reported on the Act, echoing King's claim in the first number of the *Gazette* that compulsory arbitration was *ultra vires* the federal government. It argued that the legislation 'goes a considerable way, even as a voluntary measure, in the direction of conciliation and arbitration,' and proposed some amendments 'to make the act effective.' These were basically attempts to smuggle compulsory arbitration in the back door by making it applicable to those areas over which the federal government could conceivably be argued to have jurisdiction: companies bonused by the government and firms working under government contract. The Executive also wanted it mandatory that both parties to every dispute submit a report for publication in the *Labour Gazette* and the departmental annual reports. The Committee on this report recommended that the amendment relating to government contracts should be adopted.[44] The Manitoba Provincial Executive, however, expressed dissatisfaction with the Act, especially in connection with recognition disputes, and called for full compulsory arbitration

44 *TLC* 1901, 16f, 79.

legislation. But the only report on a specific intervention made to the 1901 convention was that of the Nova Scotia Provincial Executive: 'A strike among the coal workers of Sydney, C.B., at one time took a serious turn. Mr. King, Deputy Minister of Labor, Ottawa, arrived in the Province at the time and proceeded to Cape Breton, where, having ascertained the particulars of the grievances, effected a settlement shortly after his arrival.'[45]

A similar report was presented in 1902 by the same Provincial Executive, which informed the convention that in the Halifax longshoremen's strike, King 'was not many days in effecting a settlement satisfactory both to the unions and to their employers.' The convention discussed new amendments to be proposed to government, and again there was an attempt to smuggle in compulsory arbitration of a sort, notwithstanding that convention's general stand on the subject. The amendment, which had been introduced by the Winnipeg labour MP, Arthur Puttee, would change the arbitration section of the Act to make the appointment of arbitrators follow on the application of one, not both, parties to the dispute. The award of the arbitrator would be made public through the *Gazette*, but would not be binding on the parties. This was an interesting foretaste of the IDI philosophy. Puttee had drafted a bill containing these amendments, together with one which would make it possible for the government to appoint a conciliator without the request of either party, and another forbidding the arbitrator to make abandonment of union membership a condition of the award, and had presented it to the House in March.[46] Its fate there at the hands of the CMA lobbyists is adequately described in *Industrial Canada*:

Your committee opposed this very strongly owing to the difficulty always experienced in securing proper arbitration and also because the measure laid undue emphasis upon the protection of union membership without providing in any way for recognizing the rights of the employer. Owing to the representations made by the Association at Ottawa, the Bill was not passed.[47]

Puttee reintroduced the bill in the following session and although, as the TLC commented, it did not stand a chance of passing third reading, it gave the CMA a run for its money. *Industrial Canada* reported:

Extreme regret was expressed that a Committee of the House of Commons had passed the amendment to the Conciliation Act introduced by Mr. Puttee. Steps were

45 *Ibid.*, 37, 49
46 *Ibid.*, 1902, 42, 22f, 26, 29f
47 *IC*, Sept. 1902, 90

taken by the executive council to make a still further effort to have the Bill defeated. The council expressed its regret that so many members of the House, and even members of the Cabinet, had appeared to be so partial to the interests of organized labor in the issues before them; they had either remained silent during the discussion of these measures, or had raised their voices in favour of granting additional powers to irresponsible organizations which were even now hampering severely the industries of the country.[48]

On the whole the TLC was satisfied with the wording and practice of the Conciliation Act: its only complaint was that it did not go far enough. Some of the individual unions which had first-hand experience with the Act and King's methods were sufficiently impressed to write congratulatory letters to Mulock. Indeed, that champion of the spoils system was himself popular enough to rate a warm accolade from the TLC on the occasion of his retirement from the Labour portfolio, and it seems unlikely that it was the retirement which was applauded.[49]

It should not be imagined, though, that the TLC was completely autonomous of the Laurier government, making these proposals from a position of lofty independence. Lib-Lab politics, as we have seen, played a large part in the pre-Berlin Congress, and after that convention the Liberal interest retained some considerable influence. It does seem, however, that the party contact-man changed: before Berlin it was Mulock; after, it was King.

King received his introduction to TLC wire-pulling very early in his career in the department. Just before the federal election of 1900, when King had been barely a month in his job, Mulock showed him some private correspondence which had recently arrived: 'from Fitzpatrick a Grit wire puller & labor agitator offering to pack the Labor Convent'n here with Grit representatives to overbalance the tory ones whom the elected representatives are trying to bring. But he wanted their expenses paid. No doubt this will [be] done out of a fund, tho M. said nothing to me of this. I felt it was in his mind.'[50] King was properly shocked – 'One sees here how the working classes are really duped in their organizations & are the creatures of politicians. How statesmen, mayors, agitators etc. all pull together in the party struggle. One feels that the devil in such a case can only be fought with his own weapons. What is needed is honest indept. action, but that requires leadership' – and no doubt Mulock exhibited the letter in order to test his protégé's squeamishness.

48 *TLC* 1903, 16; *IC*, June 1903, 480
49 *TLC* 1904, 9
50 Diary, 26 Aug. 1900

King's call for independent political action need not be taken very seriously, for he maintained his old view that politics and unionism make a corrosive and unstable mixture. Three weeks after Mulock's lesson in practical politics, King was attending the TLC convention as an observer: 'The discuss'n was on the subject of indept. pol. act'n in the election & an amendt. against it was lost. It was plain to see the political schemers at work, the Congress was full of them & I could see that one section was seeking to defeat the other while playing a false game with the labouring classes as a whole.'[51] 'The [labour] question is much to the fore during this election,' he noted during the campaign, 'but with the exception of Mr. Mulock, most of the cabinet seem to be afraid of touching it. The Unions are more active in the no's of their indept. candidates. The fair wages & anti-sweating mvt. & the Department of Labour, and Labour Gazette are the main features, with some stress on the enforcement of the Alien Labour Act.' Echoes of his mistrust of independent labour politics are heard throughout the diaries. Thus, in 1906, King commented very favourably on an article by W.H. Mallock about labour members of the British parliament. Mallock argued that 'the best way of insuring the nation against demands on the part of labour that are unreasonable, is to satisfy, and if possible to anticipate, those that are just and reasonable.' 'I never saw the truth represented better,' wrote King. And when he launched his first search for a constituency, he thought it ought not to be one with a heavy labour vote, for 'it might be necessary to legislate in the interests of labour & the country in a manner that some labour men might not approve of.'[52]

King realized, however, that, so long as independent labour politics was likely to cause more damage to the Tories than to the Liberals, it could safely be encouraged. In August 1906, Robert Glockling, a long-time Conservative labourite and sometime TLC president, resigned in disgust from the Ontario Bureau of Labor because of the CMA-sponsored barriers the provincial Conservative government put in the way of its work. King immediately suggested to TLC President Alphonse Verville that Glockling be run as a labour candidate in Toronto, and repeated the suggestion to Draper. 'The tories have made a fatal blunder in letting him out.'[53] On another occasion he made a similar suggestion to Frank Sherman, the UMWA organizer, urging him to run as a socialist.

51 *Ibid.*, 20 Sept. 1900
52 *Ibid.*, 9 Oct. 1900; 6 Sept. 1906 (W.H. Mallock, 'The Political Powers of Labour,' *The Nineteenth Century*, vol. LX [August 1906] 202–14); 4 Dec. 1906
53 *Ibid.*, 31 Aug. 1906

King's relations with the leadership of the TLC were mixed. His assessment of John Flett as an agitator has already been quoted, and he was convinced Flett was behind the charges that he had campaigned for the Liberals during his first intervention under the Conciliation Act – the charges from which Ralph Smith had had to rescue him. Another influential TLC leader, Patrick Draper, was his warm ally. Draper, who represented the Ottawa labour council, was elected TLC Secretary-Treasurer in 1900, and retained that crucial post throughout King's career in the Labour Department. In 1901 he asked King for a biographical sketch to appear in the Ottawa Labour Day souvenir programme, and already King had identified him as an ally against Flett. King supplied part of the copy for the TLC's Executive Report in 1901, and it appears that the Conciliation Act amendments calling among other things for compulsory arbitration in government contract work were King's idea. This close working relationship persisted, so that in 1907, when King was actively lobbying to be appointed Minister of Labour if he won a seat, he enlisted Draper's aid in heading off such other claimants as Ralph Smith and Alphonse Verville. King was behind the TLC's strong resolutions in favour of an autonomous labour department, and he treated the leading figures on the executive who supported the idea to a 'little dinner' at the Russell House to keep the pressure on. Nine months later he was agitating still: 'Had a short talk with Draper of Trades & Labour Congress re getting thro resolution Dept. of Labour.'[54]

The secret diplomatic history of King's rise to the Cabinet might be told, without too much exaggeration, as the story of his successful attempts to supplant Ralph Smith as labour's leading Liberal. (At one point, he had even tried to get Smith to abandon his seat in his favour.[55]) That he could do so without being a trade unionist or an MP himself was a testament to his ability to accommodate his programme to those of several powerful interests: labour, business, and his Cabinet masters. This ability to accommodate, however, was not simply a sign of opportunist flexibility in King: it was inherent in the programme of industrial peace itself. Before turning to King's greatest claim to be the father of industrial peace – the IDI Act – it will be well to examine his conciliation practice in a little more detail.[56]

54 *Ibid.*, 11 March, 12, 10, 15 Aug. 1901; 14 and 15 Jan., 10 Sept. 1907
55 *Ibid.*, 15 March, 4 April 1906
56 Cf. Canada, Department of Labour, 'Labour Legislation in Canada: A Historical Outline of the Principal Dominion and Provincial Labour Laws,' Aug. 1945, p. 10: 'The great bulk of the work accomplished under this [Conciliation] Act is, necessarily, unknown to the general public.'

8
War on the periphery

Safe in his power, whose eyes discern afar
The secret ambush of a specious pray'r;
Implore his aid, in his decision rest,
Secure whate'er he gives, he gives the best.
[Samuel Johnson, 'The Vanity of Human Wishes']

No industry was so torn with strife during the formative years of Canadian labour policy as coal mining. Both in Nova Scotia and the west, coal miners struggled throughout the period to establish and preserve their organizations, and this meant not only bitter conflicts with some of the most intransigent employers in the country, but internecine warfare as well. As John Mitchell's United Mine Workers of America attempted to bring AFL unionism to the coalfields, it battled competing organizations on both coasts. In the east, the Provincial Workmen's Association finally succumbed to UMWA raids in the wake of its debilitating 1909 strike. In the west, conflict between the Mine Workers and the syndicalist Western Federation of Miners was eventually resolved by a jurisdictional agreement assigning coal mines to the former and hard-rock mines to the latter. Throughout the seven years during which the Conciliation Act was the principal expression of federal disputes policy, however, these conflicts continued unabated.

Coal mining was carried on at the periphery of Canadian industrialism. Particularly in the west, in the pit camps and company towns of Vancouver Island and the Crow's Nest Pass, the miners' daily experience gave the lie to pat homilies about the mutual interests of labour and capital. Working under conditions of great danger and deprivation in a highly competitive industry which epitomized the staples cycle of boom and bust, their position further threatened by the flooding of the labour market with Oriental contract

TABLE 1 Department of Labour Interventions, Western Canadian Mining Industry, 1900–1911*

Year	Act[1]	Company and locality	# Workers	Industry[2]
1901	C	LeRoi, War Eagle, Centre Star mines, Rossland, BC	1000	M
	C	Alexandria Mines, South Wellington, BC	260	C
1903	C	Crow's Nest Pass Coal Company, Fernie, Morissey and Michel, BC	1500	C
	R	Crow's Nest Pass Coal Company, Fernie, Morissey and Michel, BC	1500	C
	R	Western Fuel Company, Nanaimo, BC	600	C
	R	Wellington Colliery Company, Ladysmith and Union, BC	300	C
1905	C	Western Fuel Company, Nanaimo, BC	700	C
1906	C	Alberta Railway and Immigration Company, Lethbridge, Alta.	500	C
1907	I	Canada West Coal and Coke Company, Taber, Alta.	150	C
	I	Western Canadian Coal Operators Association:		
		Canadian American Coal and Coke Company, Frank, Alta.	250	C
		Crow's Nest Pass Coal Company, Fernie, Coal Creek, Michel, BC	1800	C
		International Coal and Coke Company, Coleman, Alta.	370	C
		West Canadian Collieries Limited, Lille, Bellevue, Alta.	350	C
		Breckenridge and Lund Coal Company, Lundbreck, Alta.	125	C
		H.W. McNeill Coal Company, Canmore, Alta.	300	C
		Pacific Coal Company, Bankhead, Alta.	400	C
	I	Alberta Railway and Irrigation Coal Company, Lethbridge, Alta.	400	C
	I	Canadian Consolidated Mining and Smelting Company, Moyie, BC	400	M
	I	Hillcrest Coal & Coke Company, Hillcrest, Alta.	70	C
	I	Hosmer Mines, Hosmer, BC	100	C
	I	Canada West Coal and Coke Company, Taber, Alta.	150	C
	I	Domestic Coal Company, Taber, Alta.	50	C
	I	Duggan Huntrods & Company, Taber, Alta.	40	C
	I	Strathcona Coal Company, Edmonton, Alta.	40	C
1908	I	John Marsh et al., coal mine operators, Woodpecker, Alta.	100	C
	I	Manitoba and Saskatchewan Coal Company, Bienfait, Sask.	50	C
	I	Western Division Collieries, Taylorton, Sask.	90	C

Year		Company		
	I	Standard Coal Company, Edmonton, Alta.	20	C
	I	Galbraith Coal Company, Lundbreck, Alta.	30	C
1909	I	British Columbia Copper Company, Greenwood, BC	225	M
	I	Nicola Valley Coal and Coke Company, Middlesboro, BC	150	C
	I	Western Coal Operators Association, comprising 7 companies, Alta., BC	2100	C
	I	Canada West Coal Company, Taber, Alta.	300	C
	I	Edmonton Standard Coal Company, Edmonton, Alta.	75	C
	I	James W. Blain, Cardiff, Alta.	60	C
1910	I	Alberta Coal Mining Company, Cardiff, Alta.	35	C
	I	British Columbia Copper Company, Greenwood, BC	350	M
	I	Canadian–American Coal and Coke Company, Frank, Alta.	262	C
	I	Crow's Nest Pass Coal Company, Fernie, BC	3000	C
1911	I	Western Coal Operators Association, BC and Alta. (UMWA Dist. 18)	6000	C

SOURCE Canada, Department of Labour, *Report*, S.P. 36 and 36a, 1901–1913

NOTES

* To end of Laurier government, Oct. 6, 1911.
1 C: Conciliation Act, 1900
  R: Royal Commission on Industrial Disputes in British Columbia, 1903
  I: Industrial Disputes Investigation Act, 1907
2 M: Metal Mining
  C: Coal Mining

labour, western miners turned to direct political action and radical syndicalism to safeguard their interests. Like their fellows elsewhere in the world, Canadian coal miners were unusually militant, unusually committed to collective action, and unusually hostile to industrial capitalism.[1] As much for these reasons as because their industry was the essential supplier of fuel for the homes, mills, smelters, and railways of the west, the miners became the recipients of unusually frequent doses of Mackenzie King's soothing syrup.

This chapter examines a few instances of federal intervention in the Conciliation Act period. It is intended to provide further illustrations of the conciliation policy in practice, and to clarify King's role in the struggle between John Mitchell's market-oriented business unionism and the radical syndicalism of the Western Federation. It ends with an account of King's intervention in the strike which inspired the passage of the Industrial Disputes Investigation Act and helped set the stage for the closing irony of his career in the labour department.

I

The Western Federation's most important local in British Columbia at the turn of the century was the Rossland Miners' Union. After 1899, hard-rock operators in the area began a concerted attack on the union, employing spies, informers, armed police, and provocateurs. In July 1901, the miners struck in a last-ditch attempt to preserve their union, and in sympathy with strikers at the Northport, Washington, smelter that handled Rossland ores. In response, the mine managers imported strikebreakers, in violation of the Alien Labour Act, and obtained injunctions against the strikers in local courts. 'Union officers were subpoenaed and ordered to produce their records in court; their refusal to comply brought contempt charges and imprisonment.'[2] The employers were clearly gaining the upper hand and, at the end of October, the union's executive committee wired King to come to Rossland 'to act under Conciliation Act, 1900, to investigate and adjust strike here at the mines.'[3]

When King arrived at Rossland on 9 November, he found that the mine managers had been able to replace the strikers, many of whom had drifted

---

1 Cf. Ben Selekman, *Postponing Strikes: A Study of the Industrial Disputes Investigation Act of Canada* (New York: Russell Sage Foundation, 1927), 88ff; Jamieson, 97ff
2 A.R. McCormack, *Reformers, Rebels, and Revolutionaries: The Western Canadian Radical Movement, 1899–1919* (Toronto: University of Toronto Press, 1977) 39. The court case is briefly described in chapter 6 above.
3 *LG*, Dec. 1901, 362

away. The situation was not one calculated to win King's sympathy. He made certain findings of fact – that the strikes had been called without due regard for the relevant clauses in the union's constitution, that the major issue involved was recognition of the union committee, and that the Rossland strike was in large part a walkout in sympathy with the Northport local – any one of which would have been enough to put the action beyond the pale. 'As to public sympathy with the men,' he told Mulock, 'I am unable to find any traces of it. I asked the committee to give me the names of half a dozen reputable citizens who would say that they were right in their demands and their present attitude, but they were unable to give them.'[4] King believed the men to be 'entirely in the wrong. I have told them so and have no sympathy with them, that is to say, the agitators, for this is clearly and simply an agitators' fight.' He recommended that, although there had certainly been violations of the Alien Labour law, the government should not bother investigating or prosecuting them.

'I have obtained a new point of view in regard to trade unionism,' King wrote to Harper, who was holding the fort back in Ottawa. 'The situation here is one of the grossest tyranny of a labour organization, and the dealings of those who have manipulated the affair are as crooked as they can be. I would never have been able to explain conditions in British Columbia rightly, much less comprehend the present situation, unless I had come here, and for this reason I think the purpose of my coming has been fully met.' The letter continued to outline the essentials of King's new comprehension 'of the obstacles with which industrial development in B.C. has to contend.' These included political unrest, and the 'embarrassing legislation,' presumably Oriental exclusion, 'which has followed in consequence'; 'trade union tyranny, caused in part, through the interference of American organizations in Canadian affairs'; the Alien Labour laws, stock manipulation by investors, and 'the possible monopoly of coal and coke.'[5]

For the first time in his career in the Department of Labour, King had come across a union which did not meet his rather stringent criteria of legitimacy. King's first impressions of the Western Federation were to be lasting, and his litany of complaints – violation of union constitutions, irresponsible agitators, recognition disputes, sympathy strikes – was to be enumerated again and again in the years to come.

4 King correspondence, King to Mulock, 18 Nov. 1901
5 King to Harper, 18 Nov. 1901

II

King's next involvement with the Western Federation came in 1903. The Crow's Nest Pass Coal Company, operating mines at Michel, Morrissey, and Coal Creek, BC, was the main supplier of coal and coke to the British Columbia metal mining and smelting industry. Workers at the three camps organized a WFM district federation in November 1902, and drew up a new wage scale to be presented to management. The company's general manager, however, declined to deal with the union and a strike was called on 10 February 1903. As it progressed, the entire mining industry in the region was affected by coal shortages. The Fernie Board of Trade and the premier of the province both offered to intervene in order to attempt a settlement. Although neither the union nor the company had requested intervention under the Conciliation Act, King was sent to the scene at the insistence of BC Senator Templeman.

Once he had investigated the situation, King decided that since recognition was at issue, in the nature of the case 'conciliation or arbitration could do little, if anything, towards effecting the termination' of the strike.[6] The refusal of the company to meet with the union committee, and the refusal of the strikers to abandon their union, precluded any hope of settlement other than what might result from a trial of strength. On 28 February, King left Fernie.

King had not been able to meet with the general manager of the Crow's Nest Pass Company, for he had gone to Victoria to attend the founding convention of the British Columbia Mining Association. Having adopted a constitution permitting it to 'use its good offices in adjusting and settling mining labour difficulties,' the association decided, the very day that King left for Ottawa empty-handed, to intervene in the Fernie strike. By the end of March, it had arranged a settlement which included a form of recognition of the miners' union. The Crow's Nest Pass Company agreed to meet with union committees from each of the camps and from the district executive, so long as only company employees sat on these committees.[7]

The Mining Association also passed a resolution requesting that the provincial government appoint a commission 'to examine as fully as possible into the existing relations of employer and employees engaged in the mining industry in this province, and to gather data on the question of capital and labour therein employed; the said commission in the meantime to be regarded as a

6 *LG*, March 1903, 673ff
7 *Ibid.*, April 1903, 775–7, 799ff

conciliation board in any mining labour troubles that may occur ...' The BC government was evidently willing to accede to this request but, in the event, it was a federal Royal Commission that inquired into the province's labour scene. A great deal has been written about the Royal Commission which investigated coal-mining strikes led by the WFM in Vancouver Island and the Crow's Nest Pass, and the CPR strike organized by the related syndicalist union, the United Brotherhood of Railway Employees.[8] Here it will be sufficient to briefly review the main features of the inquiry and the final report, and to describe King's role.

The appointment of the commission seems to have been instigated by concern in Cabinet about radical American unionism in the west. King's masters were not quite so sophisticated as he in being able to discriminate between good unionism and bad – for Laurier and Mulock, at least up to 1903, the distinction to be drawn was between American and Canadian unionism. Thus Mulock to Laurier: 'perhaps it would assist to disillusion [Canadian workers who had "come under the domination of the AFL"] if an intelligent commission ... were to point out the injuries that have come to them because of the interference of the American unions.'[9] On 18 April 1903, only a couple of weeks after the Mining Association had settled the Fernie strikes, the government appointed the Hon. Gordon Hunter, Chief Justice of British Columbia, and a Methodist minister, Rev. E.S. Rowe, commissioners under the Inquiries Act. Mackenzie King was appointed secretary of the Royal Commission, and he was a very active secretary indeed. He has been credited with – or blamed for – drafting its final report.[10]

The inquiry got off to a less than wholly auspicious start, when Chief Justice Hunter suggested that the Vancouver Island strikers abandon their WFM local and return to work quietly while the commission went about its business. Needless to say, the miners politely refused. The commissioners toured the Island and held two weeks of hearings at Vancouver, where the proceedings often appeared more like a trial of the WFM and UBRE than an impartial inquiry into the causes of industrial unrest. King 'became quite roused and excited in a quiet way at the bias' he thought the commission was showing in permitting the mine owners' counsel to cross-examine the

8 See, *inter alia*, Jamieson, 112ff; Allan D. Orr, 'The Western Federation of Miners and the Royal Commission on Industrial Disputes,' unpublished MA dissertation, University of British Columbia, 1968.
9 Quoted in Jamieson, 119
10 Cf. Dawson, 138, and 139n where it is stated that 'the concluding section of the report, however, embodying general recommendations and conclusions was not written by King alone, but in collaboration with the Chief Justice.'

miners 'as if unions were being tried for their right to exist.'[11] Mackenzie King, of course, had had a similar experience himself in the aftermath of the Toronto student strike, and he knew what it was like to be on the stand. While the commission was investigating the Vancouver Island situation, King's sympathies – and, he thought, those of Hunter and Rowe – were fully with the workers. Story after story of the exactions imposed by James Dunsmuir, principal colliery operator and sometimes premier of the province, was retailed from the witness stand as the commission piled up what was to become some 800 pages of printed testimony. On 8 May, King told his diary that 'If Comm'rs had to report tonight it wd. all be in favour of the men & against the Dunsmuir Co.' A few days later, he summarized his analysis of the situation:

A selfish millionaire, has become something of a tyrannical autocrat. To satisfy a prejudice of greed he has undertaken to make serfs of a lot [of] free men, [by] compelling them to live at a place of his own dictation miles away from their work. Owning everything & possessing all but absolute power, he will let his men possess as little as possible. Every attempt they have made to form a union he has frustrated by dismissing leaders, to be more secure in their position these men have at last joined the Western Federat'n of Miners, to have a moral & financial backing. For this the mines of the owner have been closed. To my mind the right to live where a man pleases, & the right to join a lawful organiz'n are legal rights, which for an employer to deny because of monopolistic power is a social wrong. To be free from Individual Autocracy, these men are embracing Socialism, it is a natural and inevitable step.[12]

Natural and inevitable though it might be, in King's view it was highly unfortunate. He had great admiration for the WFM's local organizer – 'he made a splendid witness, answering important questions frankly & directly and admitting nothing on Cross Exam'n that could prejudice the miners' case'[13] – but he concluded that while 'these men are true martyrs, sacrificing much to a cause which they believed true & noble,' socialism was a disease bred of reactionary employers. King could at one and the same time celebrate 'the tremendous nature of the organiz'n movement among wkgmen. gradually uniting all workers into one great brotherhood,' and deplore the miners' refusal to abandon their union and return to work.

11 Diary, 13 May 1903
12 *Ibid*., 10 May 1903; this was a Sunday entry, which may partially account for its particularly righteous tone.
13 *Ibid*., 6 May 1903

When the commission began its sittings in Victoria, and then crossed to the mainland, King's perceptions began to change. He became convinced that American syndicalists 'used the Canadians as a sort of cat's paw for their own purposes.' 'The question of "Union Recognition" seems to be the one rather than a quest'n of wages or conditions. The relation of American organizations the main question.' King began to sort out his thinking about industrial peace:

The solution to the problem of strikes seems to me to lie along the line of a kind of business partnership arrived at by long term agreements between responsible leaders of organized capital on the one side & organized labour on the other. The trade unions must be incorporated and limits put on the right to strike without compliance with safeguards in the constitution, as, for example, 3 mos. notice, vote of ⅔ majority of men over 21, who have been members of union for 6 mos. ... Conciliation, compulsory investigation, and then compulsory arbitration seem the steps absolutely necessary, in view of the interdependence & interrelation of industries & public welfare.[14]

Once at Nanaimo, King's heated perception of the miners' nobility and the coal companies' rascality, fanned by the extremes of the Dunsmuir situation, died down. Socialism, British Columbia style, was not the celebration of mutual brotherhood he had once imagined it to be, but merely a stubborn refusal to recognize the necessary solidarity of all classes in the community. Most businessmen were not dinosaurs in the Dunsmuir mould, but just ordinary folks. King's sense of social justice could best be aroused when there was a clear fight between Good and Evil. He needed dragons and maidens to stimulate his imagination: in their absence, he fell back on a somewhat despairing defence of the everyday:

It is distressing to see the hold that Socialism has on many of the working classes thro' this island, it is not a healthy sort, but a social unrest which begets the most intense unhappiness, and bitterness between classes. 'The class conscious struggle' has been urged to the extent of making many irreconcilable elements in the community, and with the sort of leadership there is there can [be] little else save a following of wandering fires. Two or three minor witnesses were also called & the Manager of the Fuel Co. He seemed a very ordinary person, with little to commend him any way, a combination of good nature and headstrongness.[15]

14 *Ibid.*, 12 and 15 May 1903
15 *Ibid.*, 21 May 1903

When the Commission's *Report* appeared, it proved to be a very odd document indeed. It postulated a complex, almost Byzantine, conspiracy among the various affiliates of the American Labor Union to disrupt British Columbia industry, and if this conclusion demonstrated the Chief Justice's grasp of elementary rules of evidence, then the quality of justice in the province must have been strained indeed. While testimony before the inquiry had catalogued a hair-raising collection of instances of the most vicious and tyrannous employment practices, the *Report*'s conclusions focused almost exclusively on the perfidy of the unions. The commission had learned, among other things, that Dunsmuir had forced the miners to relocate their homes and then shut down his mines rather than recognize the union; that the other mine operators had used these and other tactics to try and break their workers' organizations; that the CPR had employed professional spies and provocateurs and had hounded one sick and weak unionist to his death. But when it came time to make recommendations, the commission barely slapped employers on the wrist. They were told they ought to make 'considerable sacrifices, if necessary' in the interest of industrial peace, that they ought to meet with committees of their men, that they ought to employ 'persons of tact and discretion in all the offices of superintendence,' and that workers are 'sentient beings who have, equally with themselves, senses, affections, desires, doubts and fears.' Nothing was said about intelligence; perhaps it was asking as much as could be expected to request recognition of sentience.

When it came to the unions, it was another story. The commission came down hard. It began by condemning the WFM strikes in the familiar terms: they were recognition strikes, they were fomented by foreign agitators, they were called in violation of union constitutions, they were sympathy strikes. It then proceeded to draw the line between legitimate and illegitimate unionism:

And here, it may be remarked, lies the essential difference between the legitimate trade unionist and the revolutionary socialist: the former realizes that he has a common interest with the employer in the successful conduct of the business; the latter postulates an irreconcilable hostility and is ever compassing the embarrassment or ruin of the employer, all the while ignoring the fact that capital and labour are the two blades of the shears which, to work well, must be joined together by the bolt of mutual confidence, but if wrenched apart, are both helpless and useless.[16]

16 Royal Commission on Industrial Disputes in the Province of British Columbia, *Report*, S.P. 36a, 1903, 65f. Fifteen years later, in *Industry and Humanity*, King again used this metaphor of the shears.

The commission recommended that syndicalist unions like the WFM, the United Brotherhood of Railway Employees, and their federation, the American Labor Union, be declared illegal organizations, since they were 'really not a trade union at all, but a secret political organization.' It did not stop here, however, but went on to recommend limitations on the power of 'legitimate' trade unions as well: incorporation, a statutory cooling-off period, prohibition of the boycott and sympathy strikes, and, in certain special circumstances, compulsory arbitration. It urged Canadian workers to 'exercise extreme caution in their decision to join any given organization,' and to 'be careful in the selection of their leaders.' While the commission decided on balance not to prohibit international unionism *per se*, it recommended serious penalties for locals which went on strike at the instance of international headquarters. In a final attempt to sugar the pill, the commission recommended a statutory reduction of the hours of labour: 'of course this ought to be done gradually.'

That the commission had not only condemned the syndicalists, but had come close to tarring legitimate unionism with the same brush was anathema to the AFL unions. Gompers expressed his indignation, 'that we should be classified and come under the category of such concerns which the Commission has exposed to the contumely of the civilized world.' King reassured him that there could be no question of 'the honor, integrity, and faithfulness of any organization affiliated to the American Federation of Labor or upon any of its men.'[17] King's friend A.B. Lowe, organizer for one of the railway unions, wrote to disagree with the recommendations about incorporation.[18] Ultimately, of course, few if any of the commission's proposals became law. The American Labor Union affiliates were not outlawed, although for the time being they sank into obscurity following the failure of their strikes. Unions were not required to incorporate, nor did the various measures to outlaw international unionism introduced from time to time in the Senate achieve success. On the other hand, Alphonse Verville's persistent attempts to get an eight-hour day bill through the Commons were equally unsuccessful. Compulsory investigation and the cooling-off period were to become law a few years later, but King had already been thinking about them before the commission was constituted. The Royal Commission on Industrial Disputes in British Columbia was most significant for its role in clarifying the distinction between good and bad unionism. Its outcome was to be a shift away

---

17 Quoted in R.H. Babcock, *Gompers in Canada: A Study in American Continentalism Before The First World War* (Toronto: University of Toronto Press, 1974), 110
18 King correspondence, 28 Dec. 1903

from making the Canada–US boundary the defining factor, towards discriminating between market-oriented business unionism and unionism founded on 'class prejudice.'

III

With the weakening of the Western Federation in the BC coal fields, the United Mine Workers of America began to take over the territory. Like the WFM, the Mine Workers was an industrial union. Unlike the WFM, it remained within the AFL fold and eschewed syndicalist class notions. Although some local leaders within the British Columbia UMWA district were ardent socialists whose politics remained attractive to many workers in the industry, the dominant figure in the Mine Workers was its president, John Mitchell. Mitchell was not only a pioneer in industrial unionism and collective bargaining; he could speak Mackenzie King's language, too. After the great Pennsylvania anthracite strike of 1902 he wrote a book, *Organized Labor*, for an evangelical publishing house. The very first sentences set out Mitchell's conviction that industrial capitalism was here to stay, and that trade unionism must find its place within it: 'The average wage earner has made up his mind that he must remain a wage earner. He has given up the hope of a kingdom to come, where he will himself be a capitalist, and he asks that the reward for his work be given to him as a workingman.' 'There is no necessary hostility between labor and capital,' Mitchell wrote; 'Neither can do without the other ... the interest of one is the interest of the other.' Mitchell recognized that 'many persons ... divide labor organizations into three classes, respectable, semi-respectable, and disreputable.' 'This classification is like dividing men into adults, youths, and children. The child becomes a youth, and the youth a man, and in the same manner the unions now denounced as radical and unreliable will in due time attain to complete and full fledged respectability.' It was all a matter of mutual respect and fair dealing. Mitchell was generally opposed to compulsory arbitration as a substitute for the strike, but he argued that in some essential industries, like the railways, 'the power of the state might occasionally be exercised in order to secure the country from incalculable damage.'[19] It was President Roosevelt's intervention in the Pennsylvania strike that had won the UMWA both organizational gains and public respect.

19 *Organized Labor: Its Problems, Purposes and Ideals and the Present and Future of American Wage Earners* (Philadelphia: American Book and Bible House, 1903), ix, 84f, 345

Mitchell could speak the conciliatory language that King had made his own: at the same time, he could be a very tough trade unionist. It took King some time to realize this, and it was to occasion some embarrassment. But if there had to be unions in the western coalfields, certainly the UMWA was a vast improvement over the syndicalists. The Royal Commission had played the two off against one another in its report, to the great advantage of the Mine Workers. When King met Mitchell at a National Civic Federation convention in Chicago in 1902 or 1903 they made a pact: should UMWA attempts to organize in the western Canadian coalfields give rise to a situation that King felt must lead to an attack on international unionism, he would contact Mitchell immediately.[20] Occasion for this soon came. In late 1903, the UMWA raided the WFM in the Crow's Nest district, and by 1905 it had taken over organization in the Nanaimo area on Vancouver Island. The Nanaimo union had begun as an independent organization: as such it had sent Ralph Smith to the BC legislature and then to the House of Commons. In 1903, it had been swept into the Western Federation movement and had been radicalized sufficiently to deny Smith credentials to the Trades and Labour Congress. Then it passed to the Mine Workers and, on 24 September 1905, Mackenzie King arrived to settle a dispute.

The two major coal-mining properties on Vancouver Island were owned by Dunsmuir and, until 1903, by the Vancouver Coal and Land Company. The former was irreconcilably hostile to trade unionism: the latter, under the management of S.M. Robins, had enjoyed a working relationship, including a union shop, with the Nanaimo union, and had been warmly commended by the Royal Commission for this. In 1903, the Vancouver Coal Company's properties were taken over by the Western Fuel Company, domiciled in San Francisco, and after a time Robins was fired to be replaced by a Mr Stockett. Apparently Robins was too soft on unions. In October 1904, while the local union's affairs were in disarray due to the weakness of the Western Federation, Stockett introduced a number of changes at the mines. Real wages were reduced, the miners were required to pay for their tools, and the working hours for about half the men were extended. It was apparently the miners' dissatisfaction with these changes and the inability of the WFM to respond to them that had led to the organization of a Mine Workers local.

When Ralph Smith left the BC legislature for Ottawa, the Nanaimo miners elected J.W. Hawthornethwaite as their Independent Labour MLA; in 1902, Hawthornethwaite joined the Revolutionary Socialist Party. Notwithstanding the 'impossibilitist' theoretical stance of the party, the Nanaimo representa-

---

20 King Papers, MG 26 J4, vol. 13, file 82, memorandum on Nanaimo strike

tive proved to be a hard-working advocate of labour reform in the local legislature. He was returned again in the October 1903 BC election, and managed
to secure passage of an Act providing for an eight-hour day in the province's
coal mines. (The eight-hour day for metal miners had been legislated
earlier.[21]) This enactment was to furnish the immediate matter for the 1905
Nanimo affair. The Western Fuel Company argued that, owing to the peculiar geology of its mining properties, the eight-hour law discriminated against
its business in favour of other BC coal mines. Moreover, the company
claimed that, since its miners had elected the MLA responsible for the act,
they should be required to bear the discriminatory burden of the legislation.

At first the company had threatened to shut down its mines entirely in an
attempt to forestall passage of the Act. When this proved ineffective, it
decided to shift the burden of the legislation by closing one of its shafts and
requiring all miners to enter the workings from Protection Island, the cost of
transportation to be borne by the men. By rearranging the mode of entrance
to the mine, the company argued that it was able to avoid the discriminatory
provisions of the eight-hour law, which timed the hours of work 'from bank
to bank.' On 27 May, manager Stockett provided the miners with three alternatives: the mines would be closed down, or the men must accept the new
mode of access and pay the costs of transportation, or there could be a general 10 per cent wage reduction for all underground employees. The miners,
worried that this was just another in the long series of attempts to undermine
their position, turned down all three alternatives, and on 1 June the company locked them out. The UMWA local attempted on several occasions to
open negotiations for a settlement, but Stockett refused to recognize a union
committee. At bottom, it was a capital strike against the BC mines legislation.[22]

Four months after the mines had been closed down, Mackenzie King
arrived on the scene. Once again, he came without an invitation from either
the company or the miners. He began by revisiting an old acquaintance,
ex-manager Robins, who told him that Dunsmuir had arranged with the
Western Fuel Company to supply its customers' orders for the duration of
the dispute, and that the president of the Fuel Company, a Mr Howard, had
experienced difficulties with unions in San Francisco and so would not consider recognizing the UMWA at Nanaimo. Robins had suggested that the
company sign a binding time contract with the union, but Howard had

21 McCormack, *Reformers*, 64
22 This paragraph, and the rest of this account of the Nanaimo affair, are based for the
most part on the Nanaimo memorandum in the King Papers.

refused to consider it. Robins told King that Hawthornethwaite 'was a very dangerous man, and that he had been responsible for most of the trouble, he also said that there was no doubt that the amendment to the Eight-hour law produced by Mr. Hawthornethwaite had worked an injustice to this Company so far as vertical shaft mines were concerned.'

King next went to visit Mr McLean, the secretary of the UMWA local. The circumstances of their meeting could not have been better calculated to win the immediate sympathy of the Deputy Minister, who 'found him returning from Sunday School with a bouquet of flowers, there had been a children's service and he had been teaching a class, some of the flowers had been sent to the hospital, he had brought a few home for his wife and children.' McLean explained to King that the miners had decided the previous week not to resume work by a vote of 247 to 9, since Stockett refused to make any alteration in this earlier conditions. King immediately formed a plan – a plan that was to become a part of his general practice when recognition disputes involving 'legitimate' unions were concerned:

I was surprised, however, to learn from [McLean] that Mr Stockett has gone so far as he would meet a committee from the men, so long as they did not come as representatives of the United Mine Workers, they might, however, all belong to the United Mine Workers, this gave me the first view of an opening through the situation, this meeting with Mr Stockett was prepared to let the men have their organization, although unwilling to recognize it, and I at once made up my mind to proceed on the lines of pointing out a distinction between being allowed to have an organization, though not having the organization recognized and the Company absolutely refusing to allow any men in its employ to belong to an organization which is Mr Dunsmuir's attitude where an organization has outside affiliations.

The next day, King met with members of the local UMWA committee, who explained the history of their union and the events leading up to the lockout. King sympathized with their opposition to the October 1904 reductions, but told them it was now probably too late to do anything about them. The miners claimed that Stockett was trying to play the Western Federation off against the Mine Workers, although the WFM no longer had more than 20 or 30 members in Nanaimo, while the UMWA was paying relief to some 360 members. According to King, the committee admitted that the eight-hour law worked somewhat to the disadvantage of the Nanaimo mines, although it resisted the company's attempt to make the workers bear the cost and argued that the transportation charges the company wanted to impose were much too high. The committee suggested that, had the law timed the eight hours from pit base instead of bank, it would have been fairer to the Western Fuel Company: 'I immediately took a cue from this point and got them to repeat that they thought some unfairness in Hawthornethwaite's amendment ... I also emphasized the subject of Hall's amendment [base instead of bank] as being a line on which perhaps we might proceed in dealing with the Company, thinking that perhaps if we could get from the men a statement endorsing Hall's amendment the Company might [be] prepared to waive the cost of transportation ...'

Thomas Gibson, the UMWA organizer, attended this meeting and exchanged some remarks with King afterwards, leading the latter 'to size him up as a professional agitator.' There was a worm in McLean's rosy apple, a worm whose later turning was to cause acute discomfort for King.

That afternoon, King had his first meeting with Stockett. As he had earlier with the union committee, King told Stockett that he had come at the instance of the government, and was 'prepared to do anything in my power in helping to a settlement if they [company and locked-out men] were willing to accept my services, but if they were not of course I could do nothing.' King's typescript memorandum displays some intriguing lacunae at this point in their discussion: Stockett 'began by saying that the Company had taken a very decided position in this matter and were not going to have any [blank space] brought to bear on them, I told him that I had not come for the purpose of bring [blank space] to bear, but to do what I could to relieve [sic] the situation.' Given that there had apparently been an earlier exchange of telegrams between the Labour Department and the fuel company, and that the blank spaces were sufficient for a twelve-character word to have been eradicated, it appears likely that what King suppressed was 'intimidation.'[23] The manager was evidently in a fighting mood. He blamed Hawthornethwaite for the trouble, and insisted on an 'unalterable' position upon which the reopening of the mines must be based: the men must pay transportation; they must accept the conditions of work as they had been in May; and 'individual contracts, also no recognition of any Union whatever.' Stockett insisted that, while the men might belong to any organization they wished, be it church or union, the company 'would like ... to fight the labor organizations, and that they objected strongly to the American interference, that they were afraid of the men here being drawn into affiliations with the United States which would bring them out in case of any difficulty on the other side.'

23 There are other gaps in the memorandum, but, with one exception to be mentioned later, they do not disrupt the sense; they appear to be the typist's. The exception is in a context very similar to that noticed here.

King asked why, in that case, he was willing to deal with the Western Federation, 'as I thought they were a worse gang than the United Mine Workers, that the latter organization was in every way a reputable one compared with the Western Federation,' and Stockett's reply convinced him that the UMWA committee's charges in this respect were well founded.

King attempted to summarize affairs for Stockett's benefit, saying that there were really only two points at issue: union recognition and the eight-hour law. Stockett agreed, but wanted to add individual contracts as a third issue. King argued that it was unfair to ask the men to bear the whole cost of the eight-hour law: here Stockett insisted that since they had elected Hawthornethwaite and had signed a petition supporting the bill when it was before the legislature, 'they should be made to bear the cost of it, unless they were made to bear the cost they would not try to have the law repealed at the next Legislature, which the Company was scheming to have done.' This gave King another opening for compromise: 'I said to him supposing we could get from the men a resolution stating that the law worked harshly so far as these mines were concerned, would not that be worth more to him than the cost of transportation ... it might be possible to get such a resolution, but I would not undertake to try to get it unless he would agree to waive the cost of transportation, that such a resolution would be a heavy pull to Hawthornethwaite and certainly would be worth much to the Company.' King suggested that this idea be put to a mass meeting of all the men, irrespective of their union affiliation, and that this meeting elect a committee to negotiate a binding contract with Stockett. The contract would include a resolution opposing the eight-hour law, and would be signed by each of the men, thus overcoming the problems of union recognition and individual contract. Stockett agreed to think this over, and King left him 'feeling that along these lines we would probably get a settlement.'

King had now to sell the idea of a mass meeting to the union representatives. He told them that since the vast majority of the miners were UMWA members, the union should have no difficulty electing its nominees to the proposed negotiating committee. Gibson, naturally enough, opposed this abdication of recognition. Then King went on to sell the idea of a contract to be signed by every miner: here he had to overcome the patent objection that this would be a weak substitute for a collective agreement signed by company and union representatives. King represented it as a compromise between Stockett's insistence on individual contract and the union's interest in a true collective agreement, and he gilded his argument quite ingeniously:

I pointed out that in this way if the committee which was a United Mine Workers' committee formed a contract, then every man whether he was Western Federation or not would have to sign that contract as made by the United Mine Workers committee, this would have a tendency to break up the Western Federation altogether and would strengthen the United Mine Workers in their efforts to make a cohesive Union. I laid emphasis on the fact that what they should seek to preserve was their Union, that they must keep in mind the alternative of this fight being continued which might mean that the Company being very strong the men after waiting another month or two would become disheartened and some would break away from the organization altogether ... I thought however, by making a contract for a period of 2 years that they would insure themselves against any further exactions on the part of the Company during that time.

Eventually the UMWA committee was to agree with King's suggestion, although Gibson did not approve. In the meantime, King enlisted Ralph Smith's assistance in bringing pressure (not, it is to be assumed, intimidation) to bear on Stockett to accept the replacement of transportation costs by a resolution against the eight-hour law. King also entertained a delegation from the Western Federation of Miners, who supported the mass meeting idea and asked to have a representative on the resulting committee. King let them off the hook gently: no matter how much he might wish to have their union represented, he told them, the election would be solely in the hands of the meeting. They asked him where Hawthornethwaite came in: 'I replied that Mr Hawthornethwaite was a politician and that my mission had nothing to do with politics and I thought it would be better that both Mr Hawthornethwaite and Mr Ralph Smith should not be allowed to attend the meeting.'

Later, King met again with the UMWA committee, in Gibson's significant absence, and they gave their approval for the mass meeting. But they were concerned that they should not be asked to give in to what was obviously unjust in the company's conduct. King's answer was revealing of the hidden catch in the impartial umpire's role:

I pointed out that however hard the fact might be it was nevertheless true that in matters of this kind one could only consider the ethical side of the question in the light of conditions as they are, that I had always found working men ready to ask themselves the question 'is this right', I had found capitalists ask themselves the question 'does it pay' and that before the question of right could be determinded [sic] in telling the men who were free to put their capital where ever they wished transferred it from one business to another, the question of 'does it pay' would be one which would be necessary to consider at all times ...

The company had decided that union recognition and the Hawthornethwaite law just did not pay: for the union to try, on the basis of some ethical conception of fairness or justice, to battle this would be sacrifice akin to suicide. King went on to press for a resolution denouncing the eight-hour law as it stood in favour of the Hall amendment, which would time work from the pit base. When some members of the committee, 'apparently Hawthorne-thwaite men,' opposed this, King reminded them that they had earlier agreed that the law operated unfairly at Nanaimo. 'I reiterated the importance of saving their organization and again pointing out what would be the probable outcome of a failure to settle it this time that it meant a long struggle, the breaking [away] of the [men] from the organization and individual contracts when work was resumed.'

After much diplomatic negotiation with Stockett, King believed himself to be in a position to call a mass meeting: the manager would meet with a committee elected by such a meeting, and a settlement based on repudiation of the controversial clause in the eight-hour law would be acceptable to the company. Stockett stipulated that McLean should not be on the committee, and that the government would agree not to prosecute the company for violation of the eight-hour law. King also arranged with the UMWA local president and Ralph Smith that any agreement negotiated by an elected committee need not be referred back to a second mass meeting for ratification. He met with Hawthornethwaite, who told King 'that if the men wished the law changed, it was in their hands.' Everything seemed in order for the mass meeting, when a couple of snags arose. Stockett told King that, while he was willing to meet with an elected committee for the purpose of reaching a contract, once that contract had been signed he would not recognize the committee. King made up his mind 'to go as far towards a settlement with Stockett as possible taking up this matter last, and if he held out on this point I would throw the onus of the failure to effect a settlement on him believing that he would hardly face a [intriguing blank].' Then the UMWA local president, Johnston, and Ralph Smith informed King that Gibson was hostile to the mass meeting idea, saying that the union was fully capable of negotiating a settlement by itself:

I immediately began to look around in my mind as how I could get Mr Gibson out of business, I felt strongly that if a settlement failed on account of any words of his, I would have to come out strongly against the interference of agitators from the United States, but before doing this I had made up my mind to communicate with Mitchell pointing out [what] such a course might mean in the way of mitigating [sic] against international unionism in Canada. As Mitchell and I talked over this matter in Chicago some two or three years ago, and had an understanding to write him at any time that I found a danger arising [,] I felt that might be an advisable step if necessary.

The union committeemen came by to report on a UMWA meeting that had been held that morning. They had had a difficult time getting the membership to agree to the mass meeting and the other elements in King's strategy, but they had been successful: they were 'empowered to settle on any basis that might seem fair providing that the following conditions were carried out. 1. Contract to be for one year and no longer. 2. Transportation to be paid by the Company. 3. No discrimination against the men on account of the present strike [sic]. 4. Company to recognize the committee appointed in connection with differences which might arise through the year.' There were apparently some other difficulties, the natures of which are obscured by gaps in the memorandum, but these were overcome. Finally, the stage was set for the mass meeting.

Some four or five hundred men filled the Nanaimo Grand Opera House on the afternoon of 27 September. King explained his view of the situation and his conviction that unless a settlement was made according to his plan, the men's prospects looked hopeless. He proposed that somebody move a resolution calling for the election of a committee of five and, once this had been done, 'pointed out that I did not think there was any need for discussion'; the resolution was passed unanimously, and nominations were called for. A slate prepared by the UMWA committee was elected by acclamation. There was one final item of business. Just before the meeting broke up someone moved that John Burns, the British trade unionist who was visiting Victoria at the time, be invited to Nanaimo. King promised to send a telegram to Burns.

King was understandably enthusiastic about the outcome of the meeting. He was especially impressed at 'the fine respect shown by everyone, not one man interrupted during the whole hours talk and all removed their hats as soon as I began to speak, they were also generous in their applause at the close of the meeting.' King learned of suspicions that company men had sneaked in to the Opera House and concealed themselves in a box: 'I thought I will send to Victoria and get a detective, put him on to this matter and if I find out that they were present in this way I will give the fact out to the public.' Gibson aside, King was clearly on the side of the men who had applauded him so warmly. The following day, though, he found himself quarrelling with Hawthornethwaite, who was none too pleased with the turn events had taken and who probably felt himself betrayed by his constituents in the matter of the eight-hour law. King bullied him a little, saying that in all the four months of the lock-out he had made no move towards a settlement, and that the onus must lie on him. But Hawthornethwaite was merely a bystander: King had got his meeting and his committee, and the end was well in sight. He could afford to bait the socialist politician.

Three days after the successful mass meeting, the Grand Opera House saw another gathering of Nanaimo miners. Once again Mackenzie King stood on the platform, now with the elected committee ranged uneasily behind him. This time there was an innovation: King had sent for a stenographer from Victoria to record the proceedings verbatim, so that there could be no question later as to what had been said. Although it had originally been agreed that there need be no second meeting to ratify a contract, a second meeting had been called for that very purpose. Evidently something had happened in the interim to make this impressive event, Victoria stenographer and all, necessary. What this something was King now endeavoured to explain.

Thanks to his anxiety that there be no later possibility of misrepresenting the proceedings, we have a verbatim record of King's performance.[24] It was a wonderful oration, perhaps the greatest he ever delivered. His prime ministerial evasions in the House of Commons pale to incoherence against this address to the miners of Nanaimo in Opera House assembled. What made his speech so stirring and decisive was not any particularly powerful use of language, but its rhetorical structure. Its closest analogue is the speech Shakespeare gives to Mark Antony over the bloodied corpse of Caesar. King spoke over the bloodied corpse of his projected settlement, and his speech was if anything more effective than Antony's, for it brought the corpse to life. King spoke of his hopes for a settlement and stirred the hopes of his audience. He hinted that these hopes had been wholly frustrated and plunged his audience into despair. He pointed to the agent of frustration, Hawthornethwaite, and roused the indignation of his listeners. And then, with a final flourish, he unveiled the settlement that had finally been reached and, lo and behold, if it was not so good as his audience had hoped, it was not nearly so bad as he had led them to fear. Relieved, they voted to accept it – not unanimously this time, but by a comfortable margin – and gave him the final burst of applause from which he had heretofore requested them to abstain. It was a great performance and the applause was deserved, if not for the substance of the presentation, at least for its style. That substance may be briefly, if undramatically, told.

Following the election of the committee, negotiations had begun through King's mediation. The two sides did not meet: King interviewed one and then the other, and carried messages and suggestions back and forth between them. They were able to agree on many things, but one issue still posed difficulty. This was the question of transportation costs versus the withdrawal

---

24 The transcript, which runs to sixty pages, is appended to the Nanaimo Memorandum, in the same file. It is numbered consecutively with the memorandum.

of the offending clause in the eight-hour law. King, anxious to avoid a stale-mate, decided to take up Hawthornewaite's offer of a few days earlier, to assist in the settlement. He visited the MLA and asked him whether, if the miners' committee wished it, he would be willing to withdraw his amend-ment. According to King, their meeting was friendly, but no sooner was King's back turned than Hawthornewaite posted a bulletin attacking the pro-posed settlement. It is difficult to make out just what this bulletin said, but it included charges that King was a Liberal seeking to make political capital out of the lock-out, that he was opposed to the eight-hour law on principle, and that the committee, under his influence, was betraying the miners.

King had visited Hawthornewaite without the elected committee's knowl-edge. When he was finally able to bring the two parties together and arrive at a final settlement, he realized that Hawthornewaite's double dealing had alienated the confidence of many of the miners. Hence the second mass meeting. King had laboured long and hard, a settlement had been reached which was the very best that could ever be arrived at, and, while some things in the contract might appear unacceptable, they were counterbalanced by other things which were more than had originally been hoped for.

The settlement removed the worst feature of the company's docking sys-tem; it increased the minimum wage for men picked by the company to work a particular seam; it provided for non-discrimination and for the company's recognition of the elected committee as an ongoing grievance committee; and outside the formal contract the company agreed to reduce the charges for tools. These were real, if somewhat minimal, gains. On the other hand, the men were still to be charged up to a dollar a month for transportation until such time as the offending clause in the eight-hour law was rescinded. In fine, while some real concessions were made to the miners, the company had won the main point in its strike. And King insisted that, were this settle-ment not to be accepted in its entirety, the mines would be closed down. This was the burden of his speech; the peroration deserves to be quoted in full:

This afternoon, as I walked up to the Manager's Office, for the last time, I got a first glimpse of the mountains across the lake, and of the scenery beyond, and I could not see the beauty of it all, and I thought to myself [:] All this week you have been here you have not been able to see the beauty across there; there was nothing bright, and I thought that tomorrow you will enter on another month, and I wondered whether the struggle would still be on, and all would be dark, or whether you would see the same kind of brightness in front of you as I saw this afternoon. I trust for your sakes it will be bright gentlemen. Now I will leave you with the agreement.

It was truly a marvellous speech, but the mood King had created was rather abruptly broken when the following exchange took place:

GENTLEMAN IN AUDIENCE: We still have to pay the $1.00 for transportation in going over to Protection?

MR. KING: The payment of $1.00 for transportation will be for the transportation across to Protection – for No. 1 and Protection – not Northfield mine.

SAME GENTLEMAN: I believe that is what we went out on strike for, isn't it?

MR. KING: I don't like the tone of speaking ...

Of the 329 ballots cast, 236 were in favour of a settlement. The strike – or lock-out – was over.

But something must be said of the aftermath. Hawthornethwaite was returned again by the miners of Nanaimo at the next provincial election.[25] The contract arranged by King remained in force for seven years. Finally, in 1912, the United Mine Workers organized a massive strike in all the Vancouver Island coal mines. The strike lasted two years, an extremely bitter and violent affair involving the widespread use of imported strikebreakers and Oriental contract labour, military intervention, and, finally, the disappearance, at least temporarily, of the UMWA from the Island collieries.[26]

This was all in the future. Immediately, King found himself embroiled in an argument with John Mitchell. Gibson had written Mitchell his account of King's involvement, charging that the Deputy Minister had called the Mine Workers a 'foreign organization' which 'had no business on this island,' that the unionists were 'agitators' who, if they were not careful, 'should be put in jail.' Mitchell's reply was read at a meeting of the Nanaimo local. 'Referring to the settlement itself,' he wrote, 'I fear that your Deputy Commissioner [sic] of Labor is not a very loyal friend of the workingman and I think his influence was used to save the company from complete surrender.'[27] Local president Johnston and Ralph Smith both wrote to King informing him of this letter: there ensued an angry correspondence between King and Mitchell, in which the former denied having said any of the things ascribed to him by Gibson, and demanded an apology. Mitchell promised to make an enquiry, and, in December, King received a letter from a member of the elected committee:

25 McCormack, *Reformers*, 63
26 See Jamieson, 123ff, for an account of this strike.
27 King correspondence, Mitchell to King, 9 Nov. 1905, reporting on Mitchell's correspondence with the Nanaimo local

What I want to tell you is this that our United Mine Workers Union in Nanaimo has received a second letter from John Mitchel President of the United Mine Workers of America stating that some one has wrote a letter to him complaining about Gibson's conduct while in Nanaimo and our union has passed a motion and sent it to John Mitchel stating that Gibson's conduct was alright while in Nanaimo. I think that this is misleading to John Mitchel, I raised a protest against it and told them in the meeting about it. I told the meeting that to pass a motion exonorating Gibson from all blame was equal to passing a vote of senture on yourself and also the committee.[28]

But Nanaimo, for all its temerity in re-endorsing his sworn enemy, did not mark the end of King's dealings with Mitchell and the Mine Workers.

IV

The decline of the Western Federation and its replacement by the Mine Workers after 1903 was not confined to the Vancouver Island collieries. On the mainland, in the Crow's Nest Pass and Lethbridge areas, the UMWA established District 18, organized by the Socialist Party of Canada member, Frank Sherman. In 1906, District 18 went on strike against the Crow's Nest Pass Coal Company at Fernie and Michel, and against the Alberta Railway and Irrigation Company at Lethbridge. The strikes were fought for improved wages and conditions, and for union recognition. While the Crow's Nest strike was ended without Department of Labour intervention, the dispute at Lethbridge was finally settled through the good offices of Mackenzie King. This was the strike that provided the immediate stimulus for the Industrial Disputes Investigation Act. It also marked a new, and rather extraordinary, stage in King's relations with John Mitchell.

The strike began early in March 1906. For three months, the company merely shut the mines down. Then, having refused a union offer of arbitration, the company proceeded to hire 'green hands' to work the mines, albeit very inefficiently. The RNWMP was called in to prevent intimidation of the strikebreakers, and one unpleasant incident occurred when a Mountie non-com ordered his patrol to draw their pistols before a group of fifty strikers. The striking men, however, restored order of their own accord and the incident was not repeated.[29]

The Alberta Railway and Irrigation Company was the principal supplier of coal to rural Alberta and Saskatchewan, and as winter approached the pro-

28 *Ibid.*, Booth to King, 1 Dec. 1905
29 *Ibid.*, Smith to Laurier and enclosures, 25 March 1906

spect of a fuel famine for the homesteaders mounted steadily. The situation was worsened by the fact that the winter of 1906 was an unusually harsh one,[30] and local politicians became very worried. Before long, a flood of telegrams and personal representations descended upon Ottawa, and at one point the government seems seriously to have considered sending in strikebreakers to get the coal out of the ground.[31] In November, Mackenzie King was asked to go to Alberta, not on the request of either of the parties to the strike, but at the immediate demand of the Premier of Saskatchewan. King faced a dilemma:

When I learned of the fact that I might have to intervene in these strikes [news of the Fernie settlement had not yet reached Ottawa] and knowing how strong a prejudice the United Mine Workers had against me, without cause, over the settlement of the Nanaimo strike and seeing also on file a telegram from Sherman, who was managing the Fernie and Lethbridge strikes that the miners at Fernie and Lethbridge did not want Mackenzie King at any price; I determined that the first step to take would be to go direct to John Mitchell, the President of the United Mine Workers of America and discuss the situation with him, clearing up old scores, and bring him to an understanding as to my attitude towards his organization; also to let him see for himself how critical the situation was in the Canadian West; and in what peril his organization might be placed, if they were to maintain an unreasonable stand.

King left to see Mitchell at the AFL convention in Minneapolis, armed with a letter from Saskatchewan Premier Scott saying that 'so serious was the situation in his Province that if necessary he would have to send in men protected by Police to work the mines at Lethbridge rather than let the people freeze to death in their homes.' King hoped to convince Mitchell that unless the strike was quickly settled the union could not hope to win against government-supported strikebreakers, and 'so strong would Public Opinion become against the United Mine Workers that it might be difficult for his organization to retain any hold in Canada.' He arrived in Minneapolis on 19 November and immediately arranged a meeting with Mitchell and another UMWA official, to whom he explained his run-in with Gibson at Nanaimo and his actions during the lock-out. Then King set out his view of the Leth-

---

30 Cf. T.D. Regehr, *The Canadian Northern Railway: Pioneer Road of the Northern Prairies, 1895–1918* (Toronto: Macmillan, 1976), 184, n61
31 The account which follows is based on King's 'Confidential Memorandum Re Lethbridge Strike,' King Papers, MG 26 J4 vol. 13, file 80.

bridge situation and the likely action of the Saskatchewan government. He asked Mitchell whether the UMWA would insist that all the miners become union members, and, according to King, he replied that it would not, unless the company absolutely refused to permit the men to join a union. 'Mitchell seemed quite uneasy during part of the interview which I had with him. I was a little surprised at his want of composure ... I was less impressed with Mitchell than when I met him before. It seemed to me that he had [hardened] somewhat both in appearance and manner.'

King was still worried that Mitchell and the other members – Sharp and Burke – of the UMWA executive board did not trust him, so he suggested they speak to the Canadian delegates at the AFL Convention. Glockling was there, as were Lynch of the Typographical Union and Sam Landers, the TLC's fraternal delegate. 'I think the hearty manner in which all of these men greeted me gave some re-assurance to Mitchell and Sharp and Burke.' Mitchell arranged that Sharp should go to Lethbridge to help in arranging a settlement, and King was convinced that he had won the latter's confidence after discussing the situation. 'We arranged that my having been at Minneapolis should be kept secret; that I would leave that night for Winnipeg and that Sharp would meet me on the train at Moose Jaw the following day and we would go together to Lethbridge.'

When King arrived in Winnipeg he went to visit A.M. Nanton, managing director of the Alberta Railway and Irrigation Company. Despite his agreement with Mitchell, he told Nanton of his visit to Minneapolis, saying that he had gone there 'in view of the strong prejudice which Mitchell's Union had against me.' Perhaps he felt that Nanton might find out anyway about the trip, and by putting it this way King could imply that he was at odds with the union leading the Lethbridge strike: supporting this interpretation is the fact that King told Nanton of Sherman's injudicious telegram to Ottawa. He explained that in his view a settlement would be possible on the basis of making conditions at Lethbridge the same as at other mines in the district: this would be 'fair,' and its resemblance to the Department's Fair Wages policy is evident. 'As to the question of a Union I said that I had always taken the attitude of allowing men to belong to an organization if they wished; on the other hand that they had no right to insist upon a Company employing only Union men and to compel all men to belong to a Union whether they wished to or not. I took this stand from my belief as to what is the true liberty of the individual, viz; the right to join or not to join an organization as one might deem best.' Nanton was apparently not wholly convinced. In the 'Confidential Memorandum' which he drew up describing his intervention in this strike, King explained his strategy up to this point:

The purpose of my interview with Mr Nanton as also the purpose of my interview with Mr Mitchell was to give each of the parties at the outset an impression that I was desirous of being quite fair and impartial and was not unfriendly to either; also to let them see that I appreciated clearly their side of the case. It is one of the first essentials in conciliation negotiations to let each party see clearly that you understand all the things that have aggravated, angered and incensed them; that you appreciate all the obstacles with which he has to contend, leaving to a secondary stage in the proceedings the weak parts in his position.

King now proceeded to Lethbridge. On the way, he reviewed the correspondence on the strike and concluded, influenced perhaps by his recent conversation with the urbane Nanton, 'that the manner in which the strike had been called was anything but in keeping with the Constitution of the ... United Mine Workers. It appeared to me that the Union Officials had taken a very arbitrary and objectionable stand, and that the Company in self respect could hardly have dealt with them at the time.' When Sharp joined the train at Moose Jaw, King 'dwelt pretty strongly with him upon the impossibility of any settlement being made on the basis that only Union men should be employed and of the probable difficulty of getting any agreement signed with the Union.'

At Lethbridge, King embarked on the usual round of meetings with the company manager, P.L. Naismith, and the strikers' union committee. He inspected the mines and concluded that while the strikebreakers were very inefficient miners, the strikers were not attempting to intimidate them or interfere in any way, the company's claims notwithstanding. There was a deluge of telegrams awaiting him, describing the developing coal famine and the hardship it was causing to homesteaders. Without going into all the details of the negotiations, it may be stated that the company's refusal to recognize the union committee and establish a union shop was the final hurdle before a settlement. The question of working hours was evaded neatly, when King prevailed on the provincial government to introduce an eight-hour law for coal mines: what had been his downfall at Nanaimo was thus turned into a trump card at Lethbridge. The company proved willing to grant a general 10 per cent wage increase. When negotiations deadlocked on the recognition issue King, remembering Mitchell's concession on the union shop, decided to pay the UMWA leader another visit. He travelled to Indianapolis, but did not need to see Mitchell since an acceptable settlement was reached during his absence from Lethbridge.

During his stay at Lethbridge, King seems quite to have won the heart of Frank Sherman. They spent a pleasant evening together with the Deputy

Minister reading excerpts from *The Secret of Heroism*. Following the settlement, King and Sherman maintained a friendly, if desultory, correspondence: Sherman addressed King as 'Dear Friend' and indicated his approval in principle for the IDI Act. They exchanged photographs and King sent Sherman *Alton Locke* and Toynbee's *Industrial Revolution*.[32]

The immediate occasion for the IDI Act came, of course, at Lethbridge. The picture of thousands of poor homesteaders freezing to death in their sod huts all because of a recognition dispute at the mines could hardly fail to excite King's instinct for the melodramatic. 'As I lay awake in the early hours of the morning,' he wrote in the 'Confidential Memorandum,' 'I conceived the idea that when I got back to Ottawa whether the strike was settled or not in my report I would draw attention to the nature of legislation making it impossible for such a situation to arise in the future.' In his official report, published in the *Labour Gazette*, he did indeed make a recommendation to that effect. It was here that he first used the powerful phrase that was to emerge again later from the woolly sophistries of *Industry and Humanity* like a blade thrust through the fog:

When it is remembered that organized society alone makes possible the organization of mines to the mutual benefit of those engaged in the work of production, a recognition of the obligations due society by the parties is something which the State is justified in compelling if the parties themselves are unwilling to concede it. *In any civilized community private rights should cease when they become public wrongs.* Clearly, there is nothing in the rights of parties to a dispute to justify the inhabitants of a province being brought face to face with a fuel famine amid winter conditions, so long as there is coal in the ground, and men and capital at hand to mine it. Either the disputants must be prepared to leave the differences which they are unable to amicably settle to the arbitrament of such authority as the State may determine most expedient, or make way for others who are prepared to do so.[33]

The official report in the *Gazette* corresponds poorly to the account in the 'Confidential Memorandum.' This is true on a number of points, but nowhere more notably than in regard to King's original visit to Mitchell. The official report mentions the second trip – and later accounts of the strike have noticed this – but that first journey to Minneapolis was effectively buried. Only a handful of people – Mitchell's executive board colleagues, three or four

32 See, e.g., King correspondence, Sherman to King, 25 Nov. 1907; King to Sherman, 10 June 1907; also Diary, 19 April–6 May 1907
33 *LG*, Dec. 1906, 647ff; emphasis supplied

Canadian delegates to the AFL Convention, a couple of politicians, and A.M. Nanton – had any hint of the steps Mackenzie King took to clear his name after the Nanaimo fiasco.

But Lethbridge did not mark the last King was to hear of the evil Mr Gibson. Early in 1907, he received a letter from Harriett Reid, who worked in Mitchell's office:

> Just a line in passing to tell you that I met Mr. Thomas Gibson, who was a delegate to our recent convention.
>
> In my ten minutes' conversation with him, I was unable to determine for myself whether or not he has a lack of moral sense. In this event, I could not, of course, decide whether he was born without this essential attribute, or had lost it in the labor movement in the endeavour to be a diplomat. I take comfort in the thought, however, that being an Irishman, and in all probability never having read the Shorter Catechism, Mr. Gibson will never know what he may lack or what he may have lost.[34]

The letter is stamped 'Answered,' but there is no trace of a response in the King papers. Perhaps Mackenzie King had the last word after all.

V

Following the passage of the IDI Act, and particularly after his election to the Commons in 1908, King's personal role in disputes settlement was reduced. There were exceptions, however, one of the more important of which is discussed in chapter 10. Apparently the pressure of other work kept King out of the field: when Sherman complained to King about a hold up in the working of an Investigation Board at Lethbridge in 1907, King replied, 'One other thing. You speak of sending for me. Please do not do this if you can possibly help it ... I would very much prefer not adding to my troubles by being drawn into yours.'[35]

This exchange is of interest for another reason, of course. It seems to indicate that the UMWA, at least, was satisfied with the outcome of King's interventions – there would be no more telegrams urging the government not to send him 'at any price.' This notwithstanding the fact that King's interven-

---

34 King correspondence, Reid to King, 8 Feb. 1907
35 *Ibid.*, King to Sherman, 9 Oct. 1907. This new dispute at Lethbridge seems to have followed from problems in administering a new contract signed earlier that year, in a settlement made during the process of constituting an Investigation Board.

tions almost always resulted in the failure of the union to achieve official recognition, and that the arrangements King made have been denounced by recent writers as 'company unionism.'[36] Mitchell and his advisers seem to have been convinced by King's argument that certain employers, especially in the coal-mining industry, were so opposed to unionism that to fight them on the recognition question would lead to the inevitable destruction of their organizations and the end to any possibility of improving wages and conditions, or of eventual recognition.

Of course, the government may be faulted for not introducing legislation making recognition and good-faith bargaining compulsory, just as it may be faulted for not removing the unions' common law disabilities by statute. But this is surely another matter altogether from the question whether King's idiosyncratic way of going about the settlement of strikes within the existing legal framework was helpful to trade unionism or not. Mitchell and others seem to have felt that, in the last analysis, it was helpful. Whether their view was correct or not, it was surely one that had some effect on King.

King had a difficult time with the United Mine Workers, but he clearly considered it an acceptable alternative to the Western Federation, and he acted so as to enhance the ability of the former to displace the latter in the western coal fields. King must be credited, too, for changing the Liberal government's view of what constituted an acceptable trade union. As we have seen, he decided early in his intellectual career that the AFL was the very model of the modern trade union, and he insisted that unions must be discriminated among, not on the basis of nationality, but on grounds of 'legitimacy.' In this way, he played his part in cementing the hegemony of Gompers in Canada. Of course, King made use of business and government opposition to American unionism to put pressure on the AFL unions – in the cases examined here, the UMWA – to settle disputes on his terms. Acceptance of state involvement in the industrial relations process was one of the prices American unions had to pay for legitimacy in Canada. Before 1911, if the Mine Workers may be taken as a case in point, they did not consider that price exorbitant.

36 For example, Jamieson, 70.

9
'A very far-reaching and potent right'

Three symbolizes spiritual synthesis ... It represents the solution of the conflict posed by dualism ... It is the harmonic product of the action of unity upon duality. [J.E. Cirlot, *A Dictionary of Symbols*]

The Industrial Disputes Investigation Act of 1907, or the Lemieux Act as it is sometimes called (after the Labour Minister of the time) was King's lasting statutory contribution to Canadian industrial relations policy. It epitomized Canadian disputes policy until well into the Second World War, and its major concerns – compulsory conciliation, the 'cooling-off' period, the tripartite board, and special treatment of 'public interest' disputes – remain entrenched in the labour relations statutes of most Canadian jurisdictions, albeit they are now coupled to the Wagner Act principles of union certification and compulsory collective bargaining. In the beginning, the Act was applied primarily in disputes affecting railways and coal mines, but during and immediately after the First World War its scope was extended significantly. The Act was successfully challenged on constitutional grounds before the Judicial Committee of the Privy Council in 1925, but the consequences of disallowance were evaded by an amendment inviting the provinces to hand over their industrial relations jurisdiction to the federal government. Most did this, and it was not until 1950 that the Supreme Court ruled that provincial powers could not be delegated in this manner to the central government. By then, the IDI Act itself had been superseded, but its major provisions, in one form or another, have exhibited remarkable staying power.[1]

---

1 There is a useful brief review of the constitutional history of the Act in H.A. Logan, *State Intervention and Assistance in Collective Bargaining: The Canadian Experience 1943–1954* (Toronto: University of Toronto Press, 1956), chap. 1.

Almost from its first reading in December 1906, the Act was greeted with much interest and controversy.[2] In part, this was due to an intensive advertising campaign launched by King,[3] but much of the debate took place between eager advocates of its adoption in other jurisdictions, and their no less dedicated opponents. The British government sent a special commissioner to investigate the Act,[4] while the United States Bureau of Labor compiled several detailed reports.[5] An 'Association in Favor of a Law for the Investigation of Industrial Disputes' was formed in Massachusetts,[6] and a law modelled on the IDI Act was passed to regulate mining disputes in the Transvaal.[7] Popular magazines and scholarly journals conducted symposia on the Canadian act[8] and, as we have already seen, Gompers employed some of his choicest language to denounce it before the Walsh Commission. Some authors practically made a career out of the debate on the IDI Act: Selekman, for example, published at least four versions of his account of its operation, including his doctoral dissertation.[9] The debate on the Act

2 When the bill came up for third reading on 14 February 1907, Lemieux was able to read into the *Debates* editorials from newspapers in New York, Brooklyn, Lethbridge, Toronto, and Montreal.

3 King published articles on the principles of the Act and its operation in a number of American magazines and gave frequent speeches on it. For an example of the former, see *World's Work* (Aug. 1913), 438–44; for the latter, see the report of his talk to the Boston City Club, *Boston Journal*, 15 Jan. 1910, or the published text of his speech at a banquet given in his honour 'by Representative Business and Labor Men of Cincinnati,' 18 Sept. 1913, in King Papers, MG 26 J5, vol. 1. King enlisted the departmental staff in this publicity blitz: see, e.g., Acland's article in *National Review* (Oct. 1909). Even his father was not left out: see John King, 'Industrial Peace Legislation in Canada,' *Green Bag* (Dec. 1907).

4 Sir George Askwith, *Report to the Board of Trade on the Industrial Disputes Investigation Act of Canada, 1907*, Cd. 6603, 1913. See also his *Industrial Problems and Disputes* (London: John Murray, 1920), chap. XXIV.

5 *Inter alia*, V.S. Clark, 'The Canadian Industrial Disputes Act of 1907,' *Bulletin of the Bureau of Labor*, 76 (May 1908); a shorter piece by the same author and with the same title, *Bull. Bur. Lab.*, 86 (Jan. 1910); an anonymous piece with the same title, *Bull. Bur. Lab.*, 98 (Jan. 1912); and B.M. Squires, 'Operation of the Industrial Disputes Investigation Act of Canada,' *Bulletin of the United States Bureau of Labor Statistics*, whole no. 233 (1918).

6 Two of this association's pamphlets are included as enclosures with King correspondence, Pierce to King, 7 Feb. 1910.

7 See King Papers, 'Memorandum re I.D.I.A. amendments,' MG 26 J4, vol. 15, 10447f.

8 *Survey*, 31 March 1917; *Annals of the American Academy of Political and Social Science*, vol. 69 (1917)

9 There is a useful, although incomplete, contemporary bibliography of the Act in Ben Selekman, *Postponing Strikes: A Study of the Industrial Disputes Investigation Act of Canada* (New York: Russell Sage Foundation, 1927), app. D.

long outlived its place on the statute books, persisting with a little less heat to this day.[10]

Canadian businessmen and trade unionists maintained, for the most part, an attitude of cautious approval towards the IDI Act throughout the period covered by this study.[11] It is true, as we shall see later on, that the TLC demanded its repeal in 1911, only a week before the Liberal defeat, but this demand arose not so much out of opposition to the principles of the legislation, as in reaction to that old bugbear of the union movement, unfavourable judicial interpretation. This is not to say that there were no dissenting voices raised in the labour movement before 1911 – the Act was a regular subject of extended debate at TLC conventions – but that until 1911 its supporters managed to hold the field. The later attitude of the unions lies outside the scope of this study, for it would have to be founded not only in an examination of the later experience under the Act, but in a thorough study of the Borden government's approach to industrial relations and of the new economic and social forces that began to take shape in the pre-war recession. This chapter, then, deals with the origins of the Lemieux Act (so called after its sponsor in the House, Postmaster-General Rodolphe Lemieux, although there is no question but that King was its author) and its first four years of operation.

I

If the Lethbridge miners' strike of 1906 fathered the IDI Act, one of its grandparents was the railway disputes legislation of 1902–3. It will be recalled that in 1902 the government introduced legislation for compulsory arbitration of railway strikes and lock-outs, and that the TLC, conscious of Gompers' characterization of compulsory arbitration as a species of slavery, and spurred on by the railway brotherhoods' lobbyist, successfully opposed it. The following year new legislation, dropping the compulsory arbitration feature, passed through Parliament to become the Railway Labour Disputes Act, which was consolidated with the Conciliation Act in 1906. It is necessary here to look at the RLDA and its unfortunate predecessor in a little more detail.

10 For recent discussions see, *inter alia*, Jamieson, 128f.; H.D. Woods, *Labour Policy in Canada* (Toronto: Macmillan, 1973), 341ff: Bruno Ramirez, 'Collective Bargaining and the Politics of Industrial Relations in the Progressive Era, 1898–1916,' unpublished doctoral dissertation, University of Toronto, 1975, chap. IX, has a discussion of US response to the Act. Ramirez's claims about 'the actual political bargaining surrounding the enactment' of the IDIA (p. 262) are, however, unsupported by evidence.
11 Business and labour response is discussed below.

It is not entirely clear how the compulsory arbitration bill came to be introduced, but on the basis of what evidence is available some plausible guesses can be made. Once again, a particular strike furnished the occasion for the introduction of the legislation. In this case it was the recognition strike of five thousand maintenance-of-way men against the CPR's operations across the country, lasting two and a half months in the summer of 1901. The spectre of a nation-wide rail strike certainly haunted the Laurier government, but there were other factors as well. Pressure from various quarters had been mounting for a compulsory arbitration law. In January 1901, well before the CPR strike, Smith Curtis, the former BC mines minister, called on King to press for compulsory arbitration legislation, but King 'let him see that I do not favour this tendency, & was inclined to feel that it were better to leave industry more alone, save in laying down rules & restrictions against unfair play, & also subjecting it to the influence of public opinion where this could be focused thro' a Department or other means as e.g. in Conciliation.' Curtis persisted, however, occasioning this further reflection by King: 'I think tho' that he is mistaken in regarding compulsory arbit'n as a great panacea. Most men who consider & advise it see only the seeming immediate effect upon stoppage of strikes, they fail to see that a strike may after all bring greater good than its prevention. I cannot believe [in] the compulsory adjustment of wages schedules. No judge unless he be an economic divinity could regulate rightly wages in any trade of importance for 1 year.'[12]

Another source of pressure was Ralph Smith who, until September 1902, could advance compulsory arbitration as a long-standing demand of the TLC. Smith had continued to press the government for such a law, not only in his public expressions of disappointment at the Conciliation Act, but in private visits to the labour department as well.[13] A third possible source of interest in such a measure, although here there seems to be no direct evidence to go on, was the fact that Mulock had paid a lengthy visit to Australasia in 1901, and may have returned impressed with the compulsory arbitration legislation there.

But the immediate pressure for legislation outlawing railway strikes came from Sir Thomas Shaughnessy, president of the CPR. He wrote to King in February 1902, saying that he 'would like very much to have a chat with you on the labour situation,' and they met in Montreal on the fourteenth of the month. They apparently discussed Sir Thomas's ideas about labour legisla-

---

12 Diary, 11 and 12 Jan. 1901. Curtis linked his demand for compulsory arbitration to nationalization of industry. See also *ibid.*, 21 and 23 Nov. 1901.
13 *Ibid.*, 30 Sept. 1901, and *passim*.

tion and agreed that Shaughnessy would meet with C.M. Hays of the Grand Trunk to find some common ground. King wrote to Shaughnessy on the eighteenth to say that Mulock was desirous of a short session, so that any legislation they might wish to bring forward should be submitted soon. King also informed him that the views of the railway workers would have to be canvassed, and that this would cause delay. The tone of the letter seems to indicate a courteous hesitancy about the proposal. Shaughnessy wrote back to say that Hays was not ready to have 'such legislation as we discussed' brought forward at that time: 'Of course, the Grand Trunk lines are not in the same position as our own, by reason of the fact that they serve a more thickly populated territory.' He suggested that the matter be left in abeyance for another year. 'In the meantime, some plan may be devised that would be acceptable to both employers and employees.'[14]

Nevertheless, Mulock forged ahead and presented his bill to Parliament on April 29.[15] There is no evidence that King had anything to do with the drafting of the bill besides his meeting with Shaughnessy: his diaries and correspondence are silent on the subject. Given his opposition to Smith Curtis' machinations throughout 1901, it is unlikely that he approved of the measure. Perhaps his opinion was canvassed, for the bill was introduced with markedly little enthusiasm. Mulock stressed that the government would not attempt to have it passed during the session, that it was purely a tentative measure, and, obliquely, that it could do with a lot of improvement: 'It was presented to parliament and to the country at the time in order that it might receive consideration at the hands of the public, the railway companies and their employees during the recess, and the minister stated that the government would welcome any suggestions tending to perfect the measure ...'

The *Labour Gazette* opened its account in this way, and closed it in a similar fashion: 'It is to be borne in mind, however, that in considering the whole or any part of the Act that the measure in its present form is tentative, and that, as stated by the minister, the government will be pleased to receive suggestions having for their object the improvement of the measure.'[16] Evidently the government was not entirely pleased with the prospects of its new child. Why then, especially since Shaughnessy had backed down, was it introduced at all? There can be no final verdict on the basis of the papers available, but two or three plausible hypotheses may be advanced. The gov-

---

14 King correspondence, Shaughnessy to King, 4 Feb. 1902; Shaughnessy to King, 13 Feb. 1902; King to Shaughnessy, 18 Feb. 1902; Shaughnessy to King, 19 and 21 Feb. 1902
15 *LG*, June 1902, 769
16 *Ibid.*, 738. The bill was published as an appendix to this issue of *LG*.

ernment might be seen to be responding to the CPR president's suggestions; it may have felt it could no longer ignore the clamouring of Ralph Smith and his supporters; it was undoubtedly aware of the developing rift within the TLC and may have chosen this method of testing the waters.

The bill, short-titled 'The Railway Arbitration Act,' prohibited strikes and lock-outs on the railways. It would establish permanent arbitration courts on the Australasian model. There would be seven tripartite provincial boards, each to consist of one representative elected by employers, one by employees, and a third appointed on the nomination of the other two or, failing that, by the government; these boards would have jurisdiction over disputes affecting railway employees within the boundaries of a single province. A five-member dominion board, seconded from the provincial ones, would deal with inter-provincial disputes. The constitutional problems that had been the federal government's excuse for making the Conciliation Act a purely permissive measure were avoided by providing for provincial consent to the Act's operation. All in all, it was quite a drastic measure and the railway brotherhoods lost no time in voicing their disapproval.

In July the locomotive engineers, meeting in Toronto, decided to oppose the bill.[17] A correspondent to the firemen's magazine warned that the law would 'mean the dissolution of railway organizations,' and the trainmen's journal urged its Canadian lodges to oppose it.[18] Harvey Hall of the conductors led the fight at Berlin, and the preamble of his resolution left no doubt about the brotherhoods' interpretation of the bill's consequences. It would 'rob the employees of their constitutional rights, destroy their organizations and place them absolutely in the hands of the railway companies, at the same time depriving them of that citizenship which is so dearly prized, and which is the inherent right of all free-born British subjects.'[19]

Following this trouncing of the arbitration bill in the halls of labour, King got down to work on an alternative:

Worked for a while on the preparation of a draft bill for the settlement of Labour Disputes by some form of arbitration. I worked on this for about 1½ hrs. tonight, reading over Illinois State Arbitration Law & evidence in regard to same. My present feelings are against the apptmt. of a Permanent Board, as increasing machinery which at the stage is not necessary, and as likely to be less competent than the board chosen

17 *LG*, Aug. 1902, 80
18 J.H. Tuck, 'Canadian Railways and the International Brotherhoods: Labour Organization in the Railway Running Trades in Canada, 1896–1914,' unpublished PH D thesis, University of Western Ontario, 1975, 298f
19 *TLC* 1902, 59

with view to particular pursuit. I wd. rather make the whole an addition to Conciliation, thereby strengthening the power of the former & minimizing the need of arbitration. Machinery is nothing, personality everything.

A day later, the notion of arbitration seems to have been supplanted in
King's mind by the possibility of investigation:

I worked almost the entire time on the bill for the Settlement of Labour Disputes. I
think a measure of this kind should be brief, and with as little machinery about it as
possible, its aim should be to afford a means of the public getting an intelligent view
of the facts of the situation and of bringing an enlighted [sic] public opinion to bear.
In this connection I would like to make the *Labour Gazette* given [sic] greater
service.[20]

He wired to Charles F. Adams in Boston requesting a draft of his proposed
arbitration bill, and wrote to his old Harvard patron, Charles Eliot Norton,
who replied that Canada was far in advance of the United States in labour
legislation because the 'Canadian system of administration has the advantage
of being comparatively unhampered by legislative acts and purely political
considerations.'[21] And in the middle of January, a delegation from the railway brotherhoods was entertained in Ottawa to discuss King's new bill:

I read it through aloud first then we took it up section by section. We had only
finished the preamble & part of the interpretation when lunch was served. The Minister had the table in his dining room arranged like a banqueting table with flowers,
etc., the sight of all the men on either side with the Minister at one end was a fine
one ... After lunch, we continued the discussion of the Bill there being free discussion
on every point. Discussion lasted till after 4, when adjournment came. Mr. Hall on
behalf of the men made a speech thanking the Minister for his hospitality & for his
interest in the measure. The Minister then made one of the best little speeches I have
ever heard him make. He told them that it might seem strange to them, his cham-
pioning their cause, but whatever his means, his heart was with them & for the public
good ...[22]

King's bill, the Railway Labour Disputes Act, was introduced on 17
March, 1903, and received Royal assent on 10 July. It was designed to find a

20 Diary, 2 and 3 Jan. 1903
21 King correspondence, Adams to King, 10 Jan. 1903; King to Adams, 13 Jan. 1903;
    Norton to King, 26 Jan. 1903
22 Diary, 17 Jan. 1903

happy medium between the Conciliation Act, ineffective because it was purely permissive, and compulsory arbitration. The latter was inadvisable, the department's Annual Report stated, because of 'the difficulties besetting the enforcement of awards, and the liability of error arising in the judicial determination of relations which, in the interests of the parties and the business community must ultimately be determined by economic forces.' An alternative method was needed, 'better suited to the end in view,' the method of 'compulsory investigation.' The Act provided for the establishment of two tripartite boards in any dispute, each to consist of one representative of the employer, one of the employees, and a third member appointed on the mutual nomination of the other two or, failing that, by the government. Any dispute threatening to bring about a strike or lock-out could be referred by the Minister to this two-stage machinery. The first board, a Committee of Conciliation, would be 'limited to the lending of friendly offices,' and if it failed the matter would pass to a Board of Arbitrators, with the power to compel the production of documents, examine witnesses under oath, and issue an award. But the arbitrators' award was not to be binding on the parties. It was to be, instead, 'an impartial adjudication carrying with it the sanction of public opinion.'[23]

King believed that the existence of such a measure would itself serve to prevent strikes, and in the Annual Report a rather questionable gauge of its success was suggested: 'It was contemplated that the existence of such a measure would of itself give to the parties likely to be affected by it a strong reason for settling their differences between themselves, without allowing them to reach a point where the public might be given opportunity of probing into the private or business affairs of either. The success of the measure as a means of preserving industrial peace is to be estimated, therefore, by the absence of any reference under it, quite as much as by the number of cases which may be referred and the awards given.'[24] This particular attempt to have things both ways was, as we have seen, not an isolated example of King's logic.

As it turned out, the Act was a tremendous success by the first criterion. Only one dispute was referred to it from its passage until 1907, when the IDI Act appeared on the statute books. This was a conflict between the Grand Trunk and the telegraphers in 1904, successfully settled at the arbitration stage. There was some trouble afterwards in the implementation of the agreement, but the TLC, in 1905, generously absolved the department of

23 Canada, *Sessional Papers*, 36, 1903, 59, 71
24 *Ibid.*, 71f

blame. It commended 'the Government's action in introducing legislation endeavouring to prevent conflict between employer and employee, and sincerely regrets that the G.T.Ry. management did not honorably carry out the award of the arbitrators ...'[25] An officer of the telegraphers' union visited King to tell him 'he was pretty well satisfied with the result,' crediting the Act, and King immediately asked him to put his satisfaction in writing.[26]

The significance of the RLDA lies not in its success as measured by one or the other of King's criteria, but in the fact that it was a sort of rough draft of the IDIA. The *ad hoc* tripartite board, the appeal to public opinion, ministerial initiative, and the unenforceable award were all brought together for the first time in the railway act. The Industrial Disputes law which followed in 1907 added only two new features; the broadened scope of 'public utilities,' and, more importantly, the postponement of a work stoppage. Compulsory investigation, introduced in the RLDA and reinforced by the BC Royal Commissioners' report, came into its own with the 1907 Act.

II

'I conceived the idea that when I got back to Ottawa ... I would draw attention to the nature of legislation making it impossible for such a situation to occur in the future,' King wrote in 1906, on a sleepless night in Lethbridge. The very day of his return to the capital he called on Lemieux and 'told him he ought to introduce a compulsory investigation measure.' With Lemieux's approval, he went to see the Prime Minister. 'I told him I thought the Gov't should make an investigat'n compulsory, he said at once he agreed, to draft the measure.' (King then put in another bid for a seat and a Cabinet post.) A few days later he was working on 'certain recommendat'ns I am thinking of putting in my report on the Lethbridge strike. I intend advocating legislat'n to compel an arbitration of points in dispute. I find it hard to do this work to my liking under pressure, but now is the time, it must be done – I will be the father of a coal mines dispute act, if all goes well.'[27]

This was 9 December. On 17 December, Lemieux moved in the House for leave to introduce 'Bill (No. 36) to aid in the Prevention and Settlement of Strikes and Lock-outs in coal Mines and Industries connected with Public Utilities.'[28] King had worked very fast to prepare the outline of an Act which,

25 *TLC* 1905, 44f
26 King correspondence, King to Mulock, 20 June 1905
27 Diary, 4 and 9 Dec. 1906
28 *Debates* (1906–7), 1036

in its final form, was to consist of seventy complicated clauses.[29] Under government sponsorship it passed through Parliament very quickly. First reading in the House took place on 17 December, 1906; second reading was proposed on 14 February, 1907; and it passed third reading after lengthy debates in committee on 19 March. It was introduced into the Senate on 20 March, passed second reading the following day, went into committee, and passed third reading that evening. It received Royal Assent on 22 March. This speed is all the more surprising since in the House debate it got entangled with a Conservative resolution for a select committee on strikes and lock-outs, and in the upper house with Senator McMullen's latest attempt to ban American union organizers from Canada.

King continued to work at the bill while it was before the House (it had received first reading in blank). On 16 December he was reading Gilman's *Methods of Industrial Peace*, and immediately after the New Year he was back at work; 'reading thro the New South Wales Arbitration Act, & Act passed in Ont. in 1894 re Councils of Conciliat'n & Arbitration, – a long affair copied from New Zealand legis'n with mostly all of its essential features left out. After lunch Giddens came down and we worked from 2 till 5.45 drafting additional clauses of the Industrial Disputes Compulsory Act. Many important points suggest themselves as we go along. We completed most of the provisions, some of them in rather rough form, we will make a final revise tomorrow. By rights I should have another two weeks to carefully consider and revise the sections.'

The bill was completed and sent to the printers on 3 January, some two weeks after first reading. This was not all that was odd about this government bill: 'The Bill has thus gone to the printers without the Minister or a member of the Government, or a soul save Giddens & myself aware of what is in it. Ralph Smith has seen some of the clauses, and father, but no one else, every line of it has been written out or rather drafted by myself.'[30]

There is a long set of quotations and citations from various sources bearing on the Act in one volume of the 'memoranda and notes' series in the King Papers.[31] Some of these seem to have been put together in preparation for amending legislation later on, but others were probably prepared in the original drafting process. They include quotations from Gilman and other writers, reviews of labour legislation in other jurisdictions, and extracts from state-

29 6–7 Edward VII, chap. 20
30 Diary, 16 Dec. 1906, 2 and 3 Jan. 1907; N.P. Gilman, *Methods of Industrial Peace* (Boston: Houghton, Mifflin, 1904)
31 MG 26 J4, vol. 14, 9434–10232

ments by various interested groups. King's own estimation, however, was that the measure was in all important respects original:

Many of the suggestions, & much of the phraseology as well as some of the sections being taken from other Acts, the New Zealand legis'n in particular, saving this however the measure is my own. The ideas embodied in it were mine before I knew they had found expression in legis'n elsewhere. So far as I know now no country has legis'n just on the lines of the main features of this bill, – an investigat'n after the manner of our Courts & prohib'n to strikes or lockouts prior to or during such investigat'n, proceedure [sic] as to exchanging statements, manner of serving same etc, all this last is quite original. As I have got underway with the drafting I have found suggestions or similar legis'n elsewhere, but I can honestly say no suggestion from an outside source that I can recall was in my mind when I suggested the main features of the measure, so far as Canada is concerned, it does not owe its origin to other countries, their methods or their ideas.

King's earnest enthusiasm for his own work was expressed in the familiar way: 'God has given me the opportunity, had used me as His instrument to frame the measure, & I have done it along lines & in a manner which I believe will further His Will among men.'[32]

Given this interpretation of the bill's significance, it is understandable that King should have been a little put out that nobody in the Cabinet seemed to want to see it. Lemieux even asked him to send a copy to Borden, the opposition leader, without having seen it first himself: King insisted that he read it. The message must have filtered through, for a few days later he was called to the Council Chamber where Laurier, accompanied by Aylesworth and Lemieux, told him it was 'a splendid piece of legislation.'[33] It was a season for compliments to King. Borden told the House, as he tried to push through his resolution, that King's personality rather than the Conciliation Act machinery was responsible for the settlements he had achieved.[34] But there was still some opposition to the bill.

The most important opposition came from the railway brotherhoods in the running trades, and it was abetted by Lemieux's ineptness in marshalling the bill through the House. When the proposed legislation was first announced, it was to apply to coal mines only. Then, during the first reading debate, Lemieux moved to amend the title (which was all there was to the bill at that

32 Diary, 3 Jan. 1907
33 *Ibid.*, 5 and 10 Jan. 1907
34 *Debates* (1906–7), 1175, 3035, Diary, 9 Jan. 1907

stage) to include other public utilities, including electric (street) railways. W.F. Maclean, the Toronto *World* editor who had been read out of the Conservative party in 1905 and sat as an independent nationalist in the Commons, asked whether 'public utilities' would include 'general railways,' and Lemieux answered that 'We already have a Bill which provides for the settlement of labour disputes in connection with railway companies.'[35] By this, as later debate showed, he meant the RLDA of 1903.

In the meantime, and before the bill was printed, there had been some conversation between Lemieux and J. Harvey Hall, the legislative representative for four of the brotherhoods in the running trades. Hall, understanding that the Act was not to apply to the railways, did not oppose it. When he received a copy of the printed bill, however, and found that it did indeed apply, he circulated a letter to the locals of each of the brotherhoods he was representing. This letter, dated 19 January, stated that 'the measure is one that may have very serious effect in the operation of our organization, and is the second step made by the present government towards compulsory arbitration.' It cited the long delays that might be expected from the proposed machinery, and ended with this summation: 'The principal objections that I see to the Act is [*sic*] the enforced delay and the creation of additional expense upon the membership without any possible adequate return. I think that you should consider it from this standpoint, and also that of compulsion, but whatever you do lose no time as it is important that I should have your views on the question at as early a date as possible.'[36]

The immediate consequence of Hall's circular was that opposition speakers were soon armed with letters, telegrams, and petitions from railway union locals across the country denouncing the bill. Hall sat in the visitors' gallery watching the proceedings and antagonizing Lemieux. The labour minister got himself into hot water almost at the beginning by attempting to argue in favour of the IDI Act by showing how effective the Laurier government's labour legislation had been in the past. Had not the RLDA prevented railway strikes, so that not one had occurred since its passage? The opposition, of course, took him up on this to ask why, if there was already so wonderful a law on the statute books, it was necessary to include railway workers in the new one. After all, the railway brotherhoods were themselves very happy with the RLDA. Lemieux sputtered a bit, and then decided that the bill should be amended so as to make it optional in railway disputes to invoke either the RLDA or the IDIA. But when his amendment reached the

35 *Debates* (1906–7), 1036
36 Quoted in *ibid.*, 3366

floor, it became apparent that it would import the IDIA principle of a prohibition of strikes or lock-outs pending investigation into the old Act. He protested that the cooling-off period was an essential component of the legislation, that it would be futile to legislate for public utilities without including railways, and that anyway the brotherhoods would have the option of choosing between the two different types of board machinery. But Lemieux was cowed by Hall. He wrote to the brotherhoods' legislative representative inviting his support for the amendment and then procrastinated during the committee stage waiting for an answer. The opposition insisted that the bill should move out of committee of the whole into a special committee that could hear witnesses, but Lemieux refused. Finally, in the debate on third reading, in the midst of last-ditch attempts by the opposition to kill the legislation, the labour members of the House came to Lemieux's aid.

Alphonse Verville, president of the TLC and member for Maisonneuve, spoke first. He spoke against hearing testimony from employers and workers on the bill, and announced that he would rather have 'imperfect legislation than no legislation at all.' He spoke against an opposition amendment excluding railways from the bill. His very short speech, which contained no matters of substance whatsoever, was intended no doubt to place the TLC imprimatur on the legislation. Verville was followed by Ralph Smith, and a much longer speech. Smith argued that the railwaymen had had sufficient opportunity to explain their position, and he denied the justice of their claims. They objected to the machinery of the bill; well, they could have the RLDA machinery if they chose. They objected to the principle of compulsory investigation: 'That, Sir, is the principle of this Bill, and I submit that if the railway men are entitled to be exempted from the operation of that principle, we should not apply it to any other public utility ... There is no industry in the country which is half so much a public utility as a railway. There is no business that affects directly public interest, life and limb and business and commercial interests of every description, to anything like the same extent as does the operating of a railway ...' But the principle of compulsory investigation was a good principle. The railway men had been misled – 'I do not say that any man personally and directly sought to deceive the railway men' – into equating it with compulsory arbitration. If they really understood it, they would support it. But there is no time to educate them now, he implied with a last flourish for the gallery: 'There is a possibility at present of tremendous labour struggles in this country. I am not speaking officially or because of any direct information that I have, but I have good reason for knowing that there are great probabilities of very serious industrial strikes within a few weeks. I would recommend the government to get the legislation through as soon as possible, and apply it, and we shall get practical evidence of its benefit. There is a possibility of a struggle in the coal fields of the west on a much more extensive scale than when the question was originally considered in this House.' Shortly thereafter, the legislation passed third reading.[37]

Why did the railway brotherhoods oppose, and the TLC executive support, the bill? Verville's speech on third reading was not the only indication of TLC support, for the Congress's annual cap-in-hand had come in the midst of the debate on the bill. King was present when the delegation met Laurier and Lemieux on January 15:

Draper spoke on the resolut'n re the creat'n of a separate Dept. He spoke of how the work of the Dept. of L. had grown, of the importance of the work, and the good it had done, & how it was appreciated by the working classes. He spoke of Mr. Lemieux's interest & the activity he had shewn, but urged strongly for a separate portfolio. He spoke also of the Industrial Investigat'n Act which he said the Exec of the Congress had carefully studied & strongly endorsed excepting clause re non-union labour – Simpson spoke on this also & said excepting 2 clauses I interrupted & said 1 & he said Yes, – the other was in their favour but wd have in justice to go out. Simpson spoke of disciplining [?] Union members. O'Donoghue as Sol'r of Congress also endorsed bill, excepting clauses, but sd they reserved their right to suggest small amendments. Draper congratulated the Minister & myself on the Act, & said it was the best piece of labour legis'n they had ever had, that whoever drafted it shewed that he had a knowledge of industrial conditions & needs throughout the whole country. Verville's only object'n was that the bill did not apply to all industries & trades. O'Don. endorsed clause allowing its extens'n by O-in-C.[38]

To provide a slight gloss for this report, it should be explained that the clause objected to by Draper and Simpson was one prohibiting strikes 'because of employment of persons other than union members,' while the other with which it was paired and 'wd have in justice to go out' prohibited dismissals of employees on account of their membership in a union.[39] Both these clauses were dropped in committee stage. 'Extens'n by O-in-C'

37 For the entire debate on the bill and on the Borden resolution with which it became entangled, see *ibid.*, 1036–44, 1150–83, 2590–3091, 3278–368, 3696–8, 3802–38, 3843–82, 3978–4007, 4458–518, 4772–86, 4978–5016, 6005–8. For the Senate, see *Hansard*, 1906–7, pp. 500f, 526–46. The Senate debate is of little interest. Ferns and Ostry's comment that the House debate was 'brief' (p. 74) is inexplicable.

38 Diary, 15 Jan. 1907. King spoke to a delegation of locomotive firemen later that day, and felt that they would support the bill.

39 Sections 62 and 63 in the bill as drafted: see *Debates* (1906–7), 4006f.

referred to a clause permitting the Governor in Council to designate additional industries as 'public utilities,' and therefore subject to the Act; this was, if not totally expunged, at least watered down in the final draft.[40]

The TLC delegation had an opportunity to present its views on the Act to its constituents at the September convention. Verville reported that the executive had approved the bill:

Organized Labor does not want to strike to enforce its demands if the consideration of them can be attained without recourse to that remedy. The strike has been our last resort, and as the Bill continued our right to strike, but assured a fair hearing of the demands of the workers, there was nothing to do but to give our support to it. Nor is organized labor blind to the fact that in every great industrial struggle the public have a large interest as well in the result as in the means adopted to reach that result.

Parliamentary Solicitor O'Donoghue seconded these sentiments:

The full importance of this Bill has not, probably, been fully understood by all the constituents of the Congress. In my opinion organized labor has gained much by its passage into law, if for no other reason than that by it, the grievances of workmen are publicly ventilated while, at the same time, they are enabled to remain at work and receive their daily wages. Moreover, unincorporated trade unions are officially recognized by the Bill and their representatives are entitled to a hearing before the public body constituted under it. In this regard the Bill marks a great advance in public opinion and to that extent will deprive individual employers of an argument that is very often resorted to by them to avoid recognition of a trade union.[41]

But the executive did not have an easy time of it at the convention. Whereas in 1906 only one representative of each of the shopcrafts locals (one carman), the maintenance-of-way men, and the running trades (one trainman) had attended the convention, this year twelve delegates from these crafts attended. There were three representatives of the maintenance-of-way men, four carmen, two locomotive engineers, and three trainmen. The maintenance-of-way men, led by King's friend A.B. Lowe, opposed the running trades by supporting the IDI Act. Appropriately enough, when the question of the Act's principle came up, it was Lowe who moved that the TLC, 'in consonance with the oft-expressed attitude of organized labor in favour of investigation and conciliation,' accept the Act.[42] A three-hour

40 See section 68 of the final Act.
41 *TLC* 1907, 10, 45
42 *Ibid.*, 55f. The Report has 'A.B. Lane,' but this is a misprint.

debate ensued, in which the running-trades representatives, supported by a delegate from the cigarmakers, Gompers' own union, attacked the executive's position. The debate, at least as it was reported by the *Manitoba Free Press* on 20 September 1907, was not marked by any great evidence of labour statesmanship. It was characterized by unsupported allegations and personalities, climaxing perhaps with Congress vice-president Simpson's offer to continue the discussion outside, but in this it differed little from several of the scenes enacted some months earlier in the House of Commons. Hall's old allegation, that the IDIA was a step in the direction of compulsory arbitration, was the principal substance of the opposition. At the end, on a standing vote, the convention declared 81 to 19 in favour of the principle of the Act. A special committee was struck to propose amendments, and the following day these were considered. While the report in the TLC *Proceedings* is somewhat obscure, it appears that the convention wanted the Act to be extended to cover all industrial disputes.[43]

Aside from Hall's insistence that the Act was the prelude to compulsory arbitration, it is not easy to piece together the reasons for the running trades' concerted opposition. But one set of considerations came up time and again in the debates. The running trades, the aristocracy of the North American labour movement, were almost alone among the unions in having regularized relations with their employers. They had no worries about union recognition or having to wage lengthy strikes merely in order to establish bargaining relations. They insisted that they had managed to develop an intricate and institutionalized mechanism for resolving grievances and carrying on collective bargaining, and they were concerned that the compulsory features of the Act would disrupt this. In a way, it might be argued that the railway unions in the running trades had crossed Hobsbawm's second watershed well ahead of their counterparts in the labour movement. They were fully fledged business unions and as such were opposed to state intervention in their affairs. Other unions, the maintenance-of-way brotherhood in the railway industry and most organizations in other fields, were in no such position. They were still struggling for their lives, and when the IDI Act came along with its promise

---

43 *TLC* 1907, 69, 73; amendment no. 4. 'It was explained that what was sought was such amendment to the Bill [sic] as would make it applicable, not only to public utilities, but generally to all industrial disputes. On the Solicitor stating that the amendment did not cover what was desired, a vote was taken on the proposition to extend the operation of the Bill to all industrial disputes, the vote resulting in favor of the extension and against [sic]. The Solicitor was instructed to draft an amendment accordingly.' The solicitor's report to the 1908 convention did not report on the Congress' 1907 amendments to the Act: cf. *ibid*., 1908, 90. Clark (May 1908) says the resolution passed.

of forcing a hearing of their grievances and demands, and its apparent *de facto* recognition of their organizations, it seemed likely to circumvent the weary cycle of recognition strikes that had so often been lost. They were still caught up, as well, in the notion of right rather than bargaining power, and they were perhaps too ready to place their faith in the impartiality of an IDI board. The concept of fairness which underlay their celebration of the Fair Wages Resolution some years before was still a strong part of their outlook. Revolutionary socialists like R.P. Pettipiece could condemn the Act 'on the ground that there was an irrepressible conflict of interests between the owners of property and the workers, and this battle had to be fought to a finish,' but he was in a minority of one. Moderate socialists like Simpson could support the Act for much the same reason as the labourites at the convention: 'I would not admit for a moment that we have a right to place our stamp of approval on a system of capitalism by acknowledging a certain system of arbitration: but when it comes to putting the suffering of wives and children against the means whereby the settlement can be made, I am ready to sink my own personal opinions to bring about a better state of affairs for those women and children.'[44] The great run of trade unionists was willing to put off the inevitable hardship and likely defeat of a strike in favour of a hope of settlement through the IDI machinery. The running-trades brotherhoods, which declared they did not need to strike to win their demands, opposed it. Ironically, when they did have to turn to a strike on the collapse of IDI proceedings in 1910, it was not the Act but King's ever-ready zeal to go beyond the letter of the legislation that sealed their defeat.

III

The Industrial Disputes Investigation Act of 1907 provided for the investigation of disputes by a tripartite board, consisting of one representative nominated by each of the employer and union, and a chairman chosen by these two or, failing that, by the government. No strike or lock-out could take place until the board's report had been handed down. The board's report was not binding on the parties, but if it was not accepted it would be published so as to bring the weight of public opinion to bear. The board was armed with quasi-judicial powers of inquiry, and beyond this it was empowered, in the words of the Act, 'to bring about a settlement of the dispute, and to this end ... the Board may make all such suggestions and do all such things as it deems right and proper for inducing the parties to come to a fair and ami-

44 *Manitoba Free Press*, 20 Sept. 1907

cable settlement ...' Before turning to an examination of how boards attempted to fulfil this mandate, two features of the Act's philosophy need to be considered. These are the notion of 'public utilities' and the idea of arbitration by public opinion.

Although the term 'public utilities' appeared in the title of the Act, it was not formally defined in the body. 'Employer,' however, was defined as 'any person, company or corporation employing ten or more persons and owning or operating any mining property, agency of transportation or communication, or public service utility, including, except as hereinafter provided, railways, whether operated by steam, electricity or other motive power, steamships, telegraph and telephone lines, gas, electric light, water and power works.' In the Commons debates Lemieux argued – along lines developed in King's memorandum cited above – that public utilities embraced monopolies and oligopolies:

The intention here has been to group together under such economic terms as appear to be sufficiently specific, those industries and classes of industries upon the continuous and uninterrupted operation of which the welfare of the general public and other industries are dependent ... For economical reasons, this service, in a number of cases, is best performed by a single or limited number of individuals or companies; in other words, it partakes of the nature of what may be termed a natural monopoly ... in public-service utilities the element of competition is, either for a natural or economic reasons, or reasons of public policy, eliminated to a greater or lesser degree.[45]

The notion of public utilities seems to have been, to stretch a technical term, overdetermined. Two reasons for treating them apart from other industries were given: their uninterrrupted operation was essential to the community, and they had certain monopoly-like characteristics. But the first of these was what motivated the Act. It served double duty too, inasmuch as it provided an argument in favour of the bill's constitutionality, a question that arose more than once in the course of the Commons debate. If an industry was one on which 'the welfare of the general public [was] dependent,' then surely it must be for the 'general good of Canada' and subject to federal jurisdiction. Indeed, the opposition criticized a provision of the bill permitting the government to widen the definition of public utility by Order-in-Council, pointing out that these powers already resided in the government by virtue of section 92(10b) of the BNA Act.

45 *Debates* (1906–7), 3014f

The argument to monopoly was drawn on, in all likelihood, to answer the Jevonian question: 'why, in general, we uphold the rule of *laisser faire*, and yet in large classes of cases invoke the interference of local or central authorities.' To invoke an answer to this (silent) question was useful in a broad ideological sense, as it served to legitimize government interference with free enterprise and economic freedom in general, the catchwords Harvey Hall had called upon in criticizing the railway arbitration bill for trampling on the rights of all free-born British subjects – a turn of phrase, incidentally, that was echoed in one of the running-trades local's protests about the IDIA. It will be seen, too, that the general definition of public utilities as being in the nature of natural monopolies was a little far-fetched. In the coal-mining industry, for example, while possession of any one seam would entitle the owner to rents as well as profits, the industry as a whole, with its proliferation of small mines, was a highly competitive one. Where competition was restricted in this industry it was often more in the nature of monopsony, with dependence on railway contracts, than monopoly. In any event, the restricted competition argument could not in itself suffice to define the scope of the Act, for with the developing merger movement and the flight to cartels that preceded it numerous monopolistic and oligopolistic corporations emerged beyond the reach of the Act.

It might be noted, however, that compulsory investigation was made use of in industrial disputes in two of the largest of these, although not through the IDIA machinery. The Bell Telephone Company was the subject of a Royal Commission investigation early in 1907, and the case was made much of during the IDIA debates. Later, in 1908, another Royal Commission enquiry was launched into labour relations at the Dominion Textile Company, which by that time had grown to incorporate the greater part of Canadian cotton manufacturing capacity.[46] King served on both of these commissions. Finally, in 1910, he introduced the Combines Investigation Act, a totally ineffective attempt to apply the IDIA machinery to anti-trust purposes. There is a sense, then, in which King's concern with regulation by investigation was turned towards the emergence of large-scale industry in general. And while the IDIA did not encompass within its scope all monopoly-power firms, it did bear on many of them. The railways, after all, were the first giant industrial corporations, and the Canadian state had gone out of its way to ensure that they would become, if not natural, then at least economic monopolies.

---

46 For an outstanding discussion of conditions leading up to and following on this enquiry, see Jacques Rouillard, *Les travailleurs du coton au Québec 1900–1915* (Montréal: Les Presses de l'Université du Québec, 1974).

Thus the argument that public utilities ought to receive special treatment as monopolies merges into the argument that they should receive special treatment because their continuous operation is necessary for public well-being. Both of these, it will be seen, are part and parcel with King's general conception of the community as party to industry. In the first place, inasmuch as monopolies are creatures of public policy, public policy has a right to a say in their operation. In the second place, since the community is dependent on the operation of these monopolies, the government, representing the community, has the duty to intervene in favour of continuous operation. If the definition of public utilities given by Lemieux was overdetermined, it was because he, or more likely King as his speech-writer, was determined to show both right and duty.

Finally, in this connection, the special poignancy associated with the term 'public utilities' for many Canadians in the first decade of the century must not be forgotten. In the state-organized development of Ontario's new staples, as Nelles has shown, a complex constellation of political ideas and slogans centred on 'efficiency,' 'the people's share,' and public ownership of critical resource industries; 'public utilities' was at the core of the progressive business publicists' appeal to popular support for extensive government intervention in such areas as forest conservation, mines development, and the creation of Ontario Hydro. The state's role in accumulation was transmuted in this ideological constellation into the legitimation of the new industrial order: 'it was the duty of the state,' Nelles points out in connection with the conservation movement, 'to protect the public interest against the rapacious instincts and ignorance of its citizens,' while bankers and industrialists 'naturally responded to the conception of social efficiency, that business might confidently continue forever under professional, scientific management.' Similarly, the campaign for Hydro, for all its rhetoric about 'the people's power,' was organized and orchestrated by businessmen on the assumption, typical as we have seen of the CMA's understanding of the state, that their interests were coextensive with those of the larger community. And just as Lemieux was shepherding the IDI Act through the Commons, the by-law campaign for Hydro was heating up in Ontario, a campaign in which 'the religious rhetoric fused to the hydro myth transformed the public power movement into a crusade against evil forces and villainous men who were constantly scheming to deprive the working man of his inalienable right to hydro-electricity at any cost.'[47]

47 H.V. Nelles, *The Politics of Development: Forests, Mines and Hydro-Electric Power in Ontario, 1849–1941* (Toronto: Macmillan, 1974), 187, 190, 277.

The language of public utilities was peculiarly potent in the political conjuncture of the moment, and for all the federal Liberals' discomfort with the events taking shape in Ontario, there can be little doubt that this verbal magic was seen and used as something to conjure with. By linking the disputes investigation policy to the language of public utilities, all the glamour of the strongly supported Ontario campaign could be had without its liabilities. Thus there may have been here a sort of subliminal lexical appeal to all classes of the community, something that the argument to monopoly could only reinforce. That King was sensitive to this may be seen in a letter he wrote to Mulock in 1904, setting out some ideas for a speech to a labour audience. He urged Mulock to 'offset any capital which the Conservative party is making out of the alleged direct opposition of the Liberals towards public ownership'. 'I believe that, on the whole, public ownership people – who, as you know, are numerous throughout Ontario and the West – incline in their sympathies to the Liberal party. On the other hand, many of them are public ownership first and party afterwards, and will go with the side they think most likely to give effect to their advocated reforms.'[48]

But there is a second, a negative, side to the definition of public utility. In one sense, the IDIA represented a *retreat* from state intervention in the industrial relations process, inasmuch as the special treatment of public utilities meant that they were hived off from the general run of industries. We have already noted that the Conciliation Act provisions were to all intents and purposes abandoned after 1907. The IDIA did, to be sure, have a clause permitting its machinery to be invoked in other industries on the joint agreement of both parties to the dispute, but of the 124 applications for boards received by the registrar in the five years from 22 March, 1907 to 31 March, 1912, only four were referred under this clause.[49] For whatever reasons, then, the sweeping range of the department's services over all sectors of the economy was truncated after the passage of the IDIA. The Act established and set apart a special public or quasi-public sector in the economy. Intervention in this sector was justified in terms of the two claims to public-utility status described above, but of these the first – the dependence of the com-

48 King correspondence, 20 Oct. 1904
49 Of the four cases, three were from the Quebec boot and shoe industry. The IDIA was evidently seen as a more acceptable procedure than Archiepiscopal intervention. The fourth was from the Montreal Cotton Company at Valleyfield, a long-standing client of departmental conciliation services. In a number of other cases, applications for boards made by one of the parties to disputes in industries not covered by the compulsory features of the Act were rejected owing to the failure of the other party to agree. The registrar's report for 1907–8 listed six instances of this, five of them from Quebec.

munity on continuous operation – was clearly paramount. Royal Commissions were, after all, extraordinary occurrences, and the requests by trade unionists that the Act be extended to all industries went unheeded.[50] The argument from monopoly, as we have suggested, implies that *laissez-faire* is to be the rule, and King's stricture on compulsory arbitration, quoted earlier, that 'it were better to leave industry more alone, save in laying down rules & restrictions against unfair play,' points in the same direction. It would appear, then, that extensive intervention in the public sector was introduced without interfering in any way with the free play of market forces in the private sector, and, to take the argument a step further, that intervention in the public sector tended to support the viability of market forces in the private sector.

The link between public utility and public opinion is to be found in the overdetermination of the former. So long as 'public utility' was not simply the precise use of scientific terminology – and Lemieux's attempts to define it degenerated during the debate into the final admission that 'there appears to be among economists a difficulty in giving an exact definition of the word'[51] – it is clear that some non-scientific criterion must be invoked in connection with it. The notion of community or public fitted this requirement. Since the Act is to operate on behalf of the public, and the investigation is to be an investigation for the public, the outcome must be decided by the public. The decision of the investigating board, in the absence of a settlement, would not be imposed on the parties. It would be left to the higher court of public opinion. During the Commons debates, the concept of public opinion became talismanic, a touchstone of faith. H.S. Beland gave unmistakable evidence of a background in the *collèges classiques* when he reminded the House of 'the philosophical proposition that common consent is a criterion of truth,' and demonstrated by a process of deduction from first principles that public opinion as created by the Act would be at least 'a relative criterion of truth.' 'Everybody admits,' urged Lemieux, 'that the moment you put the facts before the public, which is the great third party in every quarrel, you are certain that the quarrel is pretty satisfactorily settled.' Later on, hard pressed by Borden's exposure of flaws in the board process, he found his feet again on the solid rock of public opinion: 'My hon. friend must

50 In 1913, King told a meeting of Cincinnati businessmen that the Act 'is not made applicable to all industries, because as a Federal measure its provisions apply to all parts of the Dominion, and there would be difficulty in administration at such long range if all industries were included.' This is the only reference I have found to such an explanation. 'Industrial Peace,' in MG 26 J5, vol. 1, p. 11 of the pamphlet.
51 *Debates* (1906–7), 3015

remember that public opinion is always watching over these proceedings, and parties who will make an abuse of these settlements will find public opinion turn against them.'[52] It is understandable that elected politicians should have elevated public opinion to the status of a household god, and this may explain why the term was not uttered once in the Senate, but the relation between the minor deity and the projected operation of the Industrial Disputes Investigation Act deserves further exploration.

Three nested levels of public involvement in the disputes settlement process were implicit in the Act. In the first place, the Board of Conciliation and Investigation was itself a public agency. Although two of its members were appointed directly by the parties to the dispute, these members were supposed to be 'disinterested,' at least in the limited sense of having no pecuniary interest in the outcome. Moreover, it had the option of holding its deliberations in public. Second, within the board, the chairman was the special representative of the public, holding the deciding vote. Finally, the public as a whole was called upon to enforce the board's award in cases where the parties did not come to a settlement. Section 25 of the Act provided that when no settlement was concluded, the board should submit a full report to the Minister, including its 'recommendation for the settlement of the dispute according to the merits and substantial justice of the case.' This is glossed in King's memoranda:

Under this section the public will be enabled before a strike or lockout is actually declared, to form an unprejudiced view of the attitude of the parties and be in a position to know to which side its sympathies should be extended. Instead of receiving through the press, biased or inspired articles it will have before it the calm, deliberate statement of a body of responsible men, who have already looked carefully into the case, and as judges and trusted public servants have given their views upon it.

Later in this series of notes, evidently those on which Lemieux based his speeches in the debate, the power of public opinion is discussed in light of the Bell Royal Commission:

The effect of public opinion cannot be better demonstrated than in the recent telephone investigation in Toronto, where, after the company had declared it would not be bound by the findings of the Board, public opinion was of such influence in the matter that, out of deference to it the company joined in what appears to be a very satisfactory settlement. Nothing but public opinion did it.

52 *Ibid.*, 3085f, 3812, 3872

The public interest was defined by example in an argument about why the railway employees must be included in the Act:

Moreover, a strike on a railway may prevent shipments of coal or supplies being brought to factories, or disturb and lead to a general cessation of industrial operations in mines, factories and industrial plants of one kind or another. In the interests of all industries dependent in any way on the railways, it is desirable that railways should be included in this legislation.

King took some pains to provide a liberal justification for the inclusion of the other industries in the Act. 'If one will study the teachings of the economists of the John Stuart Mill school, best known as the English individualist *laissez-faire* school, he will find that the liberty of the individual is conceded only where the liberties of others are not infringed in consequence.' Thus the act was a perfectly liberal one:

Where a strike in a coal mine takes place or on a railroad [*sic*] and in connection with gas works, electric light or water works, and people are prevented from getting fuel, receiving their food supplies and having drinking water or a city from having its fire protection, etc., it is perfectly clear that in all these cases the liberties of a great many people are being infringed in consequence of too excessive liberty on the part of others. This measure proposes to restrict individual liberty only at a point where, if it is exercised at too great a length, the liberties of others are thereby infringed.[53]

The public interest, therefore, amounts to an interest in the uninterrupted operation of the businesses on which public well-being is in some measure dependent. This interest is expressed in the first instance in legislation designed to 'get at the facts' in a dispute, and if investigation is not sufficient to bring about a settlement the expression of opinion by the public, at least in the great majority of cases, will see justice done. How is the interest in settling a dispute translated into the carrying out of justice? Public opinion will support the findings of a disinterested board which, having heard the arguments of both sides, will rule on the merits of the case. To refuse to accept this award will, all other things being equal, be *prima facie* evidence of vice. Public opinion is opposed to vice.

It will be apparent that the logic of legitimation behind the Act depends on two assumptions: a monolithic public and a radically 'disinterested' board. During the Commons debate, E.M. Macdonald, a Nova Scotia lawyer and

53 King Papers, MG 26 J4, vol. 14, 9955, 10023, 10031, 10028

prominent Liberal, expressed the sense of this first assumption in terms that could not be bettered:

We have in this country a public opinion free from all the entanglements that are to be found in the older lands, clustering around the differences between the classes and the masses, clustering around old claims and old rights ... Such terms as the classes and the masses, the lower, middle or upper class are misnomers in Canada ... One day a man is a railway navvy, the next a railway owner; one day a brake man on a railroad and the next the manager of that railroad, and so I could take you through all the various phases of industrial life and show you that we have in our country conditions which do not exist in the older lands beyond the seas ... Under the magnificent democracy which we are developing in Canada not only will every man get a square deal but public opinion will see that he gets it ...[54]

This view of the classlessness of society corresponds to King's notion of community. Another view, expressed in the same debate, corresponds in part to his notion of the public. E.J. Bristol, a Conservative lawyer and director of several mining companies, argued for the existence of 'other great interests' besides labour and capital:

For instance, suppose a question arises in the west where coal mines are shut down. It is not in a particular instance the owner of a mine or the workingman who is suffering most, but it is the large mass of the population who are left to freeze while these gentlemen fight out their disputes. There is therefore an enormous class of people outside the labour and manufacturing classes who are interested in this legislation, a legislation which is exceedingly important in the interest of the whole country rather than of any particular class.[55]

Bristol's stress on the 'particular instance' parallels King's 'public' as we have treated it, but the notion that there is a 'class' outside capital, management, and labour is foreign to King's view, although certainly justified within the political economy of turn-of-the-century Canada. Independent farmers and fishermen, small businessmen and shopkeepers constituted a sizable element in the community, although for King, at least by the time of *Industry and Humanity*, they were of little account, being outside the great law of progress, the ever-increasing scale of industry: his comment while still a student, that the small store must go to the wall, suggested much the same

54 *Debates* (1906–7), 3054, 1182
55 *Ibid.*, 1182

stance. King himself never sought to enlarge the scope of the community beyond the other three parties to industry, despite the elaborate confusion in which this landed him. Indeed, Bristol's comments exhibit a similar confusion: he leaps from those not directly involved in a 'particular instance' to 'an enormous class of people outside the labour and manufacturing classes,' and whatever may be thought of these propositions taken separately, his 'therefore' is certainly specious. The concealed logic of *Industry and Humanity*, the distinction between community and public, underlies the dualities implicit and explicit in the notions of public utility, public interest, and public opinion which served to legitimize the Act. The overdetermination discussed above, then, is a consequence of the two faces of King's 'public.'

The second assumption, that of a radically disinterested board, follows from these considerations. It is tempting to discuss the constitution of the board, which is both representative of the public and contains a representative of the public, in terms similar to those attributed to Porson when a buggy came by with three men in it. 'There,' said his friend, 'is an illustration of the Trinity.' 'No,' Porson rejoined, 'you must show me one man in *three* buggies, if you can.' But the reader will consider that there is altogether too much metaphysics in this chapter already. It needs only to be pointed out that in fact the chairman was the decisive figure on the board. The other two members were advocates of special interests, those of the parties to the dispute, before they could be advocates of the general interest. Their public responsibility, then, was to be 'calm,' 'deliberate,' and 'responsible,' to use the adjectives employed in King's memorandum, quoted above. The chairman, possessing the casting vote and, as we shall see, more than occasionally involving himself in active mediation of the dispute, was the great representative of the principle that public utilities must maintain continuous operations.

Between 1907 and 1911, twenty chairmen acted on more than one board. The most frequently appointed by far was Adam Shortt, professor of political science at Queen's until 1908, when he was appointed to the new Civil Service Commission. He served twelve times. Two judges, McGibbon and Fortin, each sat on seven boards, while Judge Gunn sat on six. Among those who sat on two to five boards, two are of particular interest. J.E. Atkinson, King's boyhood friend and editor of the Toronto *Star*, served four times, while King's university acquaintance, Rev. C.W. Gordon ('Ralph Connor'), sat on three boards as chairman. Among the twenty repeating chairmen, twelve were members of the bench. Several representatives of either employers or workers also served on numerous boards. The record among employer representatives was held by Wallace Nesbitt, a corporation lawyer, who sat for railway companies on ten boards. J.G. O'Donoghue, the TLC solicitor, represented employees on no fewer than nineteen boards, all of them in railway disputes, while F.H. Sherman of the UMWA represented coal miners on eleven boards. For men like O'Donoghue and Sherman representation on IDIA boards became an absorbing part of their responsibilities to the labour movement, and they accumulated a great deal of experience with the Act's workings. It is to the operation of the IDIA machinery that our attention must next be turned.

IV

Evidence on the critical minutiae of the IDIA machinery in practice is not so readily available as, for example, that for King's interventions under the Conciliation Act. One reason for this is that boards were actively discouraged from compiling a stenographic record of their activities[56] and, especially when they terminated successfully, chairmen did not file detailed reports with the department. The nature of the disputes referred under the Act and their disposition by boards were summarized in the annual reports of the registrar,[57] and there is piecemeal information about particular aspects of the process in other sources, to be discussed presently. One further source of especial value considering the general dearth is Adam Shortt's memoir of his numerous appointments as chairman. The otherwise surprising absence of comment on the boards in King's diary is explained by the fact that shortly after the passage of the Act he was sent abroad on government business, and after his return he was immediately occupied with the search for a parliamentary seat. Before going abroad he made a second trip to Lethbridge to attempt a settlement of a new miners' strike which had erupted in violation, and probably in ignorance, of the provisions of the new Act, but he was not involved in the board process itself there.

The registrar's report for fiscal 1911 summarized proceedings under the Act to March 31 of that year. Since the act was proclaimed on 22 March 1907, this very detailed summary report covers four years of operation. One hundred and six applications for boards had been made, three of them on voluntary joint applications and one in a civic employees' dispute. These four were settled through the IDIA machinery. The remaining 102 'public-utility' references are tabulated in Table 2. Ten disputes, unresolved by the IDIA

---

56 Cf. King Papers, MG 26 J4, vol. 14, 9911, a letter of instruction from Acland to board chairmen.
57 Published as Sessional Paper 36a, various years

TABLE 2 Proceedings under Industrial Disputes Investigation Act,
22 March 1907 to 31 March 1911

Industry	Disposition		Total
	Success[1]	Failure[2]	
MINING			
Coal	32	4	36
Metal	5	2	7
TRANSPORTATION, COMMUNICATIONS			
Railways	37	3	40
Street railways	6	1	7
Longshoremen	3	0	3
Freight handlers	2	0	2
Teamsters	1	0	1
Sailors	1	0	1
Ship liners	1	0	1
Deck hands	1	0	1
Commercial telegraphers	2	0	2
	91	10	101[3]

Proportion of total references		Proportion of total failures
Coal mining	35.6%	40.0%
All mining	42.6	60.0
Railways	39.6	30.0
All transport	57.4	40.0
Railways and coal mines	75.2	70.0

SOURCE Adapted from s.p. 36a (1912), 80

NOTES
1 Success: 'Strikes averted or ended.'
2 Failure: 'Strikes not averted or ended.'
3 One dispute, unresolved because employer went into liquidation during investigation, has been excluded.

machinery, led to strikes. There was one case of this kind in each of 1907 and 1908, and four in each of 1909 and 1910. Moreover, the summary statistics tend to obscure the fact that on several occasions strikes were initiated in violation of the provisions of the Act and boards were constituted during the course of these illegal strikes. The penalty clauses of the Act, however, were not invoked by the government in these situations.

It is clear from what evidence is available that the boards were simply another institutional form for the active mediation developed by King in his Conciliation Act interventions. For all the rhetoric about public opinion, the practice of withholding board proceedings from the public eye was instituted early in the history of the Act. The Department's *Annual Report* for 1908 published, in an appendix, a long letter by Adam Shortt recounting his experience as chairman of one of the first boards constituted under the Act, in a dispute between the Grand Trunk and its machinists in April 1907. Shortt's strategy was to mediate the dispute, developing a form of settlement through detailed discussions of the points at issue with the other two members of the board. King considered this intervention 'an illuminating example of procedure' under the Act.[58] In 1916, Selekman interviewed Shortt about this board. He had been determined to over-rule technicalities raised before the board by the two lawyers representing the parties, O'Donoghue and Nesbitt, and he announced early in the proceedings that 'the board was meeting not to interpret the law but to help bring about a settlement.'[59]

Shortt's approach to the IDIA machinery precluded an appeal to public opinion, inasmuch as it tried to avoid public discussion of the proceedings in the belief that this might obstruct the mediation process. In a 1909 article discussing his extensive experience as board chairman, Shortt wrote:

In the case of all the boards presided over by the writer, it was arranged that there should be no newspaper reports of the proceedings before the board. The objection to such reports has been that the very calling for a board implied that there were more or less radical differences of opinion and assertions of right, which the respective parties were about to lay down and defend, but which, in the course of the proceedings before the board, must be given up or at least greatly modified on one or both sides if a settlement were to be reached.

This was no less true when the conciliation aspect of the board process failed to arrive at a settlement of the dispute, the situation in which the original discussions of the Act had most clearly called for the cleansing light of public opinion. It was replaced, in Shortt's practice, by active mediation:

It might seem that, having reached this stage, the board has nothing further to do but to sum up the facts and arguments, reach a decision, and frame an award, leaving to the parties the option of accepting or rejecting it. In our boards, however, the incident was never regarded as closed when we had submitted our proposals for a settlement

---

58 SP 36a (1908)
59 *Postponing Strikes*, 108

and they were not accepted, as sometimes happened. The parties were seldom brought together again, but negotiations between them were conducted by the board with the chairman as a common medium, assisted, in dealing with the employers, by their representative on the board, and, in dealing with the employees, by their representative. Occasionally, however, the chairman conducted the final negotiations alone. The object of these negotiations was to find, on either side, the lines of least and also of most resistance, to overcome prejudice, to plead what seemed to the board or the chairman as the just cause of each side with the other, and gradually to break down or dissolve away the barriers between the parties until so little remained that it was not worth while to risk a great and uncertain struggle for so small an ultimate advantage, even if successful.

Once the claims of justice were satisfied, the over-riding purpose of the board's intervention was the prevention of a work stoppage. If the final settlement could be considered 'fair,' that was very satisfactory, but the real intent was to serve the public interest by preventing a disruption in the orderly operations of essential industries. This is at least implied by Shortt in the following:

... in the negotiations special emphasis was placed on the fact that the real question was not one as to agreement or non-agreement, but as to agreement with or without a strike, and it was urged that it were better to have reasonable concession without loss than concession to mere superior strength, which might or might not be on the side of justice, and where loss was certain to be multiplied manifold.[60]

In brief, procedure under the Act from the beginning was as Mary van Kleeck described it, on the basis of almost two decades of experience, in 1927:

Although the law is called the Industrial Disputes *Investigation* Act, and its theory has been that if the facts could be made known public opinion would stimulate a reasonable attitude in both groups, as a matter of fact investigation for the enlightenment of public opinion has not accompanied the administration of the act. Representatives of the government have sought ... to bring employers and employees together. They have believed that publicity would jeopardize the settling of differences. What the act has done has been to impose an obligation not to strike until this method of negotiation and conference can be tried. The act, therefore, is an experiment in conciliation

60 'The Canadian Industrial Disputes Act,' American Economic Association, *Publications*, Series 3, vol. 10 (1909), 161, 164, 165

rather than a trial of the method of current investigation and publicity by governmental bureaus.[61]

There is some direct evidence that Shortt's practice was not idiosyncratic, that other chairmen in the first experiments with the Act placed stress on mediation at the expense of public opinion. For example, V.S. Clark interviewed 'an eminent lawyer, formerly a justice of the Dominion supreme court, who has served on several boards,' evidently Mr Justice Stuart, in 1907–8. He deprecated insistence on technicalities and legal formulae in conducting board proceedings as tending to 'prevent conciliation.' Clark concluded that 'the most successful boards in conducting proceedings, have interpreted the act as a statute for conciliation by informal methods, looking toward a voluntary agreement by the parties as its object.'[62]

Some modern commentators have taken this to mean that the Act was really intended or administered so as to encourage collective bargaining. That the Act in practice meant mediation rather than investigation directed towards the formation of public opinion is certain, but there has been some debate about whether that practice was directed towards anticipating the compulsory bargaining features of the Wagner Act or towards the prevention of strikes and lock-outs. The collective bargaining interpretation has been advanced in a fairly weak form by H.D. Woods and in a somewhat stronger one by C.B. Williams, whose position on the Conciliation Act has already been discussed.

Woods argues that the 'primary purpose' of the IDIA was 'the establishment of a bargaining relationship, and not, as commonly supposed, the delaying of the strikes or lockout.' However, he goes on to point out that 'there was no requirement to recognize the other party or to bargain in good faith, although there was the compulsion to meet together in the conciliation-board proceedings. In other words, except for the limitation on the use of the work-stoppage and the compulsion to participate in conciliation, public policy left the parties alone to work out their own destiny and interfered again only as a result of a subsequent serious dispute. This was essentially a public-interest emergency-dispute policy and little more.' Furthermore, he concedes that 'while the act encouraged a form of recognition, it did not mention unions,' and that 'once the particular dispute had been dealt with, the formal situation was as before the intervention.'[63] Woods does not

61 Introduction to Selekman, *Postponing Strikes*, 16
62 Clark, (May, 1908), 666
63 Woods, *Labour Policy*, 341, 343, 342

explain how these admissions can be squared with his former assertion that the primary purpose of the Act was not strike or lock-out prevention, but the establishment of a bargaining relationship. It seems evident that the 'compulsion to meet together in the conciliation-board proceedings' was not, on Woods' own showing, intended to foster the development of a permanent bargaining relationship, but had as its purpose the settlement of the particular dispute without recourse to a work stoppage.

Williams' position, as we have seen, is based on a semantic analysis of alleged changes in the denotations of certain industrial relations terms over time. His discussion of the IDIA is by no means as clear as that of the Conciliation Act:

The important point is that the Act set out a one-step compulsory procedure only: compulsory investigation by a tripartite board of arbitration. This compulsory investigation coupled with a compulsory postponement of a work stoppage during the investigation is what we today call 'compulsory conciliation.' The suggestion is that the meaning of the word 'conciliation' in the term compulsory conciliation, as used today, is not the meaning given to the word in the debates on the Acts of 1900, 1903, and 1907. Also, the dispute settlement device which we today call compulsory conciliation was called compulsory investigation in both the 1903 and 1907 Acts.

This is rather muddled: investigation is both the same as conciliation and quite different. The problem is accentuated by Williams' attempt to use the language of parliamentary debates to clarify the meaning of the legislation, since for the IDIA as much as for the Conciliation Act this fails to come to terms with what was actually done under the provisions of the Act. Williams argues that the Acts of 1900, 1903, and 1907 are all much of a muchness, making up a single policy orientation that persisted unchanged until 1944, when the Wagner Act principle of compulsory collective bargaining was tacked on to it. In this view, then, compulsory collective bargaining was a later arrival, and the earlier policy was something else. But it is far from clear what Williams takes that something to be. We have already seen that in his view the Conciliation Act was 'not more than what we today call collective bargaining.' If this is the case, then it is hard to see that the pre-1944 policy and the new principles introduced subsequently constituted 'two distinct ... policies.'[64] While Williams' criticisms of postwar policy seem substantially valid, his derivation of them from the earlier legislation is highly suspect.

64 Williams, 'Notes on the Evolution of Compulsory Conciliation in Canada,' *Relations Industrielles*, 19 (1964) 315, 322

If some modern commentators have seen in the IDIA the origins of collective bargaining policy, others have interpreted it as a stumbling block to the emergence of mature bargaining practices. Jamieson, for example, brings this indictment:

While unions were thus temporarily deprived of their main bargaining weapons [i.e. by the prohibition of strikes pending investigation] there were no effective restraints placed on employers to prevent the familiar practices of imposing yellow-dog contracts, blacklisting, discriminatory discharge of union members, and employment of non-union members or strike-breakers. On balance, it appears to have operated adversely to the strength and effectiveness of organized labour in Canada. There are other, perhaps more charitable interpretations of the IDIA and the objectives of its chief architect, W.L. Mackenzie King. H.D. Woods ... concludes that the latter's main purpose was to encourage, by degrees, the establishment of unionism and collective bargaining in Canada. That is to say, legislation such as the IDIA, which required the parties to a dispute to nominate representatives who would meet together in a Board of Inquiry [*sic*] under a neutral chairman, was conceived of as a means of giving unions some official status and forcing employers to grant them at least limited recognition. One could argue, on the other hand, that the Act may well have given employers encouragement to resist giving full recognition to unions, in so far as it prevented the latter from striking or picketing at the most strategic time, while failing to protect them from employer attack. The Act thus may well have delayed the evolution, in Canada, of mature collective bargaining.[65]

Jamieson's analysis differs from the others we have discussed, not only in his assessment of the Act but also in that, while Woods and Williams discuss intention and outcome as though they were the same thing, he is content to describe the supposed consequences of the Act. This is an analytic advance, to be sure, and he is able to identify certain significant shortcomings of the legislation. His general claim, however, while it is certainly a plausible one, requires some qualification, at least for the period of this study. In attempting to determine whether the Act 'operated adversely to the strength and effectiveness of organized labour,' the two principal groups of organizations directly subject to the Act must be borne in mind. The railway brotherhoods, for all their resistance to the 1907 bill, soon made their peace with the Act and managed to retain their position as the aristocrats of the Canadian labour movement notwithstanding the fact that they were singled out for special treatment by the law. They had already established institutionalized bargain-

65 Jamieson, 128f

ing relationships with their employers, and they were not faced with recognition problems under the Act. It will be argued in the next chapter that federal disputes policy did preclude the development of 'free collective bargaining' in the railway industry, but this was a consequence not of the IDI Act *per se*, but of the fact that the railways' obstinate refusal to bargain in good faith was unwittingly abetted by the government's insistence on going *beyond* the mandate of the Act. It was not the IDIA, but the broader insistence on maintenance of operations, which distorted the industrial relations process on the railways. However this might be interpreted, it remains true that the railway workers, particularly in the running trades, were the most highly and effectively organized workers in Canada, and that the IDIA seems to have had little effect on this fact.

Coal miners, the second significant group covered by the Act, were also more effectively organized than most groups of Canadian workers, although by no means as much so as the railway workers. In the western coal fields, the miners came up against the only significant employer opposition to the Act, resulting in some instances in the refusal of employers to nominate representatives to or appear before the boards. In these cases, even the very limited *de facto, pro tem* recognition implicit in the board proceedings was some improvement. F.H. Sherman, in his capacity as president of the western Canadian district of the UMWA, was for some time favourably disposed towards the Act, although the attitudes of western miners were by no means always thus, as we shall see later in this chapter. In eastern Canada, as the UMWA moved in to raid the PWA, it encountered difficulties with the Act, to be described below, and these led to its demand for repeal. In some cases, the IDIA impeded the coal miners' struggles, and in some cases it seems to have expedited them. Once again – and again, subject to various interpretations – it was during the IDIA period that the United Mine Workers managed to extend their organization to cover most Canadian workers in their industry.

The point is not that the IDIA was responsible for the organizational successes of the railway or mining unions, but that these unions were more successful than most in developing and maintaining their organizations. If the analysis Jamieson introduces was a *determinate* one – that is to say, if the weakness and ineffectiveness of organized labour were *caused* by the IDIA – then one would expect those unions directly affected by the Act to be particularly weak and ineffective, and this was patently not the case. Of course, it might be argued that these unions were strengthened by the necessity to fight the Act, but this would have to be demonstrated and in any event is quite distinct from Jamieson's argument.

There might be another approach to Jamieson's conclusion, an approach which would in effect stand it on its head. We have noted already that the IDIA had a negative implication in restricting the scope of government intervention to, for the most part, public utilities. It might be argued that *this* weakened the trade union movement in industries not affected by the Act: that the withdrawal of federal conciliation services made it that much more difficult for these unions to wring concessions out of their employers. This raises, among other things, the very awkward question of how the effects of industrial-relations legislation can be measured, a problem to which we must turn shortly. Before doing so, however, it will be useful to examine an assumption of Jamieson's that bears on the general problem, raised elsewhere in this study, of union advocacy of thorough-going state intervention in the disputes settlement process. Jamieson criticizes the Act for delaying the evolution of 'mature collective bargaining,' and collective bargaining was the focus of the Woods and Williams discussions as well. The implication is that free collective bargaining, presumably on the Wagner Act model, is the predestined end-state of the evolution of industrial relations systems, or, at the very least, that it is a consummation devoutly to be wished. We have already noted that, among the alternatives available, liberal bargaining systems may not always and everywhere be the one best way: the Australasian experience was our example. If this is true, then free collective bargaining has no *a priori* claim to serve as the yardstick against which other institutions may be measured. This view has been eloquently expressed by Pentland, discussing the IDIA in the context of his analysis of Canadian preference for the paternalistic state:

The persistent call for compulsory state intervention in Canada ... rests heavily on the concept that the father state can and should set things right. It is true that the advocates of intervention have typically had an inadequate appreciation of the advantages of unrestrained collective bargaining as a means of resolving differences and constructing an effective industrial relations system. It is true that intervention has been advocated with particular readiness by those whose bargaining power is weak. And it is arguable, and has certainly been argued on both these accounts, that the cry for intervention is the mark of immaturity in industrial relations. On the other hand, these observations are not quite as derogatory as sometimes made out to be. There is nothing sacred (except, perhaps, in an American conception of society) about perfectly unrestricted activity, or completely untrammelled bargaining. Despite a good deal of strong talk to the contrary, state intervention even including compulsory arbitration does not "destroy" collective bargaining, though certainly modifying its character. From a father state point of view, the modification may be decidedly for the better if the awards reflect relative indifference to comparative bargaining power, and rest instead on a moral conception of social entitlement to share in pecuniary and other benefits ... From the father state viewpoint, it also misses a good deal of the point to emphasize that full-blown compulsion, as in Australasia, has not eliminated strikes. The Canadian preoccupation with prevention of work stoppages and the inadequate appreciation of collective bargaining which it denotes have been stressed in this Report. But this Canadian impatience with stoppages can also be seen, and in many cases should be seen, as a conviction that the father state should supply a better way, not only more peaceful but more equitable. Reflecting this concern for equity, Canadian compulsion has been much less prone than American to deny the compelled groups any alternative except acceptance of the employer's terms.[66]

But even this, for all its usefulness as a corrective to other positions, fails to come to terms with one of the essential characteristics of the IDIA policy. The emphasis in Canadian policy on the prevention of strikes or lock-outs has meant that disputes settlement has been diverted away from a quest for equity or the recognition of 'social entitlement to share in pecuniary and other benefits,' towards the *ad hoc* suspension of hostilities. That this may in some instances have resulted in compromises approximating to 'fairness' need not be denied. The naive workerist view that the IDIA always meant the victory of rapacious employers over deserving employees[67] will not hold water, especially when it is contrasted with other available mechanisms of settlement. But the IDIA conception that the public interest is to be identified with the orderly operation of industry entails, no matter what the fortunes of individual employers or groups of workers, a generalized defence of private property rights by the capitalist state. The public interest is the bourgeois interest in two related senses. First, in the 'community' sense of the community/public duality, the general interest is identified with the expansion of bourgeois property relations and general economic growth. As Miliband puts it, 'Governments may be solely concerned with the better running of "the economy." But the description of the system as "the economy" is part of the idiom of ideology, and obscures the real process. For what is being improved

66 Pentland, 164ff
67 This was one position among several put forward in a series of petitions from UMWA locals in Nova Scotia demanding repeal of the Act in 1911: 'As was to be expected this piece of lobe-sided [*sic*] class legislation with its high sounding and hypocritical pretensions has resulted always, each time it has been tried, in bitter disappointment and defeat for the workers.' Laurier Papers, MG 26 G, vol. 659, 179122f

is a *capitalist* economy; and this ensures that whoever may or may not gain, capitalist interests are least likely to lose.'[68]

Thus an industrial relations policy founded in the view that the trains must run on time, no matter what particular restrictions it may place on 'management's rights,' tends towards the more 'efficient' operation of a *capitalist* economy. Seond, in the 'public' sense of the dichotomy, this tendency is effectively masked by the inherent assumption of classlessness, the pluralism of economic particles that classifies the industrial relations system not on class lines, but according to who is and who is not engaged in a particular dispute at any particular time. Both of these imply restrictions on bourgeois property; in the first place, on the unfettered right of the owner to ride roughshod over his hired hands, and in the second place on the putative interest of all members of the class (and this is equally true, of course, of the working as of the employing class) who may stand to benefit in general from a victory won by one of their number. But these restrictions, to quote Miliband again, are 'not in "fundamental opposition" to the interests of property: [they are] indeed part of that "ransom" of which Joseph Chamberlain spoke in 1885 and which, he said, would have to be paid precisely for the purpose of *maintaining* the rights of property in general.'[69]

In general, then, the outcome of interventions in particular disputes is of less importance than the particularity that the mode of intervention imposes on all disputes. Even were the workers to win some sort of 'victory' in every case they brought before the boards, we would not be justified in concluding that the bourgeoisie 'lost' by it, although admittedly there might be some difficulty in convincing businessmen that that was so. In fact, the IDIA would be an effective guardian of bourgeois property precisely to the extent that workers were satisfied with it. But this satisfaction was hampered by the immanent contradiction between the stress on continuous operation of public utilities, on the one hand, and the dictates of fairness in settlements, on the other. This contradiction was only capable of resolution within the framework of the Act when the employer proved susceptible to the chairman's mediation efforts. And this was the real contradiction of the Act, of course: that in the long run employers could only win by giving in, if not all of the time, then at least part of it. When employers had a long run of bad luck – that is, when they consistently refused to give in – the unions demanded the Act's repeal.

68 Ralph Miliband, *The State in Capitalist Society* (London: Weidenfeld and Nicholson, 1972), 79
69 *Ibid.*, 78

Before turning to this, however, there is another body of criticism of the Act which requires some consideration. There is a large literature which takes the promise of the Act to prevent strikes at face value and attempts to measure its success in this. It has generally been found wanting, particularly so far as the coal-mining industry is concerned, where strikes remained frequent after the passage of the Act. But there is an inescapable problem with all such analyses. For all that the legislators declared the Act to be an experiment, it was not a particularly well-designed one. The pertinent variables were not – of course, could not be – isolated, so that it is really not possible to tell what would have happened 'if' the IDIA had not been passed. If the outbreak of a single strike despite the machinery of the Act is enough to brand it as a failure in these terms, then it was a failure many times over. But no statistical assessment of the effectiveness of the Act is possible. Perhaps the most well-founded conclusion within these limitations was Selekman's, as it was summarized by a reviewer of his book: 'In the coal-mining industry, for whose peaceful ordering the provisions of the Disputes Act were originally designed, there is a record of frequent and bitter disputes. But, if in this field no visible successes can be claimed, there are a number of other industries within the scope of its working, in which the relations of capital and labour have visibly been improved ...'[70] at least to the extent that occasional negotiations took place under its auspices. But any evaluation of the Act requires that there be a yardstick against which to measure it, and it is difficult to see that there could ever be agreement about what that yardstick might be. We can say, weakly, that some strikes which might have taken place in the absence of the Act did not take place, and that perhaps there were others which would not have taken place, or would not have lasted so long, were it not for the delays imposed by the Act. And it is difficult to see why, unless we are willing to swallow the presuppositions of the Act whole, we should want to say more.

V

Throughout the period considered in this study, the Canadian Manufacturers' Association supported the IDIA, at least to the extent that it 'would be sorry to have it repealed.'[71] During the spring of 1907, while the bill was before the House, the CMA's parliamentary committee decided to withhold comment, in part because railways and coal mines were 'lines of business in

70 Review by G.E. Jackson, *CHR*, vol. IX, 2 (1928), 181
71 *IC*, Feb. 1908, 555

which members of the Association are but indirectly interested,' but also because of the experimental features of the legislation: 'While generally speaking, the principle of conciliation is to be approved of, the boards constituted under the Act are, so far as Canada is concerned, a decided innovation. It is plainly the part of wisdom, therefore, to go slowly, to test them out carefully in a narrow sphere of action before giving them a wider application. The Act is now on trial, and its operation will be watched by manufacturers with deep interest.'[72]

Industrial Canada accepted this watching brief. In May 1907 an article headlined 'The Conciliation Act [*sic*] on Trial' warned, in connection with the illegal strike at Lethbridge, that 'if the employees refuse to submit to the provisions of the law, which compels them to work during the time of investigation, then the public will expect the full enforcement of the penalties for their refusal.' The following month, under the heading 'Successful Conciliation,' the journal published a letter from Adam Shortt describing his part as board chairman in settling a dispute between the GTR and its machinists: 'An important and complex labor dispute, involving feuds of more than two years standing and not improving with age, had been settled to the satisfaction of both parties without the loss of a day's work to the men, or a dollar to the company, and above all without disturbance to the public service. Thus was every object of the Lemieux Act secured.'

Again in November, when Springhill coalminers struck in violation of the Act, *Industrial Canada* warned that the legislation was working in a one-sided way. 'You can compel an employer to continue operating ... How can you compel five hundred or a thousand men to continue work if they do not want to?' But the article took great pains to point out that 'the measure has been received most sympathetically by employers. It was the general feeling that everything possible should be done to facilitate its operation. And no doubt much good has resulted from it.'

In February of the following year, the CMA journal pointed out that the Act in operation 'has developed some features that were not expected of it by those who had a hand in its making. One of these is the killing effect it has had on the closed shop propositions of the labor unions.' In a speech to the National Civic Federation in New York, CMA secretary G.M. Murray expanded on this serendipitous bonus: 'Speaking solely from the employers' point of view, therefore, we have three good reasons why the act is acceptable: First, it has compelled unions to abandon the principle of the closed shop; second, it has compelled unions to abandon the principle of the stan-

72 *Ibid.*, Oct. 1907, 212

dard union wage; third, it has compelled unions to abandon the principle that they have the right to nominate the men who shall fill certain positions. To this extent the act has undermined some of the fundamental doctrines of trade unionism ...[73] Entitling his speech 'The Solution of Labor Troubles,' Murray averred that 'the consensus of opinion, even where everything did not go the way the employer wanted it, seems to be that the act on the whole is a very good thing.'

The effect of the Act on the closed shop was anticipated by the TLC leadership, of course, in their discussion of the two clauses which 'wd have in justice to go out,' during the drafting stage. The other two consequences Murray identified were, interestingly enough, not mentioned in the reported debates on the Act at TLC conventions. The first of these, if Murray was correct, has some bearing on the Act's role in particularizing the disputes in which it was invoked, while the second may speak more especially to the breakdown of artisanal notions of job control discussed in an earlier chapter.

A second 'unexpected feature' identified in *Industrial Canada* had to do with the administration of the Act. The journal recognized very early on that it was mediation, rather than public investigation, that lay at the heart of the Act's operations: in fact, it quite consistently referred to the IDIA as the 'conciliation' law. 'The tendency of all the more recent investigations,' it reported in February 1908, 'is in the direction of bringing the two sides together in an informal way, and letting them have it out between themselves. It is a curious development from the first ideas [i.e., of publicity,] and indeed from the intention of the Act; but it is a development along the lines of least resistance, and is, therefore, one that is likely to produce the best results.' It recognized that this was largely Shortt's doing, noting that under his method of administration, 'the Act serves a useful purpose ...' In October 1909, CMA president R. Hobson told the convention that 'the Act, of course, is only an old friend under a new name – Conciliation, under the guise of Compulsory Investigation.' He suggested that the government go a step further in the direction of industrial peace, by taking 'immediate and effective measures to bar the doors of the Dominion against the foreign agitator.' Mackenzie King, who, as Minister of Labour, was an honoured guest at the convention's banquet, thanked Hobson for his praise of the Act and suggested that the real next step should be the voluntary creation of permanent conciliation and arbitration boards, in place of further compulsion.

73 *Ibid.*, Feb. 1908, 554

The following year, *Industrial Canada* furnished a favourable comparison of the IDIA with Australian compulsory arbitration[74] – this in the middle of a serious railway strike – and a month later produced an assessment of another board experience in which one can almost physically sense the cigar smoke and brandy-and-soda assurance of the complaisant, indeed complacent, businessman:

> Through that excellent British quality of not knowing when he was defeated, Judge Barron, as Chairman of the Board of Conciliation which sat on the dispute between the Toronto Street Railway Company and its employees, achieved a notable success in averting a strike when all prospects of peace seemed to have vanished. In his work of conciliation he was ably assisted by Mr. Mullarky, whose good judgement was responsible for the favourable presentation of the company's claims, and by Mr. O'Donoghue to whose moderation and wisdom is to be credited the restraint and spirit of compromise which characterized the attitude of the men. We must believe that out of the strivings and experiments of many minds some scheme will be evolved eventually whereby the public's interests will be at all times protected against the calamity of strike or lockout on a public utility. Until such a time arrives, however, we must trust to the efficacy of conciliation, which in the hands of the present Board has proved so satisfactory.[75]

V

In his 1927 book, Selekman declared that there were two periods in Canadian labour's attitude to the IDIA. From 1908 on, labour disapproved of the Act, culminating in demands for its repeal in 1911, 1912, and 1916. Then a reversal occurred, and labour demanded that the scope of the Act be extended in 1919, 1920, and 1921. When the Act was declared *ultra vires* in 1925, the labour movement demanded its reinstatement. The period of this study, then falls in the first half of Selekman's 'period of disapproval,' and ends with the first united call for repeal. It is argued here that the 'period of disapproval' really began in 1911, when adverse court decisions triggered the release of pent-up grievances against the Act. Before 1911 the labour movement as a whole, and in particular the TLC, while it was not unanimously enthusiastic about the Act, was not overwhelmingly hostile either.

74 *Ibid.*, Aug. 1910, 38
75 *Ibid.*, Sept. 1910, 120

Besides the TLC convention proceedings, there is a useful source of information about labour attitudes to the Act in two reports prepared by V.S. Clark for the United States Bureau of Labor. Early in 1908 and again a year later Clark attempted to gather attitudinal data through interviews with various union spokesmen and other interested parties. In 1908, he reported that while 'many union officers have little information of the practical working of the act and no intelligent opinion as to its effect on labour interests,' 'those who have made a study of the subject are favorable to the law.' The railway brotherhoods were still unhappy about being made subject to it despite the fact that 'the practical value of the law seems to have been more clearly shown in railway difficulties than in any other kind of labor disturbances.' Although the PWA adopted a resolution opposing the Act immediately after its passage, presumably because the Act conflicted with the Nova Scotia arbitration law, Clark found in private conversations with members and leaders of the association that they were now favourably disposed. He quoted a 'leading official' of the PWA as writing, 'I believe it [the Act] is destined to become popular in Canada.' Clark found that the UMWA in western Canada had overcome its original dislike for the Act, especially since it had received some favourable settlements. But in the UMWA, the leadership was more satisfied with the law than the rank and file. The Western Federation of Miners was opposed to the law and demanded its repeal. There was a general pattern of eastern Canadian support and western Canadian opposition, reflecting the conservative trade union traditions of the former and the strength of the syndicalist and socialist movements in the latter. In general, Clark found that 'the attitude of workers becomes more friendly to the act with longer experience,' although those in trades directly affected by the Act were more hostile than those in others. But on the whole, and perhaps most interesting of all, Clark found that 'sentiment in its favor is probably stronger among the rank and file of the workers than among the leaders. Such casual information as one can pick up through talking with the men indicates this. In one list of interviews, including miners and railway men, every one of the workmen – thirteen in number – was favourable to the law.' This may well have had to do with reluctance to risk the strike weapon, for one railway man told him that 'middle-aged and married men, who have responsibilities, welcome the law.' Clark qualified his account, however, by noting that 'it would be impossible to say definitely whether or not a popular vote of the working people of Canada, especially of those directly affected by the law, would indorse [sic] the act at the present time.'[76]

76 Clark, (May 1908), 672–6

A little over a year later, Clark found that there was 'less unanimity of opinion and more positive opposition' among workers than among employers, although among workers 'the trend of sentiment is more difficult to detect': 'The views of different unions differ, and in each union there is an official opinion and an opinion of the rank and file, which do not always correspond. Finally, nothing whatever is known of what unorganized labor thinks about such legislation, if it thinks about it at all.' He noted that the TLC had become more equivocal about the Act in 1908, and that this may have had something to do with the fact that the AFL was officially opposed to the legislation. He found that the railway unions were less opposed to the Act than they had been, and one 'leading union official' in the industry told him, 'To give the devil his due, the act has worked very well.' Clark noted that the response of union leaders to the Act depended very much on what their own experience had been, and that they would switch from opposition to support on receiving a favourable settlement, and back again with an unfavourable one. All the same, Clark reported an 'appreciable' change in the attitudes of railway unions and workers. Miners, on the other hand, were becoming somewhat more hostile to the Act, 'due to special causes, peculiar to each particular locality.' The UMWA, just beginning its raid on the PWA, supported the Act in Nova Scotia, although for immediate tactical reasons. The attitude of the UMWA in the west was complicated by the fact that the socialists had taken the district out of the TLC: 'In this section union leaders were agreed that a referendum of their members would be overwhelmingly against the disputes act, and this was confirmed by talks with the miners themselves. Back of this opposition lay Socialist doctrine and distrust of the fairness of the government, which was believed to have a class bias in favor of capital. It was not unusual to meet miners who thought the law would be an excellent measure if it could be administered with absolute impartiality. In spite of this attitude, however, the miners in this district are continually applying for boards.' He added that Sherman, who had acted on so many boards himself, 'has on occasions commended the influence of the law.' The Western Federation opposed the Act on revolutionary syndicalist grounds, and the international conventions of both the WFM and the UMWA had condemned the law, reportedly on the insistence of their Canadian delegates. But Canadian socialists must be expected to oppose the Act on political grounds, he argued, as much as the Conservatives denigrated it in order to play down the Liberals. Clark's summary is worth reproducing:

In résumé, therefore, observation and interviews with different classes of people in all parts of Canada indicate that the disputes act has with some exceptions the support of the general public and of employers and of the parliamentary 'laborists' and of the unions not directly affected by its provisions. The officials of the railway orders are divided in their opinion, but on the whole are more favorably inclined toward the law than when it first went into operation, and the rank and file of these orders is probably even more friendly. The leaders and the aggressive membership of the western mining unions are vigorous opponents of the act, although there is a considerable quiet element in these organizations that probably regards it with more favor. The Nova Scotia miners officially indorse [sic] the law, and it has support among their members, but the result of a referendum vote upon it would be difficult to predict. Some public men regard it as significant that at the last general elections the Liberal party lost seats in several important labor centres, such as Glace Bay, Cobalt, Winnipeg, and one or two other points farther west, where the act had recently been applied to serious local disputes.[77]

Clark's testimony is significant not only for its substance but also for the caveats it imposes on our reading of the TLC position. The Lemieux Act was a party political issue; union leaders' views often diverged from those of the rank and file; labour opinion was fickle, changing with each award and settlement; extraneous factors, like the opinion of Sam Gompers, crept in to some evaluations. Notwithstanding all of these very real cautions, of course, there can be little doubt that the government took the TLC's official expressions of opinion as the voice of the Canadian labour movement, and they bear examination for that if for no other reason.

The heavily weighted vote in favour of the IDIA at the 1907 convention, and the debate which preceded it, have already been described. In 1908, John Flett published an article about the Act in *American Federationist*, the AFL house organ. He criticized delays in establishing boards, and the requirement that unions conduct a strike vote before applying for a board. He was unhappy, as well, with the tendency of some chairmen to attempt conciliation rather than carry out a searching investigation of the issues in dispute: what *Industrial Canada* celebrated was cause for condemnation to at least one unionist. He summed up by admitting that the Act had occasionally been beneficial to labour, but insisted that it required amendment to make it truly effective. But it might never amount to much: 'As a protective enactment it is of little value to labor. After all, in order to have any status before the boards, labor must be thoroughly organized and powerful to command attention. As Napoleon is credited with saying, "The Lord is on the side of the heavy battalions."'[78] The article is interesting, first because it makes the call

77 Clark, (Jan. 1910), 9–16
78 Reprinted in Toronto *Star*, 30 May 1908

for amendment rather than repeal, and second because the amendments it demands are just those adopted by the TLC some months later.

When the convention met at Halifax in September 1908, the Alberta executive expressed dissatisfaction with the Act, pointed out that when a local mining company violated an IDIA agreement with the UMWA local, the provincial Supreme Court ruled that the union, having no legal personality, could not sue for damages, despite the *de facto* recognition of unions in the IDIA. In response, the miners' unions' solicitors in the west met to discuss whether they should submit to the Act at all so long as agreements made under its auspices remained unenforceable.[79] Later in the convention, Frank Sherman moved, supported by delegates from the mine, railway, street railway and – somewhat incongruously – tailors' unions, and by the Calgary and Fort William trades and labour councils, as follows: 'That, whereas, the workings of the Lemieux Act – as at present constituted – is detrimental to labor, as a whole, we therefore demand its immediate repeal.' Sherman spoke to the resolution, and O'Donoghue had a few words as well, but the matter was put off until the following day, when Simpson and Draper moved a substitute: 'That the Trades immediately affected by the Lemieux Act, and which are affiliated with the Congress, be requested to submit to the Executive Council of the Congress the necessary amendments to make the Bill effective, from the working-class standpoint, and that the Congress Executive be instructed to obtain these amendments to the Act, and that in the event of the Government refusing to grant these amendments, a referendum on the advisability of repealing the Act be submitted to the Trades affected by the Act, and that the Congress pledge itself to abide by the result of that vote.'[80]

Simpson and Draper were both King supporters, for all the former's socialism, and a few days before the convention Simpson had called on King and offered him assistance in his bid to become Labour Minister. It seems unlikely that they would not have discussed the IDIA and the coming convention, and if King says nothing of this in his diary it is probably because he was preoccupied with the search for a constituency to run in – there are pages and pages about this. Simpson's visit occurred on the very day that, to use King's phrase, 'the Unseen Hand ... revealed itself,' – in other words, the day that Laurier finally agreed to establish a separate Department of Labour.[81] In any event, whatever unseen hands may have been meddling in the background, the substitute resolution passed.

79 *TLC* 1908, 16f
80 *Ibid.*, 78f, 81
81 Diary, 6 Sept. 1908

In 1909 the TLC executive reported that it had presented a set of amendments to the government, which had decided to hold them over until the next session. The executive told the convention that only one member had submitted amendments in accord with the previous year's resolution, a representative from the CPR shopcrafts, and that the UMWA, which had been so solicitous for changes, had since left the Congress. The amendments which were presented to the government had been drawn up by the executive without the assistance of affected trades, and the executive was confident that they would pass. O'Donoghue itemized the proposed changes in his report: they were technical adjustments to the machinery of the Act which did not affect its basic principles.[82] There appears to have been no general discussion of the Act at this convention, but perhaps thè absence of the western miners put a damper on the occasion. The following year, the Congress was able to congratulate itself on having had most of its amendments adopted, but once again there was no discussion.[83] It was the calm before the storm, and in 1911 the western miners returned.

In the interim, two events involving the UMWA had occurred, one in the west and the other in the east. In the west, eighteen locals of the union had struck the eighteen members of the Western Coal Operators' Association simultaneously on 1 April, in violation of the Act. A board was hurriedly constituted by April 18 under the chairmanship of 'Ralph Connor,' and it proved completely unequal to the task. There is a long exculpatory letter from Gordon to King, explaining why it was that the board took so long – 43 days – why it cost so much, and why it was finally incapable of reaching a settlement. Gordon believed that the mines were badly managed and did not pay, and that the miners had been receiving excessively high wages even before the strike.[84] The proposed settlement was rejected by the men, and the strike continued until the middle of November, after the TLC convention and after the federal election. The miners had failed again to win union recognition, and Lethbridge was once more the sore spot it had been in 1906 and 1907. The Act had failed in the very industry and locality that had inspired it, and the UMWA was not amused.

In the east, things were even worse. The UMWA had successfully raided the PWA in several localities, and then found that the courts prohibited it from opening negotiations for new agreements since the settlements signed by the PWA under the auspices of IDIA boards had not yet expired. But the worst blow had come during a UMWA strike in Inverness in 1909. A provin-

82 *TLC* 1909, 10, 12f, 55f
83 *Ibid.* 1910, 13, 53
84 King correspondence, Gordon to King, 7 July; King to Gordon, 18 July 1911

cial judge had convicted a union officer for paying out strike benefits, in violation of a section of the IDIA assessing penalties on 'any person who incites, encourages or aids' strikes or lock-outs in violation of the Act. Two attempts to have the Act amended to wipe out the effects of this judicial interpretation had failed, and an issue more powerful than any complaints about the tedious slowness of the Act had been created. Moreover, the 1911 convention was held in Calgary, almost in the centre of western labour radicalism, and there were seven resolutions condemning the Act on the order paper.

The attack began with a guarded feint from the executive, urging 'careful enquiry' into the complaints of the western miners about the Gordon board, and suggesting that perhaps there ought to be some changes in the Act. The Alberta executive followed with a much longer account but refrained from any general comments on the Act. On the second day of the convention a special committee, most of whose members were delegates of trades directly affected by the Act, was appointed to consider the numerous resolutions that had been submitted concerning it. Three days later it made its report. It was very brief:

The committee recommends the following as a substitute for resolutions numbers 13, 2, 32, 33, 38 and 80: –

'That this Congress instructs its Executive Officers to press for the repeal of the Industrial Disputes Investigation Act.'

It was debated, and on a roll call vote defeated, 65 to 70. Then O'Donoghue moved a substitute:

While this Congress still believes in the principle of investigation and conciliation and while recognizing that benefits have accrued at times to various bodies of workmen under the operation of the Lemieux Act, yet in view of decisions and rulings and delays of the Department of Labor in connection with the administration of the Act, and in consequence of judicial decisions like that of Judge Townsend, in the Province of Nova Scotia, determining that feeding a starving man, on strike, contrary to the Act, is an offence under the Act: – Be it resolved, that this Congress ask for the repeal of the Act.[85]

At 1:30 PM on 14 September 1911, O'Donoghue's resolution passed unanimously. Just one week later Canada's first full-time labour minister, William Lyon Mackenzie King, was unemployed.

85 *TLC* 1911, 14, 24f, 63, 88, 91

10
Beyond investigation

> Congratulations, with a ring
> Once more to great Mackenzie King!
> We all today his health have drunk,
> And *I* create him Lord Grand Trunk!
> From *labor* now he ought to be
> For months at least, entirely free;
> Without a striker or a *haze*
> Around him whereso'er he strays.
> We'd recognize his royal rank
> If he could come to *Athol Bank*.[1]

With these lines William Murray, Hamilton's 'Bard of Athol Bank,' celebrated the end of the Grand Trunk railway strike and praised the man who took the credit for it. Had Murray possessed a crystal ball, he might well have stayed his pen. For in little more than a year, Laurier's government was to go down to defeat at the polls and his Labour Minister King would lose his seat in the process. The Grand Trunk affair, with many of its issues still outstanding, was to play its part in ending fifteen years of Liberal rule. To compound the irony, King's disastrous role in the strike negotiations would later become, by transubstantiation, one element of the package that would win him the leadership of his party and, ultimately, the prime ministership.[2]

In some respects, the dispute on the Grand Trunk railway system in the summer of 1910 was a very ordinary strike. It had its quota of riot scenes and

1 King correspondence, Murray to King, 3 Aug. 1910
2 Cf. John Lewis, *Mackenzie King, The Man: His Achievements* (Toronto: Morang, 1925), 45–7, for the Liberal party's later version of King's role in the strike.

organized strikebreaking, suspected sabotage and military intervention, but in this it was little different from any of a score of other industrial disputes in those years. In the two weeks it lasted, the strike's impact on the economy seems to have been relatively negligible, and it gave birth to no major innovations in union or employer tactics or in legislation. Notwithstanding this superficial resemblance to many hotly contested but soon forgotten strikes, that on the Grand Trunk marked a milestone in the history of Canadian industrial relations. It was, perhaps, Canada's first 'modern' strike.[3]

It was a modern strike because, possibly for the first time, it involved many of the elements that characterize 'mature' industrial relations in the Canadian economy today. There was the railway itself: a huge foreign-owned corporation, the second-largest business enterprise in the country, with considerable political influence. The strike took place in a government-regulated industry providing what was deemed to be an essential service. The workers involved belonged to large and powerful international unions, formally recognized by the employer, and run from American head offices by full-time paid officials.

The Grand Trunk strike was remarkably modern, as well, in the more limited context of industrial relations on Canadian railways. In his study for the 1968 Task Force, Peitchinis surveyed the history of disputes settlements on the railways since the passage of the Industrial Relations and Disputes Investigation Act in 1948. The IRDIA combined the compulsory investigation and delay features of King's IDIA with the compulsory collective bargaining provisions of the wartime Order-in-Council, PC 1003. Peitchinis concluded that government insistence on the *prevention* of railway work stoppages, on the 'maintenance of operations,' had permitted the railway corporations to shirk their statutory obligation to bargain in good faith: 'In essence, there has been no real collective bargaining on the railways.' Measuring experience since 1945 against his ideal of 'free collective bargaining,' he isolated a number of specific criticisms of the settlement process in the industry:

3 Two other accounts of the strike are available. Ferns and Ostry (Chap. v) did not have access to the range of sources that inform the account presented here. Nevertheless, their conclusions parallel in several respects those reached here. Tuck ('Railway Brotherhoods'; also, 'Union Authority, Corporate Obstinacy, and the Grand Trunk Strike of 1910,' *CHA Historical Papers*, 1976) focuses on the role of the international brotherhoods. His version differs in a number of particulars from that presented here, particularly with respect to the impact of the strike on the 'public.' In general, Tuck tends to accept King's version of the affair at face value, an approach which leads to an underestimation of the effects of his intervention. As the title of Tuck's article shows, he places little weight on the government's role in determining the outcome of the strike.

... it would not be an exaggeration to suggest that the employment practices of the railways during the past twenty-five years can be summarized as follows: there should be no particular policy on wages, benefits and other terms of employment, they should not bargain with the Unions on the renewal of contracts involving issues on terms of employment, agreements would be concluded only after government involvement, and a commitment on its part to either permit compensatory increases in charges or provide subsidies; and whenever the trend in traffics or road transport competition, or both, make it inadvisable to increase charges, the increase in labour costs should be offset through technological and operational changes.

Peitchinis' criticisms of the impact of government intervention on railway industrial relations closely resemble Jamieson's assessment of the negative impact of the IDIA on the development of collective bargaining. Peitchinis goes beyond Jamieson, however, in recognizing that not only the imposition of delay but also the *positive* intervention of the state as conciliator has tended to weaken union power in negotiations. Railway managements, by consistently refusing to meet union demands with counter-offers, have eschewed the bargaining process in favour of the imposition of settlements made by conciliation boards: 'The conciliation proceedings were relied upon to accomplish two purposes: to determine what constituted reasonable wage rates for railwaymen, ... and at the same time to provide "neutral" justification for an increase in railway charges.'[4] Management could then offset the burden of increased labour costs – imposed from 'outside' – through the introduction of technological and operational changes, whenever increased rates or subsidies were unobtainable. The upshot of this was inevitably the inability of the railway workers, through the participation of their unions in a bargaining process, to exercise control over terms of employment.[5]

Peitchinis pointed out that the provisions of the IRDI Act alone were not sufficient to enforce this pattern: it became the norm because government was consistently willing to intervene directly beyond the requirements of the Act in order to safeguard the 'public interest.' He noted that 'since the intent of the IRDI Act was to safeguard the national interest, the necessity for direct government intervention as well, implies that the Act has failed to provide effective protection.' The Act failed, he argued, 'because the parties did not find it possible or elected not to abide by one of its main provisions, namely,

4 Stephen G. Peitchinis, *Labour-Management Relations in the Railway Industry*, Task Force on Labour Relations, Study no. 20 (Ottawa: Privy Council Office, 1971), 269, 271, 269
5 Recent amendments to the Canadian Labour Code may strengthen the unions' position in this respect.

to bargain in good faith. The consistent failure of the railways to make counter-proposals to the demands of the unions, precluded the possibility of bargaining either prior to the institution of, or during conciliation proceedings.'[6]

The practices Peitchinis described had become institutionalized and routine by the 1960s. Fifty years earlier they were informal and quite novel. But King's intervention in the 1910 Grand Trunk strike parallelled in many important respects this modern system of railway industrial relations. In particular, his willingness to carry intervention beyond the compulsory investigation prescribed by the IDIA, and his identification of the public interest with the maintenance of operations, shifted the balance in favour of the railway corporation.

There were three active parties to the Grand Trunk dispute: the company, the unions, and the federal Department of Labour. Of the three, the railway corporation proved the strongest, largely because it was able to turn the supposedly impartial conciliation and mediation processes to its advantage. Often in the past, the Canadian government had demonstrated its ability to break strikes on behalf of the employers. Now, in 1910, with public opinion on the side of the strikers, the government was to prove itself unable to protect workers against a determined and powerful corporation.

I

Discussions between the Order of Railway Conductors and the Brotherhood of Railroad Trainmen for co-operation in industry-wide bargaining began in 1907. The railway unions wanted standardized operating rules and rates of pay throughout North America, and they wanted to be paid on a mileage basis rather than on an hourly rate. This last demand arose from the modernization of equipment by most of the larger railways, with the result that operating speeds were substantially increased. The unions established three regional committees to bargain with the railways: the Eastern Association of General Committees, ORC, and BRT, included lodges on some sixty railways in Canada and the United States, among them the Grand Trunk.[7]

In January 1910, the Eastern Association presented its demands to the railways involved. In the United States, where union-management co-operation was more highly developed and where there was no IDIA to delay settle-

6 Peitchinis, *Railway Industry*, 272 (his italics omitted)
7 Eastern Association of General Committees, ORC and BRT, Minutes of meeting held at Buffalo, N.Y., October 18th to 20th inclusive, 1910, copy in King correspondence

ments, the railway managements adopted standardized rules and rates effective 1 April. In the cases of a few US railroads in financial difficulties, the unions agreed to postpone the introduction of the new rates, following voluntary arbitration procedures. Some delay occurred in Canada, but in time the Canadian Pacific, the Père Marquette, and the Toronto, Hamilton & Buffalo railways concluded similar agreements.[8]

One Canadian railway system was adamant in its refusal to concur with the Eastern Association demands. The Grand Trunk and its subsidiary, the Central Vermont, would not participate in the industry-wide agreement and insisted on maintaining the old operating rules and rates of pay.

On 7 March 1910, the Grand Trunk conductors, baggagemen, brakemen, and yardmen applied for a Board of Conciliation and Investigation under the Industrial Disputes Investigation Act. They nominated the leading labour lawyer, J.G. O'Donoghue, as their representative on the board: the company nominated another lawyer, Wallace Nesbitt. When the two could not agree on a chairman, King appointed his friend J.E. Atkinson, editor of the Toronto *Star*.[9] When the board completed its deliberations on 22 June, it found it could not reach a consensus. Two reports were handed down: the majority report, signed by Atkinson and O'Donoghue, endorsed the Eastern Association principle, while Nesbitt's minority report rejected it out of hand.

Atkinson and O'Donoghue based their recommendation on a version of the 'fair wages' principle of intra-regional equalization: 'The Board believes that the rates of pay upon the Grand Trunk Railway Company should be brought up to the standard paid on roads in the same territory.' They realized that this would mean a substantial increase in labour costs for the financially troubled railway, and recommended that the increase should take effect in two stages, the first to be implemented on 1 May. However, O'Donoghue pressed for an earlier deadline for the second stage than Atkinson was willing to recommend.

Nesbitt rejected the principle of rate standardization, stating that 'in this matter there seems to be no possibility of conciliation.' He claimed that since the earnings of the Grand Trunk were below those of other roads in the settlement, the railway could not afford to match their wages. He opposed the standardization of operating rules, arguing that the existing rules were

8 Order of Railway Conductors, *Railway Conductor*, vol. 27 (1910), 717
9 *Sessional Papers* (1912), 36a, 130. The same board investigated the CPR. For Atkinson and his friendship with King, see Ross Harkness, *J.E. Atkinson of the Star* (Toronto: University of Toronto Press, 1963), esp. 93, where his ambivalence about the IDIA after his experience on the Grand Trunk board is described.

'well and fairly administered.' Finally, he attacked the international status of the brotherhoods and the fact that the Eastern Association was head-quartered in Chicago:

It is no part of my business, sitting on this Board, to discuss public questions, but in meeting after meeting, the spokesman for the men has stated that there was no use of the Board attempting to conciliate: the men would not abate one jot or tittle of their demands; that when they first made the claim they made it under instructions from Chicago, and I merely draw attention to the fact to suggest that this is a situation as if the railways of France had to take orders from Berlin as to their methods and cost of operation. Put in that light, it seems like a national danger, but that seems to be the situation in this country at the present time.[10]

Nesbitt's blustering indicated that the Grand Trunk management intended to maintain its hard line. O'Donoghue's willingness to phase in the wage increase gave the lie to his claim that the unions refused to compromise, while Nesbitt's attack on American control of the Eastern Association might have carried more conviction had it not been that he himself was representing a foreign-owned corporation and one, moreover, that carried on a substantial amount of its business in the United States. In both countries, it was competing with railways that had accepted the Eastern Association settlement.

Following the submission of the two reports, further attempts were made to negotiate a settlement.[11] The apparent refusal of the company to bargain in good faith, coupled with the unions' unwillingness to abandon the general principle of uniform rules and rates, made these negotiations an exercise in futility. On 18 July 1910, the Order of Railway Conductors and the Brotherhood of Railway Trainmen declared a strike against the Grand Trunk and Central Vermont railway companies in Canada and the United States.

II

It cannot be stated precisely how many railway workers were involved in the strike. One of the union leaders, BRT vice-president James Murdock, claimed on the third day of the strike that about four thousand men had quit work.[12] The application under the IDIA had given the number as 3017, while

10 *Ibid.*, 131,143
11 See Section III of this chapter below. Both parties rejected the majority report. *Railway Conductor* (1910), 717
12 *Brockville Times Weekly*, 22 July 1910

the Labour Department's report recorded that 'about 2,500 conductors, baggagemen, brakemen and yardmen were affected on the lines in Canada and about 1,500 on the lines in the United States. The strike affected also 2,500 employés of the Wabash Railroad Company in Canada in train and yard service.'[13] (The Wabash, which had once been managed by GTR President Hays, shared the Grand Trunk lines from Niagara to Detroit.) The Montreal *Star* gave what it called 'semi-official figures' on 20 July, showing '8,200 men out of work, 2,700 of whom are on strike, the balance affected by lockout.'[14]

There were, then, between three and four thousand skilled railwaymen who had voluntarily left their posts on the evening of 18 July. Few, if any, of them had ever been on strike before; their unions had traditionally foresworn the strike weapon. Seen in this light, Murdock's announcement to the press on the morning of 20 July indicated a surprising degree of solidarity: 'The position to-day is that we have practically all the men employed in the train and yard service on strike from Chicago to Portland. I have been in telegraph and telephone communication with all the leading points during the day, and can say that there are not more men left in the train and yard service than voted against the strike – about fifty. If there are we have not heard of them and we have reports from every point.' Moreover, the unions' strike funds, practically untouched over the years, amounted to about a million dollars: '... there will be no difficulty in getting $350,000 a month to keep the strike going. The full protective Trainmen's Unions will be given with payment of strike pay of $50 a month to members of the Order of Railway Conductors and $35 a month to members of the Brotherhood of Railway Trainmen.'[15]

By 20 July, the company had had to suspend practically all its freight and suburban trains, and was trying with difficulty to keep the prestigious passenger service running with office personnel replacing the strikers. The company shut down its repair shops throughout the system, locking out the tradesmen, who promptly charged that this action violated the IDIA: a week later, the shops were reopened. From the beginning, the railway announced its intention to fight to the bitter end. 'This is not going to be a two days fight and then quit,' Vice-President Fitzhugh told the press: 'We knew what we were facing and we shall face it. There is every indication that we can get the men we need, and we shall get them as fast as we can ... We have many

13 *Sessional Papers* (1912), 36a, 130, 133. King's later estimates of the size of the strike varied; see Ferns and Ostry, 112n.
14 *Montreal Daily Star*, 25 July 1910
15 *Brockville Times Weekly*, 22 July 1910

applications for service, and we shall fill our ranks as opportunity offers, leaving the strikers to attend to their own affairs. They have left our service and our business is to fill their places as fast as we can get the men.'[16]

Fitzhugh's statement was four-fifths bravado. The Grand Trunk sent letters to conductors and trainmen it had fired over the years, asking them to come back. Few did.[17] On the first Friday of the strike the company began to advertise in the newspapers for trainmen and yardmen, offering wages in excess of prevailing rates.[18] Later, it would attempt to import strikebreakers illegally from the United States.[19]

The GTR endeavoured to protect its property and its attempts to maintain operations by posting security guards up and down the line. Notices went up at the stations warning that 'trespassers' would be prosecuted. The Thiel detective agency was retained, and the company requested additional police protection. In the railway towns, however, where much of the population consisted of strikers and their supporters, municipal governments were reluctant to appear to support the company. For example, when the mayor of Brockville, an important Ontario division point, was asked by GTR management to provide additional protection, he replied 'that no extra precaution up to the present was necessary as far as he could learn, and stated that the reports of disturbances here had been exaggerated. He questioned very much whether ten extra men could be sworn in as special constables on account of the sympathy for the strikers.'[20] Support for the strikers was not confined to the railway towns or to the working class. For example, the Berlin lawyer and Liberal party activist H.J. Sims wrote to his friend Mackenzie King to say that 'Atkinson thinks Hays is in the wrong ... I was in Toronto today and in business circles sympathy is with the men.'[21]

Sympathy for the strikers increased in the railway towns as the company continued its efforts to move the trains, and it was not long before that sympathy became a material force. At Brockville, 'a large crowd of strikers, with their friends and sympathizers, met all the incoming trains ... to get a look at the men filling their places, and while there was a feeling in certain quarters to become demonstrative nothing of a serious nature occurred.' But the next evening, at Niagara Falls, New York, supporters jeered strike-

16 *Ibid*.
17 *Ibid*., 12 Aug. 1910
18 *Montreal Daily Star*, 22 July 1910
19 King correspondence, Robertson to Berry and enclosures, 25 July 1910
20 *Brockville Times Weekly*, 22 July 1910
21 King correspondence, 19 July 1910

breakers on the Muskoka express and 'stones and eggs were freely used.'[22] Some indication of the severity of the disturbance may be gathered from the intelligence that the missiles 'narrowly escaped' hitting their targets and that it took only two policemen to quiet things down.

A similar crowd had met the Montreal train at Sherbrooke two days before. The newspapers carried reports of attacks by strikers and their sympathizers at Flint, Toronto, Niagara Falls, Clinton, Island Pond, Battle Creek, New London, South Bend, and other points. A station at Amigari, Ontario, mysteriously caught on fire. Four companies of the First Infantry were rushed to Durand, Michigan, to cope with the strike situation there. By the second Friday of the strike, the Grand Trunk had taken to patrolling the entire system with its section men, each of them responsible for one mile of track.[23]

Brockville was a centre of much picket line action. On 20 July, the first skirmish erupted when one of the strikers threw a baggageman off a train in the station. Crowds of strikers and sympathizers gathered at the depot, 'more out of curiosity than anything else.' On 21 July, the unions publicly warned sympathizers against the use of violence, but on the following day the sympathetic mass picketing resulted in the 'Brockville riot.' The incident began with 'hoots and jeers' directed at the strikebreakers by the crowd, but it became more serious when someone – a strikebreaker or a Thiel detective – fired a shot through a car window. The crew of this train, and of the next one to pull in, took refuge in the station offices. The increasingly restless crowd, angered by the display of firearms, rushed the offices, breaking down the door and smashing all the windows. At the same time, part of the crowd rushed the telegraph office, where more strikebreakers were barricaded: 'The frightened occupants held their ground and H. Pearsault, a Belleville train despatcher, one of the number, discharged a revolver shot through the window over the door. This had no effect in staying the hands of the rioters who forced the door and dragged out the frightened strangers. The police made several rescues, and to the credit of some of the strikers be it said they rendered valuable assistance ... The riotous scene lasted about fifteen minutes ...'

Thirteen people were injured, three of them seriously enough to be hospitalized with cuts and bruises. Significantly, the attack was directed against the strikebreaking conductors and trainmen and the private detectives who

22 *Brockville Times Weekly*, 22 July 1910
23 *Ibid.*, 22 and 29 July, 5 Aug. 1910

accompanied them. Neither the local station agent nor the union engineer who ran the train was molested. The crowd seems to have been composed almost entirely of sympathizers, rather than strikers themselves: 'a larger percentage of women than usual figured in the throng with the small boy mustering full strength.' The local paper editorialized the next day that 'The rioters are the very worst enemies the strikers can have, and prominent members of the striking unions emphatically repudiate their actions.' Following the riot, the local militia was called out, and within a few days they were replaced by regular soldiers. The militia men were uneasy about their apparent role in support of the company, guarding the station, and in any event were eager to return to their regular jobs. Elsewhere on the line, trains were now being moved under armed guard. The strike leaders issued a public request that sympathizers stay away from the scenes of the trouble, asking them to 'indulge in no reprehensible actions which will bring discredit upon an honorable body.' An enterprising local photographer offered picture postcards of the riot.[24]

Aside from a few dramatic confrontations like this, which were played up by the newspapers in may cases out of all proportion to their real significance – in the Montreal *Star* the 500 or so Brockville rioters became 1600, while one or another newspaper alluded to practically every minor railway mishap as a case of suspected sabotage – it is difficult to form a judgment of the broad effects of the strike. Certainly the effects on the railway company itself were immediate and devastating: freight traffic was practically immobilized and the passenger service was disrupted. According to the *Wall Street Journal*, the company was losing $117,000 a day on its own lines, and another $6,700 on the Central Vermont. This loss would be sufficient, the *Journal* claimed, to wipe out the entire six-month's surplus of the railway in a twelve-day strike.[25] But government intervention to safeguard the public interest could not be justified merely by the losses sustained by the company. What were the strike's effects on the economy of Ontario, where most of its track was located? Were other industries and consumers severely threatened by the strike, or were they, with some inconvenience, able to transfer their custom to other lines?

Newspaper reports are too piecemeal and indeterminate to be useful in answering this question. They did report some of the effects of the strike, listing a few factories as closing temporarily or laying off men, noting that some Ontario cheese producers were finding it difficult to get their produce

24 *Ibid.*, 29 July 1910
25 Quoted in *ibid.*

to market, and pointing out that there was developing a shortage of fresh fruit (in contemporary journalese, a famine) at North Bay. But the accounts are fragmentary and fail to provide an over-all picture of the strike's impact on the public.

King attempted to collect more systematic information bearing on this question. Through the Customs Department, the following telegram was sent to every collector of customs in Ontario on July 26: 'Confidential and urgent. Please inform me by wire immediately, not later than noon Wednesday, if possible, extent to which business in your locality is being affected by present strike, to what extent freight is being moved.'[26]

King's use of the replies to this request is discussed below. The analysis here is concerned specifically with the attempt to estimate the strike's impact on the Ontario economy. Although there are some ambiguities in the fifty-one telegrams sent in reply – in particular, some collectors seemed unable to make up their minds as to whether 'business' in the telegram meant local business in general or just the business of collecting customs – it is possible to draw some generalizations.[27]

First, and probably most significant, *no* cases of such serious hardship as food shortages were cited. Similarly, no authenticated cases of factory closings were reported, although in a few cases collectors indicated that if the situation did not improve, some lay-offs would probably result. The strike was having more or less impact on business operations in various localities, but nowhere was there immediate and severe personal hardship; nowhere had its impact reached crisis proportions.

A rough tabulation of the replies reveals that in some 40 per cent of the localities, the strike was causing little or no inconvenience to business operations; some 48 per cent reported some degree of inconvenience to business; while in only six cases – 12 per cent of the total – could the replies be interpreted to indicate serious disruption of local business. Closer examination confirms what might reasonably have been expected. Towns and villages with access to both the GTR and a second railway (in most cases, the Canadian Pacific) were often inconvenienced, due to delays resulting from heavy demand on the CPR system, but not severely. Areas that depended wholly on

26 King correspondence, King to ADM (Brown) *re* McDougald, and enclosures, 26 July 1910
27 The 51 replies are attached to King's memorandum, cited in note 26. Because of the ambiguity of many of them, and the frequent failure to distinguish between general freight movements and GTR movements in particular, they are susceptible to varying interpretations. In the tabulation described below, responses have been assigned to the *more* severe of any two categories when they appear to fit either.

the GTR for rail traffic were affected to the extent that local businesses depended on the railway for receiving materials and shipping their products. Some inconvenience was caused by the need to stockpile products which could not be shipped out. In some of these areas, the deficiency was at least partly made up by turning to alternative means of transport, whether by water or by teaming in to the closest CPR depot. Undoubtedly, the strike was costing businesses money and causing some irritating delays. On balance, the over-all situation seems to have been very much like that reported by the collector at Chatham: 'Business inconvenienced but not ruinously by strike, no freight moving and goods en route held up.'

From the strikers' point of view, this must have been almost an ideal state of affairs. Their strike was severely hurting the company, while its wider effects were not so grave as to turn public opinion against the unions. Disturbances like that at Brockville might have weakened their support, but this was more than made up for by the behaviour of the company. Moreover, attempts by the railway to discredit the strikers by charging violence and intimidation must have become somewhat less credible when it was revealed that, in at least one instance, strikebreakers shot up the train they were running in a perverse attempt to vilify the strikers. By July 26 the chairman of the English board of directors was on his way to Canada, presumably to rescue the railway from the financial and political damage that President Hays' obstinacy was causing.[28] There seems little doubt that, had the workers and the company been permitted to fight it out, the unions would have won their strike.

III

The investigation board's report had been received at the Labour Department on 22 June, but King had been made fully aware of its contents a few days earlier. On 20 June, he had written to the Prime Minister, saying that he hoped that the railway would accept the Atkinson-O'Donoghue recommendations. 'Should they not accept the award,' he wrote, 'they will, I fear, have a serious strike on their hands, and their action in so doing, in view of the rates that have been accorded the C.P.R. employees will be certain to cause popular opinion to be strongly with the men and against the company.'[29] Replying, Laurier was confident that the Grand Trunk would accept the report: 'They would place themselves in a very false position if they were to

28 *Brockville Times Weekly*, 29 July, 5 Aug. 1910
29 Laurier correspondence, 20 June 1910

refuse. The contrast between them and their competitors would be more damaging than the increase would cost them.'[30]

Evidently both King and Laurier believed that the railwaymen's demands for equalization of wages and rules with other roads were just and reasonable, and they expected the GTR to give in. In this, they underestimated the determination of the railway's management. In the period between the handing down of the investigation board's report and the calling of the strike, Hays and his subordinates engaged in a war of attrition with the government, fighting for delay and concessions.

On 25 June, the Grand Trunk's second vice-president, William Wainwright, appeared at the Prime Minister's office with a proposal. A wage agreement was possible, he stated, but the railway could not agree to the standardization of rules. This, he said, would 'in reality turn over the management of the Company affairs to the Company's employees.' He suggested that the government appoint a new board, under the Conciliation and Labour Act, to arbitrate the dispute. Laurier pointed out that the IDIA had supplanted the older act so far as railways were concerned and, it was reported to King, 'made it abundantly clear to Mr. Wainwright that the Government has no authority to intervene further in this dispute, and also that it is impossible for any railway system in the position of the Grand Trunk Railway to escape from the payment of the same rates of wages as have been established by competing lines.'[31]

Next, Hays and Wainwright let it be known that wage standardization might be acceptable, so long as it was phased in over an indefinite period. Perhaps the federal government would help place the railway on a sounder financial footing so that increased wages could be paid: either an increase in the rates paid for carriage of mails or removal of the duty on imported railway coal – or both – would suit this end. In making this proposal they were singing an old song. Some fifty years before, Macdonald's Conservatives had advanced $120,000 'on account of postal service in order to enable the Grand Trunk Railway to pay their men who had struck for wages.'[32]

Leaving the government to think this over, Hays turned his attention to the unions. He wrote the two Canadian vice-presidents who were in charge of negotiations, Berry of the Conductors and Murdock of the Trainmen,

30 King correspondence, 21 June 1910
31 *Ibid.*, G.H. Brown to King, 25 June 1910
32 Sir John A. Macdonald, 'To the electors of the City of Kingston,' 10 June 1861, in J.K. Johnson and Carole B. Stelmack, eds., *The Letters of Sir John A. Macdonald 1858-1861*, volume II of The Papers of the Prime Ministers (Ottawa: Public Archives of Canada, 1969), 349

saying that the railway would be willing to pay the standardized wage rates – but not for some two years, by which time the Grand Trunk Pacific would be in operation and the company's revenues would be higher. Disregarding Laurier's veto, he raised with them the possibility of arbitration under the Conciliation and Labour Act. The union leaders replied that, while they opposed this arbitration formula, they would put the wage offer to a vote of their members.[33] On receipt of their letter, Hays wrote King to say that the committee of railwaymen had rejected both arbitration and the wage offer. He claimed that the company was accepting the majority report of the investigation board, and that this was the wage offer the unions had turned down – an obvious misrepresentation of the facts.[34] He followed this up by demanding that King unilaterally appoint an arbitration board: 'I think it is his duty to appoint the Committee ... and then let the responsibility of refusing to act under it rest with the men.' Hays let it be known that if King refused to act on this suggestion, the responsibility for a strike would rest on his shoulders.[35]

At once, King rejected Hays' demand for arbitration, stating that he had no legal authority to impose the procedure.[36] The same day, Berry and Murdock wrote to King, pointing out that they had themselves earlier suggested voluntary arbitration as a means of solving the dispute, using the same panel of arbitrators – E.E. Clark of the US Interstate Commerce Commission and P.H. Morrissey of the American Railway Employees and Investors' Association[37] – as had been successful in achieving settlements on several American roads during the course of the Eastern Association negotiations. Hays' proposal of a new board under the Conciliation and Labour Act, they argued, would just lead to further delay, and would not bring any new information to light.[38]

Murdock further informed the Labour Department that Hays' interpretation of the majority report differed from that of the unions: the Brotherhoods took the wage recommendation to mean an immediate increase of

33 Berry and Murdock to Hays, 8 July 1910; this letter was printed by the Department of Labour. There is a copy located in King's Strikes and Lockouts file on the Grand Trunk dispute: [PAC] MG26 J4, vol. 13, file 81 (9131–44), henceforth referred to as Printed Correspondence. For the circumstances surrounding the publication of this group of correspondence, see below.
34 King correspondence, 13 July 1910
35 Telephone conversation, Hays to Wainwright, 15 July 1910. Copy of transcript handed by Wainwright to Brown, King correspondence, 15 July 1910
36 Printed correspondence, 15 July 1910
37 *Railway Conductor* (1910), 717
38 Printed Correspondence, Berry and Murdock to Brown, 15 July 1910

about 25 per cent, while Hays interpreted the same recommendation to mean about 18 per cent. The railwaymen were willing, as they had already shown themselves to be in negotiations with other roads, to postpone total wage standardization, but only if they knew definitely beforehand when complete standardization would come into effect, and what the exact amount of the immediate increase would be. The Grand Trunk, according to the union officials, had hedged on both these questions.[39]

Now, three days before the strike deadline, negotiations were apparently deadlocked. The Grand Trunk, it seemed, had been trying to buy time, but neither the unions nor the Labour Department were willing to get involved in yet another interminable investigation. The Prime Minister himself had made the government's position plain. But King thought he saw one way of avoiding a strike. Remembering Hays' suggestion that the railway might be able to afford higher wages if it received new postal contracts, and despite the fact that the Cabinet had already decided not to deal with the matter until the fall, King took an initiative.

He contacted his old minister, Postmaster-General Rodolphe Lemieux, hoping to get permission to promise the new contracts to Hays. Lemieux's reply, however, merely repeated the substance of the earlier Cabinet decision.[40] Still not satisfied, King sent a coded telegram to Laurier, away on a western tour, on July 16:

Probabilities are I will be asked by Mr. Hays to personally intervene to-day to prevent general strike over Grand Trunk system on Monday. It is possible only thing which may save situation will be an assurance that Government will grant Commission to enquire mail service rates. If as very last resort this step necessary to save situation would you authorize me to give assurance on condition that Company succeed in averting strike. Lemieux en route Gaspe says he cannot give an answer at this juncture because Council agreed to defer till full meeting. If authority given you can rely on my not using it unless only possible effective way of averting calamity.[41]

Laurier appreciated the fact that the Grand Trunk was, not for the first time, trying to blackmail the government into granting it special favours: 'Your telegram means that Company willing to defer to demands of men provided increased mail mileage is promised by us. Company should not

39 *Ibid.*, Murdock to King, 21 July 1910; King correspondence, Brown to King, 15 July 1910

40 King correspondence, transcript of long-distance telephone call, King to Lemieux, 15 July 1910

41 Laurier correspondence, 16 July 1910

make such request at this juncture.'[42] King's last hope of forestalling a strike seemed to have vanished. The company met the unions again over the weekend, but without reaching a settlement. According to the brotherhoods, the railway still professed to accept the majority report of the board, but refused to specify either the size of the immediate wage increase or the date when full standardization would come into effect. On 18 July the strike began.

It may help at this point to recall just what Liberal industrial relations policy formally entailed. Under the Industrial Disputes Investigation Act, strikes and lock-outs on railways were prohibited until after a board of conciliation and investigation had made its report. If this did not lead to a settlement, the strike or lock-out could proceed without further government intervention. If both parties wished it, the Department of Labour might mediate further negotiations, but the general principle underlying the policy was that the parties would be left alone to arrive at some sort of bargain in a climate of public opinion formed by the report of the investigating board.

The unions had been unhappy with the delay imposed by the initial investigation: the *Railway Conductor* had criticized the 'tedious slowness' of the Act's operation, pointing out that 'while more than fifty settlements have been effected south of the Canadian boundary since the Eastern movement started, the settlements on these two Canadian lines [the CPR and GTR] are still to come.'[43] In the pre-strike negotiations, the railway's management had tried to postpone the strike deadline even beyond that required by the IDIA. These attempts had not been accompanied by any strenuous effort to bargain in good faith. While Laurier had rejected the Grand Trunk's strategy consistently and from the beginning, King had permitted himself to be drawn into some additional delays. Now, however, the men had gone on strike, and King faced two alternatives. He could stand by the principles of the policy he had inaugurated and let the two parties fight it out. Or he could press for further government intervention.

On 19 July, King wrote to Laurier, explaining his request for postal concessions and giving an account of the progress of the strike so far. He indicated that he was thinking, even at that early date, of intervening with a proposal of binding arbitration.[44] The next day, he wrote to Hays, Berry, and Murdock, 'to ask if each of the parties will now be willing to refer the existing differences to arbitration, and to agree to abide by the award given, provided

42 *Ibid.*
43 'Eastern Association Movement,' *Railway Conductor*, July 1910
44 Laurier correspondence, 19 July 1910

that a Board of arbitration mutually acceptable can be secured; also to say that, if such a reference to arbitration is agreed upon, all the necessary expenses incidental thereto will be met by the government.' King explained to Laurier his reasons for sending this request: 'The reply received to this letter should help to clear the atmosphere, and to bring a clearly formed public opinion to bear with force upon the present situation.'[45] The 'atmosphere' was to become a little more muddied before it cleared.

Murdock wrote to say that, although he suspected the company's good faith, he would be willing to see arbitration of the dispute – but only on his earlier terms, the board to be the same as that which had reached success in the American disputes.[46] Hays replied that King's suggestion was exactly the one he had made before the strike was called, and which had been rejected by both the unions and the government. His letter carefully avoided making any statement as to the Grand Trunk's willingness to accept the arbitration proposal.[47] King sent another telegram to both parties, asking for a 'direct answer' as to whether they would agree to arbitration by a mutually acceptable board:

On Friday [July 23] I received a wire from Mr. Hays again evading the question by simply saying that he had nothing to add to his letter. From the men I received a wire which indicated that the offer of arbitration they had proposed was in accordance with instructions from the General Committee and, that, without being further authorized, they would not be in a position to agree to any other kind of a Board. On receipt of this wire, I wired asking that they refer my request to the General Committee and get a definite reply. This wire I sent on Saturday morning. Saturday afternoon I received a reply stating that they were willing to leave the matter to a Board of Arbitration which might be mutually acceptable.[48]

The unions had given in to King's request, perhaps believing that the authority of the government would be sufficient to overcome Hays' intransigence and convince him to negotiate in good faith. If this was their belief, it was to be disappointed. When Hays' reply to King's telegram finally arrived, it indicated that he was determined to dig in his heels:

45 King to Hays, Berry and Murdock, 20 July 1910. This letter was printed and a copy is
    located as an enclosure to *ibid.*, King to Laurier, 21 July 1910.
46 Printed correspondence, 23 July 1910
47 23 July 1910; copy located as enclosure to Laurier correspondence, King to Laurier,
    25 July 1910
48 Laurier correspondence, King to Laurier, 25 July 1910

While as you know from the many conferences urging your action before the strike took place and from our offer repeated and urged upon the committee we were desirous of arbitration and so avoiding the existing trouble, the time for such action has now passed and it is only necessary that we should have the protection to which we are entitled to enable us to resume the full operation of the road.[49]

Hays' letter was evidently intended to convey to the government the idea that the Grand Trunk was firmly in control of the situation and on the verge of winning the strike. With Hays' refusal to arbitrate, it appeared that King would have to give up his attempts at intervention. 'I do not see that [it] is possible for the Department or the Government to do more than this,' he wrote Laurier. 'I will keep closely in touch with the situation from day to day, and will do whatever may be in my power towards bringing the parties together later on should a favourable opportunity present.'[50] Laurier wrote approving King's actions, and complaining that 'the strike is most regrettable.' 'I do not know, from here, who is at fault,' he added, 'but if you can manage to bring on a settlement, you will have earned the gratitude of the whole country.'[51] As events were to show, King apparently took this to mean that he should push on with attempts to intervene, and a search for a 'favourable opportunity' at once commenced.

The agent in this instance appears to have been Joseph Atkinson. On 26 July, he wrote to King giving an account of a conversation he had had with A.B. Garretson, international president of the Conductors, in the presence of Trainmen's president W.R. Lee and Chairman Todd of the Toronto General Committee. Atkinson had remonstrated with Garretson over the unions' refusal to accept his board's report, and argued that his and O'Donoghue's findings had been, to all practical purposes, what the unions had demanded. On Atkinson's showing, Garretson had replied lamely to these arguments. 'It becomes, therefore, all the more inexplicable to me,' Atkinson told King, 'that the men should allow Mr. Hays to so far confuse the public mind when it would have been such a simple matter for them to have accepted the award of the Board conditionally if they liked upon complete standardization being brought about on September 1st, 1911, or whatever other date they might wish.' This discussion seems to have shaken the union leaders somewhat: they had apparently been counting on the support of Atkinson and the *Star*. The letter continued:

49 24 July 1910; copy located as enclosure to *ibid*.
50 *Ibid*.
51 King correspondence, 25 July 1910

In a telephone conversation with Mr. Berry he said they had been expecting the Star to criticise the Grand Trunk for its course. To this I replied that the men had made it difficult to advocate their cause because they too had refused to accept the Board's award. Mr. Hays' attitude regarding arbitration has given us almost the first opening & in addition to a brief editorial in last night's paper referring to the Company's attitude in that respect we have another article in today's paper. I think Mr. Hays has weakened himself with the country by his correspondence with you, & the Department & yourself have taken a course which must commend itself to everybody except of course the Mail & Empire people who have a perfect genius for taking the perverse and perverted view of everything.[52]

No doubt Berry reported this conversation to his international president: in any event, Garretson and Lee shortly sent a telegram to King, clearly intended to capitalize on public opinion about Hays' refusal to arbitrate, and to counteract Hays' propaganda about the ineffectiveness of their strike:

After careful inspection and full reports as to the conditions existing on the Grand Trunk System, the fact that is brought into most prominence is, if both sides persist in the determination to fight to a finish, that communities, industries and the public who are wholly dependent on Grand Trunk service must continue to suffer both loss and hardship thereby. Both sides should give consideration to the interests of those who suffer from the effects of the strike, and we fully approve and endorse the action of our representatives Messrs. Berry and Murdock in indicating to you their willingness to leave decision of the points of difference between the Grand Trunk Railway and its conductors and trainmen to any impartial tribunal that can be mutually agreed upon. Should this be declined by the other principal the burden of responsibility for the public injury must of necessity lie upon those who thus refuse.[53]

It seems likely that King was able to take this telegram, along with the replies to the customs telegram, to the Cabinet meeting on 27 July; given the close fit between King's plans for that meeting and the content of the message, it is not inconceivable that he arranged for it to be sent. In any event, the Garretson-Lee wire would have added weight to the interpretation King wished to place on the customs collectors' replies. He had another piece of ammunition as well: Laurier had written to complain that 'I am deluged with telegrams asking me to interfere in the strike between the Grand Trunk and

52 *Ibid.*, 26 July 1910
53 *Ibid.*, 27 July 1910

their men. Of course, I can do nothing, but the matter is giving me a good deal of concern.' He continued with what could only be interpreted as permission for continued attempts at intervention: 'I am sure you are in close touch with all parties and that you will neglect nothing to facilitate their "rapprochement", though I know only too well that your powers for effective work are very limited.'[54] It seems likely that the 'telegrams' Laurier mentions[55] came as a response to the release by King of a selected group of letters between the Labour Department, the union representatives, and Hays, all bearing on the question of arbitration, and ending with the agreement in principle of the unions and the refusal by Hays.[56] That these letters had been released before 27 July, and that their effect had been to reinforce public opinion in favour of the strikers, may be inferred from Atkinson's letter of 26 July. 'Mr. Hays has weakened himself with the country by his correspondence with you ...'

Following the settlement of the strike, King wrote a long and self-exculpatory letter to Laurier, setting out his version of the events. This document provides a summary of the state of public opinion before 27 July, and King's interpretation of it:

[The] effect [of the arbitration correspondence] as a consequence of the attitude of the parties which they helped to reveal was to draw public sympathy away from the company with which it was pretty strongly at the outset and to swing it with the men, so much so, that in almost every city and town of the Province the Boards of Trade and the Mayors of the several municipalities began passing resolutions and deluging the company with demands to refer the differences to arbitration. The voice of practically the whole press, Liberal and Conservative alike, became one in the same demand, while business concerns whose interests were suffering and such organizations as wholesale grocers, the retail grocers, canners' association and the like, addressed resolutions in unmistakeable terms to the company. Not only was the demand the same, but the position also, – the Government of the country had called upon the two parties to arbitrate, the Government represented the people –

---

54 Laurier correspondence, 28 July 1910
55 There is no trace of this 'deluge of telegrams' in the surviving Laurier correspondence. There is one telegram of the type described, from the mayor of Collingwood, to whom Laurier replied that King had the situation well in hand. King himself, however, was receiving urgent messages from mayors and Boards of Trade in Niagara Falls, Brockville, Stratford, Windsor, and Barrie urging the renewal of negotiations for the settlement of the strike. Laurier correspondence, Currie to Laurier and reply, 27 July 1910; King correspondence, Brown to King, 29 July 1910
56 This is the Printed Correspondence first referred to in note 33 above.

one of the parties had responded and it was the business of the other to do the same.[57]

In this letter, King implies that the decision to send the customs telegram was taken by Cabinet on 27 July: it is clear, however, from the dates of the telegrams and from what transpired at the Cabinet meeting that he had arranged to have the request sent out sufficiently early that the replies would be received in time to take them to the meeting. It is not clear whether there were in fact two cabinet meetings, one on the 27th and one on the previous day, but in any event the meeting of 27 July marked a turning-point in the strike.

The 27 July meeting was the point of no return for the government. King had successfully managed both the union representatives and 'public opinion' so as to create substantial pressure for further government intervention, despite the abstract principles of the IDIA. On 27 July, mediation by the Labour Department became the formal policy of the government of Canada. From that point on, with government prestige hanging in the balance, the course of the strike changed significantly. No longer was it to be a straightforward conflict between employer and unions: increasingly it was to become a diplomatic battle between King and Hays.

IV

Basing his position on the customs telegrams and other information, King argued that the strike was hurting the Grand Trunk much more severely than Hays would admit:

The value of the company's securities were daily depreciating in England and abroad; the company's system was paralysed; its losses occasioned through the crippling of its business was mounting up to the million dollar mark and over; whilst its additional expenses in seeking to man the trains with strike breakers and re-commence operations in the midst of a struggle were only adding to the burden. From the financial point of view it was to the Company's interests to settle ...

He interpreted the customs telegrams to indicate a serious threat to the Ontario economy, sufficient to justify continued attempts at government intervention; beyond this, he perhaps considered it necessary to save the Grand Trunk from its president's wilfulness:

---

57 See the 38-page letter from King to Laurier (Laurier correspondence, 4 Aug. 1910) explaining his role in the strike: henceforth cited as Report.

Practically without exception the answers came in ... to the effect that on the whole of the Grand Trunk System not a freight car had moved in or out of the several towns from the time the strike had commenced up to the time of wiring. But what was worse than that, factories and mills were closing down in many places because raw material could not be brought in or finished products sent out. It was also mentioned that shippers were being advised that the Grand Trunk could do nothing for some time. The C.P.R. and the other railways where they were paralleling the Grand Trunk had their facilities over-taxed and were not proving equal to the extra work put upon them. Customs receipts had fallen off considerably.[58]

The position taken by cabinet as a result of King's representations is stated in a letter to Hays (over the signature of Acting Prime Minister Sir Richard Cartwright) which it authorized. The letter enclosed the customs collectors' telegrams, and in effect told Hays that he was losing the strike, his own propaganda notwithstanding. It continued:

The government has been carefully considering the whole strike situation, and whilst it is the wish of my colleagues and myself to cause you as little embarrassment as possible, we cannot but feel, in view of the situation as disclosed in these messages, all of which are from an official and strictly impartial source, as well as from many other urgent representations, that it is eminently desirable that some settlement of the present dispute should be immediately effected, and that if this cannot be brought about by a conference between the parties, the matter should be left to arbitration as already suggested by the Government.[59]

This letter was to be delivered personally by Sir Frederick Borden, Minister of Militia. But King was not willing to wait for Hays' reply, nor did he seem to place much faith in a formal arbitration process. He opted, instead, for personal diplomacy and, as he later reported to Laurier, 'arranged ... to have a communication sent me by the men asking my personal intervention.'[60] Several hours after Borden had left Ottawa to see Hays in Montreal, King received a telegram from Murdock inviting him to come to Montreal to try to negotiate or arbitrate a settlement. King then telephoned the strike leaders, asking them to keep his request secret: 'I was fearful lest knowing I had been requested to come by the men, it might embarrass Sir Frederick in his endeavours with Mr. Hays.'[61]

58 *Ibid.*, 6f, 7
59 King correspondence, Cartwright to Hays, 27 July 1910
60 Report, 8
61 King correspondence, 28 July 1910; Report, 8

King met Borden in Montreal, and together they went to visit Hays. King reported at length, in his letter to Laurier, what transpired at this and subsequent meetings. For reasons which will shortly become clear, it is necessary to quote parts of this report extensively:

... we drove to Mr. Hay's [sic] residence and had a talk with him and Mr. Fitzhugh [a GTR executive] on his verandah from ten until after midnight. In the course of this conversation the whole situation was carefully reviewed, the respective positions of the parties fully gone into and explained, and we left on the understanding that *Mr. Hays was quite ready for a settlement* to be negotiated, if Sir Frederick Borden and I could succeed in bringing it about. I left Sir Frederick at the Windsor shortly after half past twelve and myself drove to the Grand Union Hotel, the headquarters of the Canadian leaders ... I found them waiting and we had a conversation of an hour or two. It was agreed that they were to come to my room at the hotel on the following morning and *we would consider what propositions it would be possible to submit to Mr. Hays.* In the meantime, as *Mr. Hays had expressed the opinion that no final settlement could be made without the Presidents of the two Orders,* who happened to be in Toronto, it was arranged that they should be sent for, so that they could be on hand for final negotiations. This was the point we had reached by three o'clock Friday morning ... At ten o'clock on Friday morning [July 29] the full Committee of the men assembled in my room at the hotel. The whole situation was carefully gone over, and *I was given authority to say* to Mr. Hays that in the event of his agreeing to reinstate all the men, excepting those who had been guilty of violations of law or destruction of the Company's property, the men were prepared to accept any of the following alternatives:

(*a*) To leave all matters in dispute to arbitration,

or (*b*) to accept the award of the Board of Conciliation and Investigation in toto, and where there might be any doubt as to the meaning of a particular clause to leave it to the Chairman of the Board to say what that meaning was.[62]

This was not the only version of these events recorded by King. There exists as well a memorandum, apparently dictated on the spot to his private secretary, F.A. McGregor.[63] There are some interesting discrepancies between the two versions that may best be explained by King's reluctance to tell even

62 Report, 8f; emphasis supplied.
63 This document, henceforth cited as Memorandum, is located in [PAC] MG 26 J4, vol. 13, file 81 (9161–75). For McGregor's presence, see F.A. McGregor, *The Fall and Rise of Mackenzie King: 1911–1919* (Toronto: Macmillan, 1962), 3: 'Here was my first lesson in the art of industrial conciliation, an art in which the instructor had proved himself to be a past master – patient, conciliatory, and impartial, but unswerving when principles were at stake.'

Laurier the whole truth about what took place in Montreal, for reasons that will be self-evident.

First, King's claim that Hays was 'quite ready for a settlement' does not fit very well with the details of their conversation as given in the memorandum. According to the latter document, Hays refused to withdraw the letter in which he had said the time for arbitration had passed; he claimed that arbitration on the basis of full reinstatement of the strikers was not arbitration at all; he gave King 'some explanation which I did not fully grasp' when the Labour Minister asked whether he was willing to accept the principle of mileage-based wages; and he evaded a similar question about standardized rules by proposing a reference to the Railway Commission – a plan unacceptable to the government. In general, Hays said he was willing 'to consider negotiations for a settlement,' but would not discuss the basis for settlement. According to the memorandum, when King went to his first meeting with the unionists he told them that 'I thought there was little hope of arbitration, that it would mean Mr. Hays swallowing himself, which I did not think he would be prepared to do at this stage.' Hays might have been 'quite ready for a settlement,' as King told Laurier; but the only settlement he seems to have been ready for, on the evidence of the memorandum, was one dictated by himself.

Again, King told Laurier that it had been Hays who wanted Garretson and Lee on the scene: the memorandum makes it clear that Hays was hostile to the two union presidents and that it was Murdock and the local officers, cautious about acceding to King's demands that they moderate their bargaining position, who invited them to Montreal. The letter to Laurier implies that it was the strikers' representatives who drew up the conditions for settlement and then authorized King to present them to Hays: the memorandum demonstrates that King and Borden had drafted these conditions before meeting with the men, and that they had spent much of that meeting in persuading the unionists to accept them. Regarding the reinstatement issue, one passage of the memorandum that in the event turned out to be crucially important was left out of King's report to Laurier:

On the question of reinstatement of the men Murdock wrote out on a sheet of paper what he thought would be the best language to be used: 'reinstatement as soon as possible so that Mr. Hays' position would be strong before the public.' I had pointed out that something of this kind would be absolutely necessary. He put in brackets 'all men to be back within thirty days', saying that this could be understood by private agreement between Mr. Hays and themselves with Sir Frederick and myself. As to the time limit Murdock seemed to think that thirty days was too long, but we finally came to a general agreement on that point. I took the slip in his own handwriting and held on to it.

Later that afternoon, King met with Hays again. First, he outlined the scheme favoured by the unions: full reinstatement followed by arbitration of outstanding disagreements. Then King outlined his own alternative plan: acceptance of the original findings of the Board as the basis for a settlement. Hays' response is described in the memorandum:

Mr. Hays did not commit himself finally, but said his main difficulty would be in the reinstatement of the men, that I would understand that on an occasion of this kind the Company would be glad of the occasion to get rid of certain employees who were troublesome, and this would be a convenient time to drop them. There were other men the Company had engaged only temporarily, and certainly they would be got out of the way, which would leave an opening for most of the old hands.

Hays complained about the Alien Labour Act, which hampered his ability to import strikebreakers from the US, and stated that it would be even more difficult to reinstate strikers on the Central Vermont than on the Grand Trunk, as it had been easier to find strikebreakers on those portions of the former railway's lines that ran through the United States. King told Hays about the imminent arrival of Garretson and Lee, and Hays agreed to meet with them, apparently because King informed him they would be easier to pin down to terms than Murdock and Berry. Then when King met with the union representatives later that day, he told them that Hays was unwilling to discuss a settlement until he could meet with negotiators who had final authority – the international presidents. King arranged to meet with the local unionists and the presidents, who were to arrive the next morning, in order to set up a joint meeting with the Grand Trunk executives.

Garretson, Lee, Murdock, Berry, and a handful of local union officials called on King the next morning, 30 July:

Garretson stated at the outset that Murdock and Berry had full authority to act, and that they [i.e., Garretson and Lee] were really in the position of legal advisers so to speak. This was said before the committee as a whole. Later, quietly, Garretson said to me that whatever he and Mr. Lee agreed to would be done, that he had the final say in matters, and that Berry and Murdock would carry out whatever he agreed to. He also said that whatever he undertook should be carried out; I might be assured he was prepared to stand by it, and could tell Mr. Hays so.

Garretson indicated more willingness to compromise and to sympathize with Hays' predicament than the Canadian officers had. King took pains to exclude Berry and Murdock from subsequent meetings with Hays: the next stage in the negotiations would be dealt with by the three American senior officers, Garretson, Lee, and Hays, with the assistance of the Canadian cabinet ministers.

Following his morning meeting with the union men, King went with Borden to see Hays in order, as he thought, to set up a joint meeting. It quickly became clear, however, that the Grand Trunk executives were not nearly so ready to sit down at the bargaining table as King had thought. Instead, Hays wanted King and Borden to act as his messengers, running proposals back and forth between himself and the brotherhood presidents. When King insisted on a joint meeting, Hays and his lawyer, Biggar, began to raise objections to the grounds for settlement that, King thought, they had previously accepted:

First of all he [Hays] spoke about reinstatement and asked whether in that connection they meant, getting back their pensions etc. He began to take the line that by contract they had lost their pensions in going out and that legally the Company could not restore the pensions; in this he was supported by Mr. Biggar. I expressed some disgust at this attitude, saying that it was too small an attitude for the Grand Trunk to assume and that Mr. Hays being the man he was could not afford to publicly take a stand of that kind. However, I was quite prepared to advise[64] the men to accept his interpretation and let the pensions go. This took them rather by surprise.

The union representatives would no doubt have been even more surprised to learn that King, without any mandate from them to do so, had traded away their pension rights. There is no evidence, however, that he ever told them that he had taken this step, and when the issue arose in the aftermath of the strike it was treated as merely another unilateral and high-handed action of the railway management, rather than as one of a host of concessions exacted from King by Hays. Characteristically, the report to Laurier, while it contains a lengthy account of this meeting, does not so much as mention the pensions issue.

Next, debate turned to the question of whether the Central Vermont should be included in the Grand Trunk settlement. The union leaders had been adamant on this point, but once again King attempted to compromise

64 In the typescript Memorandum, this phrase reads, '... prepared to inform ...'; the word 'inform' is stroked out and replaced by 'advise.' 9174

their position in the hope – by this time, obviously futile – that Hays would reciprocate. King proposed that the inclusion of the Central Vermont should be left to Atkinson, as chairman of the now long-defunct investigation board, but the proposal went unanswered as an angry exchange with Hays' subordinate Fitzhugh developed. King demonstrated his annoyance with the turn events had taken by refusing Hays' invitation to lunch. When King and Borden returned from their *déjeuner à deux*, they insisted that they would not play the role of messenger boys; the Grand Trunk officials would have to meet with the union men. Hays and the others agreed, and the two international presidents, along with two local union men, arrived. The top-ranking Canadian officers, Murdock and Berry, were excluded from the meeting at King's request.

At about this point, the dictated memorandum breaks off: the rest of the story must be told, for the most part, from King's report to Laurier, and as the foregoing suggests, it ought to be taken with a substantial lump of salt.

Following a long and difficult session, it appeared that verbal agreement had been reached on the timing of standardized rules and rates and on the inclusion of the Central Vermont in the settlement. The main outstanding issue was the reinstatement of the men: Hays insisted that the clause should read that the men be returned to work 'as soon as possible,' while the union representatives demanded that a specific time be negotiated and written into the agreement. The meeting reached an impasse on this point. Then King met privately with Garretson and Lee, and showed them the draft clause he had had Murdock draw up: 'all men to be back within thirty days,' by confidential agreement among Hays, the union officials, and the cabinet ministers: 'At once they said they would be wholly agreeable to this, that if Mr. Hays would give his word to Sir Frederick and myself that by "as soon as possible" he meant no longer than thirty days, the strike might be declared at an end on the basis of settlement which had been reached up to that time.'

That evening King met privately with Hays and secured his agreement to this modification of the reinstatement clause – or so he thought. Then the full negotiating meeting resumed, and it appeared that agreement had been reached on the various items considered. Hays carefully went over each of the points and then left the room to draft a final agreement. He came back with a letter for Garretson and Lee, which contained both forms of the reinstatement clause, and provided for arbitration as to which of them would obtain. But this was not all:

When we examined the letter Mr. Hays had written it turned out that not a single one of the propositions was what we had all understood had been the position reached.

Instead of May 1st being mentioned as the date at which new rates of wages were to come into effect, July 18th was fixed as the date. It had been agreed that C.P.R. rules as well as rates were to go into effect from January 1912, but his new draft did not mention C.P.R. rules, but made reference to rules in the award, with a clause that they might be subject to modifications to be mutually agreed on between the Company and committees representing the men. These changes which completely altered the whole agreement as it had been come to tenatively [sic] were pointed out to Mr. Hays. He admitted one mistake after the other, saying that clearly there was an error. Notwithstanding that everyone felt more or less shocked or exasperated, we got over this difficulty and back again to where we were before he took the proposals downstairs.

It became clear that reinstatement was the issue, and that Hays absolutely refused to put down on paper any commitment as to how many of the men would be taken back, or when. Evidently he viewed the issue as one of management's rights, and was determined to retain control in this crucial respect. Finally, he just got up and left the meeting, telling the others to do as they liked. His subordinates told King and Borden that Hays was 'not himself,' and begged them 'not to judge him too hastily.'

Next morning, King and Borden breakfasted together and discussed their next move. Once again, the two of them drew up a proposed agreement and, once again, they inserted a crucially important clause without consulting the strikers' representatives:

[In] order that Mr. Hays should be afforded no reasonable excuse for hesitating to make an immediate settlement, we decided that we would place as interpretation of the words 'as soon as possible' a period not exceeding three months, instead of thirty days, as giving him ample time to reinstate all the men, and also affording some measure of punishment to those who may have been offenders in milder ways.

Later in the day, they met with Hays to discuss their draft agreement:

When we thought Mr. Hays was about to sign he suddenly turned to us and said, 'Well gentlemen, where do you come in on this? I give my note for three months, it falls due and the obligation is wholly upon me; where do you come in?' Sir Frederick replied that we became the endorsers. We had a little laugh over this and thought Mr. Hays was only joking, but he went on to speak of different things, what hard luck the road had had in different directions, of the need of reduction of coal duties, of increased allowance for carriage of the mails, etc., etc. We told him that of course we could not speak for the Cabinet, that we were only two members, but that we would certainly be only too pleased to represent to our colleagues anything he might do to help out the present situation. We thought they would not be lacking in goodwill toward him for anything he might do. He then said he thought if we wanted him to take back any of the men, we should agree to take any men who had been taken on since the strike and whom he might not be able to find positions for or get rid of at the end of the three months.

King's reaction was that this was a bluff by Hays, and he was willing to go along with it. Accordingly, they made the commitment he had asked for, and Hays signed the agreement on that understanding. Then he asked them to put their obligation in writing, and King complied:

[We] understand that you undertake to reinstate within three months in their former positions in the company's service, all of the men involved in the present strike. We have your statement that since the strike commenced you have taken on a number of new men, any of whom still in your employ three months hence you will be under obligation to provide for ... We therefore undertake ... that the Government of Canada at the end of three months will relieve you of such obligation as you may still have in this respect, by providing in a fair and equitable manner for any men who have joined the Company's service since the strike commenced and who may be still in your employ and for whom you are unable to make further provision ...

The Grand Trunk president had, in effect, blackmailed the Canadian government into guaranteeing jobs for strikebreakers. But this was not enough for Hays; having gained his point he sought to press the advantage:

When I had read over this draft Mr. Hays said he did not like the word 'reinstate' and I asked him what he would suggest instead, and he said 'take back.' I said very well, it would read then, 'undertake to take back in their former positions in the Company's service.' Thereupon without a moment's notice, Mr. Hays said: 'This is not my undertaking at all: you are to look after the men out on strike; I am to take back as many of them as I can, and any whom I do not take back you are to provide for.'

Once again King and Borden remonstrated with Hays; once again he threw a tantrum. This time they did not let him stalk off in a huff, however: they warned him that if he continued to obstruct the settlement he would have to bear the responsibility of the strike and its issue, and that the Grand Trunk's relations with the government would suffer. On this note, they left for a meeting with the union committee, with whom it appears they were somewhat less than honest:

We laid the agreement on the table before them and asked if they were prepared to sign this agreement on the understanding that the words 'put back as soon as possible' meant taken back in their former positions within three months. They said they were, and we asked them to sign on this understanding which they did immediately ... We then said, 'It remains for us to say to you that Mr. Hays has given us his undertaking that this was the meaning which he attaches to these words. As soon as we are in a position to give you our word that this is his undertaking will we be in a position to say that the strike is at an end?' To this they replied yes. We then mentioned that we had not as yet secured this undertaking in a form that was entirely satisfactory, but hoped to be able to and that as soon as it was obtained we would communicate with them at once.

In securing the union representatives' signatures to the draft agreement, King had effectively ended their role in the negotiations. Behind the framework of operating rules, wage rates, and implementation schedules contained in the agreement was the foggy network of verbal promises and half-promises exchanged by King and Hays. Most of these were unknown to the unionists. With their signatures on the document they had no safe means of retreat open to them: from here on, the battle was to be between King and Hays, but its casualties would come from the ranks of the unions. It was not easy for King to extract from Hays the undertaking he had promised the brotherhood committee. It took prolonged discussion and correspondence, and there is some evidence that it also required a threat by Laurier to hold up passage of private bills submitted on behalf of the railway,[65] before an ambiguous compromise was worked out. In exchange for the railway's secret acceptance of the three-month reinstatement clause, the government would guarantee employment to any strikebreakers still on the payroll in three months' time – not only in Canada but in the United States as well. At 5:30 PM on 2 August, the strike was declared off.[66]

V

Why had Hays acted as he did? In his report to Laurier, King provided a shrewd assessment of the railway president, and unwittingly foreshadowed the complications still to come:

---

65 See Laurier correspondence, Laurier to Hays, 2 Aug. 1910
66 King correspondence, King to Berry, 2 Aug. 1910; King to Murdock, 2 Aug. 1910;
   Report, 30

... railroading in the United States is a business which with a certain school of men is run on certain principles. One is that human life, to say nothing of human feelings, is not to be considered, either as respects its loss through accident or its massacre as a means to an end. The end is the power of money as against all other powers in the world. To admit the solidarity of labour in any industrial struggle is to admit something more powerful than money, and that must not be done, no matter how great or tremendous the cost. Mr. Hays has seen himself in this struggle as the chief representative of that school. He knows full well that to win on this one point, and this one point alone [i.e., the reinstatement of the men], would mean, even if all else were destroyed in the effort, his receiving tomorrow the offer of the Presidency of a dozen different roads. He would be the one man known to labour as the unyielder in any future industrial battle, and that is the asset for which the seekers of dividends on some of the railroads on this continent are prepared to pay any price.

Hays had not relinquished his claim to be the 'unyielder' on 2 August. The reinstatement issue had not been settled by the agreement between King and Hays, and communicated to the men as a binding promise. Many of the men were not to be reinstated at all; many were to remain out of their jobs for a year or more before being reinstated; many were to be rehired only to be quickly dismissed again. Those who were reinstated were in many cases not put back in their former jobs; they received less responsible assignments or were sent to a completely different part of the Grand Trunk system, having to move their homes in order to keep their jobs. The reinstatement procedure was used punitively by the railway: when, eventually, public and government pressure forced the Grand Trunk to employ an Ontario judge to rule on the reinstatement rights of the remaining men, the most trivial offences were cited as reasons for not rehiring strikers.[67] One man was refused his job because during the strike he had urged the local minister to prosecute the GTR for 'running a way-freight train on Sunday in violation of the Lord's Day Act.'[68]

Those who were reinstated lost their pension rights. King had neglected to raise this matter with the union representatives during negotiations, although he had informed Hays that he would be willing to recommend that they give the pensions up. In his report to Laurier, King expressed shock and dismay

67 There is a large group of letters in the King correspondence dealing with the aftermath of the strike. See especially Berry to King, 21 Oct. 1910; Berry to King, 24 Oct. 1910; Berry and Murdock to King, 3 Nov. 1910 (two letters of same date); King to Henderson, 29 Nov. 1910; Berry to King, 28 Jan. 1911; King to Wainwright, 28 April 1911; BRT Convention delegates to Laurier and King, 16 May 1911: see also G.P. Graham papers [PAC] MG 27 IId8 VI, Acland to Graham, with enclosures, 20 Sept. 1910.
68 King correspondence, King to Bowman and enclosure, 10 Nov. 1910

at the railway's decision to cancel the pension rights, and recommended that the government boycott the Grand Trunk until pensions were restored.[69] Laurier agreed with King about the seriousness of the matter, but opted for personal diplomacy rather than legislation or boycott – with results that might easily have been predicted. It took twelve years and the nationalization of the railway to get the pensions restored.[70]

At the outset, the union leaders hailed the settlement as a great triumph. On the surface they did at first seem to have won: after all, the Grand Trunk had agreed to a form of wage and rules standardization. As the reinstatement process became known, and when the pension cancellation was announced, the railwaymen's sense of victory turned to a conviction of defeat. There were at least the beginnings of serious rank-and-file opposition to the union leaders who had represented them during the strike: in March 1911, for example, two western Ontario locals passed a resolution that amounted to censure of the officers' handling of the strike, and circulated it throughout the Grand Trunk system. Berry replied confirming many of the grievances expressed, but chiding the locals for not placing more confidence in their representatives.[71]

The union leaders' apparent willingness to hand over the reins to King and to compromise away practically every point of principle for nothing tangible in return is difficult to explain. Any interpretation must begin with the traditional reluctance of the brotherhoods to take strike action and their consequent queasiness about the course they had embarked on. Added to this was the fact that the Grand Trunk was the only railway of note left to settle: the strike would not set the pattern for other Eastern Association agreements, and perhaps the senior officers of the unions grew impatient with it for this reason. It is clear that the Canadian vice-presidents were both more militant and more cautious than their international presidents: more militant in their unwillingness to sacrifice principle, and more cautious in their reluctance to take a stand that had not been approved by headquarters. From the point of view of Garretson and Lee, it was most important to get the strike over with as quickly as possible: they trusted King, and, in any event, by the time they arrived on the scene it was probably too late for much to be salvaged. Too much was at stake for King and the government for a reversal of roles to take place. Garretson and Lee had a far greater vested interest than Berry or Murdock in union-management co-operation on the railways, and it is pro-

---

69 Report, 37f
70 King correspondence, Laurier to King, 11 Aug. 1910; G.R. Stevens, *Canadian National Railways*, vol. 2 (Toronto: Clarke, Irwin, 1962), 251
71 Heath to 'All Divisions ORC ...'; Murdock to ORC and BRT ... , 5 March 1911; Berry to Heath, 28 March 1911; all in King correspondence

bable that they feared a lengthy and bitter strike on the GTR would alienate railway companies in the United States. The international presidents showed that they could be 'reasonable,' and in the context of their broad strategy for industrial relations on the railways this may have been more important than winning an obscure and difficult Canadian strike.

For King, the Grand Trunk strike proved an embarrassment. The failure of the company to live up to the agreement provided the Opposition with plenty of opportunities to attack the Labour Minister in the Commons,[72] and when election time came his handling of the strike became an important issue in his own riding as well as in those of Borden and G.P. Graham, Minister of Railways.[73] Other Liberal members representing railway towns had also to defend their party against the charge that it had mismanaged the strike.[74] The 1911 election was not decided on the basis of the Grand Trunk strike, but there can be no doubt that in particular ridings the Liberal defeat owed much to the railwaymen's dissatisfaction with the outcome of the government's intervention.

Charles Melville Hays had little opportunity to enjoy his newly won reputation as the 'unyielder.' It is not recorded whether his actions during the strike and after brought him the dozens of offers of railway presidencies that King had predicted. Early in 1912, Hays conceived a grand strategy for recouping the sagging fortunes of his railway: he would negotiate to sell the Grand Trunk Pacific to the Canadian government. In the spring, he sailed for England to try and convince the Board of Directors to support the scheme. His return voyage began, and ended, on the *Titanic*.[75]

VI

It remains briefly to consider King's role in the strike. In the first instance, the strike itself was one of the very few in which he was involved that fitted his rather stringent criteria of justification. It was not a recognition strike, nor

72 There is a list of references to questions and debates in Parliament concerning the strike in King's memoranda file: [PAC] MG 26 J4, vol. 13, file 81 (9302–3).
73 See, e.g., Graham papers, Graham to King, 24 Aug. 1911 (file 322) and Graham to Wainwright, 24 Aug. 1911 (file 546). In the latter, Graham asks Wainwright to pass the word among the Grand Trunk employees to support the Liberals. Other correspondence suggests that the Grand Trunk was working against King and others involved in the strike.
74 'Nixon said that in the event of the men not being taken back it would go hard with Fred Pardee and Dr. Rankin; that their chances at the next election would be about equal to those of the proverbial snowball.' King's memoranda file, 9211
75 G.R. Stevens used the heading, 'A Crowning Mercy,' over his account of Hays' death. See his *History of the Canadian National Railways* (New York: Macmillan, 1973), 284.

was it one that could be interpreted as flowing exclusively from a clash of personalities. It was a strike for a principle, and the principle was the conservative 'fair wages' one that he had championed in the past. He supported the strike, then, but that support came into conflict with another principle in which he placed much stock: the principle of maintenance of operations as the ultimate expression of the public interest. This was a dilemma which admitted of no easy escape. In either case, intervention might be justified, but each would imply a unique form of intervention. In the first case, the government might step in either to force 'fair dealing' – although how this might have been effected is difficult to see – or directly through legislation to compel the Grand Trunk to accept wage and rules standardization. This might in principle have been accomplished through the enforcement of the old Fair Wages Resolution, since the Grand Trunk had government contracts to carry the mails. In this way, Hays' insistence on augmentation of the postal contracts might have been turned against him, but it is highly unlikely that Laurier would have accepted so severe a challenge to private property and management's rights, even if King would have supported it. Their differences on questions of this sort were evident in the correspondence about pension rights, mentioned already.

When Hays and his subordinates grounded their opposition to the Eastern Association demands in the concept of management's rights, they posed a direct challenge to the fair wages principle. In effect, they claimed to be willing to pay standardized rates, making due allowance for the financial situation of the railway, but they were unwilling on management's rights grounds to accept standardized rules. Since these rules included the payment of mileage wages rather than an hourly rate, their refusal to compromise on rules blocked an effective settlement of the wages question.[76] This in turn blocked the possibility of intervention to ensure good-faith bargaining, since the conflict of principles was one which left King in an uncomfortable position: it was a dilemma to which he was never able to find a solution. This left intervention to protect the public interest as the only opening available to him. Since Hays' intransigence precluded simple mediation of the dispute, King was left in the position of having to intervene directly to secure the resumption of operations, bypassing the union committee as far as he was able and turning his role into a personal crusade against Hays:

The Grand Trunk struggle was the biggest job I have ever had, because it was a first-hand fight with a big corporation prepared to be as unscrupulous as corporations can be. I was bound the Government would win, & I am happy to say I think I have

76 Report, 4

succeeded. After the first week, it was not so much a fight between capital & labour, as between a railway corporation & the Government. That was what made it interesting ...[77]

What made it interesting was also what made it disastrous. When King carried intervention beyond the limits of investigation, he was substituting himself and the government for the unions. But as Laurier had pointed out, his 'powers for effective work [were] very limited.' The government of Canada was not about to use the kinds of economic sanctions that alone might have been effective in securing an equitable and enforceable settlement; indeed, it had intervened in the first place in order to moderate the effects of those sanctions as they were being applied by the unions. Vice-president Berry neatly summarized the problem when he tried to explain the reinstatement catastrophe to his angry members: 'The Canadian Government cannot jail a Company for failing to live up to an agreement, even though they were mediators in the agreement.'[78]

It was this contradiction in King's policy and practice that made it possible for Hays to turn the intervention to his own advantage. In so far as he could shift responsibility onto King and his colleagues and thus distance himself from direct negotiations with the union, he was able to hold his ground, always keeping something in reserve. Of course, the government was only powerless to act to the extent that it was unwilling to act, but that unwillingness could be counted upon.

Equity and property were unreconciled elements in King's thought and practice. Compulsory investigation was an attempt to avoid this antagonism by introducing a third element, public opinion. But investigation could rarely be counted upon to eliminate the problem and in any case, as was argued in chapter 9, investigation usually involved active mediation and excluded the resort to opinion. The Grand Trunk strike took this one step further, and revealed with even more clarity the contradiction between equity and the 'public interest.' Beyond investigation, property emerged triumphant.

77 King correspondence, King to R.A. Daly, 8 Aug. 1910
78 King correspondence, Berry to Heath, 28 March 1911

11

Canadian liberalism and industrial peace

I MUST add one Word more: I know it hath been the Opinion of several learned Persons, who think well enough of the true Art of Astrology, That the Stars do only *incline*, and not force the Actions or Wills of Men: And therefore, however I may proceed by right Rules, yet I cannot in Prudence so confidently assure that the Events will follow exactly as I predict them. ['Isaac Bickerstaff,' *Predictions for the Year 1708*]

This study began with two groups of questions. One, drawing on Pentland, had to do with the why's and wherefore's of the Canadian federal government's unprecedented excursion into 'industrial peace' policy at the turn of the century. We set out to render the policy and practice of state intervention in industrial relations intelligible, and in so doing we found ourselves confronted with a second group of questions. These had to do with the significance of the ideological preconceptions brought by Mackenzie King to the making of that policy. We sought to draw these two questions together, first in the sociology-of-knowledge problematic of the relation between ideas and social conditions, and then, still more abstractly, in the problematic of social order, of the possibility of society. We argued that the legitimation of liberal society lay in equity and community, and we considered the possibility that accumulation – economic growth – could furnish its own legitimation. The role of the state in liberal society was identified with these dual functions of social cohesion, and it followed, first, that the role of the state in 'industrial peace' must bear on one or both of these special functions and, second, that inasmuch as new departures in state action with respect to 'industrial peace' emerged at the turn of the century, their emergence was in all likelihood in response to new challenges to accumulation or legitimation in civil society, challenges that threatened the cohesiveness of the society in new ways. We sought to identify the sources of such challenges in the changing structures of industrial management and working-class organization. These changes might have been expected to produce new responses at the level of the state, but it would be extremely difficult to predict from the character of these changes precisely what the state's response would entail. It is one thing to explain the emergence of *some* form of state intervention in industrial relations, and something else again to explain the peculiar form which that intervention actually took. To deal at all satisfactorily with the latter, we had to introduce two additional factors: the internal dynamics of the state system, and, once again, the problematic of Mackenzie King's ideology. We proposed that by considering King in light of the analytic conceptualization of the organic intellectual, we could derive at least an heuristic guide to the role of that ideology in the production of 'industrial peace' policy, a role that bore on the legitimation function and hence on the problematic of order.

Our first group of questions, then, can be separated into two parts. First, we may ask why the liberal state embarks on a policy of intervention in industrial relations. Then we must inquire as to why *this* liberal state embarked on this particular policy of intervention in industrial relations at this specific historical conjuncture. Our ability to answer these questions satisfactorily, to render intelligible the policy and practice of 'industrial peace,' must depend on our ability to bring to an internally consistent abstract schema the structure of concrete historical mediations in such a way that the integrity of the historical record is not violated. The specificity of the theory, that is to say, must depend on our ability to provide empirical referents, while its validity must depend on our claim not to have wrenched those referents from their historical context and to have done violence to the historical record. The following discussion speaks first to the specificity of our analysis; this chapter closes with a brief examination of its claim to validity.

I

We begin by posing the general question why the state in liberal society should embark on a policy of intervention in industrial relations. We have identified the problem of order in liberal societies as the problem of allegiance to a state, in that the state exercises its sovereignty so as to maintain the societal preconditions for order. This amounts to a function for the state in the preservation of equity and community, which we have termed legitimation. But liberal society is a class society, so that the claims of equity and community are constantly confronted by the antithetical experience of the working class. And this class society is, at the same time, a liberal society which grounds its possibility in popular consent. To the extent that the claims of equity and community are weakened by exacerbated class conflict, it falls in the final instance to the state to reproduce the foundations of allegiance. This task may be undertaken by private agencies, like the National Civic Federation in the United States, and to the extent that they are successful an active role for the state may not arise. (It seems plausible to hypothesize, in passing, that the importance of such private agencies in the United States may have represented an attempt on the part of businessmen to forestall the necessity for state action which might create an undesirable precedent for government intervention in a society which hewed much more closely to *laissez-faire* orthodoxy than was the case in Canada.) Again, if class conflict is expressed in pervasive and potentially revolutionary forms, the state may intervene with a policy of outright repression so extensive as to forfeit its claim to liberal foundations. So there is nothing inevitable about the liberal state's attempt to reproduce the conditions of consent. But in general in liberal society, new strains in the relations of classes will be met by new initiatives at the level of the state to legitimize the continued allegiance of all classes to the state. In other words, *class relations are mediated by the state*. The state need not intervene to restore or create thorough-going harmony between classes, so long as it is able to overcome the tendency for class conflict to be translated into a challenge to the state itself. It is of the essence of the liberal state that it presents itself outside and above civil society, precisely because the classes in civil society are ultimately irreconcilable. This view of the state has been a commonplace of liberal political theory since Hobbes and his production of the *dominus ex machina*, allegiance to whom offsets the tendency of the social order to dissolve in internecine warfare. But the liberal state is *sui generis* a class state, at least to the extent that the accumulation which it fosters is capitalist accumulation and the social relations for which it claims allegiance and which it seeks to legitimize are capitalist social relations. It follows that the attempt to overcome the centrifugal tendencies of class conflict by mediating class relations at the level of the state must pose a threat to the legitimacy of the state itself. 'It is of fundamental importance,' in Lord Hewart's familiar dictum, 'that justice should not only be done, but should manifestly and undoubtedly be seen to be done.' But this is only possible in liberal society to the extent that some common, and therefore necessarily limited, conception of what is just may serve to legitimize the state itself.

Class relations and class conflict have many outlets of expression in liberal society. They may take the form of support for particular political parties or affiliation with special voluntary organizations. They may be indexed by persistent inequalities in incomes, education, and life chances in general, as well as by differences in life-styles, values, and preferences. But the fundamental cleavage between social classes in any capitalist society, the distinction upon which our definition of class is based, is that between wage workers who bring to the market nothing but their capacity for labour and owners of capital in their role as direct or indirect employers of that labour power. Social relations of worker and employer are the prototype of class relations. And they are by their nature conflictual, in at least two senses. One area of conflict lies within the bounds of market relations in the attempts of both parties to regulate the price of the labour commodity. The other lies outside the market-place: it resides in the continuing possibility that while the employer must regard labour as a necessary factor of production, the worker may conclude from his experience that the capitalist employer is by no means essential – that he is, by contrast, an obstacle to the society's realization of its productive potential and its capacity for the widespread distribution of social goods. The boundary between these two areas of conflict is indefinite at best, but it is crossed when the price of being a wage worker is felt to be higher than the price one is paid for one's labour. Intensive methods of production, the attrition of customary practices and skills, and a perception that the invisible hand is weighing heavily on one side of the scales may all mean that dissatisfaction with the allocations of the market turns into dissatisfaction with the institution of the market per se. Class conflict, then, is not uniquely circumscribed by the field of industrial relations, but the original point of cleavage is at the level of the work relationship. 'Industrial relations' presupposes the containment of conflict within that relationship, and by extension presupposes its limitation within the constraints of the market relationship: when conflict spills over the indefinite boundary into rejection of the market society itself its expression falls outside the conventional rubric of industrial relations.

In so far as legitimation entails the defence of the market, then, the state's role in industrial relations amounts to the containment of class conflict within the range of dissatisfactions that bear on the allocations the market makes, preventing the spill-over into active discontent with the market mechanism itself. To the extent that it is successful in so containing class conflict, the state rescues itself from its own legitimation crisis. In other words, an important aspect of state involvement in the relations of workers and employers is its ability to circumscribe and set apart that area of conflict: to say, in effect, that these disputes are particularistic in nature, that they are confined to specific dissatisfactions bounded in time and space, and cannot properly be generalized so as to constitute a wholesale condemnation of the employment relationship in general and the society which is founded upon it. A second important aspect of the state's involvement is the provision, or reinforcement, of mechanisms for dealing with such disputes within the framework of the market relationship. At the margin such mechanisms – compulsory arbitration, for example – may require a partial abandonment of some features of the market in order to rescue the market as a whole from the spill-over effects of unresolved conflict. But even at such an extreme as compulsory arbitration, the 'just price' of the award is likely to be interpreted in terms of the market-price through inter-industry comparisons or similar standards of measurement.

It will be seen, however, that there are structural constraints on the ability of the state to circumscribe conflict and provide mechanisms for disputes settlement. We have argued that the impetus for new initiatives in industrial relations policy arises from the exacerbation of relations between workers and employers, and that this exacerbation in turn may arise from the implementation of new techniques and technologies introduced by employers to lower unit-labour costs. The impact of these techniques, we suggested, may lead to shifts in customary work practices in favour of the increased control by the employer over all facets of the work process. The market, it would seem, is incompetent to adjust the differences that must result in the quality of the employment relationship consequent to this assumption of control. But the state must retain its legitimacy both for the working class and for employers. So far as the latter are concerned, the successful exercise of the accumulation function is a *sine qua non* of the state's legitimacy. It follows that the state cannot intervene in the altered employment relationship to turn back the clock. Employers, as much as workers, pose a continuous challenge to the state's successful exercise of the legitimation function, and the decisions taken by employers in the aggregate in their constant search for lower labour costs will constrain the state's freedom of action. The state must seek to reconcile workers not just to the capitalistic labour market in general but to the specific form the employment relationship takes at any point in time.

Class relations, then, are mediated by the state, and conflict that arises in the employment relationship is mediated through industrial relations policy. At issue is the legitimacy of the state, for in making its appeal to equity and community as the justifactory foundations of working-class allegiance, the meaning of those terms must be constantly and 'legitimately' recalibrated so as not to encumber the businessmen's increasingly exacting definition of the nature of the employment relationship. There is, therefore, a sort of double jeopardy inherent in the state's legitimation enterprise. In seeking to provide an interpretation of industrial disorder consistent with the preservation of the market society, and in making available 'legitimate' channels into which disputes may be directed, the state is seeking to preserve the justificatory foundations of the society. It is this role that we would commonly term legitimation. But in carrying out this function, the state must preserve its own legitimacy through a generally convincing demonstration that its action is in the interest of the whole people, in the national or public interest. But that interest is normally bounded by the imperatives of capitalist accumulation. The range of options between the Scylla of what would in a particular socio-historical context be considered non-liberal and the Charybdis of what would similarly be considered anti-capitalist may be quite narrow.

'In a particular socio-historical context' – the need for this qualification indicates that apart from the structural constraints on the state's freedom of action that follow from the internal logic of liberal society, there are other historically specific contingencies that also bound that range. At any conjuncture, we would want to consider at least the relative strength of the various class organizations; their leaders' philosophical orientation to the state, to liberal capitalism, and to one another; the extent to which these leaders can command at least the tacit support of their members; their historical experience; the presence or absence of other deeply embedded divisions in the society; various demographic and economic considerations; the quality and pace of change in various institutional areas; and so on, up to and including the accidents of temporal coincidence and the random fortunes of war.

II

Let us return to the two groups of questions with which we began.

The first group consisted of Pentland's assertion that the labour policy articulated between 1900 and 1911 included measures which 'were more clearly of Canadian origin and more deliberately designed for Canadian conditions than those introduced at other times,' and the questions that this led him to ask: 'why a vigorous labour policy should appear at that time, what it was intended to accomplish or might have accomplished and, perhaps the most important question, why this energetic initiative was succeeded by forty years of inactivity.' We undertook to speak to the first and second of these questions directly. Let us analyse the implications of this assertion and these questions.

The assertion directs our attention to the Canadian origin of the policy, implying that this is something that needs to be explained, that the experience with labour policies introduced at other times in Canada was such that we could not simply assume that this policy would be of Canadian origin. Canada borrows many of its policies from elsewhere: why was this policy different? Our investigation has indicated, however, that at the outset the measures introduced were not of Canadian origin. Both the Fair Wages Resolution and the Conciliation Act were explicit copies of British models, and Mulock's ill-fated railway arbitration bill copied the Australasian machinery. The RLDA and IDIA, however, were unique. Their machinery and philosophy, while they owed something to foreign precedents, were on the whole original, and the approach they embodied – *ad hoc* tripartite boards, the unenforceable award, compulsory investigation and mediation, and, in the IDIA, the cooling-off period – put into place what has been characteristically Canadian in industrial relations policy ever since. So it would seem, on the face of it, that there were two different approaches to labour policy during the first decade of the century, one based in British and Australasian precedents, the other a home-grown variety. But we have seen, as well, that this distinction does not hold up in practice. Proceedings under the Canadian version of the Conciliation Act differed substantially from proceedings under the British version of what was substantially the same legislation. Moreover, the RLDA and IDIA were designed in large part to institutionalize and render more effective the practices developed under the Conciliation Act, so that there was substantial continuity throughout the policy. What needs to be explained, then, is not so much the 'Canadian origin' of the measures, as the conditions under which foreign legislation was first transformed in practice and then replaced or supplemented by new statutory formulations.

Pentland asserts not only that these measures were of Canadian origin, but also that they were 'more deliberately designed for Canadian conditions' than was true of legislation introduced at other times. The implication here is that the transformation and then supplantation of the foreign legislation was a deliberate response to Canadian conditions. Our reformulation of the first part of the assertion, looking to the conditions under which these changes occurred, complements this formulation of the second part. But what kinds of 'conditions' – what contingencies – are we to seek? The answer to this question should take us a long way towards answering Pentland's inquiry, 'why a vigorous labour policy should appear at that time.'

It is evident that a host of contingencies, material and ideational, could be put forward as being among the conditions in question. In chapters 2 to 6 of this study, we have chosen to emphasize a few. In broad terms, we considered four 'actors': the organized businessmen, organized labour, the Canadian state, and Mackenzie King. Throughout the study, we have drawn attention as well to some pertinent characteristics of the stage on which they performed: among these, the inherent vulnerability of the staples economy, and the dependence of the Canadian political economy on imported technique. Both of these had special implications for class relations and for the role of the state.

While the characteristics of the staples economy had immediate consequences for class organization – the regional fragmentation of the labour movement, for example – and for the state's active role in infrastructure development, what was perhaps most significant from the standpoint of industrial relations policy was the historical impetus it gave to the willingness of both organized business and organized labour to look to the state for solutions to their difficulties in dealing with their problems, particularly their problems in dealing with each other. This in turn, of course, redounded directly on class relations. Hence the manufacturers' programme of collaborating with labour on the tariff and lesser 'industrial questions,' like technical education, and their relative lack of interest in private-sector institutions for containing class conflict in contrast to their American counterparts. The irony here was that, in the American context, manufacturers developed institutions outside the state both to prosecute class war – the NMTA, for example – and to further the cause of reconciliation, as in the National Civic Federation. In Canada, while individual manufacturers experimented with 'welfare work,' manufacturers as a class looked to the state rather than to special private institutions for an agency of harmony. Despite the proliferation of employer associations, the manufacturers' umbrella organization eschewed active warfare with the unions in order to keep the possibility of joint lobbying on 'industrial' questions alive. A similar argument can be made for the labour organizations. It is perhaps noteworthy that while both Britain and the United States published offical labour statistics journals, they were under the jurisdiction of the Board of Trade and a Department of Labor without cabinet representation, respectively. The United States established a cabinet-level Department of Commerce and Labor in 1903. Although Canada's Department of Labour was at first headed by the Postmaster-General, it was even then formally separate from the Post Office department. It became a completely separate ministry in 1909 with the appointment of Mackenzie King as Minister of Labour: the United States did not follow suit until 1913. Britain's Ministry of Labour was established in response to the demands of wartime manpower allocation in 1916.[1] Throughout the first decade of the century, then, Canada was the only member of the North Atlantic Triangle to respond fully to labour demands for a cabinet-level department concerned solely with labour policies.

1 Sir Godfrey Ince, *The Ministry of Labour and National Service* (London: George Allen & Unwin, 1960); Jonathan Grossman, *The Department of Labor* (New York: Praeger, 1973)

That Canada should take the lead in establishing such a department and in developing new policy initiatives like the RLDA and IDIA might seem paradoxical when set against the second feature of the stage fittings, the reliance on imported technique. We have seen how business technique – scientific management, 'industrial betterment,' and employer associations – flowed into Canada from the United States, and we have seen as well that the trade-union movement in Canada accepted some important aspects of AFL technique, even if sometimes half-heartedly. The Canadian state was not exempt: Laurier's and Mulock's appeals to British precedent in introducing the Fair Wages Resolution and Conciliation Act harked back to Macdonald's introduction of the Trade Union Act a generation earlier. But while the Canadian innovations in labour policy might appear puzzling in contrast to the apparent willingness to look elsewhere for leadership in other fields, the paradox is more apparent than real. The staples orientation of the economy, which had created the preconditions for the special relationship of the 'industrial classes' to the Canadian state, both encouraged the import of technique and set limits to the extent to which imported technique could be utilized. Thus Canadian manufacturers could import American managerial techniques, but stopped short of fully adopting the techniques of American employer organizations because of their reliance on the interventionist state. Canadian workers could import such American trade-union techniques as craft autonomy but stopped short of the negative excesses of Gompers' 'pure and simple' unionism because of their historic experience with state intervention. In the organizational philosophies of both the TLC and the CMA the state occupied a central role, although as we have argued that role was interpreted differently by the two bodies. Since the continued viability of the Canadian economy was inconceivable without an activist state, neither the Manufacturers' Association nor the Labour Congress had an interest in the import of techniques that would substitute private agencies for the state. There was a possible exception to this in the abortive negotiations between the TLC and CMA in 1904 and 1905, when 'Civic Federation' appeared on the agenda: if so, this is an exception which, in its failure, proves the rule. Since the problems for which in other countries private agencies were developed fell to the state in Canada, the innovations in labour policy were but another consequence of the staples vulnerability which implied openness to imported technique.

Thus the question why a vigorous labour policy should have appeared at the turn of the century may be at least partly answered in terms of exogenous and endogenous factors both of which have their roots in the broad imperatives of the staples economy. Class conflict was exacerbated in turn of the century Canada by the consequences of the utilization of imported technique. The AFL's aggressive organizing drive led to the rapid growth of the union movement in Canada and its endowment with substantially enhanced financial and organizational resources, regardless of a net drain of funds to the United States. At the same time, Canadian manufacturers' appropriation of the techniques of scientific management aggravated relations with the unions as it broadened the employers' claims to work-place control and undermined the craft principle of labour organization. The growth of working-class organization on the one hand, and the extended appeal to management's right on the other, converged to produce an unprecedented wave of strikes, many of them for union recognition. Both employer and worker organizations turned to the state for aid, despite the availability of models for private agencies of industrial war and peace, in a response typical of class relations in the Canadian political economy. Equally typically, the state complied. Exacerbated class conflict was understood to be a tripartite concern in the Canadian context.

Pentland's second question asks what the labour policy 'was intended to accomplish or might have accomplished.' We might answer this very simply in terms of our theoretical schema: it was intended to legitimate liberal society in equity and community, and at the same time resolve the state's own crisis of legitimacy. But as we saw in elaborating these concepts, there are both formal and contingent constraints on the performance of this function. We identified a formal constraint in the employing class's insistence on accumulation as a component of legitimation, a constraint that reflects the inherent tension, if not contradiction, between the two functions. But this formal constraint has its own contingent features. It is not accumulation in some objectively specifiable sense with which we must be solely concerned, for there is no justification in historical experience for assuming that the developmental programme of the dominant class or some powerful fraction of it at any point in time must have the material consequences that its promoters expected. A familiar example in Canadian economic history, and one bearing on our period, is the inducement to foreign direct investment in manufacturing created by the protective tariff. Canadian manufacturers at the turn of the century welcomed the coming of the branch plants and celebrated every new movement of American industry across the tariff wall as another proof of the wisdom of their national strategy. But there is an unassailable case to be made for the negative impact of foreign direct investment on the structure of Canadian manufacturing in the medium to long term. Had the Canadian state embarked on a developmental strategy which would in retrospect have avoided these difficulties, it is likely that the manufacturers would have opposed it. So we must not make the error of imputing to our actors the long-term class interests we can divine from theory or hindsight. Manufacturers at the turn of the century required of the state that it operate in the interests of capitalist development, but what this meant to them must be understood as historically specific and therefore contingent.

A similar point must be made about the state's imperative to equity. As we argued earlier in this study, the TLC seems to have meant by equity something rather different from what the CMA meant, and both of these surely intended something quite different again from what our formal analysis of the class-divided liberal society would specify. In formal terms, the society was characterized by widespread structured inequalities, and while it is important that we are able to make this determination, it clearly does not follow that the underclass rises in revolt to cast off its chains. Our formal discussion permits us to inquire why that consummation is lacking – we would have no other grounds for posing the question – and once again we come back to contingent features of the situation. We sought to explain why the working-class organizations, while they were fiercely committed to the pursuit of equity, defined it in such narrow terms, and we found a partial solution in the market orientation of business unionism and the defensive emphasis of craft autonomy. We noted, as well, that in conceding to trade-union demands for the Fair Wages Resolution and an end to sweating, the state's legitimacy problem was postponed by accepting, and thereby reinforcing, their limited definition of equity. Here, then, is an example of containment which was, at the same time, an appeal to legitimacy *via* accumulation so far as employers were concerned. In seeking to define the problem as an 'abuse' of the industrial system, the preconditions in legitimation and accumulation for thorough-going industrialism were served.

But aside from contingent qualifications of structural imperatives, there are contingencies pure and simple. The desire of governing parties to secure votes and distribute patronage; the timing of a judicial decision; the choice of venue for a labour convention: these and a host of other historical accidents helped to determine the character of Canadian labour policy. If we permit ourselves to exercise the hypothetical counterfactual, it seems likely that, while Canada would surely still have had an industrial relations policy in the first decade of the century, it might have been a rather different one. For the sake of the exercise, let us tweak Cleopatra's nose. What might have been the consequence, say, had Gompers not decided to purge the TLC in 1902? Imagine him putting the decision off one year. Or even more plausibly, imagine that the 1902 convention took place not in southern Ontario, but in the west. In either case, one can project a scenario whereby Ralph Smith becomes Minister of Labour and Canada experiments with compulsory arbitration of railway or mining disputes. Such an eventuality, one imagines, would have redoubled Gompers' zeal to exercise even more stringent control over Canadian locals, but he might have had a more difficult time of it once the damage had been done. Had Ralph Smith become Minister of Labour, Mackenzie King might well have resigned to take up his teaching job at Harvard. Had King gone to Harvard, he might well have unleashed half a dozen *Industry and Humanity*'s upon the world: there is some mercy in the historically factual after all.

III

Let us go on to consider our second group of questions, those having to do with the role of Mackenzie King. We argued that King's policy was informed by a sophisticated ideology, but that this in itself was formally insufficient to explain his ability to translate that ideology into policy. Rather cryptically, we suggested that there was some goodness of fit between his policy and its ideological basis, on the one hand, and Canadian society at the turn of the century on the other: that how King made sense of society somehow made sense for society as well. This led us into a discussion of the sociology-of-knowledge problem of the relationship between consciousness and social existence. We determined to investigate King the intellectual, and this led us into a discussion of the intellectual as a social role. We used Gramsci's analysis to arrive at an heuristic hypothesis which saw King as an organic intellectual operating within the state system.

Before we pursue the implications of this analysis, it may be important to clear up one point. It is unnecessary to posit a complicated counterfactual to reject the 'great man' hypothesis about Canadian industrial relations policy in general. The question whether there would have been some form of state intervention in industrial disputes had King never existed need not arise, for the adequately compelling reason that the Conciliation Act was introduced in his absence and, on his own showing, in the absence of any suggestion on his part. While the Fair Wages Resolution and those sections of the Conciliation Act bearing on the collection and publication of wage statistics can be traced in part to his immediate influence, he appears to have played no part, great or small, in influencing the government to introduce the conciliation features of the Act. On the other hand, it seems to be an unavoidable conclusion that, in King's absence, the specific nature of the Canadian state's industrial relations policy would have taken a rather different form. What sort of difference this might have made in the long run is something we shall have to consider below.

Gramsci considered the organic intellectuals, who are created alongside new social groups 'on the original terrain of an essential function in the world of economic production,' to have the role of functionaries in the superstructural institutions of civil society and the state. 'The functions in question are precisely organizational and connective. The intellectuals are the dominant group's "deputies" exercising the subaltern functions of social hegemony and political government.' It will immediately be seen that there is a link here to our earlier discussion of the state's role in industrial relations. Class relations are mediated by the state in its role as the agency of legitimation, a function that is 'precisely organizational and connective,' as against the centrifugal tensions of class conflict. The state's successful solution of its legitimacy problem hinges on its ability to reproduce a constrained definition of equity and community to recapture the allegiance of all classes, a concern which parallels Gramsci's notion of 'social hegemony.' The organic intellectual role, in this formulation, is created by new social relations of production and the disorganizational and disconnective conflicts they create. We have located the exacerbation of class conflict in our period in the confrontation of imported managerial with imported trade-union technique, bounded by the structural imperatives of the staples economy. Can we identify new social groups emerging 'on the original terrain of an essential function in the world of economic production'?

Our analysis has indicated that in the context of the increasing scale of industry and more intensive production methods, the modern professional manager emerged to replace the capitalist entrepreneur at the organizational nexus of production. This transformation, enhanced by imported technique and by the flight from competition, was expressed *inter alia* by the developing schism within the CMA. As the appendix on census data demonstrates, however, this transformation was only partial during the first decade of the century. While some industries experienced remarkable increases in administrative overhead, an index of the proliferation of management functions, others underwent relative declines. Moreover, we argued that to some degree the enthusiasm among Canadian businessmen for 'system,' 'efficiency,' and even for the organic merger followed more from the prevailing fashion than from stern economic calculation. We shall have to deal with the implications of this imperfect transition below, but for the time being we may identify the modern 'scientific' manager as the emergent actor 'on the original terrain of an essential function in the world of economic production.'

Gramsci's schema would predict the creation alongside this new social group of a new cadre of organic intellectuals. Our earlier analysis of the history of paradigms in political economy suggested, aided by the hint from

Bukharin, some organic connection between entrepreneurial industrial capitalism and classical political economy, on the one hand, and finance capitalism and neoclassical economics, on the other. The school of political economy in which Mackenzie King received his training was transitional between these two paradigms. As we have seen, it called for an interventionist state to assist in the reconciliation of class conflict, and postulated a 'gospel of duty' which could make a virtue of the labour market's 'indifference,' interpreted as a consequence of the large-scale organization of industry and the depersonalization of work-place relations. It also imposed a mandate on the professional political economist to become involved in 'practical' work, by taking on the hegemonic tasks.

King's use of the new British and, to a lesser extent, American political economy might be seen as another example of imported technique. Here again, however, the technique was subtly altered in the transfer. Toynbee's discussion of the rise of large-scale industry, of the depersonalization of industrial relations, and of the emergent potentialities of 'indifference' had been in the context of an analysis of the English industrial revolution of the eighteenth century and its political consequences in the early nineteenth century. King seized upon the cardinal points of this analysis and proceeded to apply them to Canadian society in the early twentieth century but, as we have seen, he redirected the thrust of the argument. He adulterated it with a new emphasis on personal character which, while it may have had roots in his Presbyterian upbringing, was certainly strengthened by the teachings of Mavor and perhaps Henderson and Cummings as well, and he brought in too an embryonic analysis of the separation of ownership and management, learned from Ashley, Veblen, and possibly from Taussig and Mavor. King identified the large-scale organization of industry, with its obvious referents in the Canadian merger movement and publicity about US trust-busting, as both the immediate cause of exacerbated class relations and the dynamic upon which the boldest hopes for the future welfare of the 'community' could be centred. Where Toynbee had seen new hope for the gospel of duty in the indifference of market relations between citizens replacing the feudal class relations of master and man, for King indifference was the villain. It was in the interest of the community to reinstate the 'personal relation in industry,' to quote the title of the book by King's later patron, John D. Rockefeller, Jr. The community, through its state, could assist in the development of personal relations by removing 'abuses' and by providing such services as statistical publications and conciliation officers to help open the channels of communication. For King, industrial conflict had its root in misunderstanding, failures in communications, irrational fears and the unmanly desire of one or another party for personal aggrandizement at the expense of the community. The state must do what it could to clear up misunderstandings, assist in communication, and dispel fear, but in some few instances it might have to meet force with force. The more legitimate forms of compulsion, however, were those that would impose the groundwork for the exercise of open communication and reason. Personal relations must replace class relations: equilibrium must replace conflict.

The positive side of the large-scale organization of industry was its productive efficiency, holding out the promise of an ever-increasing wealth of goods and services for distribution among all members of the community. In this King saw the outcome of the 'organizing genius' of industrial management, and it was to management that he looked for the harbingers of a new age of peace and plenty. In his analogy between industrial and political government he affirmed, in effect, the new doctrine of management's rights, and it is clear that he was prepared to leave to management the exclusive right to control of the work process that followed from the new techniques. King's role in the state bureaucracy was a counterpart to the place of the manager in the system of class relations. His was the organizing genius and special expertise of the practical political economist exercising the organizational and connective functions in labour policy that complemented those exercised by the managers on the shop floor. The managers had another special significance for King, for in his analysis of the 'four parties to industry' they furnished the link between labour and capital which could dissolve class concepts. In the same way, King, through the labour department, mediated class relations – and very active mediation it was.

King also brought to the labour department a notion of 'legitimate' trade unionism which incorporated the organizational philosophy of the AFL and denied the claims of the syndicalists. His analysis of good trade unionism complemented his analysis of large-scale industry, in its emphasis on the caution and conservatism that bigness, at least so long as it is divorced from politics, can bring, notwithstanding the potential for 'tyranny' in the large centralized labour organization. But, as he never tired of pointing out, it was not the forms of organization, either of capital or of labour, that caused trouble, but their possible abuses. In the final analysis, both labour and capital had everything to gain from character in their representatives. Given King's version of the causes of industrial unrest and the primacy of the manager, it is unclear what role even the most 'legitimate' of trade unions had in his scenario for capitalist progress. At best, they seem to have represented working-class citizenship and a potential countervailing force to the excesses of an unrestrained gospel of wealth. King was as capable of strong language when it came to the abuses of power by men like Hays or Dunsmuir as he was in attacking 'unprincipled agitators' in the labour movement, but somehow the barbs fired at businessmen never seemed to find their mark so surely as those let off at unmanly trade unionists.

King's dual notion of community was the centre-piece of his strategy of legitimation. The community interest was the interest in accumulation, and it was assumed without question that accumulation must be capitalist accumulation. The boundaries of the state's role were therefore set by the perceived imperatives of business. King accepted that in any dispute settlement business would be constrained by 'what would pay.' The state had no business infringing on the rights of property directly, although it could aid in the creation of an informed public opinion and thereby bring community pressure to bear on robber barons. Equity meant that while employers might refuse to recognize a union (although it would be better were they to agree to recognize legitimate unions), they ought not to interfere with the rights of their workers to join any organization they pleased – a right of citizenship. Equity also meant 'fair wages,' with a commitment to the felicities of the market in allocating prices that ruled out compulsory arbitration. What we have called the 'public' side of King's community sought further to contain the range of conflict by denying the class implications of particular disputes. Each strike or lock-out was to be dealt with on its own terms and defined as a breakdown in communication or a demonstration of wilfulness. The issues in dispute were of less significance than that 'wrong ideas' needed to be corrected and innocent bystanders might suffer in the interim.

King's practice in the Labour Department followed from his ideological preconceptions, although no doubt his experience there modified to some extent some of his ideas. He used the *Labour Gazette* and other public media to proselytize for his interpretation of industrial disputes. He quickly discarded the formal structure of permanent boards provided for in the Conciliation Act and contemplated in the railway arbitration bill in favour of *ad hoc* interventions aimed at a speedy return to work. Nothing would be gained by letting the parties fight it out to the end; this would cause only further bitterness and, after all, there can be no solution of the labour problem short of 'restoring humanity.' He opened the department to consultation with 'responsible' leaders of 'legitimate' unions, again on an *ad hoc* basis, and he co-operated with them in their 'reasonable' legislative demands. His method was the method of compromise, but the balance which he drew was always between extremes neither of which fell outside the bounds of a market perspective.

King viewed the Department of Labour as the germ of a great agency of industrial peace. As its workload increased, he sought bureaucratic counterparts to his own practice of *ad hoc* mediation. In the RLDA and then in the IDIA he again rejected the model of permanent disputes settlement machinery in favour of a new species of *ad hockery*, the tripartite board. The board was a means of bringing responsible representatives of labour and capital together, of avoiding the vexed problem of union recognition, and of introducing a proxy King in the person of the chairman. The restrictions on public utility strikes were designed to give this brand of peace a chance, and were justified in terms of the potential negative consequences of railway or coal-mining strikes for the community's interest in accumulation. But as the Grand Trunk affair showed, the boards were only expected to stand in for King's personal brand of mediation, which could be called upon to supplement their activities when they failed to forestall a strike.

King's strategy of industrial peace was only partly successful. He seems to have overestimated the extent to which Canadian employers had grasped the imperatives of the new managerial capitalism, so he overestimated the extent to which businessmen would accept his logic of right attitudes. The argument in the Royal Commission on Industrial Disputes in British Columbia, that employers would extend recognition to those unions which proved themselves to be responsible, appears in retrospect to have been a cruel joke, but there were precedents in the American and British experience for making the claim. The modern corporation under the direction of professional managers was elsewhere making the discovery, albeit tentatively and grudgingly, that business unionism could be an invaluable ally in disciplining the workforce and providing a measure of stability in operations. Most Canadian employers were far from this realization, and for all that King praised the odd exception, he had no workable policy for convincing the majority. His essential liberalism precluded interference with management's rights, so he was left with bromides about the importance of right attitudes and the sovereignty of personality. This misreading of the situation led inevitably to a renewed tension between the dictates of equity, even in the narrow definition of the Canadian labour movement, and those of property, and probably contributed to a loss of labour support for the Liberals in 1911.

If King was not the 'great man' of Canadian labour policy, it is equally clear that he was more than simply a vector of historical forces. The ideological content of his policy and practice complemented to a great extent both ideas and material imperatives current in the 'industrial classes,' as we have demonstrated here and there throughout this study. There can be no doubt that King's ideology and practice reflected to a substantial extent many of the preconceptions of both business and labour, and that they derived much of their acceptability from this. In this sense at least, it can be argued that how

King made sense of his society made sense for it as well. Beyond this, we must recognize that the power of any ideology derives from those aspects of it that are true. King's notion of community, for all its question-begging confusion, reflected the historical bias of the Canadian economy towards active state intervention and the socialization of risk. It comprehended the readiness of both business and labour to look to the state, and it incorporated an awareness of the centrifugal tensions of a class society based in two nationalities and posed between two imperial centres. What is perhaps most surprising about King, though, is the extent to which in his thought and practice he rejected the state and minimized its role. The Industrial Disputes Investigation Act, its compulsory features notwithstanding, represented a contraction in the range of the state's involvement in industrial relations. King made no attempt to clarify the legal position of trade unions by statute, nor did he move towards guaranteeing the enforceability of agreements even when, as in the Grand Trunk case, they had been signed by both parties and sponsored by the state.. These were all subjects of contemporary discussion and grievance to which he made little response, if any. It appears likely that his stress on the personal factor blinded him to opportunities in his immediate environment for these extensions to the state's presence in industrial relations. And it seems unlikely that he would have encountered very strenuous opposition to moderate reform in these areas. More rigorous intervention, compulsory recognition for example, was of course beyond the pale, while the labour movement itself had yet to decide in favour of compulsory collective bargaining.

The exacerbation of class relations at the turn of the century created an imperative for state intervention, and Canada took the first step with the passage of the Conciliation Act. Mulock needed somebody to run the new department, and in hiring King he could repay a political debt and acquire one of the very few available experts in the field. If Mackenzie King did not exist, it would have been necessary to invent him or, if not him, then somebody able and willing to take on the same role in the state apparatus. It is unlikely that Canadian labour policy would have stopped with the formal machinery of the Conciliation Act, although there is no reason to suppose that anybody but King would have disposed so quickly with permanent machinery. Mulock's own predilection, after all, seems to have been in that direction. It is, of course, impossible to predict just what form labour policy might have taken in the absence of Mackenzie King. We know that there was substantial pressure from the labour movement in favour of compulsory arbitration before 1902, and that up until then the CMA had not decided firmly to oppose such a policy. There was at least a range of options open, albeit a fairly narrow one. But the problem does not end with the minutiae of labour policy: it is conceivable that the consequences of Mulock's choice in the absence of King might have had much broader ramifications, for example, in the development of the Canadian labour movement. In any event, dispensing with the counterfactual, we must accept that Mackenzie King constitutes a significant contingency in the explanation with wide-ranging consequences for the nature of class relations and the role of the state.

IV

So far we have pulled together and summarized some of the strands of argument and demonstration at the core of this study. We have discussed what we have done: now we must turn briefly to an examination of what we have not done. This study has raised many more questions than it has been possible to answer, and it has hewed rough forms out of material that would benefit from far more delicate treatment. Out excuse must be that our study has been in the nature of a first exploration, both methodologically and substantively, and while we have come across the occasional highly developed oasis, for the most part we have been feeling our way through more or less trackless wastes. Some of the tracks across which we stumbled, it might be added, proved to be dead ends. We make no apology, then, for the rude sketches that have passed for maps or for the bedraggled appearance of some of the specimens we have produced for inspection. But it would be disingenuous to pretend that our forced march through these thickets can stand for a thorough survey. In gaining a first appreciation of the lay of the land, we have accomplished what we set out to do. But there is much that remains to be done.

Our study of class relations has been extremely crude. We have concentrated, for the most part, on the positions advanced by two legislative bodies, the TLC and CMA, with only the briefest of excursions onto the shop floor. This was justified in part by the fact that in adopting our 'state's eye view' we could afford to concentrate on the organizations which represented the demands of the workers and employers before the state, but there are obvious limits to this justification. Far more work needs to be done in this area, both in terms of 'industrial relations' *per se*, and in terms of the reciprocal impact of changes in the organization of business and of labour. In particular, the problems of managerial reorganization and working-class response to the employers' technological decisions require thorough investigation. Most Canadian business and economic history has focused on problems of capital mobilization and changing ownership structures: studies of the production process itself would not be unwelcome.

Our analysis of class relations has been extremely limited in another sense, as well. We have confined our discussion almost entirely to the relations of the 'industrial classes,' to the exclusion of the far more numerous section of the workforce engaged in agriculture. Farmers constituted a potent political force in turn-of-the-century Canada, particularly as they began to articulate their demands through broadly based class organizations around the middle of the first decade of the century. This is an area that needs to be drawn into our analysis of industrial relations policy, to the extent that the agrarian interest may have imposed its own constraints or imperatives on the state's relations with workers and manufacturers. We have not begun to explore this question here.[2]

A third area of investigation bearing even more directly on industrial relations policy is the role of the sub-central, or provincial, states, and their relations to the central state within the entire state system. Several of the provinces introduced labour bureaux or similar agencies during our period or passed industrial disputes legislation. They were also active in the labour standards field, something that, barring the Fair Wages Resolution, we have ignored. Given the strained history of federal-provincial relations it would seem that our account of the state's role in mediating class relations would be open to substantial qualification on the basis of studies of provincial industrial relations policy.

Related to this is a second historical dichotomy, the relation of English Canada to Quebec and the role of the central state in mediating that relation. We have had very little to say about the development of the labour movement and of class relations in general in Quebec, but enough is available in the secondary literature to suggest that events took a rather different turn there than in English Canada. How this bears on our general analysis is something that must be left to further investigation. But it would seem, connected to this, that an informative analogy might be drawn between the state's role in mediating the relations of English Canada and Quebec, and its role in mediating class relations. The Laurier government, of course, played a critical role in both.

It seems politic to end this list before we swamp what we have done with what remains undone. But perhaps something might also be said about the King biography. We explicitly pointed out that our intent in this study was not biography, and that we intended to approach King as an intellectual. We discussed his intellectual formation in terms of his university career, but it is

---

2 But see Paul Craven and Tom Traves, 'The Class Politics of the National Policy, 1872–1933,' *Journal of Canadian Studies* vol. 14, no. 3 (fall 1979).

clear that this was only one possible approach among many. What is quite surprising in the literature is the lack of a detailed study of the consequences of the King family's brand of southern Ontario Presbyterianism for his world-view. Most of his biographers have something to say aout his religiosity, but none of them so far have been able to locate him precisely in the sectarian ferment that characterized Canadian protestantism at the turn of the century. Simply from the standpoint of our understanding of what made King tick, this is an important lack, and it may be found to have broader implications as well. It seems important, too, to test the 'intellectual' approach to King against his later career. Finally in this vein, we must point out that we have eschewed any attempt at an amateur psychoanalysis of King, for all that his diaries sometimes seem to beg for it. We have serious doubts about the usefulness of such an enterprise, whether for a fuller understanding of King or for broader purposes. However, we cannot resist the temptation to let King have the last word by reproducing without comment a diary entry that appears to have implications not only for the workings of his subconscious mind, but for his historic task as an organic intellectual in the mediation of class relations as well:

This morning I was dreaming of coming from some place to the Chelsea Station on a wheel, being delayed for a workingman who was following on a wheel, not arriving I went back for him, & found he had decided not to come. I had then to hasten through wet & mud for the train and caught it just as it was leaving the station.[3]

3 Diary, 9 July 1902

Appendix
The changing internal structure of
Canadian manufacturing, 1900–10

It was argued in chapter 4 that while the scale of the Canadian economy increased dramatically in the wheat boom period, the traditional pattern of intersectoral relationships remained largely unchanged, so that the scale increases had their greatest effects, not on the underlying structure of the economy as a whole, but on the internal organization of industry in the increasing size of the firm and the reorganization of the work process along scientific management lines. This appendix reports quantitative research using the 1901 and 1911 industrial censuses in an attempt to measure one critical aspect of internal reorganization: the proliferation of management functions.

'The most useful, single index of the internal bureaucratization of economic enterprises,' according to Reinhard Bendix, 'is the proportion of salaried employees in the occupational structure of a country'[1] The classic study in this area is Seymour Melman's 'The Rise of Administrative Overhead in the Manufacturing Industries of the United States, 1899–1947.'[2] Melman noticed a general tendency for the ratio of administrative (i.e., salaried) workers to production (i.e., wage-earning) workers to rise over time in all industrialized countries. He sought to explain this rise in administrative overhead by studying a sample of manufacturing industries in the US industrial census; he was interested both in explaining differences between industries in any one census year, and in explaining the growth of the administration to production (*A/P*) ratio over time.

Melman found that differences in the magnitude of the *A/P* ratio at any one time were independent of any characteristics of industry except size, and

1 *Work and Authority in Industry* (New York: Wiley, 1956), 211
2 *Oxford Economic Papers*, new series, III, 1951, 62–112

the relation with size was independent of any particular measure of that characteristic. In analysing the determinants of change in the *A/P* ratio over time, he found that 'large increases in average size correspond with relatively small increases in administrative overhead,' while no other aspects of business operation were systematically associated with the general increase in the *A/P* ratio. How, then, was the increase in administrative overhead to be explained? Melman rejected the explanation that 'the aggregate efficiency of administrative personnel had declined precipitously from 1899 to 1947': 'We are thus led to the inference that the increase in administration personnel, and the failure of their number to decrease as a result of mechanization [of office operations], is connected with the addition of *new functions* carried out by the administration personnel ... The added administrative functions which are indexed by our measures of increased administrative overhead evolved pervasively and at a relatively uniform rate throughout manufacturing industry ... The additional administration personnel executing such functions comprise the bulk additions to administrative overhead which we have observed.'

Both Melman and Bendix argue that a relatively steady and homogeneous increase in the *A/P* ratio, and hence the proliferation of new management functions, is characteristic of all modern industrial countries, and both authors construct tables or charts to demonstrate this. Melman explicitly cites the Canadian experience. If a generalized increase in the *A/P* ratio could be shown to hold for Canada in the 1900–10 period, it would constitute powerful evidence for the assertion that Canadian industry was undergoing an internal restructuring of the sort we have suggested in chapter 4.

Before embarking on this topic, it is well to enter some caveats. First, Melman and Bendix make use of fairly long-time series in their analyses. Here, we must consider changes in the *A/P* ratio within one decade, with data for only two points in time, the 1901 and 1911 census dates. Second, the Canadian industrial census for these years is far less amenable than the American to this analysis. Census industry definitions are uncertain,[3] and we do not know how central office staffs have been distributed within or among census industries – assuming they have been distributed at all. Whatever their shortcomings, however, these are the best data we have or are likely ever to have for this period.

---

3 *Cf.* J.H. Dales, 'Estimates of Canadian Manufacturing Output by Markets, 1870–1915,' Canadian Political Science Association Conferences on Statistics, 1962 and 1963, *Papers*, 61–91, especially 79

In order to carry out an analysis of administrative overhead in Canada, industrial census data for 1901 and 1911 were converted to computer-readable form. Each case consisted of a single census industry, with its set of variables for 1901 and 1911. During the analysis, each case record was extended to incorporate mean establishment-level values for each of the industry-level variables in the file. The A/P ratio for each industry was computed[4] and a percentage-difference variable representing the degree of change between 1900 and 1910 was added for this ratio and for a number of other selected variables. There were sufficient data for both years for about 160 census industries.

In the aggregate, the Canadian data conform to the Melman-Bendix prediction. Between 1900 and 1910 there was a mean increase in the A/P ratio for all Canadian census industries of 13.8 per cent. This seems to be roughly in the same order of magnitude as several other countries they describe.

However, when we look at changes in administrative overhead on an industry-by-industry basis, the picture is not one of steady increase. The aggregate mean growth in the A/P ratio masks some significant differences in the experience of different industries. Of the 161 census industries for which data were available, 59 experienced a growth of 10 per cent or more in administrative overhead between 1900 and 1910. Another 35 maintained more or less the same A/P ratio throughout the period, varying between increases or decreases of less than 10 per cent. The remaining 67 industries experienced *decreases* of 10 per cent or more in the A/P ratio; some of these declined by more than 70 per cent. Thus, although there is an aggregate increase in the A/P ratio for these 161 industries taken together, more individual industries experienced a decline than an increase in administrative overhead.

In the following paragraphs, 'average' establishments in each of these three groups are described as they appeared in the 1911 census and as they had experienced the process of change over the preceding decade.

4 Melman arbitrarily distributed working proprietors half to A and half to P. While the 1901 Canadian census distinguishes working proprietors from other salary recipients, the 1911 census does not. Initially, the 1901 A/P ratio was computed two ways: first, copying the Melman assignment, and second, assigning all working proprietors to A. The two measures were almost perfectly correlated although, obviously enough, they gave different ratios in those industries with very small numbers of wage earners per establishment. In subsequent calculations, working proprietors were assigned to A for 1901 to make it fully comparable with the 1911 figures.

1 Industries with declining A/P ratios

In 1910, the average establishment in this group had a fixed capitalization of about $44,000. It employed about 3 administrative and 39 (ranging as high as 171)[5] production workers; about three-quarters of the latter were adult males. Its total output was valued at about $101,000, while it paid about $48,000 for materials and $19,000 in wages and salaries. Taking these industries in the aggregate, the ratio of fixed capital to the wage bill was about 280 per cent. The average establishment in this group had experienced a small absolute decline (about 7 per cent) in the number of administrative employees between 1900 and 1910, and an increase of about 60 per cent in production workers. The total value of output had increased by 150 per cent, and materials costs by about 110 per cent. Its fixed capitalization had increased by 245 per cent, and there had been tangible increases in all categories of production workers, male, female, child, and outworkers. Among the industries with the greatest decreases in *A/P* ratio, secondary food and beverage manufacturing stood out. This group included, as well, small specialized manufacturing firms (e.g., gas machines, fancy goods) and much of the clothing industry. The mean change in *A/P* ratio for this group was −35.9 per cent.

2 Industries with stable A/P ratios

In 1910, the average establishment in this group had a fixed capitalization of about $81,000. It employed 5 administrative and 47 (ranging as high as 202) production workers; slightly more than three-quarters of the latter were adult males. Its total output was valued at about $149,000, while it paid about $65,000 for materials and $25,000 in wages and salaries. Taking these industries in the aggregate, the ratio of fixed capital to the wage bill was about 350 per cent. The average establishment in this group had experienced a 27 per cent increase in the number of administrative employees between 1900 and 1910, and an increase of about 27 per cent in production workers. The total value of output had increased by 110 per cent, and materials costs

---

5 The census presents aggregate statistics for each industry, among them the number of reporting establishments. In order to derive 'establishment level' figures, the aggregate statistics for each industry were divided by the number of reporting establishments, yielding data for a mythical 'average' establishment in each industry. Thus the maximum figure given here and in the two paragraphs following is the *mean* figure for the industry in this category that had the largest number of production workers per establishment. It follows that the largest establishment in this industry would have had a still larger workforce (unless all the establishments in the industry had the same size workforce).

by about 82 per cent. Its fixed capitalization had increased by about 200 per cent, while the fastest growing group in the work force was adult *female* in-plant workers. Typical industries in this group included foundries and machine shops, the boot and shoe industry, canneries, and plaster works. The mean change in *A/P* ratio for this group was 1.7 per cent.

3 Industries with increasing A/P ratios

In 1910, the average establishment in this group had a fixed capitalization of about $132,000. It employed 8 administrative and 71 (ranging as high as 492) production workers; more than 80 per cent of the latter were adult males. Its total output was valued at about $409,000 while it paid about $220,000 for materials and $44,000 in wages and salaries. Taking these industries in the aggregate, the ratio of fixed capital to the wage bill was about 410 per cent. The average establishment in this group had experienced a 70 per cent increase in the number of administrative employees between 1900 and 1910, and an increase of only 5 per cent in production workers. Most of this increase was accounted for by an increase in the employment of adult males, while employment of adult females had undergone a small absolute decline. The total value of output had increased 147 per cent, and materials costs by 358 per cent. Its fixed capitalization had increased 174 per cent. Among the industries experiencing the greatest increases in *A/P* ratio, the textile industry, industries supplying railways, and high-technology manufacturing stand out. This group also included a number of producers' goods industries, and industries associated with the new staples of the emerging continental economy, smelting and wood pulp. The mean change in *A/P* ratio was 77.3 per cent.

In summary, the industries which experienced increasing *A/P* ratios in the first decade of the twentieth century were larger than other industries, had a higher organic composition of capital, and relied more exclusively on an adult male workforce. Their high *A/P* ratios reflected absolute increases in administrative employment that outran the rate of increase in the productive work force. These industries were on the leading edge of the new industrialism: railway supplies, producers' goods, the new staples, and high-technology manufacturing. While there were signs, in particular the rate of growth in fixed capital, that some industries in the other two groups may have been moving to 'catch up' to Group 3 industries, the inescapable conclusion from this analysis is that the decade 1900–10 was one of markedly uneven development in Canadian manufacturing, so that the *A/P* ratio discriminates quite well among broad groups of industries. If the ratio reflects

TABLE A Census industries experiencing the
greatest changes in *A/P* ratio, 1900–10
(Percentage difference, 1900–10)

---

a) The ten industries with the largest increases in *A/P* ratio

1. Textiles, dyeing and finishing	602.6
2. Railway supplies	354.7
3. Cars and car works	166.8
4. Sewing machines	164.9
5. Electrical apparatus and supplies	163.4
6. Wax candles	162.5
7. Washing compounds	154.0
8. Boot and shoe supplies	135.2
9. Fertilizers	133.3
10. Car repairs	119.4

b) The ten industries with the largest decreases in *A/P* ratio

1. Baking powder	−91.4
2. Gas machines	−76.2
3. Condensed milk	−72.6
4. Safes and vaults	−71.3
5. Fancy goods	−70.8
6. Explosives	−67.7
7. Woolcarding and fulling	−66.0
8. Cocoa and chocolate	−65.7
9. Dies and moulds	−61.1
10. Rubber clothing	−58.4

SOURCE: Computed from Census of Canada, 1901, 1911

the proliferation of management functions, as Melman suggested, it appears
that the *fact* of scientific management and 'efficiency' penetrated to only a
small, if very important, group of industries in this period. It seems more
than likely, however, that the *ideology* of those movements was far more
widely diffused.

Index